Praise for the New Edition

"For seventeen years, I have insisted that hundreds of my clients read and use *Mom's House, Dad's House*, the 'Dr. Spock' of joint parenting books. The revised edition . . . is a must-have resource manual."

—Joel Edelman, lawyer, mediator, counselor,
and author of *The Tao of Negotiation*

"This is an upbeat, wise, eminently practical guide for divorcing parents . . . and . . . the professionals who help them. Highly recommended."

—Judith Wallerstein, Ph.D., author of *Second Chances*

"In seventeen years of family practice, I've given many books to my parent clients, but none helped them heal like *Mom's House, Dad's House*. If you want to strengthen the heart of your family . . . and come out of the divorce process a stronger, wiser, and more peaceful parent—this book is your friend."

—John Kydd, family law attorney and past president,
Association of Family and Conciliation Courts

"This is a wonderful book. In clear and eloquent language, Isolina Ricci charts a constructive course for divorcing parents. The chief benefactors of this modern classic will be the children."

—Richard Louv, author of *Childhood's Future* and *The Web of Life*

"This book should be a required textbook for every divorcing parent. If both parents would read even designated portions and have meaningful dialogue, it could result in the substantial reduction of stress in what is very often the most difficult period in one's life. At the same time it could help avoid or reduce the traumatic effects that divorce usually causes to the children."

—Michael J. Ostrow, president of the
American Academy of Matrimonial Lawyers

(continued)

Mom's House, Dad's House

A Complete Guide for Parents Who Are Separated, Divorced, or Remarried

ISOLINA RICCI, Ph.D.

A FIRESIDE BOOK
PUBLISHED BY SIMON & SCHUSTER

FIRESIDE
Rockefeller Center
1230 Avenue of the Americas
New York, NY 10020

FIRESIDE and colophon are registered trademarks
of Simon & Schuster Inc.

Designed by Irving Perkins Associates Inc.
Art by Suzanne Bean Design
Art on pages 1, 28–34 copyright © 1997 by Isolina Ricci
Art on pages 57, 79, 84, 157, 255, 329 copyright © 1997 by Suzanne Bean Design

Manufactured in the United States of America

30 29 28 27 26 25 24 23 22 21

Library of Congress Cataloging-in-Publication Data
Ricci, Isolina.
Mom's house, dad's house : a complete guide for parents who are separated, divorced, or
remarried / Isolina Ricci. — [2nd ed.]
p.   cm.
"A Fireside book."
Includes bibliographical references and index.
1. Children of divorced parents—United States—Handbooks, manuals, etc.   2. Joint
custody of children—United States—Handbooks, manuals, etc.   3. Single-parent family—
United States—Handbooks, manuals, etc.   4. Stepparents—United States—Handbooks,
manuals, etc.   I. Title.
HQ777.5.R53   1997
306.89—dc21
97-29867
CIP

ISBN-13: 978-0-684-83078-0
ISBN-10:   0-684-83078-7

Acknowledgments

I am deeply grateful to the many people who have contributed in different ways to the writing of this second edition. Some of these people are given specific mention here or in the notes; still others left unmentioned know of my gratitude. This edition is richer because of their generosity.

I am indebted to Joel Edelman, Carole Roder-Esser, Emily Brown, Francis Still, Peter Maida, Karen Raiford, Judge Susan Snow, Judge Douglas McNish, Judge Mary Ann Grilli, John Kydd, Deborah Pontisso, and Bill Hilton for their wise and incisive reviews at the different stages of the manuscript. I am grateful to Reva Wiseman and Edwina Norton for their suggestions in the early stages of the revisions; to Kira Menniger for her help with readings for parents; to my attorney, Noel Silverman, for his wise counsel; to my editor at Simon & Schuster, Caroline Sutton, for her support and encouragement; and to Amber Turner for her creative work in the early stages of the line drawings. My thanks also go to my fine staff of the California Statewide Office of Family Court Services, at the Administrative Office of the Courts, California Judicial Council, who expertly held the reins of the office during my leave of absence to write this edition.

A special thanks goes to Suzanne Bean Design for rendering the line drawings that grace this edition and to Althea Lee Jordan for her patient and clearheaded reviews. A special thanks to Arlene Halligan, my administrative coordinator, for her steadfast support and aid; to Jennie Pryne Heckman for her support with the notes and review of the research; and to Maureen Crist for her incisive editorial consultation in the last stages of the project. My most special thanks go to Kathleen Erickson, a wonderful editor and friend, who coached and inspired me while guiding this edition with grace, humor, and insight.

Finally, I want to thank all the parents who brought their courage, ingenuity, and love for their children to the task of reorganizing their lives and who shared their experiences with me. They are the ones who make this all work.

This book is dedicated to my students, my clients, my open family of relatives and friends, my children's other family, and most especially to those in my own family—my parents; my brother and his family; and my children, Cindy, Eric, Beth, Andrew, Amy, and their families.

There is a special kiss for each of my grandchildren, Jesse, Tracie, Zoe, Michael, Marcus, Caroline, Mackenzie, David, Andrew Jr., and Rachel.

Contents

Part 3
THE LEGAL BUSINESS IS YOUR BUSINESS

Part 5
REFERENCES AND RESOURCES

Author's Note

This book is my friend.
A parent

THIS is the second edition of *Mom's House, Dad's House.* It is an expanded and revised step-by-step guide for people who are dealing with the difficult and often heartbreaking experience of ending an intimate relationship and the effects of this on their children. Ready or not, parents face a tremendous number of critical decisions that will affect them and their children for years to come. As you go through the process of reorganizing your life, this book offers ways to help make *good* decisions: those that can make the crisis work for you, help your children to adjust, and help to keep you *both* as active parents.

Like the original, this edition is designed to be a friend and companion to the reader. As a reference guide, it is practical, easy to use, and comprehensive. It adds sixteen more years of experience to the original edition adding new approaches and expanding and updating concepts that have stood the test of time. The first edition, published in 1980, has been used by people from all walks of life, in different countries, with various family circumstances and professional practices. This edition can be used by parents with all types of custody and living arrangements, including those who are unmarried and parenting solo.

I have tried to maintain a balance between mothers, fathers, parents with majority residence, and those with minority time, without ignoring the importance of their differences. To protect the privacy of clients, students, and colleagues who have shared their experiences with me, all names, places, and identifying circumstances have been changed. Moreover, to allow readers to compare themselves with these parents, the examples in this book reflect representative composites of many experiences rather than individual case histories.

The practical methods found on the pages that follow are dynamic. They will continue to evolve and adapt to changes in customs, behavior, and laws that govern the changing world of children and families. *Mom's House, Dad's House* remains a process—which you can take and make your own.

—ISOLINA RICCI
San Francisco, California

Part I

TWO HOMES WITH
NO FIGHTING

Chapter 1

Building a New Family Life
The Destination

"WHERE do you live?" the middle-aged businessman asked the nine-year-old girl sitting next to him on the plane.

"I live with my dad in Oregon and my mom in California."

"I mean, where do you live?" the businessman persisted.

"I live with my dad in the summers and my mom during schooltime."

"I understand, honey," he said, "but where is your real home?"

The little girl looked as puzzled as her seatmate. Then she explained: "I have two real homes. My mom's house and my dad's house."

Many children today have had the experience of the child on the plane. She had seen her original family expand into two different homes. Her home wasn't broken—it had first divided and then multiplied. Her mother and father had developed a working relationship and a way of raising her that may seem unworkable to some outsiders. Each parent believed that he or she was heading a family, even though, as further conversation disclosed, only one had remarried. This expanded family gave the child time with each parent and the security of their commitment to her well-being. She seemed to be loved and happy.

Given any voice in the matter, younger children will almost always choose a two-parent, two-home alternative over a one-home arrangement with the other parent consigned to the sidelines as a visitor or, worse yet, faded away.

Children usually go straight to the heart of the issue, even when parents are struggling. When they "visit" their "noncustodial" parent, they stake out their territory. They leave behind books, shoes, pajamas, toothbrushes, homework. The kids are wisely, perhaps unconsciously, carving out their own place. They are saying, "I am your child. My things belong here, too. Don't forget me when I'm gone. This is my home, too." They shy away from words like "visit my dad or my mom." Instead they say they're going to "be with my dad" or "live with my mom this summer." And for good reasons: outsiders visit; families live together. "It's a bigger family," say some children. "Both houses belong to me" or "I have two homes and two families." "Yeah, I live most of the time with my mom, but I live with my dad, too," say others. Children, after they are convinced that they can't have both parents living together under one roof, will settle for both parents separated but still functioning as parents and families. One youngster, when asked what he saw as the ideal life for a child of divorced and/or remarried parents, put it simply: "Two homes with no fighting."

BUILDING A NEW FAMILY LIFE

This book will help you build this new family life, "two homes with no fighting." When parents ache with feelings of pain, guilt, or betrayal, this can seem out of reach. But in the pages that follow you will see how to transform your negative or hurt experiences into a positive force in your life. Many of the major premises contained here have been used for more than two decades by parents in many parts of the world. They have also been used effectively by attorneys, judges, mental health professionals, mediators, educators, and physicians in their work with parents. Many people have achieved what they want—a release from the pain of the past and a promise for the future—more joy, less conflict, a new life, and children who adjusted well to the separation. Their children have been given what they want— both parents, and an expanded family in two homes; more joy and less conflict and tension. What appears on these pages goes well beyond the concept of child custody, separation, or divorce; it is a redefinition of family life for today—how to organize it, strengthen it, and make it work it in Mom's house and Dad's house.

In order to use the guidelines suggested here, neither you nor the other parent is asked to take on or give up sole custody. Some children have a fifty-fifty time split between the homes, others an eighty-twenty or even a ninety-ten division. Some have arrangements where they see each parent every day, others wait weeks or even months to see a parent who is thousands of miles away. No one family is exactly like another.

Regardless of their differences, many parents have used the methods described here to learn how to stake out their own territory, set up their own standards, make their own agreements, and stay out of each other's hair. They have acquired the skills that allow them to wave a slow but definite good-bye to their former intimate relationship and develop a new one, only this time in a businesslike working relationship as parents who are living apart. They have learned how to make a new life and to keep their kids out of the middle of their problems with one another.

Parents have adapted the approach in this book to just about every conceivable circumstance—to former spouses who were friendly, angry, vindictive, possessive, dropouts; to those living down the street or across the continent; to those who were unmarried, who had remarried, who were single, or who were in living-together arrangements. Even solo parents who were completely alone have designed unique shared parenting arrangements with close friends or relatives.

The approach suggested here can function with a minimum of communication between you and the other parent—as long as it is the right type of communication. You do not have to have romantic feelings of love for your former mate any more than you have to have romantic feelings of love for your druggist in order to get a prescription filled. What you do need is a way to relate with one another that works to help you carry out one of the most important jobs anyone ever undertakes—raising their children.

A WORLD OF HURT: DEALING WITH THE SEPARATION

If you are now suffering with the pain of separation, it may be difficult to imagine you and the children in a new life. Separation and divorce are like a hurricane or flood—no matter how much warning there is, you can be hit hard by the impact. Maybe you do not want your life together to end, and you feel numb, betrayed, torn by grief. If the separation was more your idea, you may be surprised at how deeply you feel the end of the relationship or feel an ambivalence you didn't know existed. If this sounds familiar, remember that you are not the only one in this world of hurt and confusion. Your children are there, too. But the shock will wear off. Then, just as if you and your family had been victimized by a natural disaster, you will have to attend to the work of repairing, cleaning, and rebuilding.

> *Take heart.*
> *There is a way through this*
> *to a better day.*

You, your children, and your family are important. You count. Don't let feelings of powerlessness fool you into inaction—you're a parent, a powerful force. As time goes on, you may also come to see how essential the other parent is to your child. He or she may help you, too. When your child has problems, in times of illness, and when work schedules change, the other parent can help carry the load. A realistic goal? For many parents, yes. In the pages that follow, you will also find different ways to regain a stronger sense of yourself and your importance. As time goes on, there can be a renewed sense of competence and belonging that blossoms with your new life. This new identity can affect you in many ways—as a parent, in new relationships, in the work world, at your children's school, in your community.

MAKING DECISIONS: FIND YOUR OWN PACE

"Family life was full of decisions and details before we separated," said a mother of three teenagers. "Now it's a swamp of things to decide and redecide." Separation means decisions, decisions, decisions. And they are usually very important ones. Parents will say things like "I don't know if I'm doing the right thing," "I'm overwhelmed," or "It's just too much at once." While some feel overwhelmed, others want to tackle all these decisions head-on. They want to settle things *now* and may not think things through. Neither the very slow nor the very immediate approach works out in the end. Yes, the process can be complicated and difficult—sometimes you will have to move exceptionally quickly, other times it is "hurry up and wait." But there are opportunities for you to learn, to change in ways that you have always wanted, and to reorganize your life and your family. *If you want to use this crisis to your advantage, you can. You are, after all, making exceptionally big decisions, decisions that can affect the rest of your life and those of your children.* This book will help you make these decisions and find a pace that you feel you can live with.

TWO HOMES CAN WORK FOR YOU

The approach described in this book has a long history. It began in the early 1970s when, as a therapist and mediator, I began teaching my first seminars and classes for divorcing parents in a Southern California community. As the months went on, my students and clients taught me how complex it could be to pull away from an intimate relationship and reorganize one's life. They continually asked for practical, concrete information that would help them place their experiences in perspective. Parents have complicated, often stressful lives with little time or energy for theory and polemics. They insisted on easy-to-use information that helped them place their own experience in perspective and give them a sense of direction and purpose. As one father of three young teenagers said, "There has to be some sense to all of this! Where am I going, anyway?"

To answer their requests, step-by-step guidelines and principles evolved. The original guides were published in the first edition of *Mom's House, Dad's House* in 1980. Since then I have had the pleasure of meeting and working with many more people. Some parents were determined, articulate, persistent. They wanted their children, they wanted their life to go back to normal, they wanted to get through the crisis in as good a shape as possible. Others, less assertive, were devastated by events that were out of their control, feeling betrayed, discarded, worthless. They wanted relief, respect, a sense of hope. The professionals I worked with asked for even more information they could pass on to their clients. Each new perspective taught me important lessons about what worked and what didn't. This second edition has been expanded to include as much of this new information as space allows.

THE OVERALL PICTURE

A good place to begin is with the commonly held truths learned over years of experience.

1. Children love, want, and need both parents. Fathers as well as mothers are the core of their child's life. Both parents—with and without custody—are important to their children's well-being and healthy development. Of course there are many stable and loving families where one of the parents is missing. These families have learned how to adjust and make second homes or strong ties with extended families and friends where the children are loved and protected. But there are also "pushed out" or absent parents. How their absence is handled is enormously important to a child. Children do not forget a parent.

2. Each child is unique. What one child can handle, another cannot. One six-year-old child handles a change of residence fairly well, a classmate with the same situation is bewildered and confused. While there are many guidelines parents can use to make decisions about what is best for their child, their decisions must always be guided by a heightened sensitivity to their child's individual temperament, level of development, experience, and resiliency. Wise parents increase their attention and commitment to their child during these crisis months. They know that what they do heavily influences not only how well their child copes now but also the kind of adult he or she will someday become.

3. A good legal agreement cannot guarantee a good result. Even when parents or the court decide on a good and fair custody arrangement, the settlement alone means little if the parents don't know how to put it all into practice. A court award was never meant to educate parents on the process of ending a marriage and continuing their parenting any more than it can prepare people for getting married in the first place. A first-class legal agreement is at best a good piece of surgery. It does not guarantee recuperation. The agreement alone is not enough. Parents need to learn how to make agreements work in daily life.

Unfortunately, not all legal agreements are first-class, nor are they all arrived at justly. Most people have seen friends or relatives engaged in a tug-of-war over their children. The battling "exes" who drag themselves and their children through court confrontations may make good dramatic material, but in truth they are not the majority of couples who separate or divorce. The majority of parents will not take their dissatisfactions into the courtroom. One or both of them do not trust the legal process, can't be bothered, don't have the money, or don't want to take the risk of making things worse.

4. How parents relate to one another after separation is crucial. Children need parents to relate in a constructive way—married, single, or divorced. Children do poorly when their parents are engaged in open hostilities and even worse when their parents involve them in the battle. The longer and the more intense the war, the more potential long-term damage to their child. While some anger and conflict is normal in all families, hostile parents cross over the line. They may lose control, fling accusations, blame, rage. Anything goes. After separation, the stakes become even higher.

Finding a way to relate constructively is the key to unlocking a happier future. People usually feel they have good reasons for how they feel, and some cannot seem to recover their emotional equilibrium, even after a year or two. But the eventual resolution—or at least management—of these emotions is a profound but necessary accomplishment. People *do* learn how to take these negative feelings and transform them into a positive force in their lives. When this happens, everyone is the better for it. If this is not done, these powerful feelings may not fade away and instead can grow worse over time.

For example, sole custody arrangements with visitation to the other parent can leave girls and boys with "responsibility mommies" and "recreation director daddies" or, worse, with overburdened mothers and dropout fathers. This approach doesn't strengthen family life, it weakens it, and the child pays a heavy emotional price. The child's life can be reduced by one parent; the custodial parent's responsibilities are doubled; the other parent is reduced to the status of a powerless paying visitor. Such lopsided arrangements breed even more distrust, resentment, and acrimony between the parents that may actually increase when one of them remarries. Poor shared custody arrangements can harm children, too. The arrangement may put the child in the middle, stoke the conflict, or just be a way to avoid paying more child support. The children may have both parents, but they are not free to be themselves at either home. The child pays the price.

5. Divorce precipitates a confrontation with many traditional values and beliefs, especially those that define the best interests of children. Fathers and mothers spoke to me in anguish and anger and told of their frustration, their sense of powerlessness, and their search for new standards. There were feelings of bitterness, shame, resentment.

One mother with paralegal training described her experience of filing her first set of divorce papers. "I felt like I was filing a 'certificate of failure.' Failure to pay attention to the marriage, to judge my choice for a husband. When I handed in my papers, I thought, 'If this was a term paper, it would be an F.' "

People have been raised to believe that divorce meant the destruction of the family. Many feel that a one-parent home is automatically not a family but some secondhand arrangement and that society agrees. The parent with custody is viewed as heading an "incomplete" family, and the parent without custody doesn't have a family at all. Parents still face stigma and bias that demoralize their efforts. Yet both mothers and fathers *do* head complete and viable families. They *can* contribute a wealth of experience to their community.

6. There is such a thing as a "decent" divorce, and it is worth the effort it takes to get it. A "decent divorce" is not a mystery. The key? There are standards of conduct for a solid marriage, and there are also standards of conduct for a decent separation or divorce. A good marriage takes work; so does a decent divorce. It takes a major effort during the first year before the separation and at least two or three years afterward. It can be attained through systematic training, learning, and practice. Much like learning a new language or a new skill, a person has to learn the basics, then go on to the more complicated tasks. With practice comes experience and expertise. So it is with the work of reorganizing one's life and the lives of your children. There are natural yet powerful processes marked by recognizable stages, dangerous conditions, and times of contentment. As the years have passed, much more has been learned about these patterns. The basic ingredients of a decent separation or divorce are things most parents can learn. Education, practice, and persistence are the keys. It can be seen as an ordeal that one survives, or it can be viewed as a crisis that you will do your best to learn from and make work for you.

The principles and guidelines shown in this book will serve many purposes at once. Setting up a solid two-home arrangement comforts the children, allows the parents more breathing room. Developing a working relationship as parents further stabilizes the children, takes them out of the middle, and provides you a chance to pull back from what I call "negative intimacy." This also provides a good platform from which to make legal decisions, negotiate for yourself, and build a new personal life. Everything is usually related to everything else.

MANAGING THE GOAL OF A DECENT DIVORCE OR SEPARATION

MAKING THE CRISIS WORK FOR YOU

Ignoring the crisis periods or doing as little as possible to navigate the separation or divorce does not pay. "I spent too much of my life investing in that marriage," said one man, "I'm not investing in this divorce." This man was in for a rude surprise. Regardless of how much one invested in an intimate relationship, ending it usually takes a tremendous amount of time and energy and usually money. A person can attempt to turn everything over to an attorney or try to ignore the process. But the results are not particularly positive, and the process can be unnecessarily harsh.

At the end of three years, this father faced a series of things he thought would just go away by themselves. They didn't. He was still angry at his former mate, his children's poor adjustment to the divorce was now a major worry, his second marriage was limping because of the problems with his first wife and his children. Like many people who didn't pay attention to how they handled the divorce process, his life is far more complicated now than it was before. He is still attached, or "divorced to," his former partner, spending just as much or more energy on the battle as he did before. The children need him as a father. They need him to find a more constructive way to relate their mother about them. His new wife needs this settled so they can get on with their life together. This man obtained a legal divorce, but because of the bad feelings that had been generated over the last three years, he was now farther away from being finished with his first marriage than he was when he started.

There are more constructive ways to navigate the course of ending an intimate relationship. As one woman said after completing a two-day workshop with me, "I floundered for six months, then I learned about this approach. I feel I have direction now." She came to believe she could make the crisis work for her. And eventually so did the father in the earlier example. In the process, they learned things that helped them in other parts of their daily life and in planning for their future.

Two real homes with no fighting does not happen overnight. It takes work, sweat, and tears. But it's worth the effort.

What we have learned so far suggests a new family bill of rights. If you haven't already starting making your own notes, this is a good place to start.

A NEW FAMILY BILL OF RIGHTS

THE FAMILY BILL OF RIGHTS

- Each child has the right to have two homes where he or she is cherished and given the opportunity to develop normally.
- Each child has the right to a meaningful, nurturing relationship with each parent.
- Each parent and child has the right to call themselves a family regardless of how the children's time is divided.
- Each parent has the responsibility and right to contribute to the raising of his or her child.
- Each child has the right to have competent parents and to be free from hearing, observing, or being part of their parents' arguments or problems with one another.
- Each parent has the right to his or her own private life and territory and to raise the children without unreasonable interference from the other parent.

HOW THE FAMILY BILL OF RIGHTS WORKS

Based on this new bill of rights, parents without custody or with minority time with their children have learned to ignore the implications of being "visitors" and have set up real homes with their own routines. Both parents have learned how to relax, to feel less strained, less guilty, and return their attention to their children. Both parents have been encouraged to reject the myths about "broken homes," about being "second-class" families, to move toward updating their language and their meaning of family, and to understand the impact of change on their feelings and their bodies.

The next stage may be the most difficult for some parents to complete. A retreat from your former intimate relationship as mates while at the same time developing a new, civil working relationship as parents is a major accomplishment. Once this breakthrough begins to happen—and this book will show you how—everything begins to work far better. The children are happier, the parents are back in control of their lives, the legal business is more organized, and there is a brighter future for everyone, especially children.

WHEN CHILDREN DO BEST

When children are free to love both their parents without conflict of loyalty, to have access to them both without fear of losing either, they can get on with the totally absorbing business of growing up, on schedule. They can learn to master the tasks that life places before them with confidence and a sense of security. And both parents and children can learn that something as hurtful and as earthshaking as a separation or divorce can eventually be handled constructively.

Research and experience all say the same things. Children who do best are those whose parents make them feel loved and wanted in each home, whose parents have a way to relate to one another that keeps the children out of their disagreements and bad feelings, whose parents eventually learn to manage their major disputes with one another, who can support the other parent's relationship with their children, and who allow the children independent relationships with each of them. These same factors have long been central to the commonsense, two-home approach. The chapters that follow will offer you many options for meeting these challenges.

TWO HOMES COME IN MANY SHAPES AND STYLES

Years ago, when families we knew began living in two homes, my colleagues and I all questioned: "Will children be confused when there were two authorities in two homes?" "Don't children need one home base alone?" "What about the problems that come with having contact with your former spouse? Doesn't this lead to more conflict?"

The answers came quickly. Every day most children demonstrate their ability to adapt to somewhat different authorities, different rules. After all, they follow different rules at school, in their organized sports, in their neighborhood games, at camp. They live every moment of their lives in a fast-paced pluralistic world, where expectations change with settings. They learn that at one house they get carrot sticks for snacks, while at another ice cream or cookies. One dad plays baseball with the kids, and another yells at them to be quiet. Differences are the norm.

No one set of families will shape its associations like any other. Times change. Circumstances change. Parents move, remarry, get new jobs. Children grow into teenagers. A working relationship between parents living separately has its ups and downs, its good times and bad times. Given time and effort, it usually holds its course.

Parents settled into two homes do, of course, make mistakes. Their old feelings sometimes get the best of them. They may not like each other much, but now they can work together. As a result, they and their children put down the burdens of active strife and take up the tools that build the future. The children still have both parents, but now in two homes: each parent has one home, an independent private life, and a stronger hand with the children during the times they are living together. Furthermore, when the parent who moved out of the original home became an involved parent again, everyone visibly relaxed, especially the children.

IF YOU BELIEVE YOU HAVE A FAMILY, THEN YOU HAVE ONE

When children believe—because their parents believe—that they have an expanded family that includes two intact homes where they belong and are wanted, everyone gains the security of continuity as well as a sense of the parents' commitment to their parental roles. The definition of a family must, as is true in the search for so many other meanings and values, come from within. If parents think they have a family, then they have one. If parents set their sights on a decent divorce and giving their child two homes, they can do it. And they are pioneering a wave of the future.

If you are feeling discouraged about things, consider this. Even parents ordered by the court to parenting classes because of their unusual acrimony and battles with one another have learned how to relate successfully. It is not uncommon to hear a parent say at the end of six weeks of parenting education, "If I had only had this class before I divorced, I could have saved the time I lost with our child, and fifteen thousand dollars!" This book is not a substitute for counseling, mediation, or a comprehensive parenting class. But it can be a "friend" you can refer to again and again, one that can give you a head start.

One mother put her experiences in this new world of two homes this way: "Yes, people tell me it can't work, but I ask them what alternative they can suggest. All they have to offer me is isolation in one home or destructive attitudes that lead only to more hurt for all of us. The two-home approach may not work for some. But I think it's the best show in town when you're shopping for something good for you and your kids."

THE NEW PIONEERS

The family that rears children has survived in one form or another from the beginning of time. Children need to be raised to adulthood, and adults need to be supported in their child-rearing efforts. Despite the grim statistics on divorce, separation, foster care, abandonment of elders, and family violence, a present-day parent can take solace in the fact that over the course of history, families have weathered various kinds of reconstruction and reorganization and have pioneered new ways to raise their children. It wasn't too long ago that women's life spans were much shorter than men's. Those who survived carried on and raised their children under the most adverse conditions, alone if necessary or with help from assorted family members, friends, and neighbors.

All over the world, colonists, refugees, immigrants, and ordinary citizens have moved across oceans, to another region or country. Others lived their entire lives in one place but suffered enormous losses in wars, natural disasters, and epidemics. That fact alone, taken together with economic demands, crop failures, and trade debacles, meant that families had to reorganize, reconstitute, and often change residences. We all have relatives who survived a world war or global flu epidemic. Some of our grandparents or great-grandparents were orphans or adopted. The crucial quality in these survivor families was the strength that came from sharing experiences, conquering obstacles, and learning how to adapt to the new challenges. They pioneered a new family frontier, then. You are pioneering one now.

When family survival demanded it, men and women could and did set aside rigid ideas about men's work and women's work. The father of two girl toddlers didn't let them starve because he wouldn't cook their meals after their mother died. A woman who had spent years hacking a homestead out of the wilderness with her husband and children wasn't going to give it away or give up after her husband's death—not if she could help it. These families didn't see themselves—and were not labeled—as deviant or unacceptable any more than a dad and two kids who live together during holidays and summers need to be so labeled today.

Today's parents can use the same pioneering courage and ingenuity as they reorganize their family life. They can maintain pride in themselves as parents and heads of families. And by incorporating the essential qualities of family closeness, commitment, and caring into the reorganized family, they can make the transition from the family-that-was to the family-that-is with grace and hope.

HOW TO USE THIS BOOK

This is a book of options. I strongly urge all readers—parents, children, friends, and relatives—to read the whole book from cover to cover before making any major changes or decisions in their own situations. Each chapter has an important message, like a piece of a picture puzzle. Although a few pieces of the puzzle may be useful, the overall picture can remain cloudy or even misunderstood. You may not need all the pieces to get an outline of the picture, but you do need to know which pieces you are leaving out and why.

Timing may be important to the usefulness of this book. A person torn by regret or betrayal may not have the heart to read much for a while. But several months later, when faced with myriad decisions about house, children, money, and relating to the other parent, the information here becomes an important resource. Most people who have used the methods given here have found that the rapid changes they went through during their first two years of separation were eased by reviewing certain basic principles and guidelines. After a few years, people report that what they once felt was elementary became more and more profound as their lives unfolded and certain methods took on new value and increased usefulness. One parent, a writer, said: "This book is my reference manual. It sits right next to my dictionary and thesaurus."

If you are in the process of ending your marriage now, pay special attention to part 1 and the more specific information in part 2. If you are now dealing with the legal business, part 3 is important. Part 4 covers important issues about your family, remarriage, dealing with garden-variety complaints, and the years after separation. Part 5 is a reference guide.

The information that follows emphasizes an order and structure for understanding or evaluating circumstances. It is for you, the reader. Expand it, revise it, ignore it. Even your disagreements with an idea can help you focus your own point of view. The purpose of the book is to offer you more alternatives and information on how to make these different choices work for you. The final and best judge of what will be best for you and your children is—and will continue to be—you.

Chapter 2

Believe in Your Family
Dispelling Destructive Myths

Twelve Destructive Myths About Divorce
Taking Control of the Myths
Believe in Your Family

"IT can't work," said a psychiatrist when he heard about training parents to develop a working relationship after divorce. "If couples couldn't get along when they were married, they aren't going to get along after divorce." An attorney in the group nodded in agreement.

Although I first heard this destructive myth in the mid-1970s, I have heard this *"It can't work"* myth repeated in various forms too many times since. Even though today history has shown that many, if not most, couples can learn how to build a working relationship as parents, nonetheless you will still hear comments such as "If those couples can apply that kind of effort to their divorce, they should have done it for their marriage. They should never have split up in the first place."

This belief, like those described later in this chapter, is deeply rooted in our dated myths about families and what they ought to be. These myths feed our fears and hard feelings.

You may believe some of these stereotypes yourself, be tempted to play a few games, and step on a land mine or two. The negative myths and beliefs can be powerful deterrents to your progress—both individually and as a parent. They can block the development of a working relationship between you and the other parent and hinder your emotional recovery. They can lead you to believe that what you have is a second-class "broken home" rather than a first-class family. Better to set aside destructive myths and stereotypes whenever you can so you can be more creative and your progress can be steadier.

While later chapters will describe how to detour around damaging myths and take positive action, this chapter will outline some of the guises in which they might appear.

TWELVE DESTRUCTIVE MYTHS ABOUT DIVORCE

MYTH ONE: IT CAN'T WORK

As you move to explore the two-home concept, you are probably going to come up against some common but destructive beliefs that say that no matter how hard you try, you and the other parent will not be able to get along after you separate. A decent divorce may be seen as a weird or freak accident. There are still people who believe that normal separations always bring about an all-out war, or at the least a soap opera where former spouses are embittered, distrustful, or sarcastic. This does not have to happen to you. *It can work.*

MYTH TWO: YOU DIDN'T TRY

Connected to Myth One is the *"You didn't try"* myth. This one says that most couples have not tried hard enough or long enough to save their relationship. While this may be true in some cases, many couples *have* tried hard and for a very long time—sometimes as long as six or seven years. When children are involved, separation is a particularly powerful and drastic step. Most people realize that it will change their life forever. They don't do it lightly.

MYTH THREE: THE OTHER PARENT DISAPPEARS AND LEAVES YOU ALONE

One of the most misleading myths is that the other parent will either disappear or be relegated powerless to the sidelines and that everyone will be happier. Unless one parent is a danger to the other and the children, legally one parent cannot keep the children away from another parent. Educators, lawyers, and other professionals are all familiar with this myth. Parents come into their classes or offices with expectations based on TV, films, and fiction. They are startled to find out that in the real world of separation or divorce, the other parent can and will be in their child's life, whether they like it or not. The child is the primary owner of the relationship with his or her parents, not the other way around. Parents express their bewilderment: they have parted and now they still have to talk to one another? Be parents together? Yes.

As a wise and well-known family law judge said, "The reality is that marriage is not forever—but if you have children, divorce is."

MYTH FOUR: DIVORCE IS EITHER A SOAP OPERA OR A WAR

During my weekend workshops, one of the first discussions parents would have among themselves concerns the reactions of friends, neighbors, family, and professionals their separation or divorce. Commonly, parents reported both support and divisiveness describing their circumstances as a "soap opera," or war. One father, for example, described a commitment he and the children's mother had made to keep their parenting functions separate from their anger with one another, only to have her family interfere, recast all of his behavior in negative light, and push her hard for an all-out battle.

"The children's mother and I felt good about our working relationship, but her parents were outraged. They think that I should have nothing to do with the kids, that I'm a bastard for not being the son-in-law they had expected, and that the farther away I am from her and the kids, the better. Their disapproval of me is hard on her. She needs their support and understanding, so she feels she has to agree with them about me."

This couple didn't hold the old beliefs about divorce, but people close to them wanted a war. They felt he should be excluded and good riddance. The extended family did not understand how wars and soap operas take away a family's dignity and self-respect.

MYTH FIVE: "BLAME GAMES" ARE INEVITABLE

Justifying one's separation brings with it a temptation to play dirty, to play "blame games." Most people give in to this temptation during the first year of separation, but it shouldn't become a way of life. The search for reasons why marriage has ended is a natural response to a needed reassessment, but seeking reasons to place blame is an occupational hazard. When blaming becomes too strong, it can throw a monkey wrench into both your own "emotional divorce" and developing a decent working relationship with the other parent. But most of all, it hurts your children. More than you know. Children sense things, hear things, see things that tell them one of their parents is ridiculing or putting down the other parent. It feels awful. It is confusing. It is scary. It's embarrassing.

Countless times I have heard people say you need a strong reason for going through the trauma of separation or divorce. "It's a powerful experience that changes your life, and if you are going to put yourself and your kids through it, the reasons had better be damned good ones. Otherwise, when the going gets tough, you ask yourself, Was it worth it? You have to find support for your view that either what you left was so bad or what you have now is so good that you can safely say 'Yes, it was worth it.' It's seems much easier if you just say, 'I had no choice.' "

The only thing wrong with me (or the kids) was you. Blame usually looks for a single root cause, an easy answer to the "failure" of a relationship. Nonetheless, family, friends, acquaintances, and the couple themselves feel they can ask, "Who's to blame for the failure of the relationship or the marriage?" "Who hurt who?" "Who's to blame for ruining the kid's home life? *Somebody* is causing them a lot of pain." "What about hurting the kid's grandparents (or brother, or sister, or other close family member)? *Somebody* is causing *them* a lot of pain, too." "Who's to blame for destroying the family's economic solvency? For denying the children a college education?" "Who's to blame for draining the community's resources? For taking away another functioning family? *Somebody* is destroying the backbone of society." The truth is that there are few simple answers. Relationships dissolve for complex and very personal reasons.

"It's not my fault." Competition is as essential to blame games as chips are to poker. When Dad zips around in a sports car with the children's young gym teacher, Mom, to dramatize the contrast, stays home, submerging herself in household chores and bemoaning the problems of her new job. She calls him an irresponsible playboy; he sees her as a killjoy drudge. Mom wins the morality stakes; he has the fun. Both say: "See what I had to put up with?" An extension of this thinking is the proclamation "The only thing wrong with the kids was you." Still-married parents play these "your child/my child" games, too, but the potential damage to everyone is multiplied during divorce. It's important to remember that if you insist on adult blame games, you run the risk of placing your children in the center of the table as things to be won, rather than as children to be loved and protected. Blame games are too expensive for everyone.

"Failure feels terrible," said one gentle-looking man in his twenties. "You don't want to carry that around with you if you can help it. You blame the other guy and you feel better. Or you blame yourself and feel even worse."

The third alternative is viewing the situation as a problem to solve instead of placing blame. Fortunately more people are taking this "high road," maintaining their self-respect and moving more quickly to a reorganized life. But they still may have to go against the force of popular opinion. Blaming may be a favorite way of explaining things, but it usually boomerangs in the end.

MYTH SIX: THERE IS ONE TRUE VERSION OF WHY THE RELATIONSHIP ENDED

One couple nearly always means *two* versions of what happened—one for each of the people intimately involved. The tendency to see only one side of a story is natural but potentially disastrous when there is a separation. A hidden hook on which to hang the "reasons" for separation is that both people can find enough circumstantial evidence in the past to support their view or feed the blame. Surprisingly enough, the strength of these negative perspectives provides a continuing attachment between the separating couple. In part 2 and elsewhere throughout the book, you will read more about the force of these old ties, how they can have a destructive effect on your future and your children. Most people feel hurt, angry, guilty, or vindictive at different times in the separation or divorce process. Such feelings are natural. But they also mean that you are not yet emotionally disentangled from your former mate. When people are still entangled after several years, they are called "divorced to" their former spouse, not "divorced from" him or her. They are on their way to a "forever" divorce.

MYTH SEVEN: CHILDREN ARE GOOD INTERPRETERS

Some children can have their own alternatives to blame games—learning how to manipulate the adults around them. Sometimes they carry information between the parents, losing bits or introducing changes along the way to make things turn out the way they wish things were. Children might say, "Dad is so lonely, Mom," hoping Mom will make contact with Dad and renew communications. Or they say, "Mom has a new boyfriend," hoping Dad will take the cue to try to win her back. Even when children never attempt to manipulate their parents, they may innocently blame themselves for their parents' hostilities and for other unhappy outcomes of the separation or divorce. These are serious burdens children place upon themselves. *Children are wonderful observers but often poor interpreters.* Later chapters will explain what parents can do to help their children.

MYTH EIGHT: THE BEST WAY TO DO SOMETHING IS ALL OR NOT AT ALL

The all-or-nothing myth judges situations in extremes. The following is an all-too-common example of how lack of knowledge about garden-variety behavior by children and parents can lead parents to expect the worst and eventually get it.

"The kids are so rotten when they come home from a weekend with their father, it takes me two days to settle them down," said a mother of four. "Sometimes I wish he were in Alaska or Australia. Then I wouldn't have to put up with this stuff from the kids." The father's version was: "I got to thinking, What's the use? My influence is worthless anyway. She makes all the rules now that she has sole custody. Anything I do with the kids will just be wiped away after they return home. Besides, how can a man be a father without a woman, a regular house, or a yard?"

This is *all-or-nothing* thinking. Both these people are reporting common complaints of the newly separated parent. Some simple remedies could straighten out the situation, but often people are uninformed. In their frustrated search for a reason, both parents reach the conclusion that the other parent is at fault. Then they fall into the all-or-nothing trap. The parent with custody takes on the double burden of being father and mother, and the parent without custody feels they can't parent at all without the necessary equipment of house, spouse, and yard. Distrust and resentment grow.

Perhaps Mom, in desperation, tells the children that if they don't stop their bad behavior when they return from their father's place, they won't be able to see him at all. Or maybe Dad gets a chance to take a weekend vacation for the first time in three years. Secretly relieved that he won't have to face his dilemma once more, he cancels his time with the kids. The stage is set for a widening rift. Eventually Dad fades away from active involvement with the children. He can't stand the pain anymore. Mom thinks good riddance. But as the months and years go by she wishes he were involved as she witnesses the longer-term effects on the children of the loss of their father.

Later on, some parents who try to reenter the children's lives make a major error in judgment when they attempt to do so in an all-or-nothing way. Instead of contacting the resident parent and working out a gradual schedule to become reacquainted with the children, they may go for the jugular. Some file lawsuits stating that the resident parent is a poor parent and that they can provide a better home—often using their remarriage as the major reason. "He hasn't talked to the kids in two years," a mother might say, "and he wants custody?" or "She hasn't earned the right to any custody," a father might say, "she abandoned them." All-or-nothing breeds even more all-or-nothing when what is needed is a reasoned, measured approach to a middle ground.

MYTH NINE: CHILDREN ALWAYS DO BETTER IN ONE HOME, WITH ONE AUTHORITY

One particularly devastating outcome of the all-or-nothing mentality is a rigid *one-home, one-authority myth*. Parents beginning new family patterns must recognize that they may have to reinvent their mother-father united front.

Instead of yielding on some issues or seeking out some middle ground of compromise, separating parents can trap themselves in old one-authority binds, insisting that one parent's view always triumphs over the other's.

Parents may expect their children to choose one of them over the other. "This is a two-party system," said one father, "where children are expected to register with either Mom or Dad." The outcome is that many parents without custody fight for custody themselves or in time drop out, arguing: "Why pay that other parent money to keep my children away from me?" Or: "Why try to maintain a relationship with my kids when my influence is negligible and erased the minute I drop them at that other doorstep?"

The one-home, one-authority myth not only says parents cannot disagree, it also says that the children should not maintain important, independent relationships with each parent, even though such a separate bond between parent and child is a healthy development in both married *and* single families! This ability for each parent and child to develop individual relationships without the interference of another family member allows the entire family to respect personal differences. As you will see in later chapters, individual parent-child relationships are key factors in providing opportunities to build character, impart values, and foster good judgment.

A "perfect" united front about child-rearing philosophies is rare in any family. After money, the second most common reason married parents argue is over issues of how to raise their child. Yet somehow, separated parents are expected to always have this meeting of the minds or else be judged as hopelessly at odds. This is another stereotype to put on the shelf. Parents do disagree. They learn how to deal with it constructively.

MYTH TEN: THERE ARE ONLY TWO OPTIONS: TO BE THE BATTLING EXES OR TO HAVE THE PERFECT DIVORCE

A couple locked in combat is found at one end of the all-or-nothing scale that provides only two models for parents after their marriage ends—the battling exes and the perfect couple. The battling exes' acrimony and distrust cause them to act like spiteful, irrational children. According to this stereotype, the divorced parents are supposed to hold grudges against each other for the rest of their lives, with their children severely hurt in the crossfire. Their only recourse is repeated court battles, economic ruin, or for one parent eventually to retreat from it all and to drop out. The motto: "Anything goes."

The other extreme is occupied by the couple who have managed a "perfect divorce." They cooperate cordially either in evenly divided times between homes or regulated times of "visitation." No hostility, no mistakes, and no hard feelings. The children seem to express no pain, no objections. This "ideal" model is hardly attainable for most families.

Most separating or divorcing parents fall somewhere between these two extremes. Parents weary of hostilities and legal action say that there has to be a better way. Those who heartily dislike each other look at the "perfect" model and protest, "We'd never be able to do that." Fortunately they can learn how to develop a decent working relationship as parents. What these parents do not yet know is that while they may not achieve a "perfect" relationship, they can build one that actually brings good results. Many parents who initially felt betrayed, were angry, hurt, or distrustful, did build a good parenting relationship for the sake of their children. Their children grew up and are now solid citizens raising their own families.

MYTH ELEVEN: CHILDREN ARE NOT HARMED BY PARENTS WHO BELIEVE THESE MYTHS

Behind these emotional and social roadblocks, parents have small companions. Children can't pack their bags and say, "Bye, see you when you've worked it out," and walk out into the streets. Children know they need adults to survive. Their instincts will lead them to secure the basic necessities of life. They may not have to take sides to survive physically, but too often they are expected to prove their loyalty or love to one or the other parent. Then they conclude that they must line up with one parent or the other to survive emotionally. They are children. They want each of their parents to be in their lives, they want to feel safe, loved, protected. Children are hurt deeply when they become part of a soap opera or have to listen to blame games or hear relatives demean a parent—or, even worse, are expected to become part of the attack on the other parent. Children are victimized by destructive myths.

MYTH TWELVE: "SOLO" PARENTS ARE RARELY SUCCESSFUL IN RAISING THEIR CHILDREN

Sometimes one parent assumes all the rights and authority over a child's ongoing life. Sometimes this is because a parent is unmarried and the other parent is out of the picture or has just faded away. In other cases one parent has a long disabling illness, a history of child abuse or neglect, family violence, substance abuse, alcoholism, other criminal behavior. When this occurs, children must be assigned to one safe home quickly—and sometimes permanently. The remaining parent then faces the challenge of raising a child alone and overcoming the traumas of the past. Many solo parents do this well. While their experiences are more dramatic and demanding, they also face many of the same things other separating parents face. Still, these parents have to set aside the stereotypes that say solo parents can't do a good job raising their child. They can do it and they have!

TAKING CONTROL OF THE MYTHS

Destructive myths need not rule your behavior or your life as you move on to your future. Make it easy on yourself. Observe these destructive myths when they appear. If you are a person who likes to write things down, make a note of what myth you observed, how it felt. Just the simple acts of observing something and writing it down will change things a little. Then choose only one myth to put on the shelf. Putting away one myth usually leads to positive results with others. It is a domino effect. Use the suggestions in the chapters that follow to step around your myth or to put it away. Believe in yourself and your family. Build something more solid, positive, and joyful for yourself and your child.

BELIEVE IN YOUR FAMILY

What is your family to you? Take a moment to think of (and write down if that helps you) all the ideas that come to mind when you hear or see the word "family." Pay attention to one particular question: Which dominates? The family you grew up in, the one you've been raising lately, or perhaps even some slick media image you've never seen in real life? When you say "family" right now, what do you mean? If your first answer, regardless of "custody" or marital status, is "The kids and me," you're on the right track. Your family can have all the key elements: a bond of love and experience, a shared residence, commitment, family traditions, customs, responsibilities toward each other, and pride.

Forget about marriage for the moment. Marriage may have begun a family, but it doesn't continue it. Nor does divorce or separation end it. When the marriage ends, the family does not break, does not magically disappear. It can, instead, like the family of the girl on the airplane in chapter 1, expand into separate healthy cells from the same organism. The total amount of time spent together is not necessarily the most important characteristic of a family, but the commitment and caring for one another is.

UPDATE YOUR DREAM

For some of us, the original dream of family went something like this: "Marry and live happily ever after. Grow old together. Watch the kids grow up, leave home, make their own homes, and come back visiting with wonderful grandchildren."

Many parents have told me of the dreams they once had. While they had their own variations and hopes, their dreams shared certain common elements:

- The intimate relationship between the husband and wife, how we saw and filled those roles
- The parents' relationship as parents and how they presented themselves to their children—preferably the "united front"
- The relationship between the parent and the child
- The shared residence—that one home
- The shared family history, heritage, and the "old family feeling."

When a relationship ends, the family *can* retain all of the ideal elements, but arranged somewhat differently. The parents still have a residence, but they parent alone. Their children now have two residences. The parents still have their individual relationship with their child, but they are now parenting in separate residences. The family customs can be maintained or revised by each parent in his or her own home.

The major changes are that, first, the relationship between the two parents has shifted from being both lovers and parents to the single focus of being parents; and, second, that the united front of shared responsibility and authority in one home has to be revised into a new and workable form in two homes.

UPDATE YOUR ROLES

Over time you can separate your role as a former mate from your role as a parent. We know in our hearts that being lovers and companions calls forth a different part of us than does being parents. We function differently in our roles as lovers than we do as parents. You can be parents and separate individual adults at the same time, just as you can be engineers, lawyers, teachers, nurses, salespeople—and lovers, friends, sons, daughters, *and* parents. The end of the intimate bond with your mate does not mean the destruction of your bond in parenting.

LEARNING TO WORK TOGETHER

Imagine you and your children's other parent are in a leaky boat. You have a bailer and two oars. A strong current is pulling you away from shore, where your three children stand. They are fearful, watching their world with you being swept away. Everything your children need is in the boat with you. Will you bail like mad, but lose sight of the shore? Will you say, "The hole is at your end of the boat, it's your problem." Will you attack each other with the oars out of anger and frustration? Or will you figure out how to pull the oars together, bail, *and* rescue your children on the shore?

COMMITMENT: THAT EXTRA PUSH

Most parents have a spillover of hard feelings they wade through during the first year of their separation. How might they give themselves a goal to work for, some standard to follow? Some parents meet this head-on. They make a vow to keep their personal feelings separate from their roles as parents. Dozens of times I have heard people say: "No matter what we feel about each other, we will try to keep our parent-to-parent relations as wholesome and clean as possible." This heroic goal, difficult as it may be to reach at times, is still a good one to keep in mind. In many areas we must deal with difficult persons or problems we'd rather avoid—the store clerk with an irascible customer, the lawyer with an obnoxious opponent. As one father put it, "Once you accept the fact that you have to deal with that other parent, life seems to get easier."

Regardless of your circumstances, your private relationship with your child is precious. *Nothing can substitute for you in your child's life.* You and the other parent are the ones who can convince your children that they still have you as a parent, that they still have a family, that they are important, and that as a family you are still essential to others and to your community.

You are important, you are a parent, you still have a family.

This truth is one of those you might write on your mirror and look at when you put on your makeup or shave.

Chapter 3

From One Home to
Two Homes

The Map

FEW people embark on a major journey without a good map to advise them of the major landmarks and roadblocks. But ending a marriage, reorganizing a family, and setting up a new life is often done in just such a blind fashion. "A year and a half ago," said one petite mother of two teenage daughters, "nothing was new. Now nothing is familiar, and everything is new. There's got to be some order, some direction, to this chaos!" There are no package tours for this unfamiliar terrain, but adults and children alike need to know what's up ahead.

This chapter gives an overview of the stages of transition from one home to two. To illustrate what happens, a diagram called "From One Home to Two Homes" was developed for parents and children alike to use. Like a map, it shows the major landmarks, the rough roads, the smooth spots, and the points of interest. It can be used to mark progress and as a way to remember that the crooked places will straighten out. Others have gone through this; you can, too. "I like the place with the houses where it finally gets better," said a nine-year-old boy after he looked at the diagram.

Remember that this framework is to be used as a guide, not a gospel. Each person's experience is unique, as is the pace through the transitions. You and the other parent will probably not be in the same place, feeling the same way, at the same time. Sometimes the person who has advanced to a calm

THE MAP: STAGES ONE TO SEVEN

One Home: Family History 1

STAGE ONE   **The Dream Home**
(trust and respect intact)

STAGE TWO   **Problems in the Home**
(trouble and discord)

STAGE THREE   **The Dividing Home**
(severe difficulties)

STAGE FOUR   **The Divided Home**
(separation)

Two Homes: Family History 2

STAGE FIVE   **Mom's House, Dad's House**
Off-the-Wall
(troubled but separate)

STAGE SIX   **Mom's House and Dad's House**
The Reshaping Process
Settles Down
("I've survived. I'm coping.")

STAGE SEVEN   **Mom's House and Dad's House**
From Coping to Creating
(two one-parent households)

emotional stage is baited by a volatile partner in an earlier phase, and soon the two are out of control, fighting as if they were still married. A family's progress through each period is not like going from first grade to sixth. Mom will not go through this at the same pace as Dad. Everyone, young and old, seems to follow different zigzag patterns: sometimes two steps forward, three back, four forward, one back, and so on.

Children also go through these stages, but at different speeds. Many do not or cannot express their true feelings about the fact that their parents are living separately, but hold back or deny strong emotions for months, sometimes years. Other children may move slowly, often clinging to the hope that someday their parents will reunite. "My daughter didn't give up the idea until she was twenty-six years old and I remarried after sixteen years of separation," said a mother about her oldest child. "And my youngest, who was only two when we separated, was upset that I was finally divorcing her dad. I didn't realize these powerful feelings lay dormant for so long."

Let's begin with marriage and what happens as it moves toward separation. These familiar stages are the same ones that fuel the "It can't work" stories and our beliefs about single parenting and remarriage described in the previous chapters.

FROM ONE HOME TO TWO HOMES

ONE HOME: FAMILY HISTORY 1

Stage One: The Dream Home

(Trust and Respect Intact)

Most people begin their family history with Mom, Dad, and the children under one roof. Some see this stage as "the Dream Come True." If the marriage is solid, there is love, respect, and trust. Dad has a job with the county, and Mom works in an insurance office. Ten-year-old Johnny is in middle school, and eight-year-old Suzie in the elementary grades. They all enjoy backpacking, belong to a church and bowling league, and visit back and forth with relatives. They feel the economic pressures and worry about the headline stories in the news. But they feel that they can make it. When Dad gets a raise, he and Mom plan to take a second honeymoon trip. This is a stable home.

Stage Two: Problems in Your Home

(Trouble and Discord)

Dad has been working late frequently, and Mom's acting unhappy. Before school one morning, Suzie found Mom asleep on the den couch. Some type of problem troubles Mom and Dad, but no one talks about it.

Conflict is normal. Even in the happiest of marriages, families disagree either in open fighting or private arguments. Many couples resolve their differences and return to stage one with the enrichment of a successful resolution of their problems. Love is renewed, and trust and respect are deepened.

However, if trouble in the home carries over a long period, the trust and respect so necessary to intimate relationships wears thin, and tensions rise to uncomfortable levels. Sometimes this erosion is gradual, hardly noticeable, until red flags go up—overlong working hours, an extramarital affair, repeated illnesses, excessive alcohol or drug usage. One of the parents has been thinking seriously about separation, and the other parent is stunned by the news. If the discontent is not resolved, the uneasiness deepens and a return to stage one becomes less and less likely. Marriage counseling may begin. Perhaps there is talk of a trial separation.

Stage Three: The Dividing Home

(Severe Difficulties)

When difficulties seem to be irreconcilable, the marriage has entered stage three. Parents may worry, weep more, and argue. All too often trust and respect are replaced by distrust and disrespect, and the household shows signs of dividing. Mom cries a lot, and Dad loses his temper, especially at Suzie, who is very like her mother. If friends and relatives on both sides are included in blow-by-blow descriptions of Dad's wandering eye or Mom's extravagance, there may be a "soap opera" feeling. Johnny either ignores what's happening or has unexpected rages, while Suzie's asthma increases as a physical reaction to the family's emotional pain. Perhaps a series of honest discussions, a long vacation without the children, or marriage counseling can bring back some needed trust and respect, and everybody can return to stage two and then stage one for a happy continuation of the first family history.

But the longer a family remains in stage three, the more difficult the road back. The discord and tension can be intense. Sadness and the fear of separation, with all its implications, add to the building stress. Mom and Dad ask: "Should we separate or should we stay together?" Long-term indecision can be quite destructive when the stress level is too high for too long a time. Some families bounce back and forth between stages two and three for years, unwilling or unable to end the relationship or put out the effort to make it work. In other circumstances, one mate is only aware something is not right, while the other mate has already made plans to separate, perhaps to join a new love.

Ordinarily, when a couple cannot rebuild their relationship, the final decision period eventually begins. In this case Mom can sleep only two or three hours a night, Dad is having stomach problems, Suzie's home with severe asthma, and Johnny's never home at all. Everyone is feeling the pain and anxiety that comes with an impending loss and an uncertain future. Even though the home is not yet visibly divided, it is pulling apart.

Stage Four: The Divided Home

(Separation)

The physical separation has finally happened. Mom and the children remain in the original family home, while Dad sets up another temporary residence. They want to build two homes for the children, but at this stage everyone feels the psychological and physiological shock that comes with this new and strange reality. No matter how much preparation has been made for the separation, a sense of numbness, and sometimes relief, sets in. Sometimes day-to-day functioning seems impossible or continues at only marginal levels. This dysfunctional reaction is common but dangerous, as people are especially accident-prone in both this and the next stage. Mom says, "The bottom has fallen out of my ship, and I'm scrambling for a lifeboat."

Luckily this stage is finite, lasting one hour, one day, or one month. It will ease up when you start a regular routine in your residence. The question is not how satisfying these arrangements may be, but how functional. Basic survival is a vital issue. If you can get through a day at the office, get home again, and feed yourself and the kids, you are on your way. Perhaps it is makeshift and insecure, but it is workable. You may be sad, angry, depressed, or troubled, but if you are functioning, you are not broken. You have moved on to the next level, where some reality has penetrated the numbness and shock. The hard work of reorganization now needs to begin in earnest.

These four stages are familiar. Now is the time to depart from the known and begin to explore the lesser-known stages of family life *after* the separation.

The first marriage and family has produced Family History 1. The next set of steps shows the beginning of Family History 2.

TWO HOMES: FAMILY HISTORY 2

Stage Five: Mom's House, Dad's House

"Off-the-Wall"
(Troubled but Separate)

Stage five begins a new family history and two new households, Mom's house and Dad's house. This stage can be the most difficult and the longest lasting, with the first months a time of crisis.

A flood of changes demand attention in these two new homes. Everything can be affected: income, jobs, personal habits, friendships, routines, and a sense of security and of self. The stress mounts as the question of survival in the midst of this upheaval continues to loom. Everyone knows ending a marriage costs money, but until the bills pile up, few realize how severe the economic pinch can be. Feelings are raw, sometimes out of control. Mom and Dad are remorseful one minute and unexpectedly distrustful and angry with one another the next. Dad says he feels as if he's on a roller coaster. He goes through a period of bargaining with Mom, hoping he can patch up the marriage. Because of the many ways people act out of character during this time, this stage was nicknamed "off-the-wall." Mom asks, overwhelmed, "Where am I now that I need me?"

These parents are doing their best to set up two homes, working out the division of responsibilities. But, as with many people, their strong emotions about their personal relationship often pollute their jobs as parents, and they are unaware of how damaging this unconscious behavior is to their children and themselves. When the off-the-wall feelings get the best of a former couple, the kids can get in the middle and things may seem to fall apart for a while.

Mom and Dad know they need help. Mom finds a class on divorce adjustment, Dad joins one on parenting. Each counts on friends who have two-home arrangements. Johnny and Suzie are living most of the time with Mom and spending long weekends and some evenings with Dad during the early months. Their reactions to the separation vary: Suzie has said nothing at all, but her asthma is still severe. Johnny's reaction has been open and angry. He is talking back to both parents, cutting classes.

These parents have temporarily lost touch with their children's needs. When the parents settle down enough to reestablish house rules, reinstating discipline and other structures for the children and themselves, some of the tensions and fears will let up quickly. Other difficulties take far longer to even out.

During the first part of this stage, the knottiest issues may remain unsolved—property, money, custody. Finally, as feelings cool and the parents become more adept at applying the principles of a working relationship to their discussions, they develop their own negotiation style and settle all but two issues themselves. They use a mediator to come to agreement on these remaining questions and put together their own "parenting agreement." When necessary legalities are finished, everyone breathes a sigh of relief but also feels the sadness of the formal end of the marriage. When fears fade, the next stage begins. For this couple, two years elapsed from the beginning of stage four to the end of stage five.

Stage Six: Mom's House and Dad's House

The Reshaping Process Settles Down
("I've survived. I'm coping.")

At this stage life is calmer, and the sobering demands of your new life are clearer. Suzie and Johnny have settled into new neighborhoods and are more accustomed to their new lifestyle in two homes. They continue to meet and trade information with new friends in similar families. Mom has a full-time job and has made excellent after-school arrangements for the children, easing her most pressing guilt feelings about being a single, working mother. Dad moved out of his bachelor pad into larger quarters, and the children live with him on a regular basis. He is far more confident of his role and his parenting style. He and Mom are talking about the possibilities of the children living the majority of the time with him for a year or two.

During this stage parents cement a relationship where they respect one another's territory and parenting style and rarely find reasons to interfere. Old hot spots occasionally flare up between them, but these incidents are less frequent. The parents now know how to keep their children out of the middle of their disagreements. They know the difference between "spouse-hood" and parenthood.

Somewhere in this stage, most people experience a series of "flashbacks" to the off-the-wall stage, triggered by a change in circumstances, such as remarriage or a move away. But a solid working relationship can help keep these replays short and manageable. Dad has had an important love affair, and Mom is going out more. Despite a few secret thoughts of getting back together, each knows that reconciliation would not work. They must love each other from afar.

These parents are coping fairly well, but they have not yet found this new lifestyle as satisfying as the promise of their original dream. Mom asks, "Is this all there is?" Their tasks are to continue to solidify their new lifestyles and their working relationship and to develop a strong bond with extended family and a loyal circle of compatible friends.

Stage Seven: Mom's House and Dad's House

From Coping to Creating
(Two One-Parent Households)

These families have moved from coping to creating. Stage seven is a creative breakthrough for many families. Now that they know how to separate their personal lives from their parenting functions, they can nourish their own new family integrity and solidarity. Their new lifestyle is flourishing with a sense of continuity and security. The two families are not just coping, they are creating meaningful lives for each of their members. The incompatibility that led Mom and Dad out of their marriage is clearly evident now, their lifestyles are different. A new love relationship established during this stage can be born in freedom.

Mom and Dad long ago stopped competing for the good-guy prize and no longer worry that one will turn the children against the other. Occasionally they still disagree about the children, but that's par for the course in any family. They have learned tolerance, and everyone is the richer for it.

Suzie and Johnny are now Susan and John—growing up with an expanded family in two homes with both parents. Their parents' individual friendship and family circles have expanded greatly in recent years, even more so since their father's remarriage. Susan says, "I get love and advice from a lot of people." John, now in eleventh grade, plays on the school basketball team and says his cheering section has doubled in three years. Next year he will live most of the school year a mile away at Dad's house, with long weekends twice a month and all summer with Mom.

Mom and Dad say the arrangement gives them both "adult time" as well as parenting time. Though partners in parenting, they may now feel that they have little in common except some family history. They have rebuilt their trust and respect, but from a distance. A few couples become good friends in this stage; others remain working partners. Often there remains a private recognition of affection for each other, an acknowledgment of their shared past, but the emotion is carefully controlled to avoid misunderstanding.

Both parents, just like those who are parenting solo, have formed a network of strong bonds with people in similar circumstances. These people found new ways of relating to their children and reorganizing their families that allow them to be responsive and responsible parents.

Stage seven is worth the work and the wait. There is a new form of parenthood and a special blend of old and new.

THE CRISIS PERIODS FOR PARENTS AND CHILDREN: STAGES FOUR AND FIVE

Stages four and five are the critical crisis periods. The body and psyche are under stress. This time has great potential for good or ill with or without a two-home arrangement. The crisis periods can last as little as six months or as long as two years or more when complications develop.

These two periods are so important that a series of future chapters details the symptoms, treatment, and what you can do. There will be guidelines on how to identify stress points, how to increase personal resources, how to clean your wounds, how to help yourself heal, and how to make good decisions.

UNMARRIED PARENTING

"My son's mother and I lived together for six years before we parted. We are going through a 'divorce' just as if we were married!" An increasing number of parents are living together and never marry. Yet when these couples part, they go through the same seven stages of transition as do those who were married. The issues around the children will be the same; they will have to deal with their feelings, their new lives, their new parenting relationship, and questions of how to raise their children although living apart. Nor do they escape the legal business. They have to deal with legal issues, especially those around "custody," "visitation," and support.

Other parents did not have a long-term relationship and have never lived together. Whether the pregnancy was planned or unplanned, a potential two-home family history begins immediately! These expectant parents go through their own versions of stages five, six, and seven. They have the same legal issues as those people who lived together. They are living separately, they may not even know one another well, but they are parents (or about to be parents). In place of the anguish of separation after a long-term relationship, they may at first struggle with the surprise of an unplanned pregnancy, resentment or anger because of the circumstances surrounding the pregnancy, fears, doubts, accusations. Even if these feelings are not present, there is the reality of having a parenting relationship with someone you don't know very well for the sake of your child. As one mother said, "When I decided to have my daughter, I didn't realize that I was signing on to a relationship with her father for the next twenty years!"

REMARRIAGE AND A NEW FAMILY HISTORY

When a parent remarries, a second new family history begins. During stages five and six, however, adjustments may be more difficult. Unfinished emotional business from the old marriage can overburden a new union's chances for success. People who remarry thinking it will heal hurts and solve problems may find that remarriage attempted too soon creates new difficulties instead. Remarriage doesn't automatically solve anything, and with more remarriages ending in divorce, the happy ending may not be that at all.

Remarriage is often interpreted as a new stage one, "the Dream Home." But stage one cannot be re-created. Remarriage means stages five, six, seven, or later stages. The only true way back to stage one, where the children have both parents under one roof, is to remarry the other parent!

YOU AND THE OTHER PARENT:
A NEW TYPE OF RELATIONSHIP

Building a new working relationship between you and the other parent is, as was shown before, a paradoxical process of separating your old role as a lover from your continuing role as a parent; marriage from parenthood. This is what I call the "retreat from intimacy" and the development of a new businesslike working relationship. In the chapters that follow, you will see how this works and how you can put it into practice.

It helps to remember that you don't have to love your former mate to have a businesslike relationship any more than you have to love your mechanic to get your car fixed. Be patient with yourself during this disentanglement process. It takes time and is sometimes discouraging, but it is something that can be learned, and it yields to persistent effort. Give your past a chance to settle, your feelings a chance to cool, and your skills a chance to increase.

WHEN THE OTHER PARENT WILL NOT CONSIDER
THE TWO-HOME ARRANGEMENT

When the other parent is out of the picture, hostile, or apathetic toward the idea of two homes, you have a series of steps to take and then a number of options to exercise. First, if reinvolvement is something you seek, take some time to read chapter 19, "When an Absent Parent Returns," then return to this place in the book and continue reading each chapter as was suggested in chapter 1. You will find in each chapter that the techniques and guidelines for parents usually work to end the hurt and guilt whether or not the other parent ever comes around to being involved with the children. Once you have satisfied yourself that you have digested the concepts as thoroughly as necessary, you have a series of options before you—either attempt to reinvolve the other parent (or convince him or her that you should be reinvolved yourself) or develop a type of two-home arrangement with a relative or friend—adding an Aunt Alice's house or Tom and Joan's house instead of a Mom's house or Dad's house.

GUIDELINES FOR MEASURING YOUR PROGRESS

1. Aim for a decent separation or divorce. Understand the seven stages and the way families and people can change. (*Chapters 1, 2, 3*)
2. Gradually weed out any negative or unrealistic beliefs, blame games, and soap operas. Establish your own meaning of family, home, parenthood. Believe in your family. (*Chapters 2, 8, 9*)
3. Watch your language as you proceed along this road. How you say things can determine how you and others feel about them. (*Chapters 4, 11*)
4. Respect the crisis periods of this transition. Learn what you and your children need and increase your resources to meet these needs. (*Chapters 5, 6, 16, 17, 20*). Heal your wounds. Let the emotions of the end of your intimate relationship run their course.
5. Adopt new and effective standards of conduct with your former mate. Learn to separate your role as a former mate from that of a parent, and develop a businesslike working relationship and a healthy way of parenting together. (*Chapters 7, 8, 9, 12*)
6. Reorganize or set up your own home, establishing or strengthening family rituals, customs, rules, and develop your new "family feeling." (*Chapters 9, 10, 16, 17, 18, 19, 20*)
7. Aim for a solid, explicit parenting agreement and a privately negotiated settlement about your children. (*All of part 3*)
8. Provide your children with security and continuity by maximizing your love, attention, and time with them. Understand and respond to their needs, rebuild their trust, and watch for danger signals. (*Chapters 9, 10*)
9. Strengthen ties with supportive others—friends, family, associates. If necessary, seek new ties. (*Chapter 5 and all of part 4*)

Chapter 4

Watch Your Language

How Words Help or Hurt

HERE is a familiar scenario. Someone asks a divorced man whether he has a family. He is likely to say something like this:

"I used to have a family, but my marriage broke up three years ago. My wife has custody of the kids, and I have weekend visitation."

His former wife might describe her situation this way:

"I have three children, but I am raising them alone. They visit their father on the weekend. Our marriage failed three years ago."

Now suppose we changed the parents' script:

Father: "I have a family with three children. They live with me on weekends and with their mother the rest of the time."

Mother: "I have a family with three children. They live with me during the week and with their father on weekends. The children have two homes."

STINKWEED WORDS, ROSE WORDS

The words you use can help or hurt your progress. It is remarkable how much difference the substitution of a few words can make in the meaning of the statements. In the first case, father and mother are using what I call "stinkweed" words, words that are unpleasant, negative, or defensive. In the second, they are using "rose" words, words that connote confidence and a sense of pride in parenthood.

In this case, the words that make a big difference are the positive phrases "have a family" and "live with" instead of the apologetic "used to have a family," "custody of the kids," "raising them alone," "visitation," and "visit." (Remember, outsiders visit; families live together.) Since the two-home approach is not yet well established, it is equally important to say that the children have two homes—Mom's house and Dad's house—rather than the one home of the old days. Finally, as a way to relieve any guilt or shame that might be lurking in one's insides, one also might say that the marriage ended rather than that it "failed" or "broke up."

Most parents sit up and listen attentively when negative phrases are picked out of everyday speech and placed end to end. No matter how one looks at it, the language applied to divorced parents and their children usually puts them at odds, not at ease, with their society. As in any culture, new situations demand the new use of language. It is our responsibility to define ourselves positively and properly.

THE "BROKEN HOME"

The "broken home" label and the use of divorce as a scapegoat for society's basic problems don't just stop with everyday language. They are entrenched in much professional language and attitudes as well. The divorced family is still, after twenty-one years of debate about labels and negative terms, referred to as a "broken home" rather than as a family. It takes little imagination to understand how parents or children must feel about coming from a "broken home"—not good. And other words will make them feel worse. "Fatherless home," "motherless home," "incomplete family," "single-parent family" (as if the other parent didn't exist somewhere), "failure of the marriage," "shattered family," "unfit parent," "awarded custody," and "visitation rights" are thinly veiled insults that undermine self-confidence and promote a sense of societal disapproval.

To family therapists, the phrase "broken home" can elicit associations such as uncaring, incomplete, inoperable, separated, and torn. Even the term "reconstituted family," meant to describe a family of the single parent who remarries, is a problem. This phrase recalls instructions for fruit juice concentrate: Add one mate and get an instant family. It sounds as if the family that existed before didn't count as a "real" family.

Even the seemingly innocent phrases "single-parent family" and "one-parent family" are potentially destructive. Why not call a family a family instead of adding qualification about the parents' marital state? If the term "intact family" is reserved for the never divorced, no wonder divorced men and women are sometimes uncertain of their claims to parenthood! Many single people haven't realized how the day-in-day-out use of stinkweed words injures them and their children. Their sense of self, family, and parenthood is undermined. At their worst, stinkweed words can set the scene for all-out war between parents, with battles over property, children, and who was to blame. At their best, they connote second-class status worthy of pity or condescension. Of course, not all children accept the labels at face value. One bright child with divorced parents told me he did not come from a single-parent family, saying, "My parents are single, but I'm not."

Here's a beginning exercise for parents. The very next time someone asks you, "Do you have a family?" regardless of whether you have legal custody or not, think about staking your rightful claim to family life and parenthood. This claim is yours and you deserve it. Try saying "Yes" without excuses and explanations. Don't add "I'm divorced" or "I'm a single parent." If you are a parent without legal custody, don't add "But my children don't live with me." Simply by changing certain everyday words, you can improve your own and your children's sense of identity, your sense of family self-confidence. You acknowledge yourself as a person who is a parent and heads a family, whether you are single or remarried. Your children need this from you as well.

WHAT CHILDREN HEAR

To a child, getting married and having a family means people get presents and have parties. Most words about love and family exalt oneness and sharing in a "real family" where a mother and a father live under one roof with their kids. The average child accepts this easily.

Getting divorced is the reverse of all this. People get sad, yell at each other, and do other scary things. There are no parties and definitely no presents. One of the parents goes to live somewhere else, and nobody says they are going to be happy, not even after a while.

When parents divorce, the child knows the family doesn't look the same anymore. And it certainly doesn't feel good to a child to hear a teacher call his or her home broken or hear the doctor calling the child a victim of divorce or parents stating that their marriage failed. What does all this mean to a child? With negative labels come negative conclusions. The home is broken. The parents are failures. The child is, at least partially, deserted.

DIVORCE AS A CRIME

Children are also confused by legalistic language and all the mystery surrounding courts and the judicial system. For most children, courts exist to decide who is the good guy and who is the bad guy—who's supposed to be punished for breaking the law. Somebody's to blame somewhere. When you are a child, it's easy to imagine that divorce is some sort of crime.

If a child were unlucky enough to overhear a lawyer talking to a parent before going to court, he would hear such tidbits as "the best defense is a good offense" (and any sports-minded kid knows what that means!), or that most Dads "drop out" after a year, or that Mom has to "protect her best interests" so she can be prepared to "raise her family alone." How would you feel if you heard this as a child? Would you be afraid? Would you wonder whether you were loved or would be cared for? Would you feel helpless?

DIVORCE AS A CONTEST

It isn't bad enough that Mom and Dad go to court like criminals. One day Mom returns from court and announces that the judge awarded custody of you to her but gave Dad visitation rights. It isn't particularly reassuring when Mom hastens to add: "What this means is that you will be living with me and visiting Dad on Saturdays." To many children, including teenagers, it can sound like a contest in which they were the first prize.

Children don't like to talk about these things. But occasionally their confusion erupts in statements like "Daddy sold me to Mommy for two hundred dollars a month," or "Mom won the car, the house, and me."

Even parents who avoid court battles must still deal with words such as "custody," "visitation," "awarded," "child support," "investigation," and "unfit." These all sound as if they pertain to prisons, wardens, and probation instead of to families. These words alone could confirm the stereotype where one parent has all the authority, responsibility, and rights, while the other parent must meekly obey all the rules of procedure in order to gain access to the institution.

Many professionals—counselors, psychologists, judges, mediators, and attorneys—are as deeply upset with the current adversary language of courts and institutions as any single or remarried parent. Many of them have worked hard over the past twenty years to replace the harmful and degrading words with terms that more accurately and humanely describe evolving lifestyles.

The "broken home" myth dies hard, however. Even though the legal language and professional literature are slowly replacing cold or negative labels, some single and remarried parents use words that perpetuate the suspicions that surround society's attitudes about the broken home. These parents, like some professionals, have not yet been convinced how crucially important it is to clean up the language we use to describe our new family system.

A NEW VOCABULARY

All of us urgently need to develop a new vocabulary to describe family life after divorce. Although the following word list is short, you may find it hard to master. If you can convert completely from stinkweed words to rose words in two or three months, you will have accomplished something very important for yourself and your children. If you start adding your own new words to enlarge this beginning vocabulary further, you will be one of our real pioneers.

BEGINNING VOCABULARY

Instead of Saying:	Try Saying:
Visit	Live with, be with, stay with
I have children, but they live with their mother/father	I have a family
The children's mother/father left us	I have a family
The children are seeing (or visiting) their dad/mom	The children are with their mother/father at their other house, with their other family
Motherless, fatherless, split or broken home, incomplete home	The home, the family
The children have one home and their mother/father visits	The children have two homes, an expanded family
The marriage broke up, failed	The marriage ended
Wife/husband ex-wife/husband	Children's mother, children's father

---

We have talked about most of the words on the list. There are some others that need our attention. It is important to stop using the terms "wife" or "husband" after divorce. "Ex-wife" and "ex-husband" are not much better. Saying "former wife" or "former husband" or "first [or second] husband or wife" is somewhat better. *But saying "children's mother" or "children's father" is best of all.*

The right words can help you separate your old role as a mate from your continuing one as a parent. Referring to your former intimate relationship with the words *"husband"* and *"wife,"* even with *"ex"* or *"former"* in front of them, reinforces your old life together and all those emotions connected with it. Saying children's mother or children's father will help you focus on the parent-parent relationship. Perhaps later, when your emotional divorce is complete, you can use terms like "my former wife" or "my first husband."

CHANGING OLD HABITS

All habits take time to change. But when other people resist your changes by providing roadblocks of scorn or reproach, changing a habit can be more difficult. Resistance to a new set of words is painful when it comes from children's friends or from a parent or grandparent. Teenagers might resist some of the two-home vocabulary because of peer pressure and acceptance of what is "in." There are no songs on the charts about two homes or cooperative parents. Church groups do not yet extol the virtues of parents who work together well for the sake of the children.

Children of all ages might hesitate to use new terms because they assume that one parent would be hurt or vengeful if the child referred to the other parent's house as "home." Some parents or grandparents send out strong implicit messages that say "If you talk about the other parent at all, you must act as if that parent is unimportant. You must act as if your *real* home is with me and you love me best." Such hidden agendas thrive on stinkweed words. Some older children may think, I'll do what they ask, but I don't believe it for a minute. However, it takes an especially strong child to make such a distinction. Most children find themselves in the mire of a loyalty struggle, the worst affliction for children of divorce. They want to look out for their parents' best interests and to please those they love. But one parent is saying that such love can be proved only if the children dump or demean the other parent or if they lie about how they feel.

Your own feelings may also stand in the way of the new vocabulary. It is perfectly natural for a parent who has the children most of the time to resent hearing that the children live at the other parent's house, when according to the old way of talking they only visit here. You can get a barometer reading on your own degree of anger if you try the following exercise. Ask yourself how you honestly feel if you say, "My children live with me during the weekend [or the week, whatever your circumstance], and the rest of the time they live with their other parent."

If the children live with you the majority of the time, do you feel comfortable or uncomfortable with such a statement? Does it make you feel less alone, less burdened, less as if you had all the weight of responsibility on your shoulders exclusively? Or do you resent changing your language habits because you do not want to share the term "live" with someone who doesn't share equally all the heartaches and the hard work of raising children? "They don't live with their father," said one angry mother, "they play with him. With me they work and face hard reality. I resent him being the hero while I'm the villain."

This mother's barometer reading on anger was high, and for good reason. She was in a lopsided situation, and the term "live with mother" was one of her few rewards. But her anger cost her a good deal.

ADVANTAGES OF A NEW VOCABULARY

If your children live with you on weekends, do you feel more like a bona fide parent when you say: "My children live with me"? Or do you resist saying they live with you because you really don't feel like the traditional parent with the day-to-day meals, bedtimes, and homework? "Just saying, 'Live with me this weekend,' gave me a terrific boost of parent confidence," one father said. "I started thinking like a parent instead of a host with weekend guests."

This exercise doesn't just tap feelings of anger or of hope, it brings to light other emotions and attitudes that are worth your attention. Even if the rose words seem hard to say, say them and see what happens. Pay attention to what feelings and attitudes come up for you and your children. Write down the results, if you can.

In changing your vocabulary from stinkweed words to rose words, remember that old habits carry with them the old attitudes of society.

Perhaps the most touchy situations are those with friends who react to your use of rose words with "Oh, you know what I mean" or, worse, accuse you of trying to make a bad situation look better with verbal whitewash. "You know full well that one weekend a month and two months in the summer doesn't make a home," said one father who objected to the use of rose words.

These are real times of test, for they reveal the biases and show the true colors of your friends and family. Sometimes you can answer, "I know what you mean," or shrug. When you do, probably nothing has been gained and you might feel an unpleasant aftertaste. But you could answer with a polite but firm "That is the way you choose to evaluate it. My perspective is different from yours."

We all need approval and acceptance, especially from those close to us. But going along with stinkweed words is not, in the end, going to be to your own advantage. With some effort you can work out your own ways for you and your children to relearn positive words. In so doing, you may find that the rose vocabulary genuinely interests others who find its positive approach refreshing and worthwhile.

THE BENEFITS TAKE A WHILE TO SHOW UP

Sometimes people don't take the rose words too seriously. "If it's as easy as that," they ask themselves, "how can it really work?" If you fall into this category, remember, using new words is a little like caring for your teeth. You have to brush and floss regularly before the results show in a good dental checkup. It's the same way with getting rid of stinkweed words. The changes are subtle but very important to your overall health. The benefits take a while to show up.

Rose words can definitely be a boon for parents. They create an atmosphere in which parental cooperation can develop more readily. "When I said the children 'visited their father,' " one mother said, "it didn't occur to me to ask him to attend a parent-teacher conference at school. But when I started using 'lived with their father,' it dawned on me that maybe he did have a right and a responsibility in this area, too. Now I ask him to pitch in and share, and he feels freer to say, 'Of course,' and to initiate responsibilities in other situations, too, like the medical checkups and the children's summer camps."

The new language of two-home families can also be carried over into legal agreements and subsequent marriages, as I show in future chapters. But try to use it every day until it permeates your thinking and becomes an unconscious habit.

LANGUAGE POWER

Language plays a fundamental part in shaping our reality, our values, and our priorities, in giving substance to our beliefs, defining our status and our roles. It also defines the values of our culture. What we call ourselves and what we are called can shape what we become. Words exist to serve, not to oppress. If a word or phrase describes the life you want to live, keep it. If it doesn't, toss it out and find a better one. It is our responsibility to ourselves, to our children, and to all the others who will eventually join us to use words that inspire the best in us, not the worst.

Chapter 5

Your "Human Income"

Increasing Your Resources for Coping with Stress

Changes When a Relationship Ends
The Effects of Stress
Your Resources for Coping with Stress
Self-Test: What Are Your Resources?
Ten Basic Rules for Making a Crisis Work for You
How Much Change and Stress Can and Should You Afford?

WHEN stress wrings your heart and body, depleting your inner resources, how can you replenish your inner self and regain that important balance and perspective? Answer: Increase your "human income," the amount of incoming support and nurturance that you need to meet your basic survival needs for physical, spiritual, and emotional health.

When a couple separates or goes through a divorce, stress and pressure skyrocket. There are no promises for future happiness or fulfillment. During this period, fears, doubts and questions can crowd a person's thoughts. What's going to happen to me? Will I make it? Will I use bad judgment? What can I count on? How will the children take it?

As a thirty-eight-year-old man with a five-year-old daughter put it, "The question that haunted my life before I separated was, 'Would my life be any better than it was when I was married?' " These are important questions.

CHANGES WHEN A RELATIONSHIP ENDS

Consider the avalanche of changes that inevitably moves through a family when parents separate. When a relationship ends, your way of life changes from being married to being single—your intimate relationship changes from having a long-term committed relationship to being unattached. Your parental role changes from parenting together under one roof to being a single parent and parenting apart. Your identity and self-image change from being "together" to being unattached.

There may also be changes in

- neighborhood: whoever leaves adjusts to a new area, and if one stays in the previous home, they adjust to new circumstances in the same environment.
- personal habits: eating, exercise, sleep, sex, and household habits; who takes out the trash; who does the wash; sleeping alone.
- occupation and income: usually less money to live on or a need to change jobs, to train for new work, or to resume work.
- social circles: friends may take sides or drop away in time. Few friendships remain exactly as they were when you were married.

TOO MANY CHANGES

Any one of these, by itself, is a big change. In ending an intimate relationship, these changes come together in rapid sequence, draining energy and building up pressure. It is very much like a form of culture shock, like being thrust into a foreign country. This is especially true for the parent who moves out of the original family home. The parent who remains still has the familiar surroundings. "It has some of the feeling that all is going on as it was before," said one mother, "but one of the members is missing."

Still more layers of potential stress can come from society, from your friends or family, and from your own attitudes. Guilt, stigma, discrimination, the legal process, and the legacy of the broken home all take their toll. "No welcome wagon for us," said one young mother, "not at school, church, at work, or in court." Furthermore, the new single parents need to meet new people in the same boat, people who can provide them with examples for their own lives. Successful two-home parents don't wear signs that read "Watch us. We accomplished a decent divorce." As one woman said quietly of her divorce after twenty years and three children, "The experience of ending a marriage is like childbirth; you have to undergo it to understand how intense it can be. I know now what they mean by killer stress."

THE EFFECTS OF STRESS

STRESS AND ILLNESS

When stress gets too high, the body's natural resistance to illness is weakened. If the pressures are not dissipated appropriately, health problems follow. Parents who work hard at the office and return home to another four to six hours of work and responsibility have no time to relax and recuperate. There is usually too little money, too little time, too little rest. Not surprisingly, this unbalanced life often leads to depression. Furthermore, when an unbalanced life is combined with highly stressful events such as death or divorce, people may be more susceptible than usual to heart disease, hypertension, strokes, cancer, and other life-taking illnesses. Stress is not a disease, but nonetheless it can cripple, even kill.

STRESS AND DECISIONS

For many people, a high level of stress reduces the ability to make measured judgments. Yet many issues demand a decision, poor judgment or no, and the advice and suggestions of well-meaning others only seem to add to the problem. "My brother is going through a divorce," said one man, "and his judgment is awful. He distrusts everyone who tries to help him. How can he make lifelong decisions this way?" When people most need their wits about them, they are all too often at their wits' end. Relationships can become strained, resistance to illness goes down, and judgment deteriorates.

Everyone has a limit, and even the most stable, easygoing personality can be immobilized by too much too soon. Regardless of age, income, or education, the ending of a marriage nearly always brings stress—lots of it.

YOUR RESOURCES FOR COPING WITH STRESS

How much survival and human income do you think you have now to meet the stress that comes with divorce? The questions on the following self-test focus on basic survival and human needs and how well you feel you are meeting these needs.

Before you take the self-test, look at some sample situations and answers. Question 11: "Do you have an operating circle of acquaintances, friends, or neighbors who can help you out, and vice versa, when needed?" One man, John, rated himself 2. He has about six bowling acquaintances. He hasn't thought about whether they would help him out when he needed it. He simply doesn't know. John can't think of other people he might call on. He thinks his bowling acquaintances would help out, but he's never put them to the test.

Jim, on the other hand, has a group of friends that he calls his divorce buddies—people he worked with who went through divorce about the same time he did. He knows he can count on these people (and vice versa) because they have come to his aid in the past. He gave himself an 8, saying that he could always add more friends to his circle.

Jane is naturally quiet and reserved. She does not make friends easily. She is new to the area and knows no one; her family lives thousands of miles away. She gave herself a 1, but when questioned she said that she fully intended to get that score up to a 5 by the end of the month. She was already planning to get to know her neighbors well enough so that she could count on them in emergencies.

SELF-TEST: WHAT ARE YOUR RESOURCES?

Answer the following questions using a scale of 1 to 10.

10 = The best possible answer for you. The way you are meeting this need is ideal; it suits you perfectly.

 5 = An average answer. This need is being met, but there is ample room for improvement.

 1 = Things could use improvement now! Either you are not meeting this need at all, or you are as yet unable to meet this need in a way you feel is best for you.

How Do You Rate Your Survival Income?

( ) 1. Can you pay the rent, afford nourishing food, purchase adequate clothing?
( ) 2. Are you relatively safe in your home, your neighborhood, and at work?
( ) 3. Can you obtain and afford medical care when you or the children are ill?
( ) 4. Can you obtain and afford child care during the whole week?
( ) 5. Can you obtain and afford help at home?

How Do You Rate Your Human Income?

( ) 6. Can you take a day off for rest or recreation every week?
( ) 7. Can you enjoy an activity with your children at least twice or three times a month?
( ) 8. Can you afford a sitter so that you can take the equivalent of two days off a month from parenting (if the children live with you most of the time)? Or can you afford to be with them forty-eight hours consecutively one to four times a month (if they do not live with you full-time)?
( ) 9. Is the children's other parent involved in parenting the children and taking on reasonable responsibilities?
( )10. Are you and the children's other parent on good working terms?

( ) 11. Do you have an operating circle of acquaintances, friends, or neighbors who can help you out, and vice versa, when needed?

( ) 12. Do you have a group of friends or relatives who can share some of your family life, including birthdays and special occasions?

( ) 13. Can you give and receive affection and companionship from this group?

( ) 14. Does this group on occasion share with you some of the parenting of your children?

( ) 15. Do you have at least one close friend you can share just about anything with? Can you count on this person?

( ) 16. Do you have a mate or lover with whom you can give and receive affection and/or sex?

( ) 17. Do you have a spiritual practice or healing ritual from which you can gain strength, a sense of protection, or guidance?

Now, add up your scores. Scores above 95 show you feel you are operating with a reasonable "income," using your own standards. The higher you score the better, of course. However, scores below 95 suggest that you need to take some important steps to increase your survival and human income level so that you can decrease or dissipate your present stress level. The higher your human income, the easier stress may be to handle.

Survival and human needs are common denominators to everyone, regardless of their sophistication, education, or economic status. To survive we all need food, water, air, shelter, sleep, safety. We are human, so we operate best with love, support, work, friendship, belonging, security, self-respect, a sense of purpose or meaning. Sometimes the threat of losing security can be just as stressful as actually losing it. The shipwreck victim can exist on a case of canned sardines, but he can go crazy watching the sharks circling the perimeter of his rubber raft.

The challenge is to minimize the stress by identifying, first, where it comes from; second, what basic needs are either not being met or are threatened; and, finally, how to change the situation for the better.

HOW TO INCREASE YOUR HUMAN INCOME

Major changes happen at some time to everyone, married or single. Both experts and laymen know that stress can be managed to a great degree by the right attitudes and actions. When we are in crisis, we forget how important it is to take care of ourselves. We may not be able to think clearly. Yet we need to ensure our survival and, if possible, increase our personal strength. The following list of ten basic rules have stood the test of time for increasing human income.

TEN BASIC RULES FOR MAKING A CRISIS
WORK FOR YOU

1. Don't go through this long crisis period alone.
2. Learn what's going on.
3. Look for what works and what doesn't.
4. Care for your inner self and your spiritual life.
5. Take care of your body, and find safe ways to blow off steam.
6. Keep a positive but realistic perspective.
7. Increase your skills.
8. Watch your language.
9. Keep your sense of humor.
10. Encourage your children to explore these rules for themselves.

1. Don't Go Through This Long Crisis Period Alone

Support and acceptance by other people are absolutely essential during big changes. Support is perhaps the most important of all the ground rules. At least one other person must care enough about you to be supportive, to listen, to give you feedback, and to truly care. Two people are better than one, and a group is best of all, especially when your children are welcomed and accepted in the group, too. Seek out your friends, but be careful here. Sometimes old friends take sides or have a vested interest in your not changing at all. It could be that for a time you will need to create new friendships better suited for this time of change. If you are isolated for the moment, call on your minister, a counselor, or a hot line. Despite any popular beliefs in rugged independence and making it alone, to go through a crisis completely by yourself is risky. Isolation can raise the already dangerous stress level, leading to later complications and delaying your progress. Sometimes membership in an organization can be a temporary substitute for close friends, but it is not an adequate replacement for a personal friendship. Remember, "Sorrow shared, half the sorrow; joy shared, double the joy." Don't go through this alone!

2. Learn What's Going On

Use your head, ask questions, pay attention, read, learn. It is important to know when you make any change what you are getting into, especially with separation, divorce, and the legal business. Also, finding out what's going on usually puts you in touch with new people—some of them in the same boat as you. When you ask questions or observe people in somewhat similar situations, you can pick and choose among alternatives, thinking, This is a little like my situation, or, That one has totally different problems. You gain a clearer perspective.

This sharing of a common condition need not take the form of baring your innermost soul. Just your physical presence at a meeting or lecture where you can learn what's going on is action enough until you are ready for more. Given half a chance, other people will share their knowledge with you, and your own investigations will give you extra clues. In the meantime, read, learn, collect information, make observations, and ask questions. The more information you collect, the better.

3. Look for What Works and What Doesn't

Give a plus to an action or attitude that promotes personal and family growth, a minus to those toxic signs that bring pain and dissent. There are many red lights during the first two years, and observing them in others (and asking your friends and other singles about them) can help you avoid defeatist attitudes and keep you from going off track. One divorcing woman remarked during a workshop: "Nobody told me life was a series of situations to confront and review. I was taught to see situations as problems, as a sign that I hadn't done something right. Now I see that if I want to reshape my life, I have to forget about problems and failures and look at what works and what doesn't."

Ideas and new perspectives can come from anywhere, if we are open to them. One mom, separated for five months, unexpectedly got help from her son in creating a newer family life. "My son Casey suggested one summer family reunion, instead of our usual weekend trips out of town to see different relatives," said Mary, a mother of three with a very large and demanding extended family. Mary traded in her every weekend away for most weekends spent at home so she and her children could have time together as a new family and more child-centered weekend activities in the neighborhood.

4. Care for Your Inner Self and Your Spiritual Life

Provide for your spiritual needs, especially those that heal you and lead you to a strong sense of your self and your purpose. Since the complexities of transitions bring many role changes, you will face yourself alone, no longer a married parent or a married person. Make time for your inner self, for contemplation, and for quiet periods alone when these many changes can have a chance to sink in gently. Respect this period of your life. Listen to yourself. It has the potential for profound personal changes that can elevate and renew you.

5. Take Care of Your Body and Find Safe Ways to Blow off Steam

What's good for the psyche is also good for the body. Respect the need of both to take "time out" for rest and recreation. Big changes take enormous amounts of energy; if you don't rest, stress gets the upper hand. While stress can kill, it more often maims, especially when people don't take time to eat, exercise, and rest. A crisis period can lead to the "overs"—overworking, overdrinking, oversmoking, overeating—with no energy left to resist illness or depression. Now is the time to check with your doctor, especially about the right amount of exercise for you.

Baby yourself with a good book, a sports event, an afternoon with friends, a quiet walk. Find safe ways to blow off steam, ways to let some of the inner pressures escape. Some people jog, play tennis, take up bowling. Other people work out at the gym, play the piano, join baseball teams. Whatever is your way, you'll know it's working when your body feels better and your problems seem smaller.

6. Keep a Positive but Realistic Perspective

A positive but realistic frame of mind is an important key to making anything work. This does not mean blindness to problems or an unrealistic denial of their importance. It does mean taking a long view of your experience every once in a while and making conscious efforts to shake off any negative, doomsday feelings. Your situation is similar to others', but it is also uniquely personal. *You are your own best judge of what is happening.* It's your life, and you are ultimately responsible for how you see it and what you do with it. Furthermore, research continues to show that people who best withstand the stress of crises maintain supportive contacts with others and a determination to focus on the hopeful rather than the depressing sides of a difficult situation.

7. Increase Your Skills

You might agree that you need more friends, knowledge, awareness, and better perspective and that you should care for your body and your inner self. But how do you do it? Reach out to other people; ask them what they do. Observe others thoughtfully. Take classes, workshops. Use the guides described in this book. Reorganizing one's life and parenting after separation usually requires a far more sophisticated set of specific life skills than were needed when you were one-half of a couple. Your relationships *are* more complicated now. You and your children can profit from a higher level of personal skills.

8. Watch Your Language

As chapter 4 explained, the vocabulary you use to describe your circumstances is tremendously important to your children and your own sense of
dignity and direction. Look for rose words, drop the stinkweed words. It's
your responsibility to make a vocabulary that accurately and humanely
reflects your circumstances and lifestyle. If a word or phrase does not
positively reflect your new status, get rid of it and make up your own
positive term. Remember, we often become what we are called or what we
call ourselves. Call yourself someone who is learning how to make this crisis
work for you and your children. If you use any blaming terms or martyrdom
phrases, try to drop them as soon as you can.

9. Keep Your Sense of Humor

Even if you are in a crisis period now, try to lighten it up with the humor and
laughter that can mercifully release pent-up tensions and renew a sense of
hope and perspective. As serious as a crisis might be, it can't always be taken
seriously. Play with your children, relax with them, enjoy being together.
The months and years will go by quickly enough. The times together will be
the ones most likely to be remembered and cherished. These will be the
times that will say "family." You will undoubtedly find yourself in absurd
situations you honestly never thought were possible. So learn to laugh at
yourself, and let your children laugh along with you. It's okay to be human!

10. Encourage Your Children to Explore These Rules for Themselves

These basic rules are not just for grown-ups; they can be encouraged in
children as ways that they, too, can learn to weather crises. Your example
during crisis periods is not only a good teacher for your children, it can give
your children a sense of confidence in your ability to cope with massive
changes and in their ability to "take after my mom" or "be like my dad."

These basic rules cover a lot of ground, but they are interdependent. An
effort in one area usually serves more than one need; one insight influences
more than one attitude.

HOW MUCH CHANGE AND STRESS CAN AND SHOULD YOU AFFORD?

The higher the stress, the greater your need to protect yourself and to be
good to yourself. But changes don't happen overnight, and sometimes all the
talk and action of reshaping lives is just too much, too soon. That's your clue
to stop, take a rest before going on. During great change, people are very

much like sponges; they can absorb just so much at one time and no more. Later, after drying out a bit, the sponge can soak in more change.

1. Get some *real* rest by *not* thinking about your problems at all for a day or two. Distract yourself. Try to get through several hours without thinking about your former mate or your situation now. Give yourself some breathing room. Cope with your situation at your own pace, in your own rhythm.
2. If at any time you question your resilience, your durability, talk to a friend or a counselor or find a hot line. Use all the help you can get during these first couple of years. It is available, and you deserve to treat yourself to the best.
3. Respect this period of your life. It probably wasn't in your original blueprint for your life, but it's here now, so give it your most creative attention.

Remember: you are important, your child is important, and your family is important.

Part 2

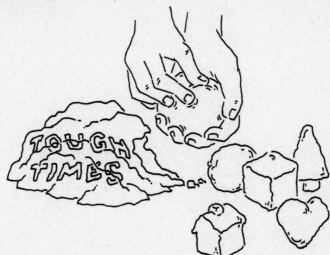

MAKING TOUGH TIMES WORK FOR YOU

Chapter 6

The Emotions of Ending a Relationship

The Wounding and Healing Process

"I DIDN'T know it would be so hard to get a divorce," said Lois, a twenty-nine-year-old mother of an infant son, separated for three months. "I thought Barry [the baby's father] would go along with my idea for two homes. People told me he'd be angry at me for wanting the divorce, but I didn't believe them. Now Barry is hostile, resentful, and I'm so mad I don't care if he never sees our son again. I'm even tempted to tell my lawyer to go for sole custody!"

Lois's surprise and reflex reaction are common. The intense emotions of divorce erupt. Barry's anger at his child's mother is as predictable as Lois's nearly automatic retaliatory response of threatening sole custody. The unrelenting string of changes that come with separations are harder to bear when there are criticisms and accusations, feelings of powerlessness, rejection, or being a failure. When once we allowed for one another's differences, now our faults and weaknesses are highlighted. The only option is to become the battling "exes." Resentment, blame, and anger obscure and threaten original goals of cooperation. As one court counselor said, "By the time some parents get to court, one or both of them are convinced that the other parent wears a tail and two horns."

When a relationship unravels, the emotions can be intense and compelling. One's judgment may be impaired because of these strong emotions. People can plunge ahead riding the crest of their intense feelings, making decisions on property, children, and support money. Many are dismayed to find that when they lose their tempers and their perspective, they can also painfully complicate their legal business and lose their savings. Parents on emotional roller coasters can also frighten their children, jeopardize their ability to have a working relationship with the other parent, and delay their emotional divorce.

If you feel there is little that you can do to contain and cope with your feelings, there is good news for you. Understanding your feelings and their effects can help you make something constructive from this major life change. The life you save will be your own!

THE WOUNDING AND HEALING PROCESS

Ending any close relationship often brings with it spiritual and emotional wounds. When a child is involved, the wounding is far deeper. No longer is it just you and your mate, now there is your child to think about. And there are grandparents, aunts, uncles, cousins, nieces, nephews, close friends, your child's schoolmates, friends, teachers, coaches. . . . The list is a long one. Your child may lose their love and protection, too.

Like a physical injury, the healing takes place in phases. To begin with, the wounds need to be properly cleansed and cared for or complications may develop. This hurts. But it does need to be done so healing can begin and strength can return. The entire healing process can be fast or slow, relapses few or many. New blows can reopen this wound and cause even further damage. How long it takes depends on how well you take care of yourself, the information you have to work with, and your commitment to yourself and your child.

You can make the most of the increased natural energy and marshaled courage of this crisis period for your own and your children's benefit. Wisdom and greater strength can come about with change. "After I finished those first two years of my divorce," said one father, "I felt I could handle anything. But before I understood about the stages of the process, I thought I was going off the deep end." Separating or getting a divorce is not something people plan to repeat. Consequently, sure that it will never happen again, they mistakenly do not pay much attention to the process itself. While divorce may not occur again, other life crises most certainly will. There may be the loss of a job, a serious illness, the end of a close friendship or another love affair, or the death of someone close. All such losses share common elements and call for similar personal skills. In other words, learning the skills to help you heal from the crisis of separation or divorce can help you later on.

SURVIVAL AND YOUR EMOTIONAL AND PERSONAL REORDERING

The major tasks during the first two years are, first, to assure your physical survival, and, next, to set your emotional, spiritual, and physical self in order. Nature helps us survive by giving our body the extra energy of the "flight or fight" response. The crisis puts our bodies into a kind of automatic red alert that increases our internal rpm. This special energy can be both healing and destructive. Higher rpm prepares us to meet drastic changes with more adrenaline, courage, and often more energy. But, unless we give ourselves adequate times to idle, to rest, or to proceed at a measured pace, ensuring an adequate "human income," the acceleration can also speed up the depletion of our physical and spiritual resources as well. Balance is the key.

WHOSE IDEA WAS THIS? WHO WAS SURPRISED?

"I tried to tell him what I was feeling for three years," said one woman. "He wouldn't believe me. Now he says I never told him anything." Her estranged husband answers, "I didn't know how serious it was. She owes me a chance to change."

The dynamics of wounding and healing are tied closely to whether or not the idea of a separation was a surprise to one partner, how long serious doubts about the relationship existed, how long the couple discussed or worked on their situation before the separation, and whether or not the separation or divorce was eventually a more or less mutual decision.

A surprise decision feels disrespectful *and* painful. This is why the hardest hit are those who didn't suspect a serious problem. They are unprepared, they are stunned, their world is in a tailspin. Experienced therapists and mediators often can predict how long it will take for a divorce or separation to finally settle based on how long each partner knew about the seriousness of the problems before the actual separation.

PRE-SEPARATION "BOOT CAMP"

There seems to be a need for what I term a "pre-separation boot camp," an often difficult time where both people try to discuss their problems with one another. Even if one person tries to explain and the other doesn't understand fully, it still helps. People expect that a committed relationship means something. They feel it deserves an honest chance to succeed. This attempt honors the original commitment, and it is a sign of respect for the partner and your life together. The person wanting the separation needs to explain why and to do so while he or she is still living there.

One partner, quietly planning for separation for a year or so, may mistakenly believe all he or she has to say is, "It's over. I am moving out," or, "I want you to move out next week." The surprised partner will not easily forgive being subject to the shock, nor the humiliation and sense of betrayal, especially if he or she finds that there is a new love waiting in the wings. These are the feelings that if left unresolved can poison the later negotiations over the children, property, and support. It is not a pretty picture.

Couples who try counseling to mend their relationship are in probably the safest form of "pre-separation boot camp." But many people don't try. They just want to escape, to start anew, to leave it all behind. It is difficult to be honest, to take the risk that you may be ridiculed, your feelings discounted or harshly judged. If you don't talk enough before you separate, you take the risk that the wounds will grow deeper and the healing period last longer. Everyone has to pay their dues, either before the separation or afterwards. Before is usually better.

REVIEW WORK AND RELEASING STRONG FEELINGS

Review work is what you do alone. It combines going back over your history, reevaluating as you go, and then—most important—releasing the emotions still stored in your memory, muscles, and nerves. Review work begins when an intimate relationship becomes seriously threatened.

Review work shows itself as a natural inclination to be preoccupied with the past (or with some present incident that seems to reflect the past) and to find yourself in the grip of strong feelings about these bygone events. Some say, "I keep having these conversations in my head and all these feelings come out." Even long-forgotten episodes can come up for review, touching and releasing any stored emotional charge left over from the unresolved past.

"Feelings welled up in me as if it were yesterday," said Dorothy about things that had happened sixteen years before. "I cried about them all over again. Then I got angry. I could see now that from those early slights, I had long ago begun to distrust his love for me. On one hand, my review work gave me a lot of insight into my marriage, but it confused and angered me as well. Why hadn't I ended the marriage then? Why had I gone on to have another child with him? What was wrong with me?"

Your preoccupation with the relationship, who was responsible for what, and what this means to you now, is natural and healthy review work. But it is *work*, like the grief after the death of a loved one. Similar in many ways, review work is also very different in that the other party is alive and a continual reminder of the relationship, of unanswered questions, unmet expectations, of a still unsettled past. "We live in the same small town. I even see her on the street sometimes," said one man. "I wonder, What is she saying about me to people? I get upset just thinking about it." If marriage is the process of selection and being selected, then divorce can be seen as being "deselected." And the living reminder of this deselection is the children's other parent. The sense of failure and disappointment can be crushing. It obscures the job of gradually separating your marriage from your parenthood.

Review work usually means allowing your past to reenter into your consciousness, and having to deal with feelings of hurt, rage, betrayal, bewilderment, failure, and guilt. These feelings might come together with thoughts of how, given another chance, you might have behaved differently. One mother doing review work said, "I feel so damned guilty now. I didn't try to have a relationship with him, I did take him for granted. I'll never be that way again." Along with guilt and failure come feelings of being unloved, unwanted, or totally alone in the world. Some say painfully, "Who am I if I am not loved?" or "No one in the world finds me important anymore." One father in obvious turmoil asked, "Where did the love go?"

Usually, review work permeates much of the first six months before (at least for the person who is considering the separation) and after the separation. If the separation was unexpected, the review work is pervasive for at least a year, sometimes more. The easiest (and most peaceful) response to review work has been described by a few people as simply coming to no definite conclusions. Not all questions have answers and not all "the whys" are worth pursuing. Asking, "What's going on here?" is more helpful than "Why?" Release and peace do not necessarily depend on taking a course of action on a position; simply acknowledging the experience can be enough.

RELEASING STRONG FEELINGS SAFELY

Give the feelings that come up a safe outlet through physical exercise, sports, activities, absorbing hobbies, or meditation, but check with your doctor first before you embark on a physical exercise regime. Any activity, physical or not, that will allow you to safely release pent-up energy and give your mind and body a chance to heal can help. As the body responds to your self-care, self-esteem and self-confidence increase. The review work seems easier, more constructive. In later chapters, the role of routines and rituals will be described. These, too, help in the safe release of feelings.

REPEATING THEMES: YOUR OLD SKELETONS

When a memory and a feeling come up repeatedly, you can be sure you have stumbled on an old skeleton from your personal closet, perhaps from your life before your marriage, perhaps from your marriage.

Pay extra attention to these relics—they give especially important clues on how to accelerate and stabilize your growth in the future. Keep a notebook or a journal on these reruns—a simple sentence will do. (Some of Dorothy's reruns were: "Feel abandoned again." "Why didn't I end the marriage sooner?") Old skeletons are often overlooked, but they can be quite useful to you in learning from the past and preparing for your next relationship.

YOUR AUTOMATIC BRAKES: DENIAL AND NUMBNESS

Because too much change and stress can be dangerous, a peculiar but completely understandable phenomenon occurs. You can become numb, and the mind either ignores or denies certain facts. This denial and numbness are the psyche's way of resting, of making the present bearable. It is a natural way of letting change proceed at an acceptable pace. Denial isn't necessarily a refusal to see reality, but a set of brakes unconsciously applied to the accumulation of too much change too fast. The transformation from being married to being a fully integrated single person and parent happens gradually, over a period of months and years. Even the most adaptable person will find this a long journey. Denial is not intrinsically bad and appears to some extent in almost everyone during the first two years. It will work for you by helping you to slow down, letting your sponge of change dry out a bit. It will work against you if you never go near the water again.

THE PHASES OF ENDING A RELATIONSHIP: THE FIRST AND SECOND WAVES

The emotions of ending a relationship seem to come in phases. Progress through these phases releases powerful but neutral energies that can work for you or against you. Some people use them to bolster their courage and motivation to make positive changes and perhaps stop smoking, lose excessive weight, or change careers. Others lighten their personal load of debilitating habits, attitudes, or beliefs. Other people are not so successful. Their unhealthy habits increase and some even become ill. Adequate information can help you choose the right alternatives for you.

THE FIRST WAVE

The emotions of divorce often divide themselves into two major time periods. For this reason, I've called the first period of time the "first wave." This usually lasts about two or three years. It begins before the separation when the relationship's future is in serious doubt. It often ends many months later, after the end of the relationship, when the new single identity, roles, and lifestyle are fully integrated and the largest share of the emotional divorce is nearly completed.

THE SECOND WAVE

The second time period, the "second wave," is a series of relapses or brief flashbacks spontaneously triggered by certain events or developments after the first two or three years. This second wave is just as important as the first wave. "Flashbacks" can happen at anytime, however, including during the first wave.

This chapter will describe the stages within the first two or three years, what to look for, and what to do. Chapter 20 will do the same for the second wave period.

The First Wave: The First Two to Three Years

1. The period before the actual separation: the beginning of a crisis period
2. The time of the separation: a crisis period
3. The eruption of strong emotions: another crisis period
4. The adult adolescence of testing new roles, new identity
5. The more mature identity and new lifestyle

The Second Wave: Flashbacks, Relapses to the First Wave

6. A general, deeper reevaluation and awareness of how your life has changed
7. When the other parent remarries, recouples, or again divorces
8. When you remarry, recouple, or again divorce
9. When the other parent has another child with another mate
10. When there is a change or threatened change in legal arrangements, such as custody or support
11. When one of you moves away from the area
12. When there is a big change in personal circumstances

TREATMENTS FOR HEALING THE WOUND

First: Follow the ten basic rules given in the last chapter to increase your human income. Be especially conscientious during the crisis periods of the first wave. In phase one, the stress level may rise to a peak just before the decision period and stay there. This high level may remain high through phase two and find a different or an even higher level in phase three. *Second:* avoid surprising your mate, and *invest in counseling or "pre-separation boot camp."* If you do decide to separate, *do your review work.* Some insight as to why things happened will help you assess your past and make plans for the future. *Third: Take care of your body and increase your "human income."* Baby yourself; pay attention to your diet, rest patterns, and exercise patterns. *Fourth: Take care of your soul and your spirit.*

- Have several friends or family members with whom you can *share your feelings.* Or enlist a trained professional. You may not feel like company, but you should be able to have it if you need or want it.
- Identify several more friends you can use as *sounding boards for decisions.* Your judgment may need perspective during this time.
- Consider *attending a class on divorce, parenting, or a support group,* or a singles group at the church or recreation center.
- Note your *old skeletons,* those repeating themes that the review work returns to and that generate so much feeling, particularly distressing feelings. Keep a brief journal.
- *Find safe and healthy ways to release your bodily tension and your strong emotions physically.* Sports or exercise, approved by your doctor, can enhance the release of emotions, as can writing in your journal or pounding a pillow.
- *Drive very carefully.* You may be accident prone.
- *Digest Chapters 9 and 10 on helping your children cope with changes.*

THE FIRST WAVE OF EMOTIONS IN DETAIL

PHASE ONE: PRE-SEPARATION (*The Decision to Part*)

Most relationships will go through an initial period of being under the weather. Many speak of this uneasy period in their marriage, saying, "something wasn't quite right," but feeling unable to put a finger on just what was wrong. (The second and third stages of the map in chapter 3.) People hesitate to admit a serious marital rift, even in the face of a deteriorating sex life, loss of communication, lack of respect, and even evidence of infidelity or dishonesty. Most people deny the symptoms as long as they can. Few people are eager to begin examining a failing relationship.

"My initial reaction was to deny that my feelings had anything to do with the relationship between my husband and me," said one mother of three teenagers. "I assumed that the trouble was my imagination or my attitude, or the kids. We would avoid each other, then become very close for a few days. It was awful and crazy."

Eventually, even with such bold attempts at denial, one or both of the partners may become aware of the marked erosion of mutual trust and respect. Pre-separation boot camp can begin. There may be scenes, accusations, tension, and fear. Bargains may be struck. But as difficult as this process may be, it will probably be worse if there is no attempt at all.

There is nearly always a strong feeling of ambivalence. You can see it on haggard faces that are struggling with bouts of anxiety, depression, hostility, and recurring illnesses. If a mutual decision to part is not reached, one partner becomes the potential leaver and the other the one who is left. The prospects of being left usually adds more grief while the leaver may feel a heavy load of guilt.

PHASE TWO: THE SEPARATION

The actual separation can be both a relief and a shock. The relief from tension and discord is accompanied by physical and emotional shock, an enveloping sense of loss. The old life together is fading fast.

The relief of finally acting on such a momentous decision helps some people, and they feel liberated, in touch with the possibilities of their new life. These are often people who covered a lot of emotional ground in the pre-separation stage and/or who initiated the separation. Others are less fortunate, especially if there hasn't been sufficient pre-separation discussion. They may feel relief from the hostilities and the indecision, but they are in shock and need time to recover. "Before the divorce, I knew everything about everything. Then when the marriage didn't turn out the way it was supposed to and the family life I loved was gone, there I was without a series of alternate game plans. I was paralyzed," said Gary, father of three.

Even those who understand and can accept intellectually the fact that the relationship has ended may effectively deny the depth of its emotional impact even in the face of physical numbness, perhaps a tightness in their throats, a hollow sensation in their abdomen, a loss of appetite. Sandy described her separation experience this way. "He moved out, reluctantly. I was relieved, but numb. Looking back now, I can see where the separation shock began and then wore off, but then it was hard to define. I couldn't sleep, cried a lot, had a couple of minor car accidents."

Other people find that the shock of separation raises their stress level to the point where some physical weakness is triggered into an acute crisis requiring medical attention. Myra, describing her siege of illness after her separation, said, "Three weeks after we separated, I landed in the hospital for emergency surgery. A week after that, I was in the emergency ward again, this time for a transfusion."

Watch for these dangerous side effects of separation:

poor judgment
accident and illness proneness, poor reflexes

depression, rage
neglect of your child
increased anger and irritability with your child

While these tendencies come and go through this stage and the following stages, they can be at their peak in stage two. For this reason, it is advisable to try to get through this stage as quickly as possible. It can last for several hours, several days, or several months. If it lasts more than a few weeks, seek professional help.

For the partner who may have been surprised by the request for a separation, these processes may be delayed and may take longer. But even for the initiator, the separation may be more difficult than anticipated.

THE WALL BETWEEN PHASES TWO AND THREE

It is not uncommon to find people who keep the separation a secret from family and friends in an effort to insulate themselves and keep the way open for a reconciliation. For example, pretending a separated husband is away on a business trip even after the legal papers have been filed.

Another form of denial that forms a barrier to the next stage is the denial of strong feelings. Some deny their grief and sadness; others hide their anger and resentments. Usually this denial of strong feelings means a bout of depression. Denial acts like a big cement lid on a bubbling pot of very real and active stored feelings yet to be released through review work. Such internal conflict is a danger signal worth paying attention to. If you do your homework and the depression still doesn't lift, consult a trained counselor.

Eventually, little blocks of the new reality will penetrate the numbness and strong emotions will escape, sometimes so strong that past restraints and traditional courtesies fly right out the window. For this reason, the next stage is characterized by intense, sometimes out-of-control emotions.

PHASE THREE: STRONG EMOTIONS

Because this period is both natural and nasty, this stage has been nicknamed "off-the-wall." It may be a time when soft-spoken women want to scream obscenities and throw things at their estranged husbands; a time when tender, caring men often spy on their estranged wives, producing wild accusations of deception or whoring. Former partners may develop a deep distrust of each other that all too often spills over into the legal arena. People may act in ways they never have before and never will again. Behavior can be exaggerated and atypical, especially if there was no pre-separation boot camp. Barry, for example, had never acted so hostilely during his marriage nor had Lois been so vindictive. The once stored anger, the sense of betrayal, of disrespect for their past together, the absence of understanding, combined with a fear of the future, can be released and aimed toward the separated spouse. Such destructive feelings and behavior are often mixed with intense feelings of loss and longing to have things the way they were.

Max described this experience: "I was unbelievably angry with her. The separation was her idea, but the divorce was finally my doing. I suppose my manhood demanded that I do something, that I act. I couldn't conceive of so much pain. But at the same time, a part of me longed to have her back. I felt that if I gave her a long enough lead, eventually she would come back to me. A part of me loved her, still does. That part wants her to grow and be happy and I wanted to ensure that my daughter would get good care."

If the parents haven't yet had a "bargaining" period, one of them may now attempt reconciliation and promise, "I'll go to marriage counseling," or, "I'll do whatever you want." When the bargaining fails, the emotions can become even more intense.

THE ROLLER COASTER

Feeling as if you are on a roller coaster of emotion is common at this stage, causing many people to fear permanent emotional instability. Others mistake the symptoms as signs that they are being punished for their failure or as proof that they still love their former mate. The intensity of feeling frightens some people and confuses most others. As one mother of six said, "It's as if all of me is in pieces, flying around in the air. But these pieces aren't landing, they just keep going. I'm scared." The off-the-wall emotions can collide with the hiring of an attorney by one or both former partners. The adversary system is not designed to manage or de-escalate feelings. Instead, it can act as a catalyst or a foil for these feelings, and the combination may be deadly. Even the most conciliatory attorneys find it difficult to persuade out-of-control clients that the legal process is not the appropriate arena for working out their intense feelings of fear, spite, or anger. Yet, such clients often say: "Things got much worse when I hired an attorney."

During this period, it's common to think that you are okay but it is your former mate who is out of control. Actually you probably are *both* out of control. This is the worst possible time to make any permanent decisions, especially legal ones. Thinking and believing the worst about each other is one of the chief hazards of this stage, and such thoughts, exaggerated and extended, can lead to serious complications. Unfortunately the legal business often demands decisions at this stage. Part 3 shows you how to deal with these legal issues, immediate and long-term.

DANGER SIGNALS AND WHAT TO DO ABOUT THEM

Men and women quite frequently feel a surge of unreasonable and irrational feelings during the off-the-wall period. Some men talk openly about "slapping some sense into her," and women talk about "making him pay dearly for what he's done." *If these are your statements, it's important that you discuss this with some trustworthy person, preferably a professional. If you have a friend who talks this way, be alert and strongly urge professional intervention.*

Thoughts of violence, suicide or homicide, are danger signals and must not be overlooked. If you have such feelings, or if you have a friend who expresses such feelings, immediately contact a suicide prevention center, the nearest free clinic, hot line, neighborhood health center, or the emergency room of the nearest hospital, fire department, or police department. Tell them you are going through a rough separation period and are temporarily out of control. You need a trained ear to listen and to advise you. You may need someone to help you control your feelings of violence or despair. Sometimes one contact is enough. Sometimes you may need a series of sessions.

Do not ignore the following danger signals.

- poor judgment and accident proneness
- strong feelings of depression, distrust
- strong feelings of anger, desire for revenge, violent feelings or thoughts
- a desire to see the other person suffer or to obey you, whatever the cost
- unwillingness or inability to express these strong emotions safely
- the ever-present temptation to take all this frustration and strong emotion into the legal arena and make exaggerated accusations
- illness or physical symptoms that increase under stress
- feeling self-destructive, like giving up, maybe then "They will be sorry."

You can help yourself by doing all of the following:

- enlist personal aid from a friend *and* a professional; do not go through this alone
- stay away from your estranged spouse, limit personal conversations
- find at least one safe way to release the pressure of your strong feelings
- avoid long-term legal decisions
- review your ten basic rules again (chapter 5) and look at how you can raise your human income

ADDICTION TO STRONG EMOTIONS

Even if your situation does not contain the elements of serious danger, this off-the-wall stage can become addictive. There is a peculiar but understandable effect after a while—people can get hooked on the strong emotions. For some people, these intense sensations make them feel alive and powerful when they may otherwise feel empty, numb, and powerless. Since rebuilding a new life takes time, everyone has a period when the emptiness gnaws away at their insides and at their hearts; the powerful surge of feeling is often a familiar, if not welcome, ally.

People can become addicted, a "junkie," hooked on anger, depression, grief, blame, guilt, hostility, or revenge—any feeling that can keep one obsessed with the other parent in either past or present times. A junkie doesn't work out the feelings in safe or structured ways; he or she keeps the feelings, and expands their meanings and effects. Or she or he ruminates over them, obsessively thinking and rethinking events to avoid strong feelings and to avoid action.

How can you identify a junkie? By the amount of time in day-to-day living spent thinking about the other parent, the situation, or about who is to blame. While the off-the-wall stage produces a certain amount of self-absorption, junkies wear their obsession like a badge of courage or martyrdom. They might believe it to be a sign of caring, commitment, or high morals. Some of the nicest people can become junkies at least for a while. Junkies usually thrive where there is a soap opera, blaming, and an all-or-nothing belief.

HOW THE ADDICTIONS CAN BEGIN

"I was afraid that my husband would stop child support, or stop seeing the children if he knew why I wanted a divorce," said Portia. "So I didn't talk to him at all. I told him he had to talk to my lawyer instead." Greg, Portia's separated husband, sought in vain for the real reasons his wife wanted a divorce. He described her to his friends as unstable and uncaring, with deep emotional problems that kept erupting in demands that he leave the house. Sometimes he wanted to punish Portia for "kicking him out." Typically he made statements like, "She thinks she knows everything; but she's not going to get her way." Then, moments later, "I hate her lawyer." Greg's feelings were so intense, he was often out in the hinterlands of communication. He feels humiliated by Portia, and he is trying to regain some self-esteem.

Portia and Greg had their own soap opera filled with blaming and accusations. Their kids' teachers were involved, so were their neighbors and co-workers. Their kids were unwilling participants. Greg's complaints and accusations about Portia were part of the "See why I divorced?" series. Portia kept repeating: "See what I had to put up with? He is totally unreasonable." Both were more and more seeing the other person as a "thing," rather than as a flesh-and-blood human being. Ordinary self-help treatment rarely reverses this damaging set of circumstances. "Junkies" need professional help.

AVOIDING THE "JUNKIE" TRAP

How can you avoid getting hooked on the blame game/junkie syndrome? The anger and hurt can last a long time. Anne, for example, didn't trust her estranged husband at all after he refused to see the children for three months. The children were hurt, angry, bewildered, acting out their fears at home and at school. To make matters worse, Anne found that few people expected the children's father to honor his parenting responsibilities. Anne reported, "The lawyer said, 'You can't make him be a father. If he doesn't want to, he doesn't have to.' People expected that he would 'not care,' and I almost went along with it because I thought the worst of him then."

"With the help of friends, good information, some new perspectives, and some badly needed practice in communications and business relations, we avoided a legal battle, and I've been grateful ever since. But I did have to let those strong feelings out somehow. So I took up jogging, washed floors, wrote pages I never read again. Sometimes I took my anger out on the kids, sometimes on myself. Only once in a while did I lash out at their father. One close friend, in particular, continually reminded me that I was going through a process, one that I could really learn from and grow through. She was right."

There is no mystery to safe passage through these stages, but everyone needs to find their own way to clean out their wound so new growth can take place. Whether it's karate, cleaning house every day, or running in place to the morning TV, find something safe that suits your circumstances, that works, and do it. In the words of one man, "People thought I was crazy, but I ran to the hills almost every day and yelled my guts out until I healed it through. But it worked."

PHASE FOUR: ADULT ADOLESCENCE

The first stages clean out the psychic wound of the past and to allow for the healing process. The adult adolescence period is set in the present.

You'll know you've reached this stage when you've become restless with the past and seek present challenges. People often find that living in the present makes it easier to ventilate their left-over feelings from the past. "There I was, happily shopping for some cheese and wine for a tête-a-tête with a new woman friend," reported one man of thirty-four, "when I came across my former wife's favorite kind of wine. I immediately had this vivid memory of the two of us together and almost cried then and there. Then, it was over and, although I felt stunned, I was okay. The whole thing took no more than five minutes, and it didn't spoil my evening. Five months earlier it would have."

The present can also bring with it feelings of euphoria, an exhilarating "I did the right thing!" One mother said, "I feel guilty because I'm so happy now." One father put it, "The worry, the loneliness I expected. I didn't expect to have such happiness emerge from the midst of it."

The term "adult adolescence" usually elicits broad smiles when people anticipate a discussion of the sexual experimentation of the adolescent, only this time with the power and experience of an adult. This is a beguiling fantasy, only sometimes realized in real life. The adult adolescent's reality is a combination of wisdom and naiveté, experience and innocence. Of course, today's divorced adult has more freedom to be sexually active with less censure than perhaps ever before, but concurrent adult responsibilities for a family or unwanted pregnancies don't vanish. Nor do the real health dangers of AIDS, herpes, and other sexually transmitted diseases.

An adult adolescent may behave like a gregarious, naive thirteen- or fourteen-year-old, like Marie. "I felt like a teenager again. I was excited about life. I felt attractive, flirtatious. I had coveted piano lessons and skiing when I was married and had never done either. I immediately signed up for both. I changed my clothes and hairstyle. I made many new friends and wanted to be out all the time. Sometimes I found out about being single the hard way. The first time I was asked to dinner, I expected dinner, not a heavy sexual pass."

A different personality, more reserved than Marie's, might be slow to meet new people, saving social times for old friends, a group outing, or a sporting event, and keep new acquaintances to a minimum. Each person's approach carries its own peculiar pitfalls and advantages. With Marie, for example, her fascination with her new life might lead her to neglect her children's basic needs. A reserved style ("the hermitage," one father called it) can promote too much isolation and a different type of parental neglect.

THE ADOLESCENT PERIOD—THINGS TO WATCH FOR

1. Ignoring the basic needs of your children.
2. Ignoring your own needs for a balanced life, not setting limits.
3. Drinking excessively, using illegal drugs.
4. Being sexually promiscuous.
5. You become the teenager in the family while the real teenagers or younger children become your parent.
6. Getting in with the wrong crowd of singles and taking on a pace or a lifestyle for which you are not ready or suited.
7. Ignoring and not taking precautions against sexually transmitted diseases or date rape.
8. Getting engaged or remarried too soon.

Former mates may react to the transformation they see after separation. "She's a mother! She shouldn't be dating like a teenager," scolded one former husband. "He's lost thirty pounds, looks fit, tan, and handsome. I had no idea I was married to someone who had that man inside of him," said a former wife unhappily.

PHASE FIVE: A NEW MATURITY AND LIFESTYLE

The psychic wound caused by the divorce has been cleansed in the first phases of the process. The last phases concentrate on the healing and mending. There is new growth, with some residual scars and some tender spots. Every adolescent is expected to grow up, mature, and begin contributing again to the family and to the community. In theory, at least, the final healing brings the ability and the willingness to take the risk to love and care for another person in an intimate relationship. In practice, most people take risks early in their separation to make new attachments, although in the early months, these attachments are less intimacy than sex, less relationship than exploration. Intuitively they know that they are not ready to make good decisions about a new partner.

Making new friends or intimates is pivotal to one's maturing identity and the evolving lifestyle. But, reconstructing one's own personal community, a sense of family, and the close circle of people who support and nurture you is the most solid foundation for your new life.

THE FINAL STAGES OF UNCOUPLING—HONORING YOUR PAST

The years you spent with your former mate were not "wasted" years. In the worst of circumstances, you can think of them as a "learning experience" and appreciate your ability to survive, rebuild, and thrive. Respect the years and respect yourself. You were at one time a couple. You had a child or children together. And now you have moved on either by choice or by circumstances. "Trying to pretend those years didn't exist was not a big help. Denying part of my past was denying a part of myself, a part of my life," said a man who had been married for eighteen years.

Anne described the final stages of her wounding and healing process. "We've both traveled a long way. It took three years for the marriage to end. Another six months getting through the initial shock and crisis period. And finally, about another two years exploring myself as an unmarried person and as a partner in parenting. Now I have established a new life and a new self-image, and am now well finished with most of the flashbacks. Parts of me are so different from what they were five years ago that old friends are amazed. I still sometimes look at the children and think, 'Why couldn't it have worked out?' But I feel that's normal. After all, I was married sixteen years, and we have three children together. We don't divorce memories, but we can learn how to live with them."

Chapter 7

The Retreat from Intimacy

How to Relate to the Other Parent

"WHEN I was married, I had a good idea of what was expected of me as a wife," said forty-year-old Peggy, separated after eighteen years of marriage. "But now that I'm separated, I don't know what is expected of me. Do I ask him for dinner when he comes for the children? Do I go along with his request to have the kids an extra night on the weekend? And what about sex? When I am angry with him, the answers are all no. But when I'm not angry, I don't know what to do. My confusion returns and nothing is solved."

Peggy has not yet separated her role as a parent from that of a wife. When she can make the two roles distinct and separate from one another, she will probably say no to sex with her former husband, no to all but very special invitations for dinner with her and the children, but a good many yeses to the father's requests for extra overnights for the children at his home. Until Peggy can make this role distinction, however, she has only her anger to help her make decisions.

NEGATIVE INTIMACY

Anger might allow people like Peggy to say no unequivocally for the first time in their lives. It might even be the primary emotion that propelled her out of her marriage, but it is not a wise basis for long-range decisions. Even worse, anger can tie former lovers together just as securely as love and take even more energy. The old saying "Love and hate are very close together" was never more true than during the early days of ending a marriage.

After a heated battle, anyone might say, "I can't stand this hostility. It hurts, it's destructive. How could he/she be this way after all we've meant to one another?" Yet despite firm resolutions to stay calm the next time, another violent disruption appears. Why does this happen?

Living a long time with another person leads to a form of emotional investment and understanding we call intimacy. To oversimplify, when feelings are loving, intimacy is positive. When feelings are neither positive nor negative, intimacy is in neutral. When feelings are negative, a paradox develops. What is happening is destructive, but there is a strong "junkie" attachment to intense negativity. I call this "negative intimacy." Most couples divorce because their history together has become too negative (or even neutral) without enough positive intimacy to act as a healthy balance.

HOW NEGATIVE INTIMACY HURTS YOUR CHILD

There is no way around the fact that your child's adjustment is directly related to how you handle your negative intimacy. Anger and frustrations are part of normal everyday life. But these episodes should be relatively civilized (even if intense) and eventually lead to constructive resolutions. Unfortunately, children of many separating and divorcing parents do not ever see this eventual resolution. Instead they witness ongoing anger that is not resolved, arguments laced with continuing sharp criticism, bitterness, contempt, lack of respect. This continual negative focus is emotionally abusive to children, and they are far more likely to develop social and psychological problems not only over the first years, but also later on in life.

Most parents grapple with their negative intimacy during the months before they separate and during the first years after the separation or divorce. They quarrel over custody, the children, money, blame one another, yell at the kids, and feel depressed, resentful, or revengeful. They have not yet separated their parental roles from their former roles as lovers.

You can find practical ways to relate to each other without being permanently hobbled by negative intimacy. This chapter outlines easy-to-use skills, giving pointers for everyday behavior and know-how that most people already have but don't yet know how to apply to a graceful redefinition of their old relationship. To begin with, take a look at how negative intimacy can fit into the larger family picture.

THAT OLD FAMILY FEELING

Each family develops its own private rituals, rules, and customs, its own blend of positive, neutral, and negative intimacy: a powerful blend I call the old "family feeling." A family feeling is when you can say, "This is home." "This is what my family feels like, sounds like, smells like," "This is how my family members behave." There are the sounds of one another's voices, the quick hug, the nighttime lullaby, the favorite music, the smells from the kitchen, perhaps a pet or two. In families, people learn what can bring a smile or a frown to another's face or how to hurt or soothe one another. There are the routines, the spoken and unspoken expectations. Some of this is spoken out loud, but much of it is subtly communicated in tone of voice, a look, or a gesture. Everyone, including the children, knows how this works, even if it is an unconscious knowing. Whether it is toxic or nurturing, the mood and the tempo of a family is unique. It is a very special music that only the members of that family know how to play.

When separation comes about, your old family feeling is disrupted, fragmented. The new family feeling has not yet emerged, and people can feel lost even when the old way was boring or destructive. If your old family feeling was positive and did not include negative intimacy, you are in luck. You can probably keep as much as you want of it for your new life. But if the old family feeling had the parents' negative intimacy as a backdrop, the old habits that pull for anger, hurt, resentment, and depression will continue to dominate and even escalate. This is because family members don't know how a positive family climate works, what it feels like, or how it sounds. So they keep what is familiar. After the separation, Mom may still talk negatively about Dad in front of the kids, the kids try to escape being caught in the middle of her blaming. Dad may tell his son not to tell Mom he is going on vacation or that he has new clothes. Or parents that used to argue late at night in their room now argue late at night over the phone.

Every family needs to develop a *new* family feeling, one that will be as positive as possible and free from the parents' negative intimacy. Until a *new* family feeling and a newer, healthier climate is pulled together under the guidance of a parent, the separation won't stop the hurt for the children or for the parent.

FROM INTIMACY TO WORKING RELATIONSHIP

LEARNING HOW TO RELATE IN A NEW WAY

"I know I'm attracted to playing all those blame games with my former wife," said one twenty-seven-year-old father of twin sons, "but what do I do instead? And how can I do it when I'm so damned mad at her, or feeling so hurt, that I can't even talk with her?"

If he didn't have children, the answer might be to leave town. But, tempting as it is, flight is rarely the best answer. The only way out is *through*. We have seen how this applies to the wound of separation and divorce. You don't pretend the wound isn't there; you help it heal. The same is true of learning how to relate to the other parent. You don't pretend he or she doesn't exist. You learn how to relate to your children's parent in a *new* way.

Many people are skilled at beginning relationships. Fewer people know how to end them or transform them. People can move from both positive and negative intimacy to a working relationship. The how, when, and where of their meetings can change. So can the why and what of their communications. Before shifting gears, people need to understand the mechanisms of relationships far more clearly than they did previously.

By looking at the way human relationships vary on a continuum of "businesslike" to "intimate," you can begin to see how to retrain yourself for your new role. Remember, it's not a sign of personal failure to feel confused about how to relate to the other parent now—the situation is confusing. But don't be discouraged, some of it will be easier than you think.

THE DIFFERENCES BETWEEN RELATIONSHIPS

To learn this new way of relating, it will help to think about the differences between relationships. Relationships usually develop according to their own sets of rules and expectations, marked by varying degrees of personal investment and expectations. A co-worker or a business associate does not become a friend overnight. People first meet as acquaintances or in a business setting. If subsequent meetings prove the relationship worthwhile, friendship might begin. Over months and years, if all goes well with the friendship, a few of these relationships might become close, perhaps one or two will become your intimates. Most people understand this progression instinctively and are familiar with how it works in daily living. If it were to be plotted on a scale from low to high, it would look like this:

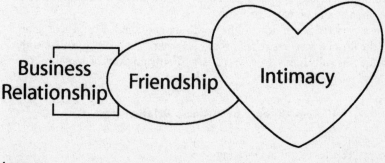

INVESTMENT AND INTENSITY IN RELATIONSHIPS

You have more invested emotionally in someone you have known for fifteen years than you have in a business contact you met last month. Of course, in a nonbusiness relationship, when for instance you have fallen in love, you can quickly become emotionally invested. But in most business and friendship relationships, the progression of a relationship carries with it a gradual increase in an investment of self and of emotional intensity. In most relationships, trust, loyalty, and respect grow *over time*. The difference in relationships is something we all know about. But a more sophisticated understanding of this difference can help you learn to relate to the other parent in a new way, one that discourages "negative intimacy" and encourages a new working relationship.

THE THREE BASIC LEVELS OF RELATIONSHIPS

THE ACQUAINTANCE AND BUSINESS RELATIONSHIP

The druggist, the vendor, your supervisor, are all people you do business with. The person you met at a party last week is an acquaintance. You both follow an implicit and explicit set of rules. When you talk with the druggist, you give him the prescription, and he fills it. She makes out the bill, and you pay it. If the druggist asks how you are, you answer, "Just fine, thank you," even if you have had a miserable day. Business associates do business efficiently and courteously, while keeping a low emotional profile. You might be friendly, but you know better than to get too close, especially if you are uneasy about the person. With an acquaintance you may be less formal, but you do not get close. It's "Hello, nice to see you."

The more at stake in a business relationship, the more explicit you must become: you operate with written agreements and formal information. If a fifty-cent purchase of chewing gum gets a cash register receipt, how much more important are explicit agreements or clear information that involve time, money, and perhaps the future.

On a personal level, despite the cordiality and familiarity that develop over the life of a business relationship, the axiom "Don't mix business with pleasure" usually holds true. Here is a shorthand way of looking at a business relationship:

Acquaintance or Business Relationship

- No assumptions
- Formal courtesies, public meetings
- Focused on the business at hand
- Explicit agreements, contracts, structured meetings

- Little confrontation, low risk, low emotional intensity
- High personal privacy, low personal disclosure
- Building and keeping a good reputation for trustworthiness is important

FRIENDSHIP—THE NATURAL NEXT STEP

"There are friends, good friends, and close friends," said a ten-year-old child. "I walk to school with friends, I play with good friends, but with my best friend, I can do everything and she knows my secrets." This child already knows that friendship comes in many shapes and with many boundaries. She already knows that many people may be friendly but few are chosen for the highest place of honor.

If a relationship with an acquaintance or co-worker moves successfully through an initial testing ground, it changes into a beginning friendship where trust and respect are building. The relationship is both formal and informal. Sometimes you make explicit agreements, and sometimes it's acceptable to make assumptions. Your assumptions about one another grow with your friendship. You are occasionally private, no longer totally public; you disclose personal information to each other, and your feelings of closeness grow.

Friendship

- Increase in assumptions and expectations
- Growing trust, loyalty, respect, understanding
- More shared feelings and personal disclosure
- Increase in private meetings, shared feelings
- More automatic reciprocity, forgiveness, and support
- Easier give-and-take
- Growing cooperation and reciprocity

As the serious friendship grows closer, you peel off more and more protective layers, revealing insecurities and faults. Your friendship can deeply move you or hurt you. When tender spots are revealed and then accepted, the friendship can deepen and another step toward intimacy is taken. When these same tender spots are stepped on or left wanting, hurt and anger arise over a friend's insensitivity and lack of caring. When your deepest fears and faults are revealed, will you stay friends? Will respect and trust remain?

On such touchy issues, many relationships falter. Unable or unwilling to take those additional steps that will mean intimacy, people fall back either to a less demanding form of friendship or all the way back to acquaintanceship. "I was so disappointed in him," said one woman of her previous lover, "I didn't want to know him at all."

But when the next steps taken are successful, intimacy becomes another dimension in your relationship. You can be partners, friends, and now also intimates.

INTIMACY

Intimacy has been described an intense, ongoing exchange of energy, affection, feelings, caring: a "safe place" where you share your vulnerabilities, dreams, hopes, joys, values. In healthy intimacy there is understanding and reciprocity. We are the most invested—emotionally and practically—in our intimate relationships. Risks diminish as trust and respect grow deeper. This can encourage ongoing openness, honesty, and flexibility in settling disagreements.

Intimacy is extremely personal and private. Couples who have the capacity for intimacy know it is not healthy to spend all their time this way. They also spend time structuring daily tasks as working partners; they spend companionable time as friends as well.

In positive intimacy, respect, trust, loyalty, confrontation, feedback, and support flourish. Each confrontation successfully addressed brings with it deeper understanding and tolerance, greater trust, a new form of respect. But not all couples are able to sustain positive intimacy over time.

Some couples find themselves entangled in a web of negative intimacy sometimes even after years of a happy marriage. "Something changed so drastically in how she treated me," said one man. "All she did was find fault. She was never satisfied. After three years, I finally had enough." Some withdraw and stonewall, others act disrespectful and annoyed with one another. Fear of losing the central relationship in one's life can undermine love further with one partner requiring continual reassurances and tests of love. Deeper dissatisfactions creep in, and perhaps one person will begin to test the other's commitment. Perhaps there is an affair and ugly scenes. Finally, the future of the relationship is in doubt and they may relate only with "negative intimacy."

Intimacy: Highest Intensity and Investment

Positive Intimacy	Negative Intimacy
Acceptance	Rejection
Positive assumptions, positive expectations	Negative assumptions, negative expectations
Trust, respect, loyalty	Distrust, disrespect, disloyalty
Privacy, informality, confidences are protected	Privacy, informality, confidences are not protected
Implicit agreements and assumptions are positive	Implicit agreements and assumptions are negative
Healthy interdependence	Unhealthy dependence
Supportiveness, understanding	Competitiveness
Disclosure is nurturing	Disclosure is destructive
Good give-and-take	All take or all give
Security, comfort	Insecurity, discomfort
Maximum intensity of emotions and feelings	Maximum intensity of emotions and feelings

If negative intimacy has destroyed their love and ability to live together, what can they do now? Must they just erase the good with the bad, the compatibility and sharing with the incompatibility and withdrawal? How can they show respect for their former love for each other, their life together, their children?

The Answer: Retreat from intimacy—both positive and negative—and go in the direction of a businesslike relationship. This permits both people, over time, to separate out their roles as parents from their former roles as mates and lovers. The goal is to create a partnership for finishing what you started—rearing your children.

THE PARENTS' "BUSINESS RELATIONSHIP"

The Goal: A decent working relationship with the other parent that meets the needs of your children

BUILDING A NEW WORKING RELATIONSHIP: THE FIRST STEPS

Separation or divorce means a definite, even if slow, ending of intimacy—both the positive and the negative. If you are hoping to reconcile, taking the businesslike approach will give you a far greater chance of recapturing the respect and trust that allows love to grow again. But trying to be friends right away is very difficult; few people can accomplish this feat. When it does happen, it happens after a solid businesslike relationship has built the respect needed for communications and give-and-take. The first steps:

1. Think of your relationship with the parent as something brand new, something to be built from the ground up. You don't return to the way you two related before you married.
2. Think of the relationship as a business relationship.
3. Realize that you have a choice about how you act and react.

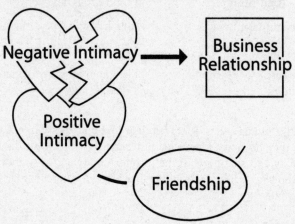

MOVE TOWARDS A "BUSINESSLIKE" RELATIONSHIP

For example, try thinking of your parenting relationship in this way. You and the children's other parent are just starting to do business together. Each of you must earn a good name for yourself. Your transactions should be mutually beneficial. It is in your children's best interest that you two parents conduct yourselves in such a way that you can take care of their needs, calm their fears, and their security. That's just good "parent-business" sense.

Most parents intuitively understand the need to retreat from their intimate relationship and rebuild a different businesslike one. Find something or some way of reminding yourself of your goal to be businesslike whenever second wave events shake up a schedule or arrangements. "I am in the 'parenting business,'" "We are partners in parenting," "What it takes to be a good father is having a working relationship with my child's mother." It is not only the most effective, but also the kindest and most rational road to emotional and economic recovery for both parents and children.

DOING BUSINESS WHEN YOU'D RATHER DO BATTLE

Often, after I introduce the concept of the business relationship to a group of parents, one will groan aloud and say something like "I hate my ex so much there is no way I could ever do business with him [or her]." If you react like this, think of your situation in another way. Pretend you need to obtain insulin for your diabetic child and you are on a frontier outpost. The only source of insulin, by a twist of fate, is controlled by someone you distrust. If you don't find a way to do business with this person, you are courting a serious medical emergency with your child. You may look for ways to get out of such a miserable situation, but you nevertheless have to do business with the supplier like it or not.

You can't afford to let your feelings endanger your child or your future. The daily tension between you and the supplier will go on. If you don't pay your bill on time or if you get an inferior batch of insulin, complications multiply. What happens today will affect tomorrow. As strange as it sounds, each of you need the other's cooperation. In your best interests, and that of your children, start learning how to develop this working relationship now.

The better you get at having a business relationship with your partner in parenting, the better your children will do. It is as simple and as difficult as that.

If all this seems unfair, it probably is. Divorce is one of the most unfair processes people experience. But seeking justice and emotional satisfaction from a former partner instead of negotiating a solid business arrangement is not going to make the result more fair. Real justice depends on a lot of hard thinking and work, not on you or the other party's lofty sense of fairness and "being right."

"I'M REASONABLE, BUT HE/SHE IS IMPOSSIBLE."

"This relationship is hopeless, he's totally illogical." "I'm willing to be reasonable, but I know she's sick emotionally." "We have so many bad feelings between us that we just have to talk through our attorneys." One parent who said he liked the idea of the business relationship said with a grin, "I just wish my wife wasn't so bent on a hostile takeover."

There is a natural tendency when emotions are out of control to see the other parent as the troublemaker, yourself the innocent bystander. Even if you are correct, the attitude alone will surely prolong the emotional divorce, keeping you attached by such emotions and beliefs to the children's other parent. As one mother said, "I had to decide: Do I want to be right? Or do I want to be free? I decided I wanted to be free." If you make this choice, then you are on the path to building a working relationship.

WHO SHOULD BEGIN?

The retreat from intimacy can be initiated by both of you or just one of you. Usually one begins alone while the other balks or invites or baits a return to the old negative ways, to the old "family feeling." There are, after all, two versions of your relationship. Even though it would be ideal for both of you to back off at the same time, that rarely happens. One of you has to take the first step.

When only one of you begins to shift to being a business partner, the other parent may protest loudly and convincingly. "It feels awful not to have you tell me what is happening in your private life like you used to," the reluctant new single may say to the one retreating. "After all those years together, to treat me so coldly is deeply cutting. Didn't we mean anything to one another?" The wail is genuine, the question penetrating. If you are the one retreating and your former mate touches you in your heart of hearts, pleading for you to stay in a close relationship, say gently: "I feel many of these same things. But we are just prolonging the inevitable. Let's try to honor what we had by respecting one another in this new way. We have decided to live our separate lives from now on, and this is part of what we have to do."

Sometimes a retreat is not so poignant, and the bait is hostility, accusations, and threats. Negative intimacy is hard to shake when each of you knows how to hit the other's weak spots. But remember, it takes two to battle. Keep doing your homework well.

Developing a working relationship as parents is the most that former lovers should ask of themselves. Friendship is nice but not necessary. For some parents, however, two or three years of a successful working relationship bring the additional dimension of a renewed friendship and a spirit of forgiveness. When this happens, the parents often consider themselves part of one another's extended family and everyone wins. Later chapters in part 4 will describe how this comes about. However, even then, this friendship has a solid businesslike working relationship as foundation.

WHEN TO BEGIN

Developing a working relationship is serious business. Hasty decisions or misplaced parental demands can do a great deal of harm. Some parents learn about the working relationship and think, "I can do that easily. All I have to do is be businesslike." Similar to teenagers with no driving experience or training, they jump into the driver's seat, step on the gas, and back right into a tree. Retreating from intimacy is not just retreating from hurt and anger, it is also the little everyday actions. Take the following self-test. When you are finished, ask a good friend of yours to answer these questions *about you.* Sometimes we don't realize how we appear or what we do or say. It's worthwhile to get another opinion.

SELF-TEST: ARE YOU MOVING AWAY FROM INTIMACY?

	Seldom	Occasionally	Often	Usually
1. Do you frequently find yourself calling the other parent "my wife" or "my husband" in conversation?	4	3	2	1
2. How frequently do you mention the other parent to others either positively or negatively?	4	3	2	1
3. Are you curious enough about what your former mate is doing to ask others about him or her?	4	3	2	1
4. How much do you depend on the other parent to support your needs in your single life?	4	3	2	1
5. How often do you find yourself thinking about your former mate during a typical week?	4	3	2	1

(continues)

(*continued from previous page*)

	Seldom	Occasionally	Often	Usually
6. Are there unsettled issues between you and your former mate that are major problems?	YES			NO
7. Are the two of you involved in *any* legal action with each other now?	YES			NO
8. Do you have a key to the other parent's home? Does he or she have a key to yours?	YES			NO
9. Do you keep or store possessions in one another's homes— furniture, art, appliances, jewelry?	YES			NO
10. Do you keep memorabilia and love souvenirs from the former mate in a prominent place in your home or office?	YES			NO

Scoring the Intimacy Self-Test:

THE FIRST FIVE QUESTIONS: Three or more answers of "seldom" or "occasionally" usually means that you are using everyday ways to gain a successful emotional separation from the past. A score of 18 is excellent. One "often" answer is not indicative of an emotional tie, but two "often" answers and even one "usually" should draw your attention.

THE SECOND FIVE QUESTIONS: More than two "yes" answers to these questions should also draw your attention.

Most people have one or two poor habits. Some of these are kept around almost as pets. But involvement that goes much beyond this limit is a sign that deeper issues need attention before the retreat from intimacy can be complete.

GUIDELINES FOR YOUR MOVE AWAY FROM INTIMACY

1. Watch Your Language

Refer to your children's other parent as "the children's father" or "the children's mother." This language can help you and the children to place your new focus where it belongs—on the parenting. The right words can help your "cooling down" process, help your retreat from intimacy, and reassure and reeducate your children and yourself. Recall chapter 4 and think about the words you use. Try not to think or refer to your "husband" or "wife" or even "ex" or "former spouse." If you refer to the children's other parent as your "wife" or "husband," you are still thinking intimacy not business relationship. Your feelings may not deny it, but your words should not encourage it.

2. Begin to Think Now in Terms of a "Business Relationship"

We usually have choices about how we act and respond to others. Remember the characteristics of a business relationship: courteous, relatively formal, low-key, public, respectful. You keep your personal life to yourself, you expect your meetings to be structured, and you expect explicit agreements, whether verbal or written. We cannot control other people's behavior. We can only control our own. Choose to be businesslike. The next chapter goes into more detail on how this can be accomplished.

3. Help Yourself to Privacy

Respect the other parent's privacy. If you find yourself asking friends or the children questions about your former mate's new life, try to stop. If such information is offered by others, politely change the subject. As for details about your own new life, keep them to yourself. Don't become the neighborhood soap opera. It is humiliating to your children and ultimately to you.

Often people are curious about the other parent's private life. People ask, "How did it happen?" It is strange that such an intimate question is asked by people you hardly know. You don't have to answer that question. Try saying, "I don't discuss my private life outside of my family, I'm sure you understand." It is your life, your privacy. It is also the other parent's private life. People outside your close circle have no right to know the details.

Privacy about sex is another problem. A father may be infuriated by the thought, "Is she sleeping with somebody now, in *my* house?" "Is he having a good time partying," a mother wonders, "while I work two jobs to keep body and soul together and a roof over my children's heads?" Keep your normal curiosity within bounds. If you want to share the details of your private life, keep them for your close friends. Don't ask for trouble by waving the red flag of sex before the other parent. When curiosity about the other parent's sex life grows excessive, negative intimacy erupts in distorted fantasies about the other's behavior, often promoting inquiries to friends or the children about the other parent's whereabouts and actions. If this happens, try to remember that you *are* getting a divorce and that knowledge about the other parent's private life is your way of holding on. As much as you may want to know what is happening in that other bed, you—and your children—are bound to get hurt if your curiosity persists. When it comes to sex, rumors are rampant, and truth is scarce. Not only is the other parent's private life no longer your business, but the version you get about it will surely be distorted.

4. Time with Your Children Is "Together" Time; It Is Not Baby-Sitting

One of the ugliest blows children suffer comes when one or both parents sees their time with the children as "baby-sitting" or "dead time" instead of valuing it as their own private together time to be parent and child.

Some parents refuse to see their children because they are angry at the other parent, wanting them to be overburdened without a break from parenting and without a chance to make or pursue new love relationships. Blinded by jealousy and revenge, a mother or father might call him- or herself a "baby sitter." They forget that they have their own distinct parent-child relationship quite separate from the other parent. Such parents are obsessed with being a former mate instead of a parent, and the children are the losers. Time with your child is precious.

5. Show Common Courtesy and Respect

Even when you don't feel he or she deserves it or needs it, show respect. Common sense says be courteous to a business associate or a co-worker, withhold rash judgment. But it is hard to be courteous and formal when inside you have feelings of jealousy or outright hate or are thinking, I distrust you, or, You are cruel and heartless, or even, I still love you, I don't want to let you go. Rudeness, sarcasm, or threats whip up the stuff of negative intimacy. Ask yourself, could you keep your job if you acted this way at work? Retreating from intimacy requires common courtesy. Although you may be right in thinking that a good blowup will temporarily clear the air, more often it's like scratching poison ivy. You may feel better for the moment, but the task of stopping the itching and bringing your poor skin back to health still lies ahead of you!

6. Act Like a Guest in the Other Parent's Home

"How do I act in the other parent's territory?" Easy. Like the guest you now are. Wait to be invited in, ask for permission to use the phone, the bathroom, and so forth. Even if the answer is, "Of course, you don't have to ask," ask anyway . . . *every time.* A parent who wouldn't dare barge past the secretary into an inner business office might not show the same courtesy to the new partner in parenting; he or she might step in uninvited and even snack on food in the refrigerator. The principles are the same, even though the circumstances are not. Respecting one another's territory and privacy is very important, especially during the first two years. Yes, it can be hard and often sad to back off and be impersonal, but it's nowhere near as hard as it could be if you don't respect the new regime. If you are not invited in, painful as it might be, don't pout or throw a tantrum. Either wait on the doorstep or in the car. This waiting can be very painful for both parents, inside and outside the house. Though time soothes, there is usually no easy way out during the first year.

Children will want to invite their parents into the house, saying "It's my house, too, and you can come in." Despite the truth to the statement, you will be wise to instruct them to get permission from the other parent, again, *every* time. Why? It's a wise formality. It builds respect with the other parent and shows your children that you have respect for their other parent. Respect for territory is good medicine.

7. Don't Expect Appreciation or Praise from the Other Parent

Approval and appreciation for a job well done is hard to come by in the early stages of a working relationship between parents. Parenting alone for the first time can be lonely. You may long for the support or approval of the other parent. Perhaps you need advice on a problem or appreciation for your tactics or decisions. When Olga, for example, asked her son's father, "What do you think about my decision to punish our son by denying him TV for a week?" she was hurt when he answered, "I think it's a stupid thing to do. You never could control him."

If you are going to fish for support, remember that you may get a kick in the pants instead of a pat on the back. You are not yet entitled to expect any kind of emotional support. While the move away from intimacy goes on, the strain of the separation seems to throw tact out the window. What you do in your home is your business. It is also your problem.

During those first months when tensions are high, better look to friends and close family for support and appreciation, even in the smaller child-rearing decisions. If you can tactfully lend your approval and support to the other parent, please try to do so. If you can't, try to withhold expressing your disapproval until you know how to do it without rocking the boat too much.

8. Be Explicit with the Other Parent

Intimacy is implicit and impressionistic, while a business relationship is explicit and detailed. A mother might say, "I don't need to be explicit for the children's father, he knows what I mean when I say I'll pick them up on Monday. Or at least he should, we were married eleven years!" This woman is still trying to write checks on a closed "intimacy account" with her former husband. It's time she closed that account and started saying explicitly what she plans to do and where. For example, "I'll pick them up on Monday at my brother's house after the children have had breakfast—between nine-thirty and ten o'clock," and then follow through.

9. Expect to Feel Strange About the New Relationship at First

Remember that many people feel strange about beginning a new relationship with an old lover. "I feel like a hypocrite," said a father of two. "I want to tell her off, and here I am being courteous and businesslike." Control of your behavior at this stage earns a plus, and if you feel the mismatch between your feelings and your actions, join the crowd. This is one of the costs to pay. This facade of neutral civility may be very thin sometimes. But as the months pass, this will change. Emotions will have cooled, your move away from your former intimacy will be well on its way, and the working relationship will have developed its first solid beginnings.

10. Don't Give Up, Keep Up Your Effort

One of my clients, Kathleen, labored for several months trying to act businesslike with the other parent, who had left her for another woman. She would begin their every-other-night phone conversations with her children's father in a businesslike manner and then fall back into the old negative intimate scene as the conversation went on. "I can't seem to get it. I know what I should do, I just can't seem to get it," she complained. I advised her to be kind to herself, she was still recovering from the shock of the separation.

One day she called me, triumphant. "I finally got it. I just have to act like I did when I worked the complaint department at the store!" She was finally in control of a miserable situation. She knew what she had in her past experience she could now draw on for today's challenge, even if she couldn't always do it one hundred percent. It takes a while to "get it." But it usually will come to you if you keep at it. And it is well worth the effort. If a conversation goes badly, end it. Make an appointment to try again another time.

11. Look at the Retreat from Intimacy as a Path, Not a Tunnel

You may feel you don't need to follow these guidelines very often. Or, if you are newly separated, you may find, like Kathleen, that the guidelines don't always bring you the immediate relief you hope for. But, as one father put it, "It isn't that the business approach is the only way you interact, but it is what you put into practice as soon as you start getting emotional or tense. It's not all you do, but it is what you get back to."

If this sounds like too much work, try thinking about separation or divorce as an auto accident. The accident resulted in a serious injury to you and your children. Without rehabilitation and consistent effort, none of you will walk or talk normally again. So you all work hard to regain your health. Little by little you regain your faculties and so do the children. But another thing happens as well. The process made you all stronger, more skilled in dealing with tough times, more appreciative of the good times and of supportive friends and family.

I urge all of you who read this to put out the effort to heal, to become stronger, to use this time to learn. And for those of you who are relatives or friends of someone who is going through this difficult time, support and encourage them. They *can* become stronger than before.

Chapter 8

The New Businesslike Relationship

Standards of Conduct for Parents

Standards of Conduct for a Working Relationship
Whether or Not to Interfere
Communications
Basic "Parent-Business" Principles
When the Going Gets Really Tough
An Example of a Good Working Relationship
How to Prepare for a "Parent-Business" Discussion

"The greatest disappointment of the first months of divorce," said one woman, "was my realization that—like it or not—I had to relate to the children's father. I had wanted him out of my life completely. I wanted never to see him or hear his voice again. But when you have children together, that is not the way it works."

The last chapter put forth the foundation and the first guidelines for your move away from your former intimacy. This chapter will look at how to use business principles to help you in your new working relationship. There are ground rules for autonomy, for respect of one another's territory and authority, for communications between you, and for negotiations within your new working partnership. Chapter 19 elaborates on the complicated problems of eventually developing a working relationship with an absent parent who wants to become reinvolved or reinvolving a parent who is a parent in name only.

Again, here is a reminder that any actual changes you are considering in your present relationship should be set aside until you read the rest of this book. Don't be in a rush to change things. Let the information and ideas soak in before you make any big changes or draft a legal agreement. Some parents, in a hurry to reach a final arrangement, assume that all they need is a good legal agreement. They feel that the law will not only set the stage for a parenting relationship, but will guarantee it. But consider this: When parents learn how to communicate and establish ground rules after divorce, their legal agreement will probably be an excellent one, and a good working relationship can result. But if they haven't mastered some basic skills, the best legal agreement in the world will not succeed in practice. Part 3 has more on this. Now let's begin.

STANDARDS OF CONDUCT FOR A WORKING RELATIONSHIP

STANDARDS OF CONDUCT FOR A BUSINESSLIKE WORKING RELATIONSHIP

Maintain your own territory, independence, and autonomy
Make your children's needs more important than your territorial rights or your independence
Respect the other parent's time with the children
Interfere if your child needs your protection
Respect the other parent's parenting style
Follow good communication guidelines
Use basic business principles when relating to one another

MAINTAIN YOUR TERRITORY, INDEPENDENCE, AND AUTONOMY

The first standard for your new working relationship is also crucial for your emotional divorce and your move away from your intimate relationship, regardless of whether it was positive or negative. Each of you should delineate and maintain your separate territories and do so with respect for your child's needs and for the other parent. Put simply, Mom's house is her territory and Dad's house is his. To preserve autonomy, you must maintain your own boundaries courteously and firmly—and you must keep your nose out of the other parent's territory as well. This doesn't mean you must tolerate neglect of your children, but it does mean you cannot dictate what happens over there.

MAKE CHILDREN MORE IMPORTANT THAN YOUR TERRITORIAL RIGHTS OR YOUR INDEPENDENCE

"It's my house, my territory, my way of raising the kids," a parent might say. But some parents are overeager to do things differently from before and are too preoccupied with their own problems to think of the children's needs. A parent may neglect or drop rituals or routines that children, especially young children, need to readjust to the new life. Perhaps they disagree with the other parent's child-rearing philosophy. Too big a difference between house-hold routines will cost you and the children over the months and years ahead. Take it easy with your changes if they are going to be far different from before. Children are adaptable up to a point, but they don't usually do well with vastly different routines and philosophies. Be considerate of their needs.

RESPECT THE OTHER PARENT'S TIME WITH THE CHILDREN

Each parent has the same rights and prerogatives. No fair making plans for the children during the other parent's time with them! And don't let the children talk you into changing times with the other parent "just this once." Exchanging times requires both parents' consent.

Here is how it works. Dad is living in the original family home with three children, ages five, seven, and twelve. Mom is taking them to her new place this weekend, Friday after school. When the twelve-year-old says he wants to go to a baseball game on Saturday with his pals, Dad tells him they need to both call his mother for permission. The weekend is Mom's time to make decisions and take responsibilities. If Mom says no, Dad does not malign "mean old Mom." He supports Mom's decision. Or suppose Dad has been given four tickets to a children's theater on Mom's Sunday. Before he whets the children's appetite for the theater, he tells Mom about the tickets. If Mom is unwilling to change plans, Dad should step back. If he really wants to smooth the waters and build everyone's sense of trust, he can give the tickets to Mom!

The noninterference principle can strengthen the parent-child relation-ship and enhance the emotional climate of family life. Parents can focus on making their relationship with the child the best it can be, rather than spending time on what the other parent is doing or not doing. It lessens nasty side effects like competition, nosiness, and manipulation. Noninter-ference gives the children a sense of security and continuity. Children know what to expect and eventually see how "two homes with no fighting" works. When parents adhere to the noninterference principle, parental cooperation is strengthened, and the children see a new, different, but still united front from their parents.

WHETHER OR NOT TO INTERFERE

INTERFERE IF YOUR CHILD NEEDS YOUR PROTECTION

Every parent has the duty to respond to a threat to their child's health or safety—whatever the cause. Child abuse, family violence, and neglect can and does happen during times of emotional turmoil. It is every parent's responsibility to exert self-discipline at these times and to protect the child if the other parent is neglectful or abusive. A problem arises when one is unable to distinguish a parent who is merely inexperienced from the one who is dangerously incompetent or abusive. Obviously a parent who raises welts or breaks bones is dangerous. A parent who swats a child's bottom once when exasperated or yells in the heat of an argument has lost some control but is probably not dangerous.

If your child is in any physical danger during this period, *seek help immediately.* Do not attempt to act without outside help when you know that a real risk exists. If you are uncertain how to proceed, call a hot line, the police, the emergency room at your local hospital, your family doctor, or a therapist for advice. You may need a professional counselor to help you decide whether the child is really in danger or whether your fears have been magnified during the emotional upheaval of divorce. If you find that your child is not in real danger, let the other parent alone. Cool it, and pay more attention to your own relationship with your kids.

The harder calls are those where a child is emotionally neglected or demeaned. Or the situation brings about childhood depression, or makes it very difficult for a child to develop normally or succeed in school or in social situations. Something needs to be done, yes, but "interference" means something less dramatic than calling the police. If you can, take your concerns to the other parent first. Find out if the other parent will join you or the child in family counseling. Or consult a counselor, mediator, or minister to help you form a plan of action.

RESPECT THE OTHER PARENT'S PARENTING STYLE

Having a different parenting style from the other parent is common. Different is just "different." After separation, you can no longer monitor the other parent's adequacy on a daily basis or insist on certain behaviors.

Eloise, a mother of daughters aged five and six, thinks that their father, Vince, is inept and unfit as a dad, even though she knows that he loves his daughters. Eloise insists that Vince present for approval a detailed schedule of projected activities for each of his weekends with their daughters. This is a surefire way to ensure trouble from the girls *and* from Vince. He may eventually seek custody himself to escape from Eloise's iron control and from the humiliation of parenting on her terms. Or Vince may just give up and fade away.

Maybe Eloise is right when she claims that Vince knows very little about child rearing. All parents can use improvement. But while her relationship with Vince remains strained, she cannot appoint herself instructor for his parent education. A counselor or friend might encourage Vince to upgrade his parenting skills, but any intervention by Eloise will probably only arouse resistance as long as Vince is resentful of her. But Eloise might be successful if she *also* agreed to take a class.

Every parent, married or single, makes mistakes. It's unreasonable to expect perfection of any parent, especially those now trying to relate to children alone for the first time. If Vince were able to communicate with Eloise, he might say something like this: "You weren't born knowing everything about being a mother! You made some mistakes in feeding the girls and training them. I have a right to make a few mistakes and to learn on my own, too." Eloise might say in return, "You reject everything I say because it comes from me. You know I know my children well. At least you could think about what I'm saying."

COMMUNICATIONS

FOLLOW GOOD COMMUNICATION GUIDELINES

Very often it isn't what is said but the way it was said that causes trouble. When you are only a few steps on the path away from intimacy, even the most innocent gesture can press on a bruise from the past, triggering a full-blown emotional reaction. No matter how firm Jim may be in his resolve to treat Jane as a business associate, he reacts to a certain rasp in her voice as he would to boiling oil down his back. His wrath rises, and instead of remaining coolly detached, he suddenly reacts with furious negative intimacy.

Fortunately, fundamental methods of communication can be learned. With a little effort and practice, many people can control exaggerated responses and diminish their vulnerability. Taking the following surveys, whether in a single sitting or one by one, will show you how to rate your own current status. The process will also give you some tips on how to increase your own communications skills.

CHECKING YOUR COMMUNICATION STYLE

The style of communication between intimates or former intimates operates according to a complex dynamic. Your answers on the following questions can give you some important information about your style as can the "Further Reading" section of part 5.

To begin, think back to the last four or five times you had reason to have some communication with the other parent. Ask yourself *how you made this contact.* Ignore for the moment why you did it, what the message was about, or how you felt about it all—just concentrate on *how* you got the message to him or her. Did you do it directly—talk to him or her yourself by phone, in person? Did you write a letter, send a note? Or did you do it indirectly, by asking a friend, a spouse, or a child to talk to the other parent for you?

Self-Test: Communications Part 1

As you think back over the last four or five times you have had a message to give to the other parent, how did you pass that message along—directly or indirectly?

Direct: You talked to the other parent yourself, face-to-face, by phone, or sent a letter or a note in a sealed envelope. Number of times this happened _____.

Indirect: You asked someone else (a friend, child, relative, co-worker) to get information for you or to give a verbal message to the other parent. Nothing was written down. Number of times this happened _____.

Donna sends messages frequently to the children's father, but never in person. Over the past two weeks, she has sent messages to him twice through a third party (his brother) and twice through one of the children. None of these messages has been written; all have been word-of-mouth. She has a score of 4 indirect messages.

Dennis has a different communication style. He has talked directly to his child's mother twice over the past two weeks, once on the phone and once in person. He has all direct scores.

Jay lives nine hundred miles from his children during the school year, and they live with him during the summers and holidays. He talked to his children every week directly but realized he had talked to their mother directly only once during that time. He had asked the children to tell their mother information for him three times. He wanted to avoid talking to her on one occasion. The other two times it seemed the natural thing just to ask one of the kids to tell Mom for him. He had 1 direct and 3 indirect.

YOUR SOURCES: DIRECT OR INDIRECT?

Now that you have an idea of how you pass on information, look at how you get information. *Think back over the past several months. Try to remember*

*where your information has come from about your children and your former mate
the last four or five times.* For example, Donna gets her information about the
children's father from his brother, sometimes from the children. The brother
also gives Donna information about how the children behaved the weekend
they were with their dad. Donna gets her information *indirectly,* and over the
past two weeks, she has gotten such information four different times.
Dennis, on the other hand, usually gets his information directly. He asks his
former mate questions himself, often in phone conversations or a note. For
example, he asked the children's mother, "Do you want me to send extra
jeans along with the kids this coming weekend?" Another parent might be
indirect in the same situation and ask the children, "Did your dad say he
wanted me to send extra jeans along with you next weekend?" Remember as
much as you can about where and how you got your information about the
other parent and record this below.

Self-Test: Your Sources Part 2

Direct: *"I find out from . . .* my former mate _____ times
Indirect: *"I find out from . . .* relatives _____ times
friends _____ times
children _____ times

How to Score Your Communications:

Look at your scores in one and two. If you have higher *direct* scores than
indirect scores, you're on the right track. *The higher the direct score, the more
you are tending to your own business rather than involving other people in your
responsibilities. And your messages, because you delivered them yourself, will be
what you want and what you mean.* The higher the indirect score, however, the
greater the chances are that you are ducking your own responsibilities or
passing them to others. When you send a message through another person,
its delivery and tone is always an unknown, as is the receiver's response.

Indirect communication usually signals some kind of game playing.
Sometimes the style is artful, based on an implicit "knowing" that character-
izes old intimacies. At other times it is clearly manipulative or a flat-out
power play. If a person won't be direct, you can't get a straight answer. You
may have to wait around, possibly losing your temper or your advantage
while you do.

Using the children to carry a message is the worst mode of communication. You
are putting your children in the middle. "Tell your mother that I'm going
to be late next week," Dad might say as he drops the kids at the front door
of Mom's house. Or, "Tell your father I'm waiting for the support check,
and he should send it with you when you come home." *Regardless of how*

legitimate the message, do not use the children as messengers. Notes passed back and forth with the children as messengers can work out all right as long as the notes are in a sealed envelope.

In workshops or seminars I have asked parents, attorneys, judges, mediators, and physicians to do a role-play: one plays the mom, one the dad, and the third the child. The people playing the mom and dad are told they are very uncomfortable talking to one another. They are to instruct the child to talk for them and to tell the other parent, "Mom/Dad needs the child support check right away." It is a painful and difficult role-play.

The people playing the two parents are shocked at how easy it is to put the burden of an adult problem on their child (even in an artificial role-play) and how easy it is to complain to their child about the other parent's demand. Those playing the child are usually shocked and surprised at how deep their feelings run for just a workshop exercise. Depending on their temperament, they are "devastated," "resentful," "fearful," "I didn't want to do this," "If I do this, Dad will yell, if I don't, Mom will yell," "I wanted to shrink away to nothing," "I am upset at the bad things my dad said about my mom," "There she goes again. What a baby!" A few felt powerful knowing they could embellish or withhold information and manipulate their parents with the tone and delivery of the message.

The moral is clear. Do your own work, Mom or Dad, and leave the kids out of it. Communicate directly with one another and keep your kids out of the middle of your problems with one another. Second-best is indirect and written. The worst is to use the children as messengers.

RESPONSES FROM THE OTHER PARENT: HARD OR EASY

Answer the first four questions by circling a 1 for a definite No and a 5 for a definite Yes. Mark 1 for the most dissatisfied, difficult, and hard No you can give. A 5 is for the most satisfied, reliable, and easy Yes.

SELF-TEST: RESPONSES FROM THE OTHER PARENT

	No	Yes

1. Overall, how would you rate your communications with the other parent? Give yourself a 5 for a pattern of excellent communications, a 1 for the poorest or if you have no contact at all.   1 2 3 4 5

2. Is it fairly easy to contact the other person—that is, if you had to get in touch with him or her for an emergency, could you do it readily?   1 2 3 4 5

3. When you have a request or a question for the other parent, do you feel you will be given a fair hearing?   1 2 3 4 5

4. When you ask a question or look for a response from the other parent, do you get a response within a reasonable amount of time?   1 2 3 4 5

5. When the other parent at first wants to avoid an issue, or avoid talking to you, can the two of you eventually work it out?   1 2 3 4 5

6. When you want to avoid an issue or avoid talking with the other parent, can the two of you eventually work this out?   1 2 3 4 5

How to Score "Responses from the Other Parent":

Add up your answers for these questions. A score of more than 18 is a positive sign, an indication that you can get in touch with one another when you need to and that you have brought about a degree of mutual respect.

If you score less than 18, your sense of respect or of trust may be strained. If you review your communication style carefully in the next set of questions, you may find some helpful clues to easing the situation.

REVIEW YOUR COMMUNICATIONS, PAST AND PRESENT

Think back on your marriage. At what time of day did you have your most positive exchanges? When did you seem to have the most difficult ones? "The worst time to talk to Harry was just before lunch," said Laura, "and there didn't seem to be any really good time." Can you give yourself some idea of the best and worst times to start a conversation with the other parent?

Then ask yourself which mode of communication seems to work best, which tr.. worst. Some people think they have their worst arguments face-to-face, others on the telephone. Some people hate getting letters and are calmed by a phone call; others find that in-person meetings clear the air.

There are no clear-cut answers. You have to decide which mode works best for you. Write them down on paper—after you have the answers to these questions, ask yourself the following:

What is the most irritating and maddening thing that he or she does, the mannerism, tone of voice, or topic that really sets you off? "Lynn is evasive—she never gives me a straight answer," "Scott is a liar; he says he put the check in the mail and it arrives a week later with a postmark of two days before." "Joyce whines. It sets me off," or, "Richard wants to talk about the separation all the time." Whatever list of irritants you make, spend some time thinking about how that parent can make you angry or upset. Then ask yourself what you do that sets him or her off. Even if you don't like to be pinned down by specifics, this time try to write it down. Then think about it. Consider yourself allergic to these behaviors. What can you do to avoid them? Or what is the antidote? Perhaps asking Joyce how things are going will give her the attention she needs, or telling Richard that setting aside a time privately to talk about the separation seems to be a good idea. Sometimes giving the other parent what he or she wants works to increase your goodwill and also may alter the way the other parent reacts to you.

Finally, ask yourself how you avoid talking about something with the other parent. Do you change the subject, refuse to answer the phone or letters, screen your calls on the answering machine, say you will get around to it (and then never get around to it)? Do you say, "I don't want to talk about it"? Do you get angry or feel like giving the silent treatment, perhaps forget it altogether? Whatever you do when you want to avoid an issue or answering the other parent's questions, it's useful for you to know what you *do*. Once you have identified some of your own responses, ask yourself, "What does the other parent do when he or she wants to avoid talking to me or answering questions?" Sometimes saying straight out, "I know I'm putting you off and I apologize. This is very hard for me," gains you some respect. But follow it up with a real-life action or negotiate more time to think about things. Taking an active step is frightening. But avoiding the subjects and the decisions will work against you. Don't take too long.

Give Yourself a Break

When you have answered the questions on each of these self-surveys, and gathered important information on how you can communicate more effectively with the other parent, why don't you give yourself a breather. You've covered a lot of ground, some of it heartbreaking. If you feel weary, take a break and come back later to this next section on basic business principles for parents.

BASIC "PARENT-BUSINESS" PRINCIPLES

BUSINESS PRINCIPLES WHEN RELATING TO ... ANOTHER

It isn't always easy for two people to do business together. If you have worked for more than a few years, chances are you have worked for a difficult employer, supervised some hard-to-manage employees, or dealt with the demands of unreasonable customers. In business we often take pride in our ability to operate successfully under difficult circumstances. And when your own happiness and that of your children are at stake, learning the skills of doing business with someone you don't like (and may not even trust) is vital to your future. Business principles may help both of you calm down and calm each other.

BASIC BUSINESS PRINCIPLES FOR PARENTS

- Effective businesspeople keep their feelings in check. They don't mix business with pleasure . . . or with displeasure.
- Effective businesspeople conduct business through an orderly give-and-take in which both adhere to a common set of courtesies and expectations.
- Effective businesspeople say what they mean and mean what they say.
- Effective businesspeople expect proof of sale or agreement.
- Effective businesspeople give the other person the benefit of the doubt but nevertheless expect delivery of promised goods and services.
- Business flourishes with reasonable flexibility and support.
- Business works with good communications.
- Business works best when people know how to negotiate and solve problems.

The impersonal business relationship seems incongruous between people who have shared a bed and a life. Yet there is a bittersweet dignity to this ability to close the book gently but firmly on your past lives together.

1. Keep your feelings in check. In business relationships, one's feelings are not to be confused with the job to be done or the goal to be reached. People say, "Don't mix business with pleasure." In order to succeed with shared parenting, you simply expand the rule: Don't mix business with displeasure, either. Rudeness, accusations, and a hot temper will get you fired on the job. And it won't advance you in this situation, either.

Some people, trained in the subtleties of business, often understand the concept of controlled emotions well. Once they are introduced to the concept of a working or business relationship with their former mates, they feel more comfortable. Others have sometimes been socialized to negotiate with feelings instead of with words and formal processes. However, these people catch on quickly once they understand the rules of the transaction.

2. Be orderly. Effective businesspeople conduct business through an orderly give-and-take in which both adhere to a common set of courtesies and expectations. Good business, like communications, requires regular schedules, protocols, business hours, expectations, and clear record keeping and memo writing. As parents you can prepare for each business transaction with thought, study, and self-control as if you were preparing to talk to an important business associate about a situation in the office or on the job. You would not want to remind him or her of past conflicts or problems. You must be willing to put the past behind you enough to promote a meeting of minds. You make appointments instead of just popping in. You write a memo at the end of your discussions. You don't leave the meeting expecting that you or your associate will remember every detail accurately. These principles work for parents as well.

3. Make no assumptions. Avoiding assumptions means checking your understandings with the other parent. Have everything explicit and put it in writing. With agreements, get a confirmation or a corrected version from the other parent. For example, a father might assume that he is going to continue bringing the boys to Little League games just as he did when they were living together, and since he has been living with the boys every other weekend, he will continue to take charge of their Little League activities.

It's Dad's job to write his assumptions about Little League in a note and mail or fax it off to Mom, asking for her confirmation or for her version of the details. When feelings run deep and strong, it's hard to remember objective details. Memos after separation are a must. Don't think, We'll take care of it when it comes up. Check out your assumptions, write them down, and then get verification.

Dad's note or letter to Mom could go something like this: "I've made the assumption that during the Little League season I'll be responsible for seeing that the boys get to the games and practices and back home, and the costs that come along with all that. I've also made the assumption that the every-other-weekend schedule we've had is to continue indefinitely, or until we come up with other arrangements. If you don't agree with this, I would like to know by the end of this week so that we can talk about it."

4. Give the other parent the benefit of the doubt. This is a close cousin to the "make no assumptions" rule. When one parent is late picking up or bringing the children, think first of a flat tire or heavy traffic. Don't immediately see the delay as a deliberate attempt to ruin your plans.

Suppose you hear from a neighbor that the other parent is going out of town the weekend that he or she is to be with the children. You wonder, "Is this parent going to cancel the weekend with the children at the last minute?" Furious, you are ready to pick up the phone and make some accusations. Take a deep breath and back off. Do your best *not* to assume that secondhand information about the other parent is accurate. Better instead to say nothing or to call after you have calmed down. The bad feelings that accompany separation or divorce can lead you to jump to the wrong conclusion. In business, difficult situations are *managed* whenever the stakes are high enough.

5. Use businesslike communications. Good business communications principles apply to parents developing a working relationship. Business is conducted in many ways: in person, by various types of mail, by phone, and sometimes, when the going gets sticky, through attorneys. Rarely does a business transaction take place with an unauthorized third party (friends, relatives, or children) carrying information. Apply the same principles to parenting. Communicating is your job. Try to make plans yourself. If in-person communication becomes too uncomfortable, retreat to those methods that feel the most comfortable but allow you to be explicit and provide the other parent a way to answer you. This is quite acceptable. Just write that you're trying to keep your feelings out of these important discussions, but you hope to resume personal contact later. *Remember, good communication is your child's safety net.*

6. Don't take the other parent for granted. As simple as this guideline may seem, it may also be the most important. Building trust with the other parent does not mean you can take him or her for granted. After divorce this becomes a dangerous form of disrespect and can rapidly lead to trouble. "I don't like being sent a bill in the mail with no explanation," says Michael. "I usually pay for whatever extracurricular activities Suzanne wants to provide for the kids, but she should consult with me, or say, 'This came up at the last minute.' It's rude."

7. Double-check your verbal understandings. Remember, during this transition time, memories fail more often. Concentration may not be what it is normally. It is not usually intentional, it just happens. Anxiety, too many things to think about at once, the emotions of divorce, are all memory busters. "It is so bad now," said one father, "I can't remember my zip code." It is this reason, not the distrust of the other parent, that should motivate you to write things down and check it out. When you and the other parent make an arrangement, say, "Let me double-check this," then repeat your understanding in *detail*. Then say, "Have I got it right?" This reinforces that you were listening to what the other parent said and that you do want to understand. Too often we misinterpret a small but important detail. Or we forget one. This little routine is a gem. It will catch a problem before it begins. And it builds respect and trust with the other parent.

8. Use basic negotiation skills. Part 3 will help you with the basics.

WHEN THE GOING GETS REALLY TOUGH

When a parent has a major problem with negative intimacy and blame games, it can be tough trying to find a way to be businesslike. You try all the things in the previous list, and although it helps, it is not doing the job. Anyone who has worked for a few years has probably had a difficult boss, supervised some especially hard-to-manage employees, or dealt with irascible customers.

Think about how successful employees handle a tough boss or a difficult co-worker. Here is what some people in my workshops or seminars say they would do:

> "Minimize contact at all levels," "Don't be a clock watcher," "Support your boss in public," "Make your dedication to the job very clear. Volunteer for things, ask what you can do to help." "Do your job, let the boss do his or her job," "Ask the boss for help," "Focus on his problems," "Be aware of your entitlements," "Eliminate all negative interactions with others about the situation," "Demonstrate a clear understanding of what the boss is saying," "Ask yourself what's going on, evaluate it. Ask, 'What are the risks?' " "Do some self-assessment. It can't always be the boss's fault," "Be sure to document everything," "Set up meetings and ask for help," "Separate the person from the behavior," "Try not to take it all so personally," "Build other relationships," "Don't play games," "Flood the boss with information so he or she doesn't get wrong ideas."

Here is how this can work with the other parent.

THINGS YOU CAN DO WHEN THE GOING GETS ROUGH

1. Avoid in-person contact.
2. Make your communications formal and direct—send faxes, beeper, or voice messages.
3. Always demonstrate that you clearly understand what the other person is saying.
4. Keep the agenda on the principle of doing what is best for the children.
5. You know what triggers a conflict or feelings of shame in the other parent. Try not to pull these triggers.
6. Look for ways to acknowledge his or her loyalty, contribution, and dedication to the children.
7. Do your job as a parent, let him or her do his or her job as a parent.
8. Confront only with great care. Choose your fights very carefully.
9. Try to be flexible. Volunteer something he or she would like to have.
10. Do some self-assessment.
11. Keep the parent a person in your mind. Don't make him/her into a monster or a "thing."
12. Do what you say you are going to do, be reliable.
13. Know your rights. See part 3.
14. Keep detailed records and a log.
15. Use a mediator. Bring your memos and documentation.
16. If mediation doesn't help, see a lawyer or go to court yourself.
17. If you can't change the situation, be sure your attitude works for you, not against you.

Simple as it sounds, just knowing what is happening is half the task. At first you may not be able to change what you do or say or how you say it. But you will know what you are doing rather than remaining oblivious of your own actions. Change takes time for everyone. Give yourself the benefit of the doubt, and try out this new way for two months. See if it will help you and your situation. Chapters 12, 13, and 14 may also help.

AN EXAMPLE OF A GOOD WORKING RELATIONSHIP

Brian and Pat, who have children ages nine and eleven, have been separated for about six months. The children live with Pat about two-thirds of each month. Twice a month they live with Brian over extended weekends, from Thursday night through Monday morning. This division of parenting is a tentative arrangement. They've agreed to try for two months and then appraise the result. They are both still in the off-the-wall stage of emotions.

Because their feelings are still so raw, Pat and Brian communicate by phone and use the fax or the mails to verify their arrangements. They need to write memos and keep records because Pat has a reputation (with Brian) for being forgetful, and Pat claims Brian often changes plans at the last minute. Writing memos is a time-consuming bore, but it prevents many accusations and excuses. The parent who slips up cannot shift the blame. Each agreement is confirmed by the memo on the desk or on the kitchen bulletin board.

Brian has a free afternoon coming up next week and wants to spend it with his daughter Tricia. He calls Pat at work and asks, "Is this a good time to talk to you, or should I call you later?" Pat replies that she's free to talk now. Her motivation is that she just wants to get the talk over with.

"I have a free afternoon next Thursday," Brian says, "and I'd like to spend it with Tricia. I'll pick her up after school and have dinner with her, then bring her home about eight o'clock. How does that sound to you?" As he talks, Brian hopes he doesn't have to persuade Pat.

Pat agrees; Brian is relieved. Then he contacts his daughter Tricia to see how she feels about Thursday. Tricia is delighted, father and daughter make their private plans, Tricia asks her mother and tells her their plan. Brian prepares a note to send to Pat.

"Here is my understanding of today's phone conversation. On Thursday, January 12, I will pick up Tricia after school and take her to dinner. I'll bring her home at 8:00 P.M. I'll call the sitter on Monday to explain that Tricia won't come home after school on Thursday. If I don't hear from you by this weekend, I'll assume this is your understanding as well. Take care of yourself, Brian."

Brian marks his calendar and makes a copy of the note before mailing it to Pat. When Pat receives it, she posts it up and also makes a note to remind Tricia that morning of her change in plans after school. There is no need for future phone calls between the parents and far less possibility of misunderstanding. Brian now has a direct line with Tricia about Thursday, and each parent has a memo to remind them of their agreement. If Brian wants to change plans, he will have to repeat the entire procedure.

Brian and Pat followed the "Parent-Business Principles" below. By making plans this way, they are acting as if they respect each other, the way people do in a simple business transaction. By using the phone and notes they could keep emotions, which were at a peak, under control. You wouldn't think twice about using this procedure at your job.

HOW TO PREPARE FOR A "PARENT-BUSINESS" DISCUSSION

CHECKLIST FOR A "PARENT-BUSINESS" DISCUSSION

- *Prepare yourself emotionally.* Since some or all of the discussion has emotional triggers, focus on being "businesslike."
- *Style of communication: Direct.* Neither children nor friends transfer or interpret information. All information comes directly from one parent to the other.
- *Expectations: A business occasion only.* No expectations for emotional support or approval. Do not take the other person for granted.
- *Preparation for discussion or transactions.* Set up appointment, have an agenda, ask for most convenient time, meet in a neutral place.
- *Content of discussion: One or two items,* about children only. No personal disclosure, keep a low profile.
- *Style of conversation/discussion: Informal, but on the subject;* courteous; specific, rather than vague; questioning, rather than judgmental.
- *Time of phone calls:* During normal working or business hours or by mutual agreement.
- *Record keeping:* Notes or memos made after each conversation to record details of agreements.
- *Verification:* Note sent to other party itemizing agreement, asking for verification.

HOW TO SABOTAGE YOUR WORKING RELATIONSHIP

Pat and Brian could have sabotaged their exchange in many ways. Brian might have called Pat late at night, and either parent might have been discourteous on the phone. Brian might have failed to send the memo. Pat might have forgotten to post it as a reminder for Tricia.

Let's imagine how such behavior might affect an ordinary business relationship. Suppose a business associate calls you at home, after you have gone to bed, to complain about the details of a contract you are negotiating. When you tell him you will discuss it on Monday during business hours, he becomes discourteous. He finally agrees to a Monday morning appointment—but he doesn't show up. When you finally get together, he snarls at you and makes snide remarks about your personal appearance. Would you do business with this person? Would you hire him? Would you fire him?

Think of the many ways people in business can be irritating and unprofessional. They don't return telephone calls, are late for appointments, misrepresent their services, don't show up or often call in sick, and don't keep agreements. They say they don't remember, or they say, "I was never told about this," when you know they were present when the topic was discussed. They bring in personal aspects, stray from the subject at hand, challenge your competence or integrity, and downgrade the competition. Everything else is more important than the task at hand. Former mates do this to one another all the time, saying "All is fair in love and war. And this is war." But it boomerangs. Their job is to do what is best for their child. This is the goal, the job description, the project. Provoking, unbusinesslike behavior will lose you a lot in the "parent" business and, more important, make your child the loser.

HOW MEMOS HELP

Most parents find "those damned memos" irritating but very useful. "The memos shaped me up," one mother said. "I couldn't blame the children's father for my own negligence." During periods of emotional upheaval, people are forgetful. They remember feelings and snatches of conversation but forget details that have not been recorded.

When Brian agreed to bring Tricia home at eight o'clock, he made a commitment not to keep her out beyond her bedtime. Keeping such promises is essential to building trust in the cooperative parenting relationship. He showed his willingness to abide by the agreement when he put it in writing. When Pat received the brief memo, she accepted it as a routine business procedure—not as a sign of scorn or distrust. (Some people misunderstand this feedback process when it occurs in private communications.) Today there are many different ways to communicate. Investigate, and use what's best for you.

Writing memos eliminates some of the verbal cues that cause tension in oral communication. "I knew he was going to give me a hard time," one mother said after a telephone call from the children's father. "His tone of voice was icy and disdainful." Familiar voice tones, gestures, and postures tell us what might be happening inside our former mates. But as accurate as we might be about his or her thoughts and motives, mind reading and second-guessing do not belong in business. When in-person talk gets nowhere, focus on the written word. Put it in writing. Get it in writing. There is another advantage to written memos. Once you work out an arrangement, you may not need to renegotiate the issue from scratch again because it is already in writing. How you worked out orthodontic care for your oldest child may work for your second child. Or the arrangements you made for insurance so one teen can drive the family car may work when the next child is ready to drive. Memos can be a good use of your time.

YOUR CHILDREN'S RESPECT

The businesslike relationship will be a boon to your children as they watch a major miracle occur. Their parents—two people they love deeply—are learning how to work together, despite feelings of anger and disappointment. When parents are at war with one another, children lose their sense of security. They can feel helpless, unsafe. A good businesslike relationship can reassure your children that the hostilities are under control. They can begin to trust again. This new ordering of priorities is a model of decent behavior sorely needed in today's world. You can teach your children by your example how to devise an effective working relationship without sacrificing personal integrity. You can prove to them that when something is really important, such as *their* health and happiness, their parents can work together.

Chapter 9

Mom's House, Dad's House

How to Make Them Homes

PUT yourself in your child's place. Your parents have announced that they are separating. What would they have to say or do that would first, help you feel things would work out all right, and second, show that you would now have two homes instead of one? Parents in workshops frequently respond by saying: "I'd want to feel that my parents knew what they were doing." "I'd want my own things, my own place, in both homes." "I'd want my friends, my school, my pet." "I'd want to stake out my own territory in each place." By the time the list is halfway finished, one person in the group will say, surprised, "This other home sounds like a real home."

Right. The other home *is* a real home for your child. Regardless of how much contact the child has with each parent, the other home can actually help stabilize the child's new life. You can get past the competition of which is the "real home" and develop a two-home safety net. You do not have to feel that you are making this effort only for the sake of your children. It will stabilize your life, too.

This chapter offers guidelines for you to consider as you go about reorganizing your life as a parent, whether you are parenting solo or hoping for a two-home arrangement. These guidelines explain ways to redesign your independent relationship as a parent with or without consulting the other parent.

TWO-HOME REWARDS

Parents who set up two homes for their children often make comments like "It made me feel I was a real parent again" or "I knew what I was doing and the children could feel it." When necessary steps are taken to reclaim certain responsibilities for our children, normal parenting is resumed. We break through some of these sex-typed barriers that have said that men cannot be nurturing and responsive or that mothers who set up another home have "given up their children" and have something intrinsically wrong with them.

When parents establish a working relationship, their children can feel that Mom and Dad are on top of this life crisis and that things are going to be okay. Then even perhaps, "Uh-oh, I guess that also means they are each going to get my report card!"

YOUR HOPES AND DREAMS AS PARENTS

A good place to start thinking about what is best for your children is to think about what you hope and want for them. This process has a way of focusing your energy. It has the potential to help us steer a course and to measure our progress. If you are feeling emotional or depressed, thinking about your hopes for your children may not be an enticing exercise. Skip this section and go to the next one, but do try to come back to this eventually. It is a keeper.

"I want to provide security and continuity for the girls," said Leslie, a mother of two girls ages four and six. Randy, the children's father, wanted to be sure that his daughters were prepared to live in today's difficult, sometimes dangerous, world. Both Randy and Leslie wanted to end their open hostilities, or at least have a working truce. They had never had to think about their hopes and dreams or put them in words before. It was a revealing process. They first discussed the kinds of adults they wanted their daughters to be, then the kind of childhood they wanted for them. It took them only an hour to come up with the first ideas, but it took two weeks for them to agree on their final selection. When they were finished, both said they were proud of their accomplishment. They knew that carrying them out would be a noble achievement.

Randy and Leslie's Hopes and Dreams for Their Daughters

1. To provide our daughters with a sense of continuity, stability, and security, especially in their concept of "home."
2. To prepare them to live in a fast-paced, changing world, to survive and thrive.

3. To give our daughters two involved, caring, and responsible parents who communicate their needs and share responsibilities for their upbringing.
4. To provide our daughters with positive role models, including one for resolving conflict and dealing with tough times.

Some couples find that they agree on several things, but that each has other hopes as well. Dad may want his son to be a team player in life, Mom wants him to be socially responsive. These couples can have *both* their individual and their mutual values. They can agree to support each other or agree to not interfere. This is one of the ways separated and divorced parents can provide their children with a new age "united front" and provide them with a sense of direction and purpose.

As you read over the rest of this chapter and the ones that follow, ask yourself, "How can this action, attitude, or state of mind contribute to fulfilling my hopes and dreams for my children, building a new, positive family feeling, and a healthy parenting partnership?"

PARENTING PATTERNS

A parenting pattern is the way parents relate to one another. It holds an important key to how well children adjust to change. If a pattern is destructive, neither equal time nor a traditional every-other-weekend visitation arrangement can protect a child. But when a parenting pattern is constructive, many arrangements can work.

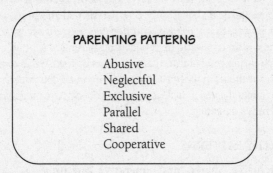

PARENTING PATTERNS

Abusive
Neglectful
Exclusive
Parallel
Shared
Cooperative

UNHEALTHY PATTERNS

Everyone knows that *abusive parenting and neglectful parenting are unhealthy*. But there are two other patterns that harm children. First, there can be a *hidden neglect*. These are the children of economically solvent parents, who are clothed, often fed, and usually sheltered, but are emotionally and psychologically abandoned by parents who are overly preoccupied with themselves, their work, social life, or activities.

Second, there is *parallel parenting*. While this pattern can be seen in never divorced families, it is a major hazard for "joint custody" families. Both parents are involved in the child's life, both have input into major decision making, but there is little or no interaction between them about their child. Parents are unable or unwilling to discuss the children's needs with one another, and their communications are strained or nonexistent. When parents live apart, their anger or distrust often rules their relationship. They contact one another only in emergencies or in case of serious illness. The children are not free to talk about their feelings or what happened to them in their other home—where they went, whom they saw. Children in such circumstances may have to act as if they do not have another parent and must choose their words carefully in the presence of each parent. Sometimes, when a child talks spontaneously about something that has happened at the other home, the parent may say, "I don't want to hear about it." These demands place a sorrowful burden on their child.

These parents will often alternate attendance at school events rather than risk a scene or bad feelings. Such parents may say, "It's too painful, or difficult, to talk to him/her," or, "Every time we talk, there's an argument," often adding, "She/he takes it out on the child" or "puts the child in the middle." In such situations the child may have two parents but may not feel at home or secure with either one. One child in such a situation said, "My safe home is the car." When I have asked children how things are going for them, or if a change would help, their answer was frequently something like "No, keep it as it is . . . at least I have them both, even if it isn't the best." Children appear to fear that if only one parent had the lion's share of the authority or power, that parent would deprive them of access to the other parent. Some children have no hope that their parents will be able to change.

Parallel parenting puts children and parents at risk. *While common in the first year of separation, families do and should grow out of this pattern into a more constructive, habitual pattern, such as positive exclusive parenting, shared parenting, or cooperative parenting.*

THE HEALTHY PATTERNS

Positive Exclusive, Shared, or Cooperative Parenting

Most parents can learn to develop positive parenting patterns regardless of the way the children's time or the parents' rights and responsibilities are divided. You may not now be in one of these healthy patterns described, but you can begin. How? Use the same tools you have been reading about in previous chapters: retreat from negative intimacy and use your new business relationship approach to build or strengthen a healthy way to be effective parents. This and the next chapter on children can be especially helpful.

Chapter 13 and the chapters in part 4 will also be useful. Try to develop one of the three positive parenting relationships described here within the next nine to twelve months.

HEALTHY PARENTING PATTERNS

1. Parents frequently share information about their child. Written notes, voice mail, and e-mail often substitute for one-on-one talks.
2. Parents' communications are respectful, usually businesslike and direct. No verbal messages are sent through the children.
3. Parents keep the child out of the middle of their problems with one another, and there is no neighborhood "soap opera."
4. Each parent supports the other parent's relationship with the child and helps the child feel free to love both of them.
5. Parents provide the child the environment, support, and love to develop normally—physically, emotionally, spiritually.
6. Parents can answer yes to nearly all the questions on the "Taking Stock" list in the next chapter.

Exclusive Parenting

This pattern is a familiar one, exclusive in that there are very clear, even rigid, boundaries between what Mom does and what Dad can do, and one parent acts as the family executive officer. A number of different kinds of families have this pattern.

The first is where the other parent is out of the picture completely. Examples: the death of a parent; the parents never married, and one of them is not interested in being a parent; the other parent because of criminal activity or abuse is prohibited from being involved; a nonresident parent has no significant time or decision-making authority either because of geographic distance from the primary home or because of legal action. An exclusive parent has a big job to do, but it has been done and is now being done successfully by many parents.

The second type of exclusive parenting is when there are two functional parents. One parent makes all the decisions, has all the responsibility, and has all the authority. The other parent pays child support and commonly has "visitation" twice a month. Perhaps the noncustodial parent gives opinions regarding major decisions in education or medical treatment, or he or she may have some limited functional authority. When the parents work well together and the child has consistent and continuing access to both parents, this form of parenting can be successful for all concerned. "I can count on him if there is an emergency, and so can the kids," say some mothers. "She knows the kids best. I wouldn't want to second-guess her," say some fathers. However, if the parent *with custody* is the "in-house" parent, the parent *without custody* often considers his or her position as the "out-house" parent, as a "visitor," peripheral and powerless. The resident parent may feel overwhelmed, overburdened, and defensive. The negative side of this pattern can be quite destructive for everyone.

Shared Parenting and Cooperative Parenting

Shared parenting is a structured businesslike working relationship. These parents may disagree, but they resolve their concerns either by agreeing to disagree or by compromise. They keep their child away from their problems with one another. Parents can attend school conferences jointly and events together. Teachers, coaches, and child guidance counselors feel free to call either parent without risk of getting caught in parental competitiveness or territorial disputes. Children can share their lives with both parents. *Cooperative parenting* goes even further. It builds on that working relationship with an additional spirit of respect, forgiveness about the past, and an easier give-and-take. Cooperative parents truly try to help each other. The well-being of their child takes the highest priority in their lives.

A healthy pattern is an important goal for all families—married, divorced, or never married. It is, like most things, dynamic. People have different styles of dealing with their anger, grief, conflict, and tension. Some try to avoid it, others confront on even the smallest issue. Some rise to most of the challenges, others sink with negativity and have to be rescued by friends. No one person has everything or does everything well. *Keep your eye on your prize—a healthy parenting pattern. This will give your child the opportunity to continue to develop normally.* So keep up the effort. Your children will benefit, and in the long run so will you.

YOUR HOME

A SENSE OF BELONGING: MY OWN THINGS

The common grumble of parents when children return from being with their other parent is that some item, a favorite toy or a jacket, has been left behind. The first, knee-jerk reaction becomes: The other parent or the child has been inconsiderate, thoughtless, or deliberately provoking. Actually, as we have seen, this forgetfulness probably stems from the child's need to stake a claim to some territory, a sense of belonging in his or her newer home.

Children will know they belong in two homes when they no longer need a large suitcase to go from one home to another. This holds true no matter how little time they spend in one home. The time spent doesn't matter, the sense of belonging does.

Children need their own space and are entitled to privacy. Even a drawer they share at the bottom of their parent's dresser can help. They need their own nontransferable toilet articles and two or three changes of clothes. They need their own place for toys and personal effects and a place to sleep. Some personal things belong in each home and stay there. Sleeping bags rolled up in a closet can be good beds if these are their own sleeping bags. A house, a yard, and an extra bedroom are just trimmings. The sense of "my own things, here" matters. So does a trust that their things will remain protected in their absence.

Many dual-home parents simply take their offspring shopping for new clothing, sleeping bags, and toilet articles. These purchases offer a way to participate in the organization of their new, other home. When money is very tight, perhaps parents can agree on which of the child's articles of clothing and personal belongings can be transferred permanently from one home to the other. Whenever possible, honor the children's preferences. If they want to carry their favorite pajamas back and forth, let them. They may change their minds after a week or two and make a switch. This maneuver usually tests out Mom's and Dad's reactions, a trial-and-error way to learn what will feel best but also what the parents will accept. Allow reasonable time to try out different schemes; observe what is easy and comfortable for the children and then agree on rules. "Usually one or two things transfer," said one parent. "Our eldest wears the same hats back and forth. Our youngest carries his blanket and teddy bear." Remember, when your children have their clothes and things in two homes you also get rid of the "suitcase conversation" with the other parent.

GROUNDWORK

Groundwork designates the time parent and child take walking together around the new home(s), exploring, familiarizing themselves with landmarks, meeting neighbors and potential playmates, discovering busy streets, and—most important—determining boundaries for roaming without an adult. Groundwork is the most basic settling-in work parent and child must do in a new neighborhood, but it may be the most ignored task of parenting. It takes no more than an hour and should be done by each parent at each home. Benefits are widespread and long-lasting.

Lecturing the child as you march over the ground won't do the job. Nor is this an activity to be delegated to nannies or sitters. Parent and child do it together. As with other shared activities, your child has an opportunity to tell you what he or she thinks. Groundwork promotes a sense of security and can also show the neighbors that you are a caring parent.

One parent admitted her shame at living in the same place for four years and never walking the neighborhood with her daughters. "I realized I had been a four-wheel parent; if I didn't see it from the car coming into our driveway or going out of it, it didn't exist. I didn't know the names of my neighbors two houses down!" When the parent walks these routes with the children, he or she can exchange phone numbers with parents of potential playmates and friendly local merchants. When Dad sends Eric to the store or neighborhood market for bread and Eric has not returned after a reasonable time, Dad—because he took a minute to get the market's number and to introduce Eric to the manager—can phone and ask if Eric has been there.

Such groundwork establishes an automatic neighborhood watch for your children. Children gain a sense of security and of belonging; their parents gain peace of mind and real information about the neighborhood. Groundwork may take a few hours, but it pays off again and again in security and continuity for you and your children.

ORDER IN THE HOUSE

A predictable, orderly structure for at least some things is especially important when people are in crisis or having a difficult time. Parents feeling anxious, sad, remorseful, or angry can let daily routines and household organization go downhill rapidly during their own times of crisis. A little occupational therapy is in order. Pick yourself up and recover a bare minimum working order in your house. Establish a routine everyone follows for getting ready in the morning, meals, homework, buying groceries and gas, for making and eating meals, for transporting kids to school or to Little League, for rest and play, and for going to bed. Everyone needs to know what to expect.

Paying attention to household management may sound like a dull remedy for the aches and pains of separation or depression, but both common sense and research support this approach as fundamental to calming fears and to the development of a new stability. A sensible routine, with regular meals and regular times for shared recreation, translates into home, being cared about, and a sense of security. "Knowing my kids needed that routine forced me to be orderly for at least part of my week," said John. "Even when I didn't think I could make dinner or read that bedtime story, I did it. It actually did make things easier not only for them, but for me, too."

This family and others who ordered their lives early on—despite their difficulties—seem to have an easier time of readjusting overall. A sensible routine not only feels safe, it also allows our minds and bodies to calm down and heal.

HOUSE RULES AND YOUR PARENTING STYLE

Parenting apart means setting up your own house rules and settling into your own style. This can be liberating, especially if you felt the other parent used to look over your shoulder too much. More than one parent, often the father, has reported that he is enjoying his children more and feeling a rapport and depth of feeling for them that had escaped him earlier.

You can start with House Rules that reflect your expectations as well as those of the children. "If I want to take the phone off the hook during dinner, I can." "If I want to have a quiet period for reading or headphone stereo listening after nine P.M., I can write it into the blueprint." Some advice: If your natural inclination is to be a relaxed and permissive parent, consider tightening up with a routine at least during your first year. Many children interpret limits as a reflection of their parents' personal stability and as a caring for their well-being. You can provide the leadership for a set of House Rules reached in a family powwow that promotes safety, health, and privacy for everyone. These House Rules can be revised anytime you think is wise.

HOUSE RULES AT THE OTHER HOME

Common sense tells you that the more House Rules you have in common with the other parent's House Rules, the better. It is less confusing to the children and more supportive for the parents. But it would be rare for both parents to have exactly the same House Rules. Try to have the same or close to the same rules on the main organization of the child's day—bedtime periods, when to do homework, TV watching, curfews.

EATING MEALS TOGETHER

Do it. Families that eat together usually do better, especially the children. This is a time to ask about how the day went, to share jokes, ideas, hardships, hopes. To be acknowledged, listened to, and listen to others is to feel like a family. Turn off the TV. This is the time to talk together, even if the kids aren't all that interested. They will be, eventually.

SAFETY RULES

Each home, regardless of how the children's time is divided, has basic safety needs. You need a clearly legible list of emergency numbers: the doctors', friends', and neighbors' numbers where the parent can be reached. Parents should familiarize children with fire escapes, routes in case of earthquakes, tornadoes, hurricanes, floods, fire, or other disasters. Set up meeting places for the family if separated. Please do not overlook these essential routines. There's no need to alarm very young children with details of such information. But they should memorize their own addresses and last names, phone numbers and the names of other family or friends to call in an emergency.

FAMILY WORK

No home can function without somebody doing the work. Besides being necessary, this work can help build security and solidity for the new family's self-image, especially when parent and children work together. When the parent scrubs the sink, the eight-year-old daughter puts away the dishes, and the ten-year-old vacuums, the burden of housework is lightened by teamwork and the growth of a new family feeling.

Participation builds solidarity, as all athletes who play team sports know well. Children of any age need the satisfaction of doing a job in cooperation with Mom or Dad. Children's family work is not a form of cheap labor for unpleasant tasks, but a preparation for an independent life as an adult. Completed tasks remind children that they belong; that they are functioning family members, trusted, appreciated, and most of all, needed to keep the household running. "I feel guilty having the children do work," said a parent. His misplaced guilt will not make them feel at home, but simple tasks and the resumption of a more realistic parenting pattern will.

Children in divorced families often grow more realistic about the relationship between caring and sharing, about how things get done in the grown-up world. When children help cook meals, do the laundry, clean the house, shop, and eat the meal they helped prepare, they know what their work accomplished. A sense of mastery and increased self-confidence can grow. Children such as these seem to be more independent at an earlier age than are children from families that have never faced adversity or reorganization.

How decisions are made about family work and family rules is different in each family. Some parents prefer to make all the decisions, others allow their children to decide. A good midpoint leaves certain areas open to discussion, but the parent reserves the right to make the final decisions, while the other areas are discussed openly by all with each child's preference given as much priority as possible.

CHILD CARE

"If the freeway traffic is heavy and I arrive late to pick up my son after work, the sitter threatens me, saying that if I'm late again, I'll have to find another place for Bobby," said one father with a weary sigh. "Then, when my son announces that tomorrow he's to be at school at ten instead of the usual eight-thirty, I'm faced with the problem of what to do for his safety between the time I'm due to be at work at nine and the time he will be allowed at school. Doesn't anyone care about us and our needs?" The world of work and the world of caring for children are not often compatible, and no one knows this better than the working single parent.

Aside from the problems of employment and income, child care is the number one concern of single parents. Most single parents whose children live with them most of the time are working outside the home. This usually means finding child care when money is at an all-time low. What to do? The choices are many: a relative; a neighbor with children the same age; a neighbor who runs a family day care center in her home; an after-school day care center in the child's school or at a local community center; a private sitter, shared with other single parents and rotating the after-school meeting place from one house to another; a nanny; taking turns picking up several children and taking care of them after school—if you can get flexible working hours.

CHOOSING CHILD CARE

The quality of the care is most important for the children's development and for the parent's peace of mind. You want the best you can find. Choosing the right place for your child will likely be time-consuming. If you are new at this child care search, or are looking for a way to evaluate your present situation, call your local YMCA or parent help line. Many communities have a Child Care Council you can contact for guidelines or information. Don't delegate this job of choosing who will care for your child. Visit the day care center, the home of the day care family, or the home of the sitter who may be coming to your house, and ask yourself the questions set forth in the guides. Appendix 8, Choosing Child Care, has a sample set of guidelines.

BREATHING ROOM FOR THE PARENT

Even with a two-home situation, a tired parent can ask, "Is this all there is?" "I can hardly wait for the weekend sometimes," confided another mother of two, "when the kids will be with their father. I am so exhausted doing everything myself." *Parents need time to rest. They also need time to be adults, not just someone's mother or father.*

Taking time for yourself seems obvious but is one of the most overlooked aspects of parenting, especially for singles. In a world where so little is consistent, permanent, or secure, the continual presence of Mom or Dad seems essential for the security of a child. But think again—adults also need other adults for balance and perspective just as children need one another. The parent who never takes a break is courting trouble.

Unfortunately, most child care arrangements don't allow parents any breathing room. You rush to get ready in the morning, to get the children off to school or to the sitter's, to pick them up at night, to return home for dinner, homework. If you are lucky, late at night you have some quiet adult time.

Granted, you may have little time and energy left over for your adult personal life when you are running your home single-handed. But you need balance in your life, and your children need the renewal you get—and pass along—from the adult times you carve out of every week.

Isolated adults can come to expect from their children the intimacy and understanding only realistically available from fellow adults, and an over-protective parent can keep a child from developing into the independent, self-sufficient individual who can survive in the grown-up world.

Parents have been known to take time for themselves at the expense of their children's safety by leaving young children alone. *Please remember young children are not safe without a sitter.* No matter how conscientiously you may have taught and warned your children about what they should do in emergencies, they should not be left alone or asked to care for younger siblings when your usual arrangements have failed you. You alone are responsible for making certain that your children are under the care of a reliable adult at all times.

HOW TO FIND TIME FOR YOURSELF

Even single parents on slim budgets can find time for themselves. Here are some successful ways other parents have worked out. Three single parents agreed to bring their children together overnight once a week, either during school or on the weekends. This meant that each week two parents had one night completely free while the remaining parent had the three children. The children loved the expanded family feeling, and since each was an only child, all enjoyed observing different parent-child relationships, "staying over" at each other's homes.

This works best with three families, but two can also manage. Sometimes children can be picked up from school or child care by the parent whose turn it is, leaving the other two free. The trading can work on weekends, too. Sometimes the other parent objects to such overnight arrangements, saying, "If the children can stay with another family, they can stay more often with me, too." But overnight arrangements with friends achieve more than simply free time for the resident parent. To see them as tricks to keep the child away from the other parent is to miss the importance of exposing the child to varying family styles and of supporting the child's natural desire to solidify friendships. One mother whose former mate complained about their daughter's overnight visits with friends decided to give him what he wanted, another overnight with his daughter. Now the ten-year-old daughter may have two nights a week away from Mom—one with friends and one with Dad. When you and the other parent have a regular schedule to be with the children, these times are much easier to plan.

Some school districts have Friday Parents' Night Out, where children are given activities and supervision at school for a couple of hours for a low fee. If you don't want to go out, you could use this opportunity to take a walk or call a friend. Investigate other community-based options at churches (you may not have to be a member) and the YMCA or YWCA. Be creative.

WHAT ARE YOUR PRIORITIES?

Single parents, desperately needing balance and respite from constant responsibilities, must examine their priorities.

Since free time to be an adult is so important to effective child rearing as well as being a basic need for adults, one wonders why parents take out loans for a new car, clothes, or furniture but not for quality child care or education. The time to have plenty of good child care, education, household help, and freedom to reshape your life is now—not later, when the children are grown. Many parents find this concept perplexing, but those who forgo material possessions to gain the security and freedom of a housekeeper or a consistent sitting arrangement know the value of the support they buy. They aren't always coming home from work to face five or six hours more of housework. And when they open up the options to reshape their lives, they can take more time to enjoy and relax with their children *and* to provide an example to them on what is truly valued in life.

KEEPING IN TOUCH WITH YOUR CHILDREN

LET CHILDREN KNOW YOU ARE THINKING OF THEM

Regardless of your children's ages, when you are away from home, even if you have a sitter or they are in day care, let them know you are looking out for them. Tell them where you are, what you are doing. If they are living with you, tell them when they can expect you back, how they can reach you, when you expect them to contact you. Use written messages, the phones, pager, answering machine, voice mail or answering service, a tape recorder on the kitchen counter with messages for the day, videotapes, e-mail, or home bulletin board. Technology makes communicating easy.

EXPECT YOUR CHILDREN TO KEEP IN TOUCH WITH YOU

When your children are old enough to contact you, expect them to do so. "The cell phone is my sitter," said one single father as I watched three calls between him and his fourteen-year-old son over a two-hour period in the early evening—one telling when Dad would be home, a second from the son to explain he had a ride home, a third to say he had arrived home. If you are delayed, call and give them another approximate time to expect you. This simple information goes a long way toward calming children who have already seen one parent go out of their original home. They need to be reassured (regardless of statements like "I don't care") where you are and that you are really coming back. "I started telling my teenagers that they expect me home from work by five-thirty," said one single father, "or know the reason why. They were blasé about it, but if I came home at five forty-five and hadn't called, they let me know about it with: 'Where have you been?' or 'You didn't call!' It *was* important to them. At first I thought it was only because they didn't want me to be anywhere but home and at work, but that wasn't the whole story. They needed simple reassurance. They even tolerated my dating when they knew when to expect me home and what I expected from them during my absence."

CHECKLIST: KEEPING IN TOUCH

When your child is living with you and you are working outside of the home, do you

1. leave notes at home for your child (if your child is old enough to read)?
2. phone, e-mail, or leave a pager message for your child?
3. get phone calls from your child to your work?

During this last week, did you do any of those things listed above? If yes, how many times?

When your child is not living with you, do you

1. do any of the things listed above?
2. send e-mail or letters if you are gone for more than a week?
3. send audiotapes or videotapes if you are separated for more than three weeks?
4. have other ways of communicating such as those described in chapter 18, Long-Distance Parenting?

During the last two weeks, did you do any of the above? How many times?

Children, even teens, think and judge in concrete terms. They do best when they have continual *tangible* evidence of their parents' presence in their lives. Frequent contact when you are separated is one way to provide that.

ANCHORS FOR TEENAGERS

An anchor comes in many shapes. When a parent is gone and teens are on their own, an anchor is someone or something the teenager can count on, trust, lean on if need be. Anchors can be a responsible adult close by who knows what to do and whom to call in an emergency; a routine of check-in phone calls between parent and child; a routine that both can count on about who is where and when; and a good set of house and safety rules. The parent who takes the time to develop these anchors is improving living conditions for themselves as well as for their children.

"AW, MOM, I'M TOO OLD FOR A SITTER. . . ."

Young teenagers often object vigorously to supervision, yet they need it as much as the younger ones. "My children are over thirteen," say some parents. "They don't need supervision when I'm at work or out in the evening. They would resent it and be difficult about it." Perhaps they would be resentful, but they may need an adult as much as the younger ones do. Older children, left alone after school and for long stretches of time during the weekends, often whine and crab over helping with housework or doing anything. Such children need more, not less, adult caring and supervision.

"You should hear the way my teenage kids talk to me," a parent might say to me at a workshop coffee break. Sometimes a good friend will add, "They are rude, condescending, and no help at all to her around the house. She works full-time trying to keep a roof over their heads. They are totally unappreciative." When such parents come as private clients, the parent (usually a mother) often describes her life in this way. She was away in the evenings several times a week and was preoccupied with housework and errands on the weekends. There were few or no House Rules, no regular communications, little working order. She had rarely done groundwork with her children. There was little or no family spirit. No one seemed satisfied.

TEENS NEED PARENTS WHO ARE INVOLVED—JUST ENOUGH

Parents can often regain control of their household and their lives by beginning from scratch. Teens want interested, aware, and involved parents—up to a point. Mom and Dad need to be firm with the big things and flexible with the little ones. They can develop safety and house rules alone, then discuss them with the children. They can begin family meetings where they can talk about electricity, gas, and security and agree on House Rules such as homework, quiet time—without TV, computer games, or phone calls—after ten o'clock at night. Instead of assigning housework to be done in their absence, parents can make it a point to start being home four nights a week and to work along with their children. At least part of each weekend can be saved for family time.

Most teens, like other children, need structured, satisfying activities outside of a classroom such as teams, lessons, clubs, or jobs. These activities cannot substitute for a parent's supervision and involvement. As parents take more control over the daily framework for the household order and safety, everyone's attitude usually begins to change. Tensions ease, there are more spontaneous fun times, and everyone feels more like a family again.

THE OTHER ADULTS IN YOUR CHILDREN'S LIVES

Have you met your child's teachers? Talked with his doctor? Compared notes with her coach? If not, do it soon. The other adults in your child's life don't see many parents—especially not many fathers. Since mothers have traditionally handled all their children's health, education, and extracurricular activities, the teacher may naturally assume that after divorce the mother will continue in the same role. "I'm sorry to say," said one junior high principal, "that I don't see much of fathers here—married or divorced. And when one does come in to ask about his child or wants to see some official records, unless I have had some previous contact with him, I'm suspicious of his motives."

Each parent will have to initiate and maintain his or her own independent communication with the school and with other organizations or persons who supervise the child's activities. Investing a few hours a year in a phone call or written questions will reap enormous benefits for you, your child, the doctor, dentist, teacher, or coach.

If you have no written legal agreement and are in the process of negotiating one, make a note that you may want all school and health records and information be made open to each parent on an equal basis (see chapter 11). Also check your state law. It may already provide for this.

If you do have a written agreement that denies access to records to one parent, stop now and consider the advantages of opening these records to the other parent. Customarily the schools will allow the parent with sole legal and physical custody to deny the other parent access to information about a child's educational progress, even though the denial of access to report cards and other formal records does not in many states fall under the custodial parent's legal authority. But because of the ambiguities, schools and other institutions such as churches, clubs, and medical treatment centers may fear legal entanglements and are likely to refuse access.

It is still true that many institutions in your family's world have not yet caught up with your reality. Many schools, doctors, and clubs do not gather complete information about your child or his or her family. Don't expect them to ask you questions—you will have to provide them with specific facts about whom they can count on to be responsible and who pays the bill. If you don't, no matter how good your working relationship with the other parent, your child may lose some benefits.

Important Note. Do you have a problem with the other parent harassing you, fear for your safety or the safety of your child? If you do, the other adults in your children's lives need to be informed. Take protective legal action and get some professional help immediately. Also, you may want to deliver a copy of the protective order to the doctor, teachers, or others in your child's life. They may unknowingly release your child to the other parent or give out your phone number and address, thereby placing you and your child in harm's way. If you have a restraining order, please advise them of this. If you are a parent who has been falsely accused of these crimes, immediately obtain the services of an attorney and begin the process of clearing your name. See part 3 for more information.

HOW THE RIGHT INFORMATION WITH THE RIGHT PEOPLE HELPS YOUR CHILD

Here are some of the situations families and school personnel face and what can happen.

When thirteen-year-old Jennie was accused of theft at school, the principal's first thought was to involve both parents. But once he saw Jennie's registration card, he realized he did not have enough information to contact both parents. Jennie's registration card showed she lived with her divorced mother. There was no requirement, and therefore no place on the registration form, for information about the other parent, Jennie's father. Nor was there a place for parents to state their desires about the noncustodial parent's involvement in school matters. The principal didn't know how to reach the father—or even if he had the right to do so. Jennie's mother was not in her office, and the police were going to be at the school within the hour. Luckily, just when the principal was about to call a neighbor listed on the emergency card, Jennie's mother was reached and she was able to get to the school in time to be with Jennie.

The absence of information and some simple procedural guidelines had taken the principal's time and energy away from Jennie's needs and directed it to the unknown politics of the divorced parents' relationship. He wondered: Are the parents on friendly terms? Will the mother be upset if the father is called without her permission? Will the father be upset if he is not notified? Are stepparents involved? What about Jennie? Doesn't she have a right to her father's support and to the support of other significant adults in her family circle?

In contrast, when ten-year-old John broke his leg in a nasty fall from the monkey bars in the schoolyard, everyone at school knew exactly whom to call and for what, even though his parents were divorced. There was no need for a teacher to guess or tiptoe past parental discord. John lived most of the time with his mother, but his father and stepfather, also now divorced from his mother, were both authorized to make important decisions, to be present in classrooms, and to have access to all official records. In case of emergency, any or all of the parents or stepparents were to be called. Given this clear-cut message, the school found it easy to support John and get him the care he needed quickly.

HOW TO COMMUNICATE WITH SCHOOLS AND ORGANIZATIONS

Each parent—separately—needs to 1) have an independent communication with school and health professionals, 2) keep copies of children's health records, and 3) have open access to the children's records and activities. If your school district or individual school declines to give you this information or access, write a formal letter of complaint to them and get some action.

With the school, for example, parents can tell what they want instead of waiting to be asked. Parents with custody can write letters to the school specifying their preferences about the involvement of the other parent; if they choose, they can also formally or legally authorize the other parent to have access to privileged information and to assume authority when necessary. Appendix 1, Information for Schools, has a sample form for schools that parents can use for identifying who has authority over a child. These parents can also use the school emergency card to list the important people in their child's life by stating first the natural parents and stepparents as authorized people to call, followed by neighbors or friends. Parents without custody can show their continued interest in their child's school life with requests for a school calendar and duplicate report cards.

Parents say that phone calls and letters to teachers work very well. Say something simple, like "I am Jane's parent, and I want to introduce myself and encourage you to call me if I can be of any assistance. When the child is living with me, I may have occasion to call you, and this letter [or phone call] is a way of letting you know where I can be reached. Please call me if you have any questions." If your children do not live with you most of the time, ask to be placed on the school mailing list. At the least obtain a copy of the school calendar and information on extracurricular faculty-sponsored activities. You can even give the school a number of self-addressed envelopes that the teacher can use to send you special announcements of school activities and copies of your children's report cards. You can ask for a separate parent-teacher conference, and many teachers, encouraged by your interest, will be happy to oblige. All parents should consider joining the PTA, supporting school activities, open house, and back-to-school nights.

When you make this contact, it may be wise to drop a note or call the other parent to let them know what you have done. Assure him or her that these actions are for information purposes and a way for you to be prepared for your times with the children. This information is not to perpetuate disagreements with your former spouse; it's for you to become a better, more informed parent. It is also so your children can be assured of your continuing involvement.

DIRECT CONTACT WITH DOCTORS, TEACHERS, AND OTHER ADULTS

These independent contacts with adults in your child's life are part of your individual responsibility as a parent. And they help you strengthen your businesslike relationship with the other parent. You can more easily move away from your former intimacy because you don't have to contact him or her about every school function, a report card, or the doctor's phone number, and you can keep your communications focused on the children's needs and emergency situations. Furthermore, you don't have to depend on your child's memory.

As you make contacts with the other adults in your child's life as part of day-in, day-out parenting, one fact of life comes through very clearly. Such direct contacts with these other adults are sometimes the only way you will know what is happening. Most children will forget, lose, and otherwise mangle papers, report cards, belongings, prescriptions, and instructions. You need these other adults to tell you what is actually happening. The lost or damaged stuff is not a devious ploy by the other parent. Instead it is nothing more than childhood at its forgetful, unconscious, or even mischievous self.

"WE BOTH CARE"

The strongest statement parents can make is to present themselves jointly to the school, the doctor, or the church or community group—either in writing or in person. In effect they are saying, "Each of us is still concerned and involved with our children." It bears repeating: Any information about what you want must come from you. Don't wait to be asked.

BACK TO A NEW NORMAL

The faster you get put together the semblance of a new "normal" routine with bedtimes, family work, house rules, and safety rules, the better chance everyone has of a quick and happy adaptation to this new life.

Of course, normal routines also include doing some things out of the ordinary, special treats, special events. Parents may feel at first that they must counterbalance the pain of separation and their fear of losing their children by promises of these extras. And you might feel that these make the children look forward to seeing you. If you do, you are underrating your children's genuine affection and attachment to you. You also run the risk of degrading the precious parent-child relationship to that of entertainer and guest.

As things settle down, parents and children feel more "at home" in their new circumstances. When the bonds between each parent and the children are maintained, children adjust more quickly and so do parents. In the words of one father, "I knew I had finally put my home together when I started reading to my daughters after dinner just the way I had when I was married."

Chapter 10

Your Children

Giving Them Security and Continuity

Choices and Changes for Your Child
Keeping Children out of the Middle
Calming Your Children's Fears and Rebuilding Trust
How to Know When Your Child Needs Help
Trust Yourself, Trust Your Instincts

UNDER the best of circumstances, raising children calls for self-confidence, patience, skill, and a sense of when to leave well enough alone. During a crisis period—like the transition process of separation or divorce—the parents' emotional state can blind them to their basic parenting responsibilities. Crisis or not, parents are still parents.

Your child can be placed at risk because of the crisis, or he or she can be strengthened by it. Therefore parents are called upon to reach for greater understanding and compassion for their child's experience but also to develop more sophisticated skills for developing a safe, predictable, and structured environment. Learning more about parenting and how children's minds and emotions develop can be a great relief to you and to your child! This is one of the ways to make the crisis work for you all. This chapter only summarizes some of the child-rearing issues that need attention when parents separate or a marriage ends. What happens between parents and children during separation or divorce is complex. The chapter notes and further reading in part 5 will suggest more resources, and your local school district can help you find parenting seminars.

"WHAT CAN I DO?"

Parents ask, "What can I do to ensure that my child is not harmed by this separation?" Over the years, research and experience have shown that parents can help their child by paying attention to certain things.

First, know your family history. What happened in your family before the separation is extremely important. Children have a history, just as you do. That history can determine how smooth their adjustment might be and where you may have to do some "catch-up" parenting. Take time to consider:

1. How well were your children doing before you separated? The greater their emotional stability and basic trust in you, the better.
2. How exposed was your child to your unresolved arguments or your problems? Was your child your confidant? In the middle? Was your child present when you express your hurt or anger about your spouse to other people? The less, the better.
3. How close and supportive was the relationship your child had with you and with the other parent? The more your child could get comfort and reassurance from you both, the better.

Second, understand the job before you. It helps to have an overview of the issues included in the following list.

WHAT AFFECTS CHILDREN

1. What happened in your family before you separated and how your child was affected by it (as explained above).
2. How well you and the other parent handle the changes and decisions you must make during the crisis period and into the future.
3. How well you can respond to what I call your child's unique "TLC" and meet their needs for love, support, and protection despite your own grief and fears.
4. How well both of you as parents organize or reorganize your home and daily routines for the children.
5. How well you keep your child out of the middle of your problems and manage your differences with the other parent.
6. How psychologically healthy you and the other parent are, especially the parent your child lives with the most time.
7. How well both of you maintain your relationship with your child despite the changes in residence and time together.
8. How successful you are in keeping the number of changes for your child to a minimum.

CHOICES AND CHANGES FOR YOUR CHILD

YOUR CHILD'S TLC

The ability of your child to withstand change is often a combination of many things you can control, including your support, your love, your care. But a child's basic makeup needs to be considered first.

Think of your child's uniqueness as TLC.

YOUR CHILD'S UNIQUE TLC

T = Temperament and resilience
L = Level of development and prior experience
C = Constitution, physical sturdiness

Parents describe their children's temperaments as active, quiet, shy, easygoing, determined, sensitive, resilient, high-strung. A child's development may be delayed, average or advanced—physically, intellectually, emotionally. His or her experiences with drastic changes may have been positive or negative. He or she might be tall, small, or average for their age; have a delicate or sturdy "constitution"; be susceptible to illness, or be rarely ill. Look at your own child's unique TLC. Knowing and paying attention to these differences are your key to helping your children adjust.

A child's TLC is not something that changes as one would a suit of clothes. We all come into this world with some degree of finality in our genes. Your child's unique combination of TLC will affect your child's ability to adapt.

Think of the changes children experience. Some school-age children are happy with new places, new people, new foods. Others become fretful or cranky when something as simple as a different breakfast cereal appears on the table. These children are more sensitive and feel changes more keenly both physically and emotionally. Infants and preschoolers are particularly affected by changes. If a schedule or routine is not suited to their TLC, they may not be themselves for months, if ever. They may regress and be delayed in their development. Even school-age children and teens with a certain TLC are more sensitive and do not handle change well.

A wise parent needs to be especially observant with a sensitive child. Frequent changes for overnights or no physical contact with the other parent over a long stretch of time are usually too hard on them. The sturdier, more outgoing child has more ballast for change, but this doesn't mean the child can take an unlimited amount. Have you ever wondered why children want to hear the same story over and over again? The story is predictable. "First this happens, then that happens, then there's the scary part, then it's okay, then it ends." Most children thrive with the predictability that comes with repetition. While children may long for the circus, visits to new places, or new videos, a seasoned parent knows that they also need time to settle down after the excitement, process the new experience, get a good night's sleep, and be comforted by their own things and their own routine. You have to try different ways to accomplish this balance of change and sameness until you find the right combination for your child.

EXPLAIN CHANGE TO CHILDREN

Children need things to be seeable, touchable. They are concrete and practical, a "different kind of thinking machine," until they are about twelve years old. Abstract terms such as "love" and "loyalty" need to be spelled out in everyday terms. When children ask, "Will I have to move, change schools, change friends?" they need simple, concrete answers, not a sad, angry, or frightened "I don't know" from a distraught parent. At the least, they need answers that give possible alternatives: "We will stay here for at least one year and then perhaps move to Eighteenth Street or maybe closer to Grandma's house." One conversation explaining changes will not be enough. Children will usually continue to ask many questions, often the same questions again and again. Their questions should be answered again, and the children should be reassured each time they ask. Don't be surprised if your children react much more to the actual reality of the physical separation than to the news of an impending separation.

TALK TO YOUR CHILD

Clarify briefly what's happening and take full responsibility for it. Children are excellent observers but not good interpreters. Not knowing how your separation will affect them can be very hard. They imagine things far worse than they actually are. Just as security is built on trust, trust needs understanding. Try to have a short, true explanation and, if possible, one that is phrased in a positive way: "Your Mom [Dad] and I have tried for a long time and have finally decided it is best for us to live apart," conveys a more reassuring message than the scary, "We simply can't stand to stay together any longer," or, "We don't love each other anymore." Do not give all the gory details of your fights or betrayals. Your children do not want to know—and they should not know—how you have deeply hurt each other. Your children love you and don't want to see anyone hurt either of you. They need to know that you both meant well.

Children need to be able to respect both their parents, now more than ever. Most of all they need to know that it is all right for them to love and identify with the strengths (not just the weaknesses) of the other parent.

Explaining a situation simply, without embellishments or excuses, gives the children confirmation of your concern for them. "Mom and Dad know what they are doing. I don't have to guess the real truth and wonder how it concerns me." Remember, though, that too much information can be confusing and can end up being as useless as too little. Make it brief, make it simple. It is usually easier for children to deal with the truth than to confront abrupt changes, whispered hostility, martyred silences, or those double messages in which your action or voice tone contradicts your words. If you are feeling sad and tell a child that "everything is fine," you are giving a double message. Better to admit, "I'm sad right now," and then reassure the child, "But it's not about you and me, it's about 'grown-up' matters." A straight answer may calm your child's fears and release him or her from responsibility. But a double message can blow up small incidents to giant proportions. Demystification of events is very important.

GIVE YOUR CHILD A SAY

Changes can make children feel unimportant and powerless. Help your children feel as if they have a voice, some control. You know your child, so use your best judgment to decide when he or she should be included in a discussion. Parents can see to it that even young children offer their preferences on small things, even those that seem insignificant. Even the youngest ones can decide which toys or blanket to bring to the new place. Preteens and teens can be shown respect by asking their opinion on where they go to school, when they will be with each parent, and what will be expected of them and other decisions you think appropriate.

When a court decision, for example, forces parents into visitation arrangements in which they have had no say, they sometimes declare, "They are my children, I'll see them whenever I want to!" Parents who make decisions about their children's lives without considering their ideas force their children to have many of these same feelings. One sixteen-year-old, left out of decision making about his time at his mom's house, exploded, "She's my mother and I'll see her anytime I like," adding, "And you can't stop me." The moral of all this is if you want a schedule to be useful and positive, ask your older children what *they want* and *how their plan would work*. Then, when it comes to making the actual decisions, consider their needs and wishes seriously. One important exception: *A parent should not ask any child which parent they want to live with or whether or not there should be a separation or divorce.*

SHOULD CHILDREN MAKE DECISIONS?

Children should not make the final decisions, but they should have a strong voice. There is an important difference between taking a child's opinions seriously and turning over the decision to a child. It is the adult's responsibility to make the decision after taking the child's wishes to heart. The teenager who exploded, once given the opportunity to say what he wanted and how it could work, described how he wanted to stop by his mom's house on his way to school in the morning, to call her anytime he wanted, to spend more (or less) time if he wanted. He didn't want absolute veto power as his parents had feared, just a chance to negotiate on his own behalf. His parents agreed to his requests in principle, but they structured how it would work. He could phone, stop by his other house, even spend extra overnights, just as long as he checked in with his dad when he wanted to stay past a certain hour. Now the son could negotiate with his mom on his own. But both parents insisted that when their son wanted to change weekend plans, they each be consulted with plenty of prior notice.

Parents should not ask their children to make their decisions. "I told my daughter I'd stay married to her father if she wanted me to," said one mother. "She told me she wouldn't blame me if I did divorce him." Such parents want adultlike support and reassurance from their children. This is not appropriate. One judge reported, "When I asked a mother her position on the father's request for more visitation, she answered, 'I don't know. I'll let my child decide.'" Asking a child for an opinion is important on some issues, but making the child responsible for a major decision is inappropriate and can be damaging to the child. Even when the child's opinion is reflected in the parent's decision, making the decision is still the parent's responsibility.

Parents can say, "We want to know what you think about this, but we will make the final decision." This gives children a voice without the accompanying responsibility of making Mom's and Dad's decisions for them or feeling guilty or caught in a conflict of loyalty whirlpool. When you involve the children, make sure they are telling both of you the same things. Remember, it is natural for many children to tell parents what they think they want to hear.

CHILDREN'S "READY" AND "NOT READY" LISTS

Just as you or the other parent have those things you are ready to negotiate or talk about and those you are not, so do your children. Children are more ready to talk about or accept certain things about your separation, and they are definitely not ready to do so about other things. Respect their individual timetables. "We set up households only a mile apart," said the mother of a three-year-old separated six weeks, "but Melinda refuses even to see her father's new apartment. Her father has to come here. It's all right with us . . . at least for a while." These are wise parents. They are allowing their young child to sort out what has happened at her own pace. This will probably result in a smoother transition for their child.

HOW MANY CHANGES CAN YOUR CHILD HANDLE?

The extent of change and loss in your child's life can affect how he or she develops and learns. Unless your child was in a neglectful, dangerous, or otherwise unhealthy environment, not having both parents under one roof is an enormous loss for a child. Every other change on top of this big one is an additional burden for your child. This is especially true for infants, toddlers, and preschoolers.

The fewer changes in the first year, the better. Parents should ask themselves how many changes they are forcing their children to make. Regardless of how sturdy or resilient your child seems to be, try to do your best to keep your child in the same house or at least in the same neighborhood for that first year. Unless the children are doing poorly in their school, the familiar and comfortable are invaluable supports during those early crisis months. The teachers, friends, activities, and neighbors combine with familiar places, sights, sounds, and colors to make a safe haven for those undergoing drastic changes within their family. Introducing a parent's new love is a major change for a child. Consider the timing here carefully. The introduction should be done very slowly, as Appendix 4 suggests in "The Children and a Parent's New Love."

Marilouise's parents separated six months ago. During the week, she lives with Mom in the same place she has always lived, goes to the same elementary school, has the same friends, and knows the same neighborhood. Her father talks to her every day by phone, sometimes twice a day. He took an apartment about a mile from the house, and Marilouise is with him every other Thursday evening to Monday morning. She's made new friends at Dad's house, and some of her school friends live near there as well. Her parents have not asked her for too many changes within a short time. Marilouise has a chance to get used to the biggest change of all, that her parents are living apart. It is not necessarily easy for any of them. But it is working out.

Too many changes. David and Ronnie's parents separated and sold their house immediately, and the boys went with their mother to live in another state.

Their father remained in the city where the boys had been raised. These children have enormous changes to contend with—not only have they lost their father's presence on a daily basis, but they will see him only every two or three months. These children will have to adjust to a new climate, a new neighborhood, and a new school and have to seek new friends. Even if children are especially sturdy and resilient, these are too many changes in too short a time. Unless a parent is fleeing from an abusive spouse, so many drastic changes in such a short time should be reconsidered. If at all possible, put some of them on hold for a while.

CHILDREN'S SELF-ESTEEM AND STATUS

Parents sometimes forget that a separation brings changes not only to a family, but also to the children's sense of social status and belonging. Children can feel like outcasts. The single-parent family, and even the remarried family, may be less valued and trusted than the original nuclear family.

"My friend's mother said I couldn't play with my friend anymore," said a ten-year-old girl, recounting a still common experience among children. "She said it was because of too much homework, but my friend told me it was because my parents got divorced." When this happens to children, it hurts. Sometimes children will tell their parents. Other times, especially if they sense their parents' pain and guilt about the divorce, they will silently keep their own pain to themselves. "I got into trouble at school, and the teacher said it was because I came from a 'broken home.' I told her my home wasn't busted, it was just fine," said a ten-year-old boy, "but she didn't listen."

Such incidents can deeply wound a child. When any part of a social setting sees single parenting or divorce as a tragedy, a stigma, or a failure, children of all ages undergo loss of self-esteem and confidence. They may hear gossip about them or their parents. If this happens, children need the warmth and support of a family circle that can act as a buffer to this critical outside world. Parents and friends need to reassure children that they and their family are still acceptable and worthy.

KEEPING CHILDREN OUT OF THE MIDDLE

YOUR CHILDREN LOVE AND NEED BOTH OF YOU

If your children know you both, and have lived with you both, then they love you both. You are their parents, and we have seen how hard it is for them to understand what has happened to your love for each other. If we think of ourselves as part our mother and part our father, it may be easier to feel how conflicting and frightening it can be to have one part inside of us hate the other part that is also inside. So if you ask your children to believe that you are the injured parent, or the good guy, while the other one is the persecutor, or bad guy, you are asking the children to distrust and dislike another part of themselves. Children don't want to choose sides any more than they want to have an internal battle or low self-esteem.

CHILDREN MAY TRY TO PROTECT THEIR PARENTS

Children often say and do what they think their parents need to hear and see. Children love their parents and want to protect them, make them happy and keep their love, even at their own expense. Children usually pick up covert signals given by anxious or angry parents and want to soothe them and make them feel better. "My daughter and I can be talking on the phone, laughing about her day," said one father, "and then, wham! Her attitude and tone of voice change right in the middle of a sentence. She becomes suddenly reserved and cool, acts like she is bored with our conversation. Then I find out that her mother has walked into the room during our conversation." This daughter is changing her attitude toward her father in midstream for her mother's benefit. Perhaps by acting bored, she hopes that Mom won't ask any questions about Dad or become jealous that she is sharing her day with her dad. The daughter is taking care of Mom by acting bored with Dad. She may be wrong about Mom, but she's not taking any chances. She is concealing her own needs and feelings and doing what she thinks Mom needs. When a child tries to sort out confusing signals from parents, it can feel overwhelming, especially if he or she is forced to choose which parent needs his or her protection the most.

KEEPING KIDS OUT OF THE MIDDLE

Regardless of the parents' marital status, children hate being in the middle. Some children describe solemnly to me how they have to pretend things for a parent because that's the way they are called "good." Other children seem initially to enjoy the power of the position but quickly learn that the middle position is a losing one and that they can be used unfairly.

One teenager expressed it this way: "They argue, and they expect me to be part of that argument one way or another. At first, when I was younger, I felt important and needed. Now it's just obnoxious. They are always asking, 'What did your mom say?' 'What did your dad say?' I'm pulling out of it. But I worry that they'll be really mad at me when I do." This teenager has valid fears. Parents who need an audience for their disagreements or want the child in the middle are unhappy when a child refuses to act out their scripts as the middleman. Such parents need to develop a positive parenting pattern. If they follow the guidelines listed here, they can go a long way to keeping their children out of the middle, release their children from trying to mend things for the grown-ups, and build a business relationship at the same time.

GUIDELINES TO KEEP KIDS OUT OF THE MIDDLE

1. **Go directly to the other parent for information or an answer.** Keep your communications direct. Do not have your child become a messenger or spy even if he or she wants to.
2. **Don't bad-mouth the other parent in their presence** or where they might overhear you. Keep your frustrations for private conversations with good friends, your therapist, or a counselor.
3. **Do not participate in your children's angry feelings about the other parent.** Let them blow off steam, but don't add water to their boiler, even though you may want to.
4. **Encourage your children to speak about their difficulties with the other parent** to the other parent. Decline to get involved in lengthy advice. Suggest the names of close friends of the other parent if they need more "talking out" time. Children need adults who are safe to confide in.
5. **Do not ask your children about the other parent's life or circumstances.** Give the other parent's motives the benefit of the doubt.
6. **Do not ask children to keep secrets about you from the other parent.** If you don't want the other parent to know something, don't let your child know it either.

KEEPING PARENTS OUT OF THE MIDDLE

"Daddy got mad at me and scared me"; "Mommy didn't give me a bath"; "Dad won't let me talk on the phone to my friends"; "Mom is drinking a lot"; "Dad is never home when I am there." When a child complains about a parent, it is easy for people to jump to conclusions. But are these statements true or not?

If your child is under six or seven, call the other parent yourself and ask what this is about. Don't jump to conclusions. Sometimes the complaints, especially from the youngest ones, are transparent. "Daddy made me be in [or out, or in a time-out] all day. I didn't even get dinner." The mother knew the father would not do that. So she asked, "Tell me about more about your time together." The five-year-old recounted her weekend with her father—visit with Grandpa, visit to the park, watching TV together, shopping together, cooking meals. The "time-out" did exist, but it lasted ten minutes. For older children, encourage your child to talk directly to the parent in question. Try not to get pulled into taking sides or blaming. Children complain about one parent to the other parent in all families. Separation and/or divorce makes the complaint more powerful. If you trust the other parent not to abuse your child, then respect his or her parenting style and encourage your child to work it out with the other parent. Nonetheless, please do not dismiss complaints about the other parent as "manipulation." Most complaints usually deserve a response or an action.

TAKING STOCK

Answer the following questions as honestly as you can.

YOUR CHILD AND THE OTHER PARENT: TAKING STOCK

1. Do you think your children love their other parent?
2. Do you think the other parent is important to your children?
3. Do you and the other parent agree on discipline for your children?
4. Do you respect the other parent's parenting style?
5. Do you think the other parent has a good relationship with your children?
6. Can you and the other parent talk about your child's needs? Problems? Development? Take necessary actions?
7. Can you count on the other parent to support your relationship with your children?
8. Do you make it comfortable or easy for the other parent to have a good relationship with your children?
9. Are you reasonably confident that your former mate will not try to keep you away from your children or alienate them from you?
10. Do you inform the other parent of emergencies or major events when your child is with you (illnesses, difficulties in school, major decisions)? Can you trust the other parent to inform you?
11. Are you reasonably confident of your children's emotional and/or physical safety when they are with the other parent?

The more "Yes" or "Usually" answers you have, the better. Think about those areas where you answered "Sometimes." Becoming lax or taking the other parent for granted may become a problem. "No" answers are your cue for some creative problem solving. If you answered "No" on the question about physical safety, you must act immediately to protect yourself and your child.

"I LOST RESPECT FOR MY PARENTS"

Some present-day adults who were once children of divorce look back in revulsion over their parents' immature behavior and addiction to negative intimacy. Several of these adults have described to me how they quietly but deliberately chose schools thousands of miles from home, took summer jobs that kept them away from parents, and eventually established their own marriages and family lives in places where they did not have to be near their own parents. "I was so disgusted with them," said one man of his own childhood experiences with his divorced parents' battles, "I just decided the hell with them. They will never again get close enough to me to use me like they did."

CALMING YOUR CHILDREN'S FEARS AND REBUILDING TRUST

Parents can help children cope with change in many of the same ways they help themselves. Adults seek to gain mastery by getting information, collecting resources, talking to others. So do children. And as their parent you can give this to them. Calming your children's fears most of all requires both parents being there (or in contact) every day in some way, either in person, by phone, by fax, by video, by e-mail, by audiotapes or videotapes, or by letter. Take advantage of new ways to communicate.

PAY ATTENTION TO YOUR CHILD

The process of separation or divorce often means less time for the children. The attention parents once paid to children may now be refocused on where to live now, on arguments, negotiations, hurts, arguments, new plans, new jobs, new loves. As one grown man said, remembering his own parents' divorce when he was eight, "There I was important one day and totally powerless the next. When you are a little kid, life is confusing enough without having your parents intensely preoccupied with their own problems." Many children can't express their sense of loss. They just feel unsettled; perhaps they withdraw or become more boisterous. Their place in their parents' lives has changed somehow. It is frightening, and they can't change it. But there are many things a parent can do to help.

Words are not enough; follow or accompany them with affection. Find comfortable ways to show affection for your children. Hold them on your lap, hold their hands, touch them, give them spontaneous happy hugs, have loving eye contact. This human warmth and comfort is a vital physical communication that brings its own special kind of reassurance to you both.

YOUR CHILDREN'S EMOTIONS

You have your emotions about your separation from the other parent, and so do the children. They have their own sadness, fears, anger, and off-the-wall emotions, and they need people who love them to help them work these through. Children also need opportunities to learn constructive ways to express their emotions. Separation is a time when a number of bad habits can take over. When a child is intensely unhappy or fearful, these underlying feelings may lead him or her to be overly aggressive, belligerent, have tantrums, fight, indulge in drug usage, promiscuity. Children can also withdraw, become depressed or supersensitive.

Children's fears can escalate during the tumult of the divorcing or separation period. Children often worry that their mothers can't cope and that their fathers are lonely. "Is Dad lonesome?" "Can he really cook for himself?" "Is Mom scared—can she really make my big brother shape up without Dad?" Demystify the change by providing your children with tangible evidence. Bring the children to the new place, let them see Dad cook and Mom take a stand with big brother.

Children can experience many feelings of guilt or disloyalty, somehow feeling responsible for their parents' behavior. It's hard for children to separate how they feel from what their parents feel, especially when parents are unhappy with one another. Yet over the next few months and years, this separation will be an important and necessary accomplishment for them.

THE CHILD'S FEELINGS OF ABANDONMENT AND LOSS

Children, even sophisticated teenagers, need adults in order to survive in the world, and most of them know it. The family provides a place that says, "You are safe, you are loved, you will be taken care of." When family life is changed by separation and divorce, the child's sense of security and continuity is shaken. Who will take care of me now? Will I still be loved? Where will I live, sleep? Where will I go to school? Will I still have a real home? Children do not yet have adult-size strength, wisdom, or economic and social power. When separation or divorce threatens their security, their impotence becomes a conscious reality; they are defenseless and need your care and some special measures of protection. This is especially true for children under five, who are especially vulnerable to fears of abandonment. All children's fears are affected by the way the adults in their lives function. When the adults are not functioning well or are behaving out of character, children develop certain fears:

1. Being denied the basics of survival—food, shelter, clothing, sleep.
2. Being abandoned or left, forgotten, or unimportant.
3. Being punished, assaulted, or hurt, or being the object of hostility.
4. Being unloved, having love taken away, or losing love.
5. Losing one's friends, one's school, or the opportunity to go to college, because of a move.

One woman remembered her preteen years when her parents separated and then divorced: "I felt like a flag in a field with these two strong winds blowing at me. I didn't know the truth here. I was alone with these shifting winds."

CHILDREN ALSO GRIEVE

Children also grieve. The younger ones feel things they haven't names for yet. Older children and adults give these feelings names—sadness, loss, emptiness, fear, longing, powerlessness, anger, resentment, even disgust. Many parents have a difficult time dealing with their child's depression. We want our children to be happy. And their grief may increase a parent's feeling of guilt. Try to spend time alone with one child at a time so that there is an atmosphere that encourages feelings to emerge. When this happens, stay with it. Without preaching or promising things you can't give, acknowledge your child's feelings as real and deep.

Parents don't want to cause their children unnecessary pain or disrupt their lives, but despite that, it happens. *Listen attentively, say you are sorry they have to go through this, that you and the other parent have truly tried and tried (if you honestly have). Tell them that you will not desert them or stop loving them.* A final suggestion: Children, like adults, need to get away from it all sometimes. Let your children spend weekends and extra time with relatives and friends where things are calm, stable, and supportive. The time away may do everyone good.

Even the most conscientious parents can erroneously expect superhuman behavior from their children during the early crisis months. A parent's sense of guilt, for example, may translate into a refusal to admit any negative impact on their child. Or some parents let their child know in unspoken ways that painful feelings, especially those about the effects of the separation, are not to be shown. "I would cry from missing my dad so much, but I had to go in the bathroom or hide somewhere," said one eleven-year-old girl.

"Mom really gets mad at me when I cry anyway, and if she thinks it has anything to do with Daddy, she gets supermad." Many children hide their real feelings from parents. Especially those who desperately need their loyalty and affection. Children may mistakenly believe that their silence or withdrawal is what their parents need or want. Sometimes the children fear the intensity of their feelings or being misunderstood. Other times they are shy.

YOUR CHILDREN MAY BLAME THEMSELVES FOR YOUR PROBLEMS

Children need to hear that the separation or divorce is not their fault. And they need to hear it many times over the first few years. Imagine how terrifying it can be for a child of any age to have the family change its composition, to have one parent suddenly gone from the house while the other parent is in alternating stages of numbness and shock, anger, and hurt. Younger children may wonder, "Did Daddy leave because of something I did?" "Maybe Mommy left because I didn't clean my room. Am I being punished by losing her?" "Who will take care of me now?" Older children and teens can wonder, "How much does Dad love me to leave me like that?" "Will Dad desert me like my friend's dad deserted him?" The younger the children, the more frequently you have to persuade them again and again that this is not their fault.

Some children are strong enough to think about these questions and settle them for themselves with an internal, "Nah, my mom wouldn't do that," or, "I know it will be okay." But some children can't do that. Do reassure your child whether or not they ask such questions. But when they ask these kinds of things, be aware that behind the repeated questions may be a storehouse of fears and a need to confide that could mean professional help is in order.

MY PARENT LEFT ME

Children sometimes feel that the parent who left the family home to live elsewhere is also leaving them and removing his or her love from the child. Other children conclude that the resident parent has forced the other parent to leave. "It's your fault she left!" As a result, anger is sometimes directed at the parent who stays, sometimes at the one who goes, and often at both. Instead of being shocked at such angry outbursts or being punitive with the children, parents can help with reassuring action and honest explanations. The children have their own need to mourn the end of their parents' marriage, and anger is a legitimate part of the process.

GOINGS AND COMINGS

Children may need a "reentry" ritual or routine or time alone to readjust when they come to be with you or go with the other parents. This is natural. It is their way of coping with the transition. Some children, even teens, are crabby when they get ready to go to or when they return from the other parent. Plan quiet, soothing things for them, or immerse them in an activity with you, or talk about what they did (or will do) at the other house. Find what works to ease their anxiety and sense of confusion. Here is what one mother with two children ages seven and ten does. "When they come in on Sunday afternoon, we have a routine. First, we hug, kiss, they wash up, and then we have dinner and talk about what happened to me while they were gone. If they want, they can tell me what they did. Then I help them with any things they want to unpack, and we settle in front of the TV to watch a video I have picked out. Bedtime is no later than eight-thirty after a bath."

These children know what to expect and can reorient themselves more easily. Just find out what works and try to be consistent. You will probably want to adjust the reentry routine as the children grow older.

CHILDREN NEED PARENTS TO BE THE GROWN-UPS

Show by your actions and attitude that you and the other parent can cope, that you are the grown-ups and are in control of what is happening to your family. Check yourself occasionally to see how heavily you may be leaning on your children for your emotional support. Repeatedly ask yourself, "Who is the grown-up here?"

Some parents are so preoccupied during the crisis periods that they overlook the children's needs for safety, consistency, and protection. If your moral and emotional support is coming primarily from your children, you may be expecting too much from them.

There is a big difference between honestly sharing problems with your children and leaning on them. Your children love you, they know you, and they care deeply. They are there when others may not be. But children are not our emotional equals, nor are they yet equipped for adult traumas or carrying adult burdens. Yet listen to some parents talk about how the children are expected to take over when the adults fell apart. "Joanne takes care of me," said one young mother of a daughter aged eight. "She makes her own meals, she asks me how I feel, and she tells me not to cry. She is all I have now that her dad is gone." This role reversal is not healthy. Find someone your own age and size to lean on instead.

Crying or honest displays of emotions from your children or yourself are natural. Crying offers release when it is spontaneous and follows appro-

Danger Signals

Age	What to Look For
Infants–2½ years	Difficulty with feeding, sleeping. Excessive crying, listlessness. Regression to earlier stages of development (needing a bottle, diapers); slower or stalled development; increased fears, especially of strangers. Tantrums, hyperactivity. Fears of abandonment are paramount. Misses the absent parent. Depression. Panic. Extreme need for physical affection and holding.
2½–5 years	Same as above. Also, there may be excessive clinging, whining, sadness, vigilance, aggression, or being too good. May feel unloved, guilty, or responsible for the separation or problems between parents. May fear basic needs will not be met. May have somatic symptoms.
6–8 years	Anger, fear of future, aggression, hyperactivity, withdrawal; problems with schoolwork, peers; depression; clinging, whining. May feel unloved, betrayed, guilty. May still fear being abandoned. May have symptoms described for younger children above.
9–12 years	Anger toward parents, trouble in school with peers, blaming, depression, fear of future and abandonment, low self-esteem, excessive worries, drug and sexual experimentation, somatic symptoms.
13–18 years	The same problems can continue from earlier years, but with greater danger to self and others, including promiscuity, addiction, criminal activity. Also may withdraw from friends and/or family, be overly shy or lacking confidence, fear their ability to make it on their own, to form satisfactory intimate relationships.

priately on hurts, frights, or spats. But adult crying in front of children, if prolonged, is very frightening to children in crisis. A tear or two from a parent seems healthy, but more than that is scary. One child of divorce, now grown and with children of her own, gave this advice to parents now separating: "Don't put a kid in a role they are not ready for— the kid shouldn't be a parent to the parent. Don't make kids grow up too soon."

HOW TO KNOW WHEN YOUR CHILD NEEDS HELP

Most children will display some emotional or physical reaction to the crisis during the first six to twelve months, sometimes longer. Children need time to adjust. While it is a natural response, it is not without its dangers. Many children recover nicely from the separation, especially those who were doing well before. But some do not do well and need additional help. Certain behaviors, attitudes, or beliefs may be signs that your child is treading in deep waters. By the time the following listed behaviors have appeared, your child may have been feeling vulnerable for some time. Renew your efforts to spend time together with your child and attempt to identify the problem. If things do not improve within a month, it is time to seek professional advice.

It is not a sign of failure to consult with an expert or mental health professional specializing in children. It is a sign of strength and good judgment to get help. Ask friends for referrals, call your HMO, local teaching hospital, or your local Family Services or counseling center for a referral. Children can't feel safe when their parent cannot deal with problems. Don't wait for things to become too serious before you act. The recovery time may be far longer.

TOGETHER TIME: LISTEN, REASSURE, GROW CLOSER TO YOUR CHILD

Your together times are times where you have golden opportunities to be a good listener, calm your children's fears, and rebuild their trust in life. These are not usually times that are orchestrated or staged. There are together times in the car as you travel to the day care center, to the store, to special classes or activities together, the e-mail exchanges, or the daily phone calls after school. Bedtimes with stories or the ritual lullaby and hugs. It can be waiting for a bus together or the tag end of the school carpool. These times are precious opportunities to enjoy your child, to listen, understand, give what he or she needs from you. What happens is natural, spontaneous, real. These are the times you can grow closer to your child.

Doing "family work" side by side is a fine opportunity for becoming closer. Questions are asked, secrets are revealed, problems are unraveled, work is done (or not). This is an important time. In our overextended world, where parents spend hours commuting and children spend hours in school or activities, "together time" is more precious than ever. It is what you and your children will remember.

In many ways, parenting after divorce is the same as before. Children seek limits, question standards, test and retest their elders, and absorb values regardless of their parents' marital status. And during a family's history there are normal stages of growth for both the children and parents regardless of family circumstances. Children grow up and parents grow older. This is the same process for everyone.

Differences between separate and married parenting do exist. But the first question a parent should ask when difficulties arise is, "Does this type of thing happen in never divorced families, too?" Often the answer will be "Yes." Some never divorced parents say, "I have a hard time controlling my preschooler." Others say, "I feel awkward trying to talk to my children about the facts of life." Such situations are common and may have little to do with whether Mom and Dad are married, single, or remarried. So when a problem arises concerning the children, don't automatically assume that it is caused solely by the divorce. Instead ask yourself these questions: 1. Does this type of thing happen in all families? 2. What part of the situation may be due to our personalities and our family style? 3. What part of the difficulty may be due to outside influences—friends, school, TV, the neighborhood?

After you have looked at those possibilities, ask yourself: 4. What part of the problem may be due to the changes brought about by the divorce (or remarriage)? 5. What part of the problem may be caused by the way we parents are relating to each other or by putting our children in the middle?

SUMMARY: CALMING YOUR CHILDREN'S FEARS AND REBUILDING THEIR TRUST

- **Reassure your children that you love them and will always take care of them and look after their needs,** no matter what happens between you and their other parent. Tell them you will always be there for them and that things will turn out all right. Explain to them that you may all have times when you feel confused, perhaps sad or angry, but that you will have happy times too.
- **Comfort your child,** be their safe haven where they can grieve and express their feelings. Be mindful of the different fears they might have and that they may blame themselves for your problems. It can help to remember, "Children are good observers, but not good interpreters."
- **Reassure your children they still have their family** but now in two homes instead of one. Use positive words like "be at your other home" or "be with Mom or Dad" instead of "visit." Explain things. Demystify what's happening with concrete information appropriate to their TLC about changes likely to occur, what will be different, what will remain the same.
- **Be the grown-up.** Show by your actions that you can cope and can be trusted. Explain that the separation or divorce is grown-up business between Mom and Dad. Do not ever imply or state that your children had any responsibility for your fights or for the end of your marriage. Keep your child out of the middle of your communications and your problems.
- **Give your child a say but take responsibility for the final decision yourself.** Respect your child's needs, wishes, and opinions. Show them that they are important and seriously consider their opinions, but do not ask them which parent they want to live with or whether or not to divorce or separate.
- **Provide structure and predictability.** A sense of order is a key ingredient in increasing security, continuity and that things are under control. Regular routines, doing "ground work," having house and safety

rules are parts of this structure. Flexibility is also important, but a reasonable structure is the base.

- **Support the other parent and make it easy for the other parent to have a good relationship with your child.** Do not bad-mouth the other parent or try to turn your child against him or her. If the other parent is dangerous or abusive, get expert help immediately and protect your child and yourself.
- **Make it easy for the other parent to know what is happening with your child.** Your child needs both of you to be in touch and aware of their needs, joys, successes, worries, health, progress. Keep each other informed, even on small things if you can manage it. It is a big plus.
- **Never threaten your child with abandonment,** not even in hopes that it will make them obey you. It is dirty fighting, unnecessarily frightening, and can result in a child's loss of respect and trust.
- **Have an easy to read calendar** the children can refer to at any time. Show them where the other home will be. Bring them apartment or house hunting. **When they move from one home to the other,** remember your child's need for a transition period.
- **Know and respond to the danger signals.** Children are resilient, but only up to a point after which they can quickly deteriorate. Be aware of danger signals and don't wait too long to seek professional help.
- **Don't lead children to believe that you may reconcile with their other parent.** Fostering false dreams does not help their readjustment to this new life.
- **Reconfirm your assurances frequently** during the first year and even into the second year after separation. Such reassurances are part of their feelings of security, especially actions and affection that say you are glad to be their parent, that you love them, and that you will always take care of them.
- **Give your child the gift of yourself.** Your time together, contact when apart, your affection, your attention, your physical presence as well as your love. Hugs, cuddles, smiles, encouragement. Try not to delegate these things to nannies, coaches, or relatives. Your child needs you first.

TRUST YOURSELF, TRUST YOUR INSTINCTS

Trust yourself and your instincts. Trust in your children, have confidence in their ability to bounce back, change, and learn. You are the best judge of what is best for you and them. If you are working on at least some of the things outlined in this chapter, you have already gone a long way in demonstrating your love for your children and in caring for their needs. Many everyday problems with children respond to genuine love and common sense.

FUN, HUMOR, AND A POSITIVE OUTLOOK

Think about what you have preserved and gained, not just what you have lost. Enjoy your children, your family. There are so many options to choose from. Lighten up with regular family fun times, your sense of humor. Play. Make as much of the new life as positive and as enjoyable as you can. In the midst of all the do's and don'ts, legal business, new pressures, you will certainly find something to laugh about that is just too crazy to be taken seriously! Laughter is a great healer, and it nearly always gives us a new perspective. Your years with your children are your treasure. Trust yourself and your instincts and . . . enjoy your children.

SUMMARY CHECKLIST FOR CHAPTERS 9 AND 10

1. Consider your hopes and dreams for your children.
2. Strive for a positive parenting pattern with the other parent.
3. Consider your child's TLC.
4. Give your children a say based on their age and temperament.
5. Keep changes to a minimum at least the first year or two.
6. Strive for good communications with the other parent and keep your children out of the middle.
7. Calm your children's fears and rebuild trust.
8. Be the grown-up.
9. Acknowledge and accept your children's feelings.
10. Read the danger signals and find help if needed.
11. Believe in yourself and in your family.
12. Trust yourself, trust your children.
13. Have fun, humor, a positive outlook. Be affectionate.

Part 3

THE LEGAL BUSINESS *IS* YOUR BUSINESS

Chapter 11

The Legal Business

The Big Picture, Custody, and

Making Major Decisions

The Big Picture
Attorneys
Custody, No Custody, Shared Custody
Custody: Some Common Legal Terms
Parents' Time with Their Children
The Children's Calendar
What Is Best for Your Child?
Ways to Share Time
Where Will You and Your Children Live?
Making Major Decisions for Your Child
Your Turn. What Do You Want?

You may be surprised to find that the legal business *is* your business. And there is a lot of it. As one father said, "It took over my life for a while. I had to do a flow chart just to figure it out!" The work of separation or divorce nearly always includes some sort of legal or contractual process. You cannot leave it all to an attorney or to someone else. You will be expected to provide information, make decisions, take actions, talk to the other parent. There are many things to do, think about, decide, act upon. There are also things you will *not* want to do. This section of the book helps you to put the legal business in perspective and make informed decisions about your arrangements, your negotiations, and your "parenting plan" or "parenting agreement" (interchangeable terms used for a "custody and visitation" arrangement). If you use a mediator or an attorney, this will be invaluable information for negotiations. If you do not use an attorney or a mediator, this will help you identify and take charge of what lies ahead.

THE BIG PICTURE

THE AMBIGUITIES OF THE LAW

While parents need to know what their rights are under the law—an important base of knowledge for private negotiations—what these rights mean in practice and how they apply in specific situations often remain unclear. Parents ask lawyers questions such as "Could I have a chance to get sole custody?" "What is joint custody?" "What about child support? Does it change if I have more or less time with the kids?" "If I took my case to court, what chance would I have that the judge would see it my way?"

The answers to all these questions may not be as specific as a parent would like. Many states have guidelines to use for a range of acceptable child and spousal (alimony) support payments (when income levels of Mom and Dad are X, and Y is the percent of time a child lives with each of them, child support per child is expected to be a minimum of Z). But the answers on other related issues all too frequently are "It depends on the circumstances, the case you build, the judge, the county, the state," and even more unsettling: "I don't know—it could go either way." One byword for what parents can expect once they give up on their own private negotiations and turn everything over to attorneys and the courts is *uncertainty*. The only sure thing they can count on is that court appearances are costly, emotionally draining, and often accompanied by long waits for court dates.

With the legal business, four major things have proved to be especially useful to remember.

THE LEGAL BUSINESS WORKS BEST WHEN YOU . . .

1. keep your emotions in check.
2. try to stay out of court.
3. know your laws.
4. separate decisions about your children from those about property and finances.

FIRST: KEEP YOUR EMOTIONS IN CHECK

Courts and feelings don't mix. *The problem divorcing people face is that the emotional, off-the-wall stage usually coincides with the time people file their court papers and declare—on paper—what is wrong with the other parent.* When emotions are raw, the temptation to blame someone or something is very strong. This predictable but nasty time often coincides with the temptation to overstate or distort your concerns in these legal papers. The combination can be lethal. The pain and bewilderment and eventual retaliation from these "overstatements" should not be underestimated. "These papers say I am not home enough so he wants sole custody," said a mother who was at school fifteen hours a week. "He works fifty hours a week and hardly sees the kids now!" This couple is poised for battle. Emotions from your separation or impending divorce can easily complicate your legal business and take the focus away from the needs of your children. At the time when you should be the most rational, you may be asked to make life-changing decisions with the least emotional or financial resources to do so. "When I was doing the paperwork for the legal forms, I felt like I was literally taking apart my marriage," said one father. "I had to identify my money, her money, my assets, her assets, my furniture, her furniture. Every time I worked on those legal papers, I would relive the original feeling of shock." To keep your emotions in check, continue your effort to retreat from intimacy and to develop a businesslike relationship with the other parent.

SECOND: TRY TO STAY OUT OF COURT

This means negotiate your issues between yourselves or your attorneys. Try to avoid court hearings with their testimonies, experts, and the adversary process. The traditional adversary process forces people to choose sides rather than negotiate. The idea—however disguised—is to compete and win. Heightened emotions can transfer easily to the legal arena. Exaggerated claims grow, fueled by impressions of TV dramas of attorneys as saviors or hired guns. The law provides perfect ammunition to parental blame games. Despite many advances in the family courts and in family law, the best advice is to do as much as you can to settle the issues, especially about the children, outside of court. You may want to retain an attorney to settle property and other financial issues, but try to keep the decisions about the children between yourselves, for your work with a mediator, or for an attorney who will negotiate out of court. Chapters 12, 13, and 14 in this section of the book suggest many options for your consideration. Chapter 15 tells you how to use mediation to reach your goal.

The best agreement can be the parents' own agreement. Even though there are notable exceptions to this rule, an agreement parents can forge outside of court will usually last longer, be more satisfactory, and save time, stress, dollars, and pain. The foundation of this belief is that parents know their strengths as parents and that they love their children and know their needs better than the courts ever can. Your own parenting plan (or parenting agreement), one you can learn to develop in these next chapters, will tell the court exactly what you think is the best way to divide or share the parenting. It not only reflects your own situations, standards, and values, but it will avoid the problems associated with the adversarial system and preempts certain intrusions by the legal system into your family. The family court will nearly always honor and accept the parents' own agreement.

Keeping control of your decisions. When parents cannot reach decisions on their own or with a mediator, the next step is to hand over their decision making to others. These may be attorneys, investigators, court-appointed psychologists or social workers, and other experts. These people will ultimately either argue your case for you or present the results of their investigations to the court. Parents could well ask themselves what beliefs these practitioners may hold. What are their views about fathers as nurturers? Mothers as wage earners? What about primary custody of infants to mothers? What about the two-home approach, the concept of joint decision making? Even when laws are specific, a parent's values can easily take a backseat to the values of those persons placed in a position of power. The traditional adversary process can force people to choose sides rather than negotiate. In order to compete and win, people manipulate the process to one's advantage. If you feel that your case is out of your control and headed for a court battle, try this first. Go spend a day yourself observing what actually happens in family court.

Maintaining your privacy. If you decide to take your dispute into court, your privacy may no longer be protected and decisions about your children will be out of your hands. Remember that anyone can walk into a family courtroom and hear about the most intimate details of a family's life. Mediation, begun early enough, will give you a good chance to negotiate your own agreement and keep your family matters private. You retain control.

THIRD: KNOW YOUR LAWS

Be aware of your rights, your children's rights, and the law.

Differences in laws. Laws and legal labels differ among states and countries. The same label can mean different things in different places. "Visitation" in one locale is called "access" in another. "Sole custody" may mean total authority over a child by one parent, or it may have built-in allowances for the rights of the other parent. Some state laws will make a distinction between "physical custody" and "legal custody," others will impose "joint custody" only with joint consent. Some states will impose joint custody if one parent wants it, others will not. A few states expect children of "tender years"—usually infants, toddlers, and the youngest children—to be with their mother. Some jurisdictions, such as the state of Washington, have pioneered new legal language, so that the labels of "custody" and "visitation" are replaced by parenting "rights" and "responsibilities."

Your laws and state guidelines. Even if you have an attorney, take the time to research the laws on custody in your area. There should be many helpful books specific to your state or country. Try to go to a library and look at the family law statutes yourself. Make a copy to take home for your reference. You may be surprised how often you refer to it. You will be able to ask pointed and knowledgeable questions and then evaluate the answers you receive. Nevertheless nothing can substitute for a consultation with a knowledgeable family law attorney who can focus on your situation. Obtain information on the following laws and legal procedures:

1. Child custody: terminology used, customary divisions of time and authority regarding the children, and whether the law has any presumptions or preferences.
2. Child support and the official guidelines for determining support.
3. Spousal support and the official guidelines for determining support.
4. Determining if a custody agreement must be drafted by a lawyer or whether a private contract between the parents will be acceptable to the court. Determining what route a privately negotiated agreement needs to take to become legal.
5. Try to identify how laws on custody may affect the division of assets such as the disposition of the family residence.

Your knowledge about the interpretations and implementations of the custody laws in your jurisdiction is essential to making sound decisions about custody. You also need to know how to safeguard for your future the arrangement you negotiate now. Custody laws are not uniform across states or countries, and parents cannot be totally confident that a judge in another state will uphold the findings of the original court, even though there are strong provisions for enforcing out-of-state court orders. A disgruntled parent may seek to put aside a shared custody order of one court and take the child to another state or country. There the parent may set up housekeeping and attempt to file for sole custody or its equivalent. Even though child snatching is an extreme reaction, just the fear of it can put an enormous strain on a relationship. Far better to understand your options from the beginning. A well-written legal paragraph by a knowledgeable family law attorney placed in your parenting agreement should lay out what you both want when it comes to out-of-state or out-of-area moves with a child.

MAJOR LEGAL DECISIONS IN DIVORCE

In a divorce, your major legal decisions will be . . .

- *The sharing or division of child-rearing rights and responsibilities and legal custody.* This holds whether or not parents have ever married.
- *The dissolution:* the end of their marriage (or legal separation). *If never married:* legal establishment of paternity.
- *The division of property and debts:* the end of their common holdings as a married couple.
- *The level of financial support:* the amount of contribution toward the care of the children (child support) and the other parent (alimony or spousal support). Child support is expected to be paid by biological parents once paternity is established.
- *How the costs of the separation or divorce are allocated:* Attorney and mediator fees, moving expenses, financial fees, household costs.

FOURTH: SEPARATE DECISIONS ABOUT YOUR CHILDREN FROM THOSE ABOUT PROPERTY, AND OTHER FINANCIAL MATTERS

Even though it has long been recommended that the decisions about the children be handled separately from the other legal decisions, a property and custody agreement are often combined in one document and, for many cases, presented as a private contract or stipulation at the time of the court appearance. The interacting effects of support levels, time spent with the children, and the presence of a family home will continue to force parents and their attorneys into overlapping bargaining positions. When parents want a lever, this leverage usually ends up being the money and the kids. With some effort, parents, mediators, and attorneys can usually separate the issues about children from negotiations over property and assets.

ATTORNEYS

Even when you have an attorney, you still do a lot of work. The law and its workings are a mystery to many people, and lawyers frequently observe how bewildered and confused their divorce clients seem. Often, separation or divorce is a person's first contact with the law or with a lawyer. Some may expect that the lawyer will know all the answers, take over all the unpleasantness of relating to the other parent, change the other parent's behavior, and somehow provide comfort for all the emotional issues surrounding the separation as well. The mere act of walking into a lawyer's office is seen as either a declaration of independence, of war, or of calling for a rescue squad.

Sometimes parents are taken aback when their lawyer tells them that, *first,* they not only need to present to him or her as complete a financial picture as possible (with past records, tax returns, and other formal documents), but that they also have to figure out their own present and future financial situation. *Second,* they are asked to think about what they want regarding their children—in detail. *Third,* even when the client must pay the hourly fee for being hand-guided through this process, the client alone will have to do most of the work of collecting information and decision making. "I didn't need to pay two hundred dollars an hour to do it myself," said one angry woman who had expected different treatment.

STAYING OUT OF COURT

Attorneys can both litigate and negotiate. Hopefully you will choose one who can negotiate for you *out of court* with the other parent's attorney and keep your case from becoming a more costly and public in-court experience. Attorneys may encourage you to use a mediator for your custody issues while they take care of the rest of the financial and tax matters. They can also be effective coaches to the parties' own private discussions or mediation sessions. One of an attorney's important functions, however, is to dispel your misplaced expectations about what the law can do and cannot do for you. What you think the law provides may not be so. The legal process is not as fast, as limited, or as dramatic as it appears on TV or in films. Remember, even when attorneys are involved, once the legal business is completed, you and the other parent are left alone again to negotiate the issues that will certainly arise in the future.

Every case is different, but as one family lawyer said, "The most successful law practitioner is the one who knows how to promote a good agreement out of court, not the one who is constantly in litigation." Attorneys know that when an out-of-court settlement is not reached and the dispute must come before the bench, the best-prepared brief in the world will still be subject to the risk of unexpected events and the personal beliefs of the judge. Nonetheless, there are cases where the best thing to do is to leave negotiations to attorneys. This is especially true if there is no trust at all between the parents or if there is a history of family abuse, fraud, or substance or alcohol abuse.

Using attorneys. Family law can be complex and demanding. Knowledgeable family law attorneys can be objective and serve as guides through complex law and legal procedures. You need a lawyer for expert advice on your rights under the law, for expert review of your mutual agreements or plans. People need attorneys for advice on tax and legal consequences of proposed options for a privately negotiated agreement. Financial issues of support for both children and a spouse are not necessarily clear-cut in all jurisdictions. Although child support usually requires the use of and adherence to state-approved guidelines, these may interact with alimony, property division, and in some states the amount of time a parent spends with the children. A knowledgeable lawyer can unravel these for you and do the actual negotiations if your own efforts fall short.

A realistic financial picture: a good start. The specter of a bleak financial future often haunts the end of a relationship. At first, few people can maintain their former standard of living after separation. There are now two households instead of one, with the same amount of money to support them. There are many more unbudgeted expenditures, ranging from transportation from one home to the other; more day care expenses; fees for therapy, mediator, attorneys, and vocational counseling; to takeout lunches, suppers, consolation shopping, or drinking sprees. The emotions of divorce seem to be at their zenith when the lowered standard of living combines with the need to talk about economics. An unequal standard of living and of economic opportunity between the two parents creates resentments and grievances. The children feel the changes in their lives and the tension and the practical fallout of the financial pinch. There is rarely, if ever, enough money. Financial issues, even more than others, can become the pot the emotions of divorce get cooked in. See appendix 3 for more information including a chart to use on how to determine the costs of raising children and accounting for child support.

CUSTODY, NO CUSTODY, SHARED CUSTODY

THE "FEAR" WORDS

When people ask, "Who got custody of the children?" they usually mean whom will the children live with, who will make the decisions, who has authority over their upbringing. They are often thinking of "custody" as ownership, where all or nearly all of these rights are vested in one parent and the remaining parent can visit only at the pleasure of the custodial parent. The term "having custody" elicits fears of an all-or-nothing future. "I insist on custody," a young mother of a seven-month-old son may say. The father may answer, "I'm his father, and I'm not going to let you cheat me out of a relationship with my son."

An all-or-nothing arrangement is usually not the optimum situation for a child (or for parents). Finding a way to share or divide the responsibilities for raising the children is worth the time and frustration. The right amount and type of detail along with the right legal label will protect you both from the fear words and an unintended all-or-nothing interpretation. Remember, whether or not you develop a detailed plan, the law will still require you to identify which of you—as your child's parents—will be responsible for your child when and for what. When parents cannot do this on their own, the court will decide for them.

THE LEGAL LABELS DO MATTER

The traditional legal terms can't begin to describe what being a parent is about. But the type of "custody" term you choose will most probably have a major effect on your life and that of your children. *Legal labels do matter.* Legally and practically there is a powerful difference between the legal authority and responsibility held by the parent with a legal paper that cites terms such as "custody," "sole custody," "primary care," "primary custody," or "primary residence," and those parents who have "joint custody," or "shared custody," or "shared residences for their children." Psychologically and emotionally the difference among these terms is also enormous and can set the tone for how you relate to the other parent.

TALK TO FRIENDS, COUNSELORS, ATTORNEYS

Ask friends, counselors, and attorneys about the pros and cons of the law, legal labels, and actual parenting arrangements. These conversations can help you try on different options. If you choose a shared arrangement, you may have to educate the other parent on how you can share parenting and set up two homes and how legal requirements for a definition of custody can be met.

CUSTODY: SOME COMMON LEGAL TERMS

Here is a simplified overview of some of the most common legal terms. What they represent and how you can amplify or modify their meaning will be described in detail later in this chapter and the next. *Please remember, the law in your area may differ from that shown here.*

Common Legal Terms About Custody	Common Interpretations—Please Remember, the Law in Your Area May Differ from What Is Shown
Primary custody Sole custody Sole physical custody	These terms usually mean that the parent has all or nearly all the authority and responsibility for the *(continues)*

166 THE LEGAL BUSINESS *IS* YOUR BUSINESS

(continued from previous page)

Common Legal Terms About Custody	Common Interpretations—Please Remember, the Law in Your Area May Differ from What Is Shown
Primary residence Primary care Physical custodians Conservator	child. This parent has the child living with him or her all or nearly all of the time. Parents will also have sole custody when the other parent has dropped out or where there is abuse or neglect on the part of the other parent.
Legal custody Sole legal custody Joint legal custody	This term is used in some states. It has to do with how major decisions are made for health, religion, and education. Sole legal custody places all responsibilities and authority for decisions with one parent who may not have to confer with the other parent. Joint legal custody means that parents share major decisions.
Joint custody Shared custody Shared primary custody Shared physical custody	These terms mean that the parents are dividing or sharing some of the authority and responsibility around raising a child. It does not automatically mean that all decisions or time are equally shared. You must be very clear what you do mean when you select these terms and provide adequate detail.
Joint custody, with primary residence with one parent	This can mean that the parents are sharing or dividing authority and responsibility, but that the children have one primary residence for the majority of the time _or_ that the residential parent has the equivalent of sole custody with the other parent involved in some decisions and possibly with significant time with the children.

Common Legal Terms About Custody	*Common Interpretations—Please Remember, the Law in Your Area May Differ from What Is Shown*
Split custody Divided custody	Usually uses when one child lives with Mom, the other with Dad. Or when children live six months a year with one parent, then switch to the other parent.
Visitation Access	These terms mean the time the nonresidential or noncustodial parent has with the child. Time should be specified by overnights, hours, and frequency of occurrence. The term "reasonable visitation" is insufficient.

JOINT CUSTODY DOES NOT MEAN EQUAL TIME

For most people, the term "joint custody" conjures up an expectation for strict and equal division of time and authority, with a child going back and forth. Nevertheless, most legal interpretations of "joint custody" are that each parent is significantly involved in raising their child. It does not have to mean equal time. Although an equal division of time between homes is more popular now than it was twenty years ago, a strictly equal division of time is chosen by only a small percentage of families. A more common division is 65–80% time in one home and the remainder in the other. *How often the children go between homes should depend on the children's TLC needs, and their adaptability.* Some of these parents will choose the term "joint physical custody" or "joint custody with primary residence." When parents use terms such as "joint" or "shared," they must be very clear and *specify* where and when the child lives with each parent.

SOLE CUSTODY

Sole custody is legally far clearer than joint custody. It is part of the one-home, one-authority tradition and has a long historical and legal precedents to define its application in practice. One parent holds most, if not all, the authority and most, if not all, the responsibility. If you do not modify this term in a parenting plan, then a number of legal assumptions may come into play. This may also include the sole custody parent's prerogative to unilaterally move out of the area or even out of the country. Sole custody is nearly always accompanied by *access* or *visitation rights,* where the other parent has times with the child.

PARENTS' TIME WITH THEIR CHILDREN

"The kids' mother talks about having the kids with her most of the time," said one father. "But what kind of time are we talking about? Does this only mean overnights? What about time after school or helping with sports? Do you count the hours the kids are in school or only when they are physically with you? If you don't count overnights and school times, I'm with the kids as much as she is." Most parents understand that having a child sleep in the same house is only part of what being a family is all about. There are many ways to measure "time" with your children.

WAYS TO THINK ABOUT TIME

How we spend time with our children or make decisions for them is often automatic. We aren't programmed to look at them piece by piece. The following ways of looking at time and parenting responsibilities have been used by many parents, attorneys, and mediators. One mother of eight-year-old twins said, "It was like taking apart a shirt I'd been wearing and examining the size of the sleeves, the front, the back, the collar, as separate pieces. I had not realized that some pieces would be better a different size." This approach to "time" has been particularly helpful for a situation where one parent wants strictly equal time and authority and the other parent does not. You can also use it in your parenting agreements to identify how you want to specify time.

STRIVE FOR BALANCE

Ideally each parent should have his or her unique mix of different types of time with the children. What you want to avoid, if you possibly can, is a situation where one of you has all of the responsibility, most of the overnights and day-to-day time, and the other parent has just activities and fun time. Or one has the overnights and the other has everything else. A perfectly equal division of all time, responsibility, and decision making is unrealistic. Look for a way to share or divide time that makes sense to you and capitalizes on each of your strengths as parents. Try to find a balance.

WAYS TO LOOK AT TIME

1. Overnight
2. Together time
3. Outside activity time
4. Holidays, special days, entertainment, and recreation
5. Time away from both parents

1. Overnights

There is something special about waking up and finding a parent there in the morning, even if the parent has to leave for work and the child goes to a sitter. Where a child sleeps has special significance to both parents and children. A child should have a sense of place, of belonging, of importance, a sense of ownership regardless of how few the overnights. A child should be able to feel that "this is my home." In a legal context, it is usually the number of overnights that determines the "residence" or "primary residence."

2. Together Time

"Together times" are the core of parenting and of family life. Mom may be balancing her checkbook and Kevin may be doing his homework. Parents and children are together in the same place at the same time. It can also be "one-on-one" time, such as Dad and Zoe playing with her blocks on the living room floor. This "together time" is precious, whether or not there is an overnight attached to it. Much of our time with our children is spent in the usual routine daily of meals, playtime, reading together, supervising home-work, driving to and from school or the market, dealing with chores, teaching values, discussing the day, and handling necessary discipline. These can all be very meaningful times for both parent and child.

3. Outside Activity Time

The third way to look at time is to consider that portion of time children and parents spend in ongoing activities together outside of the home: athletics, team sports, music, dance, or working on school projects. Far from being frivolous, the right ongoing activities for a child does a great deal more than building skills or appreciation. These can provide opportunities for building character, learning about people, becoming part of the community, and having other adults take on roles as mentors or teachers. Research and common sense says that for many children, wholesome adult role models are essential elements in a child's ability to succeed later in life. Choosing, supervising, participating in, and supporting the right outside activities are important dimensions of being a parent.

4. Holidays, Special Days, Entertainment, and Recreation

Special days and holidays are a favorite part of family life and are more than Christmas, Hanukkah, Thanksgiving, or three-day weekends. They can be a school holiday spent at the beach or taking a long bike ride together, the camping vacation in the national park, the week with a favorite relative, the birthday party, a graduation celebration. Some parents feel that holidays or vacations are the only "fun" times they can spend with their children, or that entertainment is a luxury they can't afford. But families can take walks together, watch videos, do puzzles, board games, cook treats, visit friends, take turns reading aloud to each other, visit the zoo, take a drive. The possibilities are endless.

5. Time Away from Both Parents

These times are included as part of this exercise because parents are usually surprised when they honestly add up the hours their child is not with them. You do not have to calculate this time for the court, but you should know this for yourself. The law assumes that a parent will have a normal life but does not favor arrangements where children and parents do not have much time together. *Being responsible is not enough. You have to be there.* Children seem to spend many hours away from their parents. Daniel, three, is at day care; Rosa, eight, is at school; Joseph, twelve, is practicing with the band; Caroline, two, is with her aunt; Jeremy, fourteen, is hanging out with his friends; Janine, fifteen, is spending the weekend with friends; Chris, sixteen, is "out" somewhere, but not with a parent.

Parents are not at home (or unavailable if they are) because of time spent commuting, working long hours, working second, even third, jobs. Some are bona fide workaholics, others are scrambling to make ends meet. As a result, many children do not have enough actual together time with their parents. A child may be sleeping twenty-six nights out of a typical month with Mother, but because of the mother's schedule, the child may spend only two hours a day with her Monday through Friday, one in the morning and one in the evening. The only time the child can have a span of long, unbroken contact with his mother, therefore, is on weekends or during vacations. In another example, a child may be in the care of his father Thursday evening through Monday morning when Dad brings him to school. But Friday the child is in school. Saturday is filled with baseball and swimming practices, and Saturday night Dad goes out on a date. The actual "together time" they have is Friday evening, a few hours on Saturday, all day Sunday and Sunday evening, and Monday morning. If Dad is not working during these times, he and his child have a significant chunk of potential "together time." *Together time is essential for well-functioning families.*

THE CHILDREN'S CALENDAR

The "calendar" or schedule for times and activities at Mom's house and Dad's house serves many purposes. It is a basic framework for making family plans, for ordering a week's time; the presence of a calendar showing the schedule usually gives children a sense of security and continuity, of order. The schedule, combined with common house rules, demonstrates the parents' new united front. So if all this can be true, why do some people hate schedules so much?

Children and adults alike often dislike being inconvenienced, uprooted, or regimented. They hate it most when they have no say in the matter. Separation can force this situation on people, and a schedule can symbolize it all.

SUCCESSFUL SCHEDULES ARE EVENTUALLY ADAPTABLE

During the first two years, two-home ground rules and times at each home need to be clearly written and followed as much as possible. Everyone needs to know what they can count on. But some flexibility is also necessary. As the businesslike relationship takes hold, tensions ease and a more relaxed and positive parenting arrangement can result. Seasoned two-home parents with shared or cooperative ways of relating are long accustomed to negotiating changes in plans. They often report that while they have a schedule, they may not always follow it. By mutual agreement, parents and children make changes as the need arises. But these parents also state that the written schedules and agreements are the essential foundation. As one mother put it, "If we can't agree on a change and things get tense again, we can fall back on the schedule as is. It's fair and it's safe."

UNSCHEDULED TIME

One father talked about how much he missed this unstructured time now. "When I was married, the kids and I would pass one another on the front walk, exchange comments, perhaps talk for a few minutes over a drink in the kitchen. When you don't live together full-time, you can lose this." Frequent phone calls, brief stops before or after school or work, the opportunity to negotiate for more time together, are all crucial factors that contribute to maintaining that special bond.

The problem with this unstructured contact is that it often happens during the other parent's time of responsibility or authority. *Therefore one parent always needs to ask the other parent about the time before mentioning it to the child.* Dropping by unannounced at the other home or picking up a child from school or the sitter without notice can cause problems—especially the first year. Parents need to agree on what is considered *acceptable unscheduled time* and what needs the other parent's say-so.

WHAT IS BEST FOR YOUR CHILD?

Each child is unique, and so is each family. Because each family must settle into its own pattern, there are few hard and fast rules for the division of the various kinds of time with the children. Here is an overview of the most commonly accepted guidelines:

- Both parents need to take care that each remains a real parent rather than one a disciplinarian and the other only a recreation director.
- Parents must consider how well their child handles changes when making decisions. This is the "TLC" described in the last chapter.
- School-age children and parents need a block of unbroken time together. This means significant time together, including overnights, not just a few hours during the week. This can mean as little as four nights a month to half of the time or more.
- Infants and young children need

  1. frequent "together time" with both parents, every day if possible.
  2. a protected, predictable routine, sleeping and eating schedule.
  3. a primary residence with few overnights with the other parent until they grow older.

A "TLC" REMINDER

As you consider ways to share time as parents, keep in mind your child's unique "TLC."

WAYS TO SHARE TIME

SCHOOL-AGE CHILDREN

Overnights and Together Times

The importance of a stretch of together time combined with an overnight with each parent can be understood when you look at the way children actually behave in each home. When a child gets used to sleeping somewhere regularly, he or she feels at home. When a child can find the bathroom when half-awake, pull out a familiar toy, settle down for a bedtime story read by Mom or Dad, both parent and child feel the return of the family feeling and the security and joy in waking up in the morning to find each other there. The bond of continuity from such ordinary acts brings with it a precious sense of belonging and togetherness that stays with our children all their lives. So while together and activity times are very important, overnights have a special meaning—both personally and legally. More on this later.

Sharing can range from a strict schedule of equal time at each home to a view of sharing as participation in child rearing based on quality rather than quantity of time. Your child's needs and TLC should dictate your decisions. See chapters 5 and 16 if you have older teenagers.

Equal Times at Both Homes

This equal time can be divided almost any way: for example, three or four days and overnights with one parent, three or four days with the other, or two weeks and two weeks. This split-time and overnight arrangement seems to work over long periods of time when the two homes are located close together, the children are of a sturdy or adaptable temperament, and can change households well. Parents are urged to maintain easy to follow schedules and to be flexible.

One-Third Time in One Home, Two-Thirds in Another

If thought out carefully, this arrangement can work well for most school-age children. For about eight to ten days and nights a month the children are with one parent, the rest of the time with the other parent. Often the schedule is every other weekend with one overnight during the "off" week, or two long weekends (Thursday evenings until the beginning of school the next Monday). When the eight to ten days a month are taken only on Saturdays or Sundays, parents report feeling out of balance. One parent has no together or activity time with the children when free from the work week, and, unless the children stay until Monday morning, the weekend parent has no school nights.

One-Fifth Residence in One Home, the Remaining Time in the Other Home

This is often a variation on the last arrangement—about four to six days and nights during a month's period. Usually the period begins on a Friday evening and ends on Sunday afternoon, without the Monday morning school ritual, but allowing some unbroken time for both parent and child to resume a more normal relationship and some of the weekend with each parent. It may include afternoon or evening time, and an overnight, mid-week.

One Day a Weekend

This arrangement allows a parent a brief weekly contact with the child, but almost always a guest-host relationship. Reestablishing regular parenting is difficult under this arrangement, unless the time includes an overnight stay.

Open Time Between Homes

Open time means a freedom of movement between the two homes as arranged by the children. This sometimes works when the children are in their teens, mature, and the parents are willing to accept their independent plans. It needs to be closely monitored, however. The children make their plans with the parent they want to live with (for a week, a month, or a year) and then make plans with the other parent regarding their times together. The advantages of this are that the children make the arrangements. The disadvantages are that the parents may forget to interact with each other on anything but the annual major decisions regarding finances and education. Be careful here. Be sure you can answer these questions: Whom is your child accountable to and reporting to? How does each parent know where the child is? The teenager should still benefit from your parental involvement and a firm hand when needed. Before this plan can work, both parents must believe strongly in the value of the independent parent-child relationship and have confidence in their child's sense of responsibility. The parents must provide commonsense house rules at each home.

Sunday Night Returns or Monday Mornings to School?

Many parents have complained that the Sunday night ending to a weekend together is unbearably painful for the kids and the parent. In the words of one father, "The wrench of bringing the kids home on Sunday night is just more than we can take. Is there a way to get around this awful separation experience?" Yes. Instead of bringing the children to their other home on Sunday night, take them straight to school on Monday morning. The supporters of this plan say, "It's natural for a parent to bring children to school. You can say good-bye to them more easily in the course of the routine. You go on to work and they go on to classes. There's no time to feel lonely. And I don't have to face their other parent. On Sunday I can stick to the old 'school nights' pattern, check homework. I feel more like a parent this way."

But not everyone thinks this is a good idea. Others say that children need a regular routine on Sunday night in order to get ready for the school week. "They need time to settle down from the weekend with their father," said one mother. "When they stay at their father's Sunday nights, they are too tired when they come home on Monday after school. I want them here on Sunday night in plenty of time for bath and bedtime." Then there is the issue of "stuff" for school. If the "school week home" is the home where they spend more time, they usually have more school equipment, clothing, and school papers there.

If you try either of these plans, pay close attention to how the children behave and to what they say. Be ready to adjust the plan or to try something else after a few weeks if they are not doing well with it.

NESTING

One of the most successful short-term arrangements sounds strange, but it works. The parents exchange residences and the children (and their schools and friendships) stay put. For example, Mom has had the primary residence for three years, but Dad is going to take over for an indefinite period while Mom sets up a second home for the children. Dad moves into the primary family home with his furniture and things, the children's things stay put, and Mom finds her own place. If Dad brings in his furniture, kitchen equipment, pictures, and memorabilia, it will be his home. Like the children in chapter 10, parents need personal belongings to bolster their sense of territory. The logistics of these moves hassle the adults, but as one child remarked, "Hooray! We get to stay put while you all do the moving around!"

When a two-home approach is already established, such residence changes do not seem to bring children the old fears of losing one parent while gaining another. If a joint custody arrangement with a satisfactory parenting agreement has been working well, one parent has less fear of being cut out while the other takes over. But because of the soap opera legacy, a shift like this can raise old myths about one parent abandoning responsibilities. Casual acquaintances and even family members may raise eyebrows, perhaps looking for causes of failure within the parent who is now providing the home where children will be spending the lesser amount of time. Try not to let this bother you. Your children have two homes and two parents who love and care for them. What more could children ask for in this new world?

Dividing Time During the Summer

Summertime for the two-home child can mean any number of experiences. Your plans should be based on the TLC of your child and your family circumstances. The preschooler's routines don't usually change much. But for older children it can mean many things: a total, two-and-a-half-month immersion in one parent's world; a split time between homes; summer camp away from both parents; or a continuation of what had been happening during the school year. Some children travel with one parent to different parts of the world, others settle into summer jobs or summer school or just hang out with their friends.

Often summer means that the parent who normally has less time during the school year will now have that continuous stretch of time with the children while the other parent has them on weekends. If the parents are separated by many miles, the summer-home parent will have what one father described as "plain old parenting without a break."

Some parents plan vacations with children. Some children get one trip, others get two different vacations. Other parents plan their time off without the children. Still other parents work out divisions of summertime for the children to spend afternoons with Mom and eat supper and spend nights with Dad.

Summer camps come into the picture for many school-age children, as do trips to other relatives or friends. The same principles apply, however. Whatever you agree on regarding times with each parent, remember that what one parent does on his or her time is not subject to the other parent's approval. Sometimes a parent will be upset because he or she assumed that the month the child spent during the summer with the other parent would be spent entirely with that parent. Instead the other parent decided to let the child go to camp for a week and to the grandparents for another. Unless you both agree otherwise, this is a parent's time to plan as he or she chooses.

INFANTS, TODDLERS, AND PRESCHOOLERS

The most common advice parents will hear about sharing time with infants, toddlers, and preschoolers is the following:

- Think about their TLC—their needs are paramount.
- The routine, schedule, and surroundings should stay stable.
- The child needs frequent together time with each parent regardless of where the child is sleeping.
- Overnights are all or nearly all with one parent for infants and toddlers.
- As the child grows older and into preschool, overnights with the other parent increase.

Of course parents deviate from these guidelines, but when they do, they should watch their child's development very carefully, as the last chapter explained. A set routine, schedule, and the same surroundings seem to be essential for most children. And seeing both parents frequently for together time is also essential—daily, if possible. Ordinarily, children bond with both parents, and they should not be separated from either parent very long. Most parents seem to settle into a two-home arrangement with a primary home with infants, with daily or three or more visits during a week. Parents with young children should plan on revising their time arrangements at least annually, more frequently if needed. At these young ages, children's needs can change frequently. A schedule that supports their health and development is a priority. As children get older, parents can expand their schedules for more overnights.

During the summer the littlest ones are at home or keep going to day care or to the sitters. They are not yet old enough to participate in the summertime activities of older children. For the youngest children, the same divisions of time that held for the school year usually continue during the summer.

HOLIDAYS AND SPECIAL DAYS

These times have a special meaning for many families and often require thoughtful preplanning.

Holidays

These are those school and religious holidays that may or may not mean days off from work: Halloween, Thanksgiving, spring vacation, winter vacation, Valentine's Day, and religious holidays that are important to you such as Christmas, Good Friday, Easter, Hanukkah, Passover, Kwanzaa, High Holy Days, Chinese New Year, May Day, May 5, or other ethnic or religious celebrations.

Three-Day Weekends

Usually these are tacked on to a parent's weekend. In the United States, it is Presidents Day, Martin Luther King Day, July Fourth, Memorial Day, Labor Day, Columbus Day, and Veterans Day.

Special Days

Special days can be graduations, special anniversaries, a child's birthday, a parent's birthday, Mother's Day, Father's Day, Grandparents' Day, siblings' birthdays, or other relatives' birthdays or anniversaries, days set aside for family reunions.

MAKING PLANS FOR HOLIDAYS

Mom, Dad, and the Kids Together Just Like Old Times

For holidays, use this alternative with caution the first few years. Spending more than a few hours together often becomes too painful for the adults and a dirty trick on children who harbor hopes for a reconciliation . . . and most children do. Do make an effort to have everyone together behaving themselves at a family function, especially graduations or the children's birthdays. This is the ultimate sign of "two homes with no fighting." More on this later in chapter 20, "Moving On."

One Child with Mom, the Other with Dad

This arrangement also has many drawbacks. Obvious problems of favoritism and rejection surround who chooses which child. There is also the poignant reality that on the holiday, not only does a family member get to miss the other parent *or* the children, children cannot share the holiday with a sibling. Everyone ends up missing someone. Use this option with caution.

Alternating Holidays

Alternating holidays is a favorite choice of many families. Thanksgiving Day with Dad, Christmas with Mom this year, then reverse for the next year. The children remain perhaps only one or two days with one parent and the remaining time of the holiday with the other parent.

Split Holidays

Some parents split the day of the holiday or special day: half of the day with Mom, the other half with Dad. This can be demoralizing and tiring for children, who could feel like a "thing" that is shared between two parents rather than a child who deserves his or her own holiday. Use split days with caution.

Double Holidays

Many children celebrate a special day twice, once on the day itself, the second on some day selected either earlier or later than the actual day—two birthdays, two Christmases, and so forth. For some, this arrangement works quite well, and the children like the attention. It does not work for every family, however.

WHERE WILL YOU AND YOUR CHILDREN LIVE?

THE FAMILY HOME

Many parents start out convinced that the original family home and the familiar neighborhood provide an important sense of continuity for children during the first year of separation. My experience supports this view. On the other hand, the parent who left the home may want the home sold to use his or her share to purchase a new one. The remaining parent may not have enough financial resources to stay. Houses can also hinder our efforts to put our memories into perspective. Each corner, each piece of furniture or china, can haunt the parent trying to disentangle the new life from the symbols of the past. Sometimes people need a fresh start.

How important, many parents ask, is it for children to keep the original family home as one of their two homes? For how long? There are no easy answers, only a few general guidelines:

1. Try to keep one of your homes at your old address at least the first year.
2. If you must move during the first year, try very hard to keep the children in the same school unless they are already unhappy there.
3. If, after the first year or so, you must move, plan to do so at the end of a school year to minimize the disruption for the child and the difficulty for yourself.

Children moved away from their schools, neighborhoods, and friends during the initial months of their parents' divorce have to make too many major adjustments at once. Parents and children find life easier with as few major changes as possible at a time. Continuity of everyday patterns like going back and forth to school, playing with the kids on the block, and walking the dog helps steady everybody. If there must be a move away from the original home during that first year, make every effort to keep your children in the same school as long as possible that year. More on this in part 4.

TWO-HOME GEOGRAPHY: WHO IS WHERE?

How far apart will the two homes be? Will the parents' homes be within walking or biking distance, or do the children need transportation to go from one home to the other?

The easiest situation for the children is for you and the other parent to live close enough so the kids can travel between you independently. If they can walk, ride their bikes, or take easy public transportation from one home to the other, they will feel far more secure than if they have to depend on others to make the arrangements and do the driving.

Generally, as chapter 10 describes, children do better when they can stay close to the original family pattern and setting, to old friends, to familiar faces and places. Adults, on the other hand, may be needing to expand, to reach out, to take new jobs. Parents may be returning to school or other advanced training, and such plans may entail geographic shifts (see chapter 18). There are no automatic solutions, and even parents who initially move away may move back.

MAKING MAJOR DECISIONS FOR YOUR CHILD

When parents live together, both are equally responsible and have authority to make decisions and take action. But when they are not living together, who makes the decision? Who is responsible for following through? Both parents? One of you? Which one? Under what circumstances?

The school phones a parent to say that Rachel has taken a serious fall and is on the way to the emergency room. The principal advises Dad that Michael be placed in a special track for the gifted. The doctors diagnose Nina with a serious illness requiring extensive treatment. A soccer coach advises Mom that she talk to a therapist about Lily's outbursts of extreme anger. Justin at sixteen wants to take a night job at a neighborhood convenience store. An exasperated orthodontist calls Dad to complain that Sara is not keeping her visits for adjustments and that her entire treatment is at risk.

The law will expect that a child is always under the care and control of at least one parent. That parent will be fully responsible and make all the day-to-day decisions. If parents share both physical and legal custody equally, both are equally responsible and both make the major decisions. If one parent alone has both physical and legal custody, the other parent has the responsibility for emergency care and day-to-day decisions when the child is with him or her but may or may not have any responsibility or decision-making rights at other times.

DAY-TO-DAY DECISIONS WHEN THE CHILD IS WITH YOU

Day-to-day decisions and responsibilities are those decisions parents must make in the course of daily child rearing. We all know what they are—how or if to discipline, the curfew, allowances, assuring nutrition, regular medical care, short-term activities, judgments about whom they play or socialize with that day. These are the things we do for our child in our daily existence as parents. *The common rule is that regardless of who has legal or physical custody, these day-to-day decisions are made by the parent the children are with at the time.*

MAJOR DECISIONS AND TAKING RESPONSIBILITY FOR FOLLOWING THROUGH

Major decisions are those decisions with long-term consequences and often considerable expense. While the day-to-day things have long-term impact over time, they come in little everyday pieces. What is termed here as major decisions go beyond the ordinary day-to-day issues and have to do with choices of schools, child care, doctors, camps, religious affiliation or training, critical or long-term medical treatment such as orthodonture, surgery, psychotherapy, or longer-term commitments to a sport or pursuit, important trips, educational enrichment and, for older children, job choices, purchase or acquisition of major items like cars or expensive equipment, and decisions about college. You may want to share these decisions or divide them between you. Or one parent might make all the major decisions even though he or she may consult the other parent.

YOUR TURN. WHAT DO YOU WANT?

What would you like for your own child? Here is what many parents do. First, they compare a year's calendar and the school calendar. Here is an example of what a father with an eight-year-old son, David, did.

He circled all the days on the yearly calendar that were three-day weekends, holidays, vacations, special days. Then he marked when school let out for summer and when it started in the fall. He could then see what dates were available for a summer vacation together. He looked at his own business calendar and saw that he had one important trip he could not cancel over the next six months. Then he thought about his son's soccer league and the usual times for his son's games, summertime soccer camp, and times with grandparents. He tried out different ideas for time with David on the calendar with a pencil. He erased many ideas before he felt he had found several arrangements that might work for him.

TIME WITH DAVID

Possible Times	*What I Want*
SCHOOL NIGHTS: Sunday through Thursday	Okay to be with Mom, but I want every Wednesday night to be an overnight with me
WEEKEND NIGHTS: Friday and Saturday	Every other weekend with me
VACATIONS:	
Christmas vacation—two full weeks	Either split the time or alternate years
Summer vacation—eleven full weeks	One week with grandparents, three weeks with me
Spring vacation—one week	Alternate each year with Mom
Summer camp for David	Two weeks without either me or Mom
THREE-DAY HOLIDAYS	Alternate holidays with Mom
HOLIDAYS:	
Halloween	Alternate with Mom
Thanksgiving	Alternate with Mom
Christmas Eve	Alternate with Mom
Christmas Day	Alternate with Mom

After setting out your own priorities on time with your children, think about how decisions should be made about their upbringing. Once you have considered these things, the next step is to understand what can go into legal agreements. The next chapter will take you through this step by step.

Chapter 12

Parenting Plans and Agreements

The Basic Elements

Anatomy of a Parenting Plan
What Goes into a Basic Parenting Plan
A Parenting Plan in Detail
Sample Standards of Conduct
Special Provisions
Private Contracts

"WHAT exactly is a parenting agreement, or a parenting plan?" "Is it a substitute for a custody agreement?" "Is it really important?" "What's the purpose of it?" "What options do I have?"

This chapter answers these questions, makes suggestions and lists, one by one, what a plan can contain and the decisions you will probably have to make. The next three chapters will show you *how* to make one for yourself. When you are redesigning your life, the blueprint for your legal status and financial responsibilities for your child *is* the parenting plan.

A parenting agreement or a parenting plan mean the same thing. It is an expanded "custody" agreement with the full force of the law behind it when it is filed with the court. It is *the* most important legal document you will have and deserves your deepest respect and greatest efforts. A permanent and legally binding parenting agreement or plan arrangement is required by many courts, even if you and the other parent have never legally married. It can be a page or two long or five, ten, even twenty pages. It is nearly always filed with the court or incorporated into the court order. Every jurisdiction seems to have preferences on what this document is called, so in this chapter it will be called the "parenting plan" or the "plan." Every jurisdiction also has somewhat different procedures on how to finalize your divorce and plan for your child. The level of detail and thoroughness is up to you, but there are certain minimums that courts usually expect you to meet.

Many parents like to go "window-shopping," trying on different options and discarding the rest. You can probably save a significant amount of money if you do the plan yourself. The parenting plan process usually helps parents become clearer about long-range plans and expectations for their children. This could translate into a stronger sense of continuity and security for your child and greater control for you. Finally, a detailed plan probably has the best chance of working!

This chapter also includes a section on a private agreement. This is a private contract that sets forth agreements between the two of you that do not belong in a legal agreement. The private agreement can be just about anything you want. My clients found that the process of working on these private agreements and writing them out gave them practical standards to live by and put some negative intimacy games to rest. For many, the process was healing.

ANATOMY OF A PARENTING PLAN

When one parent saw a list of what he needed to think about for a legal parenting plan, he said, "I've got to think about all this to get a divorce? I can see why people stay married." When parents are married, their responsibilities and rights blend together. When parents divorce, this bundle of parental duties and prerogatives needs to be sorted out, one by one.

Parents who remain married are rarely forced to analyze their responsibilities and their children's futures in the same way as divorcing parents. One-home parents are not required to decide on their child's college education when the child is five. But dual-home parents may need to make decisions about their children for a decade or more ahead. It's frustrating to have to think in years when you are accustomed to thinking in weeks. "How do I know where I'll be in five months?" storm some parents. "I can't tie myself down to this kind of scheduling." But the law expects that parents follow through with their responsibility to raise their children to adulthood. All parents are expected to have either a court order or a parenting plan that says *how* you will do this. Not everything you read here must go into a plan, but the more complete it is, the better.

WHAT GOES INTO A BASIC PARENTING PLAN

1. Preamble, parents' purpose of the plan, and name and date of birth of child or children
2. Standards of conduct for parents
3. Legal terms defining parental responsibilities and authority
4. Religious affiliation and training

5. Basic education and college
6. Medical care and medical insurance
7. Dental and vision care and insurances
8. Insurance (life, auto, special requirements)
9. Child care, nanny
10. Time spent with each child by each parent

   a. School year (overnights, together time, activity time)
   b. Summers (overnights, together time, activity time)
   c. Holidays, special days (overnights, together time, activity time)

11. Transportation to and from each home
12. Parents' residences, location, and terms for moving away
13. Financial contributions (child support and other)*
14. Duration of agreement, revisions of agreement
15. Resolution of disputes arising from agreement
16. Sanctions or penalties if the agreement is violated
17. Tax consequences of support and residential time*
18. State and county of venue
19. Periodic review and evaluation of plan annually or semiannually (optional)
20. Death of parents (wills, guardians)
21. Provisions for catastrophic events
22. Protracted illness
23. Drastic income loss
24. Child's surname
25. Statement of paternity
26. Parents' access to information and records

A PARENTING PLAN IN DETAIL

1. Preamble or Purpose of the Plan

The purpose of the plan, your parenting values and intentions can be stated in this section in your own words. Children especially appreciate this section when they are old enough to read and understand. This is a perfect opportunity to let your children know how important they are to you and how you and the other parent pledged to work together for their best interests.

* Some attorneys and mediators believe these sections should be in the marital settlement agreement rather than the Parenting Plan. Their concern is that these sections are too complex and hold up negotiations on parenting issues.

2. Standards of Conduct for Parents

Parents who write their own parenting plans or who use mediators will add their own version of some or all of the following ground rules. These standards help to set the tone for the plan and explain how parents expect to organize their day-to-day lives.

SAMPLE STANDARDS OF CONDUCT

A. Both parents will make their whereabouts known to _____ (the other parent or a designated person or persons) so that they can be reached in an emergency.

B. Both parents will give an address and phone number to one another and to all child care providers.

C. Both parents will have access to all medical and school records and direct contact with personnel working with or caring for the children. It is our intent that both of us know about the children's needs and education. We agree to coordinate efforts regarding transportation, conferences, and consultations.

D. Both parents will accommodate their children's desires to spend more time with the other parent for special activities or "together" time.

E. Neither parent shall do anything that would estrange the children from the other parent or impair the child's love and respect for a parent.

F. Both parents are free to attend the children's activities, even if the child is not residing with that parent at the time. The nonresident parent will not interfere in the child's schedule or with the resident parent's plans. For example, if a child is residing with his father and his mother visits him at school, she will not take the child off the school grounds. Neither the resident parent nor the school should have to be concerned about the child's whereabouts or changes in plans without prior discussion and agreement.

G. Each child will have the opportunity to spend extra time with a nonresident parent by asking either parent for additional time. The resident parent has the final say.

H. The parents agree that the child will have unrestricted phone access to a parent (or by beeper, e-mail, regular mail, and so on) and that a parent will have reasonable, unrestricted access to the child by these or other similar means.

I. Whenever appropriate, the children's wishes will be seriously considered when decisions are made regarding their times and activities with each parent.

J. The parents will communicate regularly to discuss the needs and progress of the children. They agree to inform one another of significant
events during the time the child is with them and to do so before or at
the time the children change residence. This includes information about
school, activities, events, medications, or health needs as well as the
children's feelings, moods, and physical health.

3. Legal Terms Defining Parental Responsibilities and Authority

This is the most important clause in your plan. You state how you will divide or
share responsibility for the welfare of your child and how you will make
decisions on their behalf. Your jurisdiction may require a traditional term
such as "custody" or "visitation," as explained in chapter 11, or you may use
your own terms as the parents did in chapter 14. If your jurisdiction requires
you also to designate how you will handle making decisions (as described in
chapter 11), this needs to be identified. Remember, choosing a legal term
can be tricky. These terms will determine your rights and responsibilities *if*
your plan is not detailed enough. A detailed plan reduces the significance of
the legal terminology. Read your state law. If you don't have a family law
attorney, you may want to have a consultation with one to advise you on
your choice of terms.

4. Religious Affiliation and Training

*Instructing a child in a religion or a structured belief system is a major decision
and should be treated as one.* When parents disagree, they may delegate the
decision to the parent who has the greatest interest or a particular affiliation.
Many parents who wish their children to have a specific religious or philo-
sophical upbringing will write something like "We agree that the children
will be raised in the _____ [name of faith] faith." Some will also add
something like "The _____ [mother, father, both parents] will be responsible for _____'s [child's name] religious education." Day-to-day decisions
need to be made about transportation and costs associated with membership. These should be itemized with a statement describing how these will
be shared or divided. For example, "Transportation will be provided by the
parent in residence and all costs will be divided equally between the parents
[or by one parent]."

5. Basic Education and College

*Basic education means preschool and K through twelfth grade. Choosing any
school is a major decision.* Will only one or both parents attend school
conferences and receive report cards and report card reviews? Who will be
listed on the registration and emergency card, who has access to information
and records? Who will bear the costs such as fees, tuition, transportation,

uniforms, supplies, equipment, or school projects? Later in this chapter you will see an example of how these day-to-day costs can be shared in a plan. Many parents make specific financial commitments to support a college education even though the law may not require it. Parents should decide what will be funded (books, tuition, fees, transportation), whether there are requirements for student performance and behavior, and how each parent will fund his or her share of the cost for the college education.

6., 7. Medical Care, Dental and Vision Care, Insurances

Choosing a doctor, dentist, or health practitioner, decisions on long-term treatments, surgery, access to medical information, and providing medical insurance are all major decisions. Some parents share these decisions, others place them in the hands of one parent. All competent parents should have the ability to bring their child to emergency care if needed. Health insurance is often provided by the parent with the better insurance plan. Health-related costs are important to identify. Perhaps one parent is paying the insurance premiums, but there are still decisions on how the co-payments or extra costs will be paid. Will you share everything or divide costs (for example, one takes prescriptions, the other takes co-payments or costs not covered)? Appointments and transportation decisions are usually handled in private agreements.

8. Insurance (Life, Auto, Special Requirements)

Parents may want to identify the children as beneficiaries of their life insurance. Older children who drive may require additional policies or increased payments on the auto insurance. Some sports require that additional insurance be carried by a family. Identify if one or both of you will make these decisions and bear the costs.

9. Child Care, Nanny

These are major decisions and come with major costs. Will one or both of you choose child care, interview and choose a nanny? Costs can be in addition to child support or figured into the child support amounts.

10. Time Spent with Each Child by Each Parent

Time is given top priority in a plan due to its legal terms. You must itemize your overnights and the other times listed below. Do not use general terms such as "reasonable" or "frequent," be specific. Some parents use a calendar as a worksheet, and most others add the calendar to their plan. The amount of child support is often tied to the number of overnights in each home. Be sure your plan covers weekdays and weekends for all those areas shown here not marked optional:

School year (if child is of school age—overnights, together time, activity time)
Summers (overnights, together time, activity time)
Holidays (overnights, together time, activity time): Include Halloween, Thanks-
  giving, Christmas, New Year's, Good Friday, Easter, spring vacation, winter
  vacation, Hanukkah, Passover, High Holy Days, Chinese New Year.
Three-day holidays (overnights, together time, activity time): Presidents Day,
  Martin Luther King Day, July Fourth, Memorial Day, Labor Day, Veterans
  Day, Columbus Day
Birthdays (child and parent), special days (child and for parents)
Provisions for unscheduled times at child's request (optional)
Provisions for unscheduled times at parent's request (optional)

Parents should consider meeting in November to create a master calendar for January 1 through the end of school year and March or early April for summer through the end of calendar year. This creates a concrete and predictable schedule that can be posted at both homes.

11. Transportation to and from Parents' Houses

This is one of those pesky items that can throw off a working partnership between parents. Costs for buses, trains, planes, gas, and wear and tear on the car can become troublesome issues, as can where to meet, who travels where, and when. These arrangements should be specific and clear.

12. Location of Residences and Terms for Moving Away

This is always a major decision. Without a legal clause here, one of you might be able to move out of the area with the children with little notice to the other parent. Check the regulations and statutes in your state. The court generally keeps jurisdiction for custody, contact, and support until the child is eighteen or graduates from high school (in some jurisdictions the age is twenty-one).

13. Financial Contributions (Child Support)

This is a major decision. Many states have set guidelines and formulas for determining child support. Usually both parents' net incomes after taxes and Social Security are entered into a table or computer program that determines the child support range per child. You and the other parent can justify any amount of support you like, but the court may not accept, or is prohibited from accepting, a figure below the lowest range. Although the legal definition of support may be different in your jurisdiction, the financial contribution to raising a child (child support) is often thought of as *direct support* and based on "support guidelines." It is money paid to a parent. *Indirect support* is where a parent pays the cost of health insurance, partial or full payment of medical, dental, and drug costs, and provisions for college or school tuition. It is money paid for a bill. This can also be part of your legal financial settlement. *Some plans include cost-of-living increases and costs for special needs or increased costs as children grow older.* Some people will put their financial matters outside of their parenting plan and into the marital settlement agreement to avoid mixing the issues.

14. Duration of Agreement and Revisions of the Plan

A parenting plan filed with the court is legally binding until one of you goes to court and obtains a modification of part or all of the plan. However, if you and the other parent agree on changes, you can simply go ahead and do them. The key words here are "If you and the other parent agree on a change."

15. Resolution of Disputes Arising from Agreement

This is a major element of a good plan. Try to include this. One popular approach is the following: "If any disputes arise between the parents concerning this agreement or regarding our children's upbringing, they will first attempt resolution by mutual discussion. If they do not agree within _____ [days, meetings, hours of discussion], they will see a trained mediator. If agreement has not been reached within _____ [number of meetings, hours, or weeks], they will submit their dispute to binding arbitration by a mutually acceptable professional within _____ days." (Or "they will consult their attorneys regarding further legal action.") Going to court should be the last resort.

16. Sanctions or Penalties if the Agreement Is Violated

This is a major element of a good plan. People can be very creative with this. Missing a scheduled time when a parent is to be responsible for the children without trading or substituting time could mean an increase in child support to cover sitters' fees. Ask others what they have done.

17. Tax Consequences of Support and Residential Time

There can be long-term consequences that should be looked at here and provided for in a good plan. Many parents discuss the tax consequences of spousal and child support or the use of "family support" assignments. Discussions with an accountant, lawyer, or financial adviser will tell you the tax consequences in the proposed Plan for time and residence.

18. State and County of Venue

This must be clearly stated in your parenting plan. The state and county of venue is a crucial decision. State laws about custody and support differ, so choose your venue carefully. If there is a problem, this is the court where you should return to try to obtain a solution.

19. Periodic Review and Evaluation

Provisions for regular reviews of the Plan every 2–2.5 years for school-age children, more often for younger children should be included in order to make adjustments for your child's development and changed circumstances. Many parents build in more frequent reviews of the Plan—for example, every six months, when they meet to set up a master calendar, as described previously in "Time Spent with Each Child by Each Parent."

20., 21., 22., 23., 24., 25. Death of Parents (Wills, Guardians), Provisions for Catastrophic Events, Protracted Illness, Drastic Income Loss, Surnames, Statement of Paternity

Making out wills and designating guardians in the case of the protracted illness or deaths of one or both parents is sometimes included in a plan. Remember, the death of one parent automatically designates the other natural parent as the sole custodian of the children. Provisions for surnames may be included. If parents are unmarried, a statement of paternity is added.

26. Parents' Access to Information and Records

A well-written clause can assure parents of continued access to medical, educational, and other records.

SPECIAL PROVISIONS

By this time you are probably thinking, I do *not* want more things to think about. I'm up to my ears now! If this sounds like you, take a break. Remember, what you are experiencing these days is nothing less than redesigning your life and the way you parent. Your parenting plan is a cornerstone of this foundation. But do come back to this later because the following "clauses" can prove useful to review even if you don't use them in your plan or your private agreements. Also check chapter 14 for an example of how special provisions were included in a plan, and appendix 4, Private Contracts, in part 5 for additional clauses.

Parents can add provisions that expand their minimum parenting plan to address certain "hot spots." These could also could be part of a private agreement, described later in this chapter. Some parents use special clauses in their plan on who keeps medical appointments for the children; others want ground rules for changing schedules, sometimes even about the children's clothing. Each family has its own set of circumstances. Don't be shy about designing your own clauses.

THE "RIGHT OF FIRST REFUSAL": MORE TIME WITH YOUR CHILD

"I get off work at four every day. She doesn't get home until six P.M. Rachel should be with me, not a sitter," said one father. "I don't want him in my house when I get home every day," complained the mother. While this couple could not agree on an everyday arrangement, they did agree that on the days when Mom would not come home until eight o'clock, Rachel would be with Dad, but at his house.

> ### RIGHT OF FIRST REFUSAL
>
> *When a parent needs to engage a baby-sitter for more than _____ hours or overnight, the other parent first has the option to have the child with him/her— the "right of first refusal." The nonresident parent is not obligated to care for the child during the resident parent's absence but does have first right to do so over that of an appointed child care worker. If the nonresident parent chooses to be with the child, no reciprocal trading is expected. If he or she does not choose to be with the child, the resident parent proceeds with his or her plans for a child caretaker.*

MAKING APPOINTMENTS OR DECISIONS THAT COMMIT THE OTHER PARENT

"David is making doctors' appointments for the kids on my times with them. He doesn't even call to ask if I can get off work to take them," said one mother. "Gemma signed Greg up for softball without even consulting me," complained one father. If this sounds like you, think about this clause.

> *A parent will not make an arrangement or commitment that will involve the other parent's time, effort, or expense without first obtaining agreement from the other parent. The only exception is reserving a spot in an activity pending the other parent's approval.*

CHANGING SCHEDULES AND TRADING TIMES

All schedules change from time to time. It's part of a normal life, and flexibility is a critical element in allowing your children to make decisions about times with each of you. Many parents find the "trades" or changes frustrating if they have not discussed how to make these changes fair to them while also meeting their child's needs.

We agree that we will change the schedule during the other parent's designated time only by mutual consent. When a change in our basic arrangement is desired, we will make it in the following manner:

1. The parent in residence during the time in question has the final say regarding any changes during his or her time.
2. When a parent desires to trade time with the other parent, it should be for "like" time—for example, weekdays for weekdays, vacation for vacation days, weekends for weekends.
3. The parent agreeing to the proposed trade must give the parent asking for the trade two or three options for the makeup time. The parent asking for the trade has to accept one of them.
4. Traded time should be made up within four to six weeks.
5. If a parent is out of town for more than two days and nights during the time the children are supposed to be with them and a trade has not been arranged, the other parent has the right to have the children with him or her with no reciprocal trading necessary.

DANGER SIGNALS AND EVALUATING HOW THE PLAN WORKS FOR YOUR CHILD

A new parenting plan after a separation is an experiment. It should always be reviewed. Some parents find that their disagreements over their children's time are settled when they agree on regular evaluations *and* the danger signals they will look for. For example, one couple with a toddler were deadlocked on overnights. The father insisted that he needed to see her often, including overnights. The mother insisted that her daughter needed to live in one place with a regular routine and that the father could see her at her home for several hours a week. They came up with a temporary arrangement but also identified what signs they would look for (see chapter 10) to gauge how well their child was doing with this arrangement. Within two weeks they were already reevaluating their plan and making changes. The toddler was fearful, not eating properly, crying excessively. Waking time with her father was increased to eight to ten hours over the week. This was more than the mother had expected. Overnights were reduced to once every two weeks. This was less than the father had expected. They agreed to try this for two weeks and reevaluate again. They were learning how to watch for the signs of what worked for their child. As the child grows older they will certainly be adjusting the times again.

PARENT MEETINGS FOR SHARING INFORMATION

In addition to provisions for reviews of the calendar and the plan, some parents put a schedule of dates for weekly or monthly meetings. For example, *"The parents will meet either in person or by phone the first and third Wednesdays of every month to discuss the children's progress."*

PRIVATE CONTRACTS

The private contract route is used by some parents. A private contract is a composite of those things that a legal contract would not contain but that nonetheless may be important to your family's reorganization. A private contract can be for two, four, six, or twelve months. It can be something you do privately or in mediation. It is most often used by parents who have been separated less than a year. It is one of the ways they structure the way they relate to one another. One example is shown here; appendix 4 itemizes several more.

SHARED HOUSE RULES

Married parents do not always agree, so it may seem unrealistic to expect divorcing parents to agree on shared house rules. But many divorcing parents insist on shared rules. "The kids now know we have the same expectations that we had before," said one father. "Their mother and I agreed we didn't want to confuse them any more than we already had. They can count on most of the same rules in both houses." If you can agree on at least *some* shared house rules, you will be giving your children more consistency and continuity.

HOUSE RULES FOR OUR CHILDREN

It is our intent to maximize consistency between our households. Although each parent shall determine the rules for the children's behavior when the children reside with him or her without interference from the other parent, whenever possible we will construct and follow common house rules and discipline guidelines. We also agree to do the following:

• Bedtimes in each home will be between _____ and _____.
• Curfew for school nights in each home will be between _____ and _____.
• Discipline for minor problems will be limited to _____. Discipline for more serious problems will be limited to _____. We agree to immediately discuss serious situations and to support one another in following through.
• If a situation arises where our child's behavior needs discipline at both homes instead of one, we will come to mutual agreement regarding that course of action and follow it up in both homes.
• We agree that if a discipline or a house rule problem arises with a child, the other parent will support the resident parent's stand. If the child calls to complain to the other parent and/or wants to leave home, the nonresident parent will support the resident parent's stand until the parents can discuss the matter.

This chapter has shown you the anatomy of a parenting plan, identified additional topics you may want to add, and explained the use of private contracts. The next step is thinking about exploring how you can negotiate your own plan with the other parent. Get out your paper and pencil. You may want to take notes.

Chapter 13

How to Negotiate Your Own Agreements

A Step-by-Step Guide

Short-Term Private Agreements
Ten Tips on How to Negotiate
Major Steps for a Short-Term Agreement
Negotiating a Short-Term Agreement
Legal Agreements and Parenting Plans
The Long-Term Parenting Plan
Guidelines for Your Negotiations
Some Final Considerations

SOMETIMES negotiations are time-consuming but relatively easy. "We did not have a real relationship for so long," said one father, "that after we separated, it was fairly easy to come up with arrangements for our daughter. We were just going to keep on doing what we had been doing as parents, only now living separately."

But other couples are not this detached. "Making all these decisions and having to talk about every little thing is hard," said one mother. Perhaps one or both parents think that continuing their former pattern of parenting is unacceptable. "I want to be a more active father," said one man. "I know I can do it well, and my kids need me."

Yet one or both of the parents may be so deep into negative intimacy that they can't even agree on who gets to keep a favorite CD. How can they come to an agreement on sharing or dividing the responsibilities for raising their children?

Well, they do. Many parents do find ways to make these decisions despite their hard feelings. This chapter is designed to help you negotiate with one another. It begins by walking you through your first short-term private agreement and offers tips on the negotiating process itself. Then, in the last half of the chapter, you will have a chance to see how a long-term, legally binding plan can be worked out.

SHORT-TERM PRIVATE AGREEMENTS AND LEGALLY BINDING PARENTING PLANS

A short-term private agreement is for a brief period of time and, unless you file it with the court, is not legally binding. It is a private agreement between you and the other parent that gives the children and you a schedule and some structure to hold things together for a trial period. You all have a chance to see how it works and think about what you want for the longer term.

Long-term parenting plans or even "temporary" agreements filed with the courts are legal documents that have the force of law behind them. In some states a temporary agreement is filed early in the process. In other states nothing is filed with the court during the separation period. In these cases, a temporary document is in the form of a private legal contract between the parties. This private contract or a memorandum of understanding is made part of the final divorce decree at the time of the divorce. That may be a year or more later.

The first short-term agreement and the later legal parenting plan are usually closely related efforts. The short-term agreement covers perhaps no more than one-third of what the long-term plan covers. But what you accomplish in your short-term agreement can be used as part of the long-term plan and help make the long-term plan far easier to design.

START WITH SHORT-TERM DECISIONS AND INFORMAL AGREEMENTS

If you are just now separating, the unevenness of the crisis months lends itself to a healthy fear of making long-term, permanent decisions. The wisest alternative is to start with short-term temporary decisions. Come to agreements you can live with (or are willing to try to) for two or three months at a time. When the two or three months are up, revise your agreement and make a second plan for another two or three months. Two or three such short-term agreement periods can give each of you a chance to weather the ups and downs of the crisis stages, give you experience in making and living with your mutual arrangements. Once you have both passed the crisis periods and have a good idea of what seems to work, you can negotiate a long-term and legal parenting plan. When that time comes, you will have already acquired firsthand knowledge of what you want, what you think you can live with, and how to negotiate with the other parent.

CONSIDER FAMILY MEDIATION EARLY

Are you especially uneasy about attempting to negotiate privately with the other parent? Are you or the other parent having major difficulties retreating from intimacy or developing your businesslike relationship? If yes, consider family mediation (chapter 15). Usually, the earlier you start mediation, the better the outcomes.

SHORT-TERM PRIVATE AGREEMENTS

ATTORNEYS AND MEDIATORS

Do you want to negotiate your agreements yourself? Do you want to hire an attorney to represent you? Do you want to see a mediator? If one parent engages an attorney, the other parent will probably feel obliged to do so, too. If only one attorney is used, the attorney can ethically represent only one of you. He or she cannot represent both of you at once. As you could see from the chapter on what goes into parenting plans, certain aspects of parenting plans and marital settlement agreements require legal wording. You will have to choose: Do you want an attorney to review your agreement for you or to represent you? You may be able to find an attorney who will provide limited "unbundled" legal consultation or services for you. Appendix 2 has a series of guidelines for choosing an attorney. Chapter 15 will help you choose and work with a mediator.

Fees for services are a major issue that can snarl any negotiation. Think through who will be responsible for the fees. Don't leave the question of who pays whose fees until the last, since this can become a major bone of contention. Realize that these professional fees may be a major item in a divorce budget, and plan ahead for them. If you can't come to an agreement on your own, have this as your first issue in mediation.

TEN TIPS ON HOW TO NEGOTIATE

1. Be businesslike, keep emotional control.
2. Find ways you can both get what you want.
3. Watch your timing.
4. Find what motivates you.
5. If he or she doesn't follow an agreement, put "teeth" in it.
6. Use the HIRT test.
7. Try to find a FASTUR solution.
8. Show your children that mature adults can resolve differences.
9. Plan meeting times, their length, and the meeting place carefully.
10. Be kind to yourself.

1. Be Businesslike, Keep Emotional Control

The legal process married you. It also can divorce you, but it will not mend your heart or soothe your feelings. Any expectation that the legal process will somehow make a person feel better is not likely to be met. Past chapters have given you some guidelines to consider and ways to soothe your feelings. Most important of all: Keep your cool. You can lose a great deal by a loss of emotional control, and you may undertake actions that will prove disastrous to you, your children, and your legal rights.

Don't let any out-of-control feelings cloud your legal status or your decisions. For instance, if you threaten your partner with harm, you may lose access to your children, gain an arrest record, and pile up more legal fees. If your feelings are leading you to a legal, physical, or emotional fight— run, do not walk, to a therapist, mediator, or counselor who will help you find a way to work it out outside of the legal arena. If that person can work with your lawyer, so much the better. Remember, feelings are feelings. They are not always good guides for action.

2. Find Ways You Can Both Get What You Want

The old competitive approach to negotiation is a "win-lose" strategy where the most clever, determined, or most powerful party wins. This rarely succeeds in getting people the results they want in a custody or divorce action. The approach that is the most constructive is one where *both people* and their children are given as much of what they want and need as possible. This "win-win" approach is, in the end, collaborative, not cutthroat. If this seems like an unlikely fantasy, think again. Keep trying to retreat from your former intimacy, and put as many of the business principles in practice as you can as soon as you can. Eventually you should be able to see some progress on the "win-win" course. No one has everything, and no one will get everything. Choose your options carefully, and *always look at what you can give to your former mate that he or she values and that is good for your children.*

3. Watch Your Timing

Timing is important. If you or the other parent are in the "off-the-wall" stages of emotions, or if you are deeply enmeshed in negative intimacy, real settlement without a third party keeping you on track will be difficult if not impossible. You might even have good discussions, but the timing is not right for one or both of you to come to an agreement. Paradoxically, methodically bringing a businesslike approach to discussions often calms things down and more agreements result! But the timing has to be right.

There is also a time when you may be *willing* to talk with the other parent, but you *may not be ready* to make decisions with him or her. Or the situation may be reversed. This hesitation is natural—be patient with yourself and, when possible, with the other parent. *You may be willing to begin discussions, but you are not yet ready to complete them.* This gradual unfolding is built into the process, thus the repeated suggestion that you read all the chapters in this book before making decisions. Motivate yourself to wait through the *waiting period* to the *settling period.*

Even when you are ready and willing to settle, your partner may not be. Common complaints heard are "He keeps losing the papers for our meetings" or "She forgets to call me back." Such things keep happening when one parent is not yet ready to move to the next stage of the reorganization process or when a power imbalance exists between the partners. In the latter situation, the only way to gain (or keep) a position of power is to stand pat or stall.

People trained in business know this matter of timing well. Their past experience has prepared them for the shifts in negotiations, the willingness to discuss, and the reluctance to settle quickly. They can draw on that experience now.

4. Find What Motivates You

Some of us may be prepared or motivated for this family reorganization marathon with a store of experience in human relations, tenacity, or wisdom developed outside the business framework. Some parents are unconsciously motivated by memories of their own parents' divorce. "My parents had a terrible divorce. I won't put my own children through what I had to suffer." "My father deserted us and I grew up without one. I won't let that happen to my own son."

Look through your own past for any experience or belief that can motivate you to be patient. While you are waiting for things to develop, remind yourself that as frustrating as this period of time may be, it is also part of the pulling apart and reorganization process and, as such, is part of the price of divorce or separation.

5. If He or She Doesn't Follow an Agreement, Put "Teeth" in It

Is keeping an agreement a problem for you or the other parent? When one parent fails to follow through, it costs the other parent time, money, reduced mobility, and opportunities, not to mention the hurt and disappointment felt by the children. The financial burden of unpaid bills or times missed with the children becomes a forced form of unawarded spousal support. How important is it for you to have "teeth" in your agreement?

"Teeth" is slang for written statements on what will be acceptable alternatives, substitutions, and compensations when the agreement is not followed. If an agreement has "teeth" built in, it may help parents keep agreements and rebuild mutual respect. The Standards of Conduct and Trading Times in the last chapter provide some examples of these consequences.

Many good and caring parents can't always keep an agreement. Dad might get the flu and not be able to take Junior on a weekend. Mom might start school and tell Dad she just can't drive Junior to his house every Tuesday and Thursday night as she had earlier agreed. Another dad might not show up at all to bring his daughter to dinner; another mother might frequently leave her son in day care past the seven P.M. closing time. There is a big difference between the actions of these parents. To gauge how hurtful your situation is, try the HIRT test.

6. Use the HIRT Test

H = How **Hurtful** is your problem? If Dad has the flu, he won't be able to look after Junior. This situation is not truly hurtful. But when parents neither show up nor call for a scheduled time with their child or frequently leave their child past the day care closing time, they are hurting their child.

I = How **Intentional** is this transgression? Dad didn't intend to get sick. When Mom agreed to the transportation, her school schedule was different. These parents do not "intend" to do harm. Yet some parents have been advised, warned, even admonished about how their actions have hurt a child, but there has been little or no change. When this happens, score one for "intent."

R = Does this parent **Repeatedly** not follow the agreement or do hurtful things to the child? The number of times this happens is a major clue to how serious the problem is.

T = Is this a **Tactical** move by either of you? Do you believe that these actions are to gain some type of undue advantage, to get revenge, or to avoid responsibilities?

If your situation can't pass the HIRT test, you must put "teeth" in your legal agreement. There has to be a change for the better for your child. Specific sanctions or remedies written in your legal agreement will help you get that change.

7. Try to Find a FASTUR Solution

F	be	F lexible and Fair
A	be	A ctive
S	use	S ubstitutes
T	make	T rades
U		U nderstand and be Understood
R	be	R espectful

Be **FLEXIBLE** and **FAIR**, but balanced. One can't expect perfection anywhere, so try to be flexible with small things. If the agreement is not honored by a parent, try to find out why. If possible, see if there is a way to work it out. Or agree to compromise for a week or a month, but not permanently. Too much compromise may not be good for your child. At some point, especially if it doesn't pass the HIRT test, you have to take a stand. Flexibility and fairness in negotiations are major virtues as long as they can more or less cut both ways and are equitable. This does not mean caving in. But an overstrict interpretation of an agreement can be self-defeating. A parent who insists on primary custody, for example, can be flexible on extra overnights and together time with the other parent.

Being **ACTIVE** in negotiations is a must—be in there! Actively develop different alternatives for how to meet your needs and those of the children. A dad who thinks up three different scenarios to consider on sharing time during the school year is being active. One of these is likely to be close to something Mom would seriously consider. Be especially active in finding ways to overcome HIRT.

Find **SUBSTITUTE** ways to solve the problem. For example, several parents have arranged for child support contributions to be at a high level when Dad can't take either of the children as agreed. The contributions are at a far lower level when he can put in the time. Time is money to some parents, and money is time. Substitution, however designed, should be fair. Some people say, "I can't put a price tag of time or money on my children." But other parents don't see the checks and balances as a price tag; they see it as a way to continue to work together while respecting each other's lifestyles. Short-term agreements are a good time to try things out.

TRADE some of the times, trade some of the responsibilities—for example, the sample clauses in chapter 12 and the guidelines for trades. Help each other out. If Dad must miss a weekend, or Mom is unable to have the children back at the designated time, have an alternate game plan. Perhaps Dad, with Mom's permission, can take a makeup weekend within a month. Mom might drop out of evening driving times with Dad's permission but pay him back with an extra day of time at Dad's house or driving the kids round trip. If you don't take the other parent for granted or impose repeatedly on one another, trades can work quite well for everyone. There is more than one way for just about anything. Look at how you can trade times when your schedules are changed unexpectedly. A quick review of chapter 11 will spark your thinking.

Try to **UNDERSTAND** the situation from the other parent's perspective and treat him or her with **RESPECT**. Most garden-variety deviations from the Plan are just normal, everyday happenings in today's world. They are not federal offenses. Try a FASTUR solution. The core of good negotiations is how we understand and respect one another. Everyone responds to situations differently, and no parent is a star in every parenting realm. *Try to build your plan for raising your children based on each other's strengths.* You probably know your former mate's habits well. Communication is not just words, it is also tone, feeling, body language. Can you communicate in a way so that he or she can understand you? And can you listen so you can understand?

If you can genuinely respect the other parent's point of view, you will be able to understand more. *You do not have to agree or even like what you understand. But step back and respectfully play back what you hear. Then ask, "Did I understand you correctly?" You may be surprised at the answer you receive.*

8. Show Your Children That Mature Adults Can Resolve Differences

When parents are in conflict, their children feel it deeply—even when they don't show it on the outside. When parents cannot eventually resolve their conflicts or at least agree to disagree, children are demoralized and emotionally injured. They often feel they are to blame. Further, children begin to believe that if their own parents can't solve personal problems, perhaps things are hopeless, and one can escape through drugs, violence, or mental illness.

When you take the time and effort to work hard on solving your differences, either with a mediator or by yourselves, you not only improve your chances of a settlement, you also give your children a role model for the future. Your children will see two people they love giving their best efforts to handle a painful and difficult time in their lives. You give them a precious lifelong gift that says even the toughest situations can be handled decently and that "things can eventually be worked out." Conflict that stays unresolved between their parents is the most damaging effect of separation or divorce on children. It can affect them their entire lives.

9. Plan Meeting Times, Their Length, and the Meeting Place Carefully

1. Remember to choose a meeting time that suits your partner and yourself. Don't make it the end of a long hard day or when you are hungry.
2. Limit your discussion time to from thirty to forty-five minutes. *Stop* at the end of that time. Emotions can get out of hand after twenty-five or thirty minutes, especially if you are working without a mediator. If you are on a roll, let it go another fifteen to thirty minutes.
3. Cover only *a few items* in one session. Agree on an agenda beforehand. For your first meeting, discuss those items you are most likely to agree on.
4. Hold the meeting in a neutral place or one where everyone feels comfortable, perhaps a public place like a quiet restaurant or a park.

10. Be Kind to Yourself

As you do all the background work needed to negotiate an agreement, a number of feelings can surface, some pleasant, some unpleasant. This is to be expected. As one man put it, "Just thinking about arrangements for summer camp reminded me of our troubles that summer we separated. I got depressed." It may be difficult to think because so many feelings crowd in. If this is happening to you, take just a few items at a time, limiting your thinking period to as little as fifteen to thirty minutes. Then go on to some other project and come back perhaps in a day or so to the next set of items. You may also want to review chapter 6.

HOW TO BEGIN

Ask yourself the following questions:

1. What issues about my children are most important (chapter 9)?
2. Will the children have a vote in making decisions (chapter 10)?
3. Do I want to consult an attorney or a mediator for a short-term agreement?
4. Who will pay the bills for a lawyer, mediator?
5. What do I want for a short-term agreement?

MAJOR STEPS FOR A SHORT-TERM AGREEMENT

1. Using the guidelines suggested, both parents negotiate a trial period of one or two months and establish a regular but flexible schedule when the children will be at Dad's house and at Mom's house. Often who stays in the family home is negotiated as well.
2. The parents develop their own standards of conduct for autonomy, noninterference, and territory. They usually agree that when the children are with one parent, that parent is to take full responsibility for their care and welfare. The children are to clear plans with each parent during his or her time. Statements of noninterference by each parent are usually restated to reaffirm respect of the other's parent-child relationship and of each other's territory.
3. A one- to three-month calendar and/or a short-term agreement is written out and copies are made and signed by both parents. Each parent keeps two copies, one for the "working relationship" file, one to spare. *A calendar or a list of times with each parent and activities should be posted where everyone can see it.* Perhaps on the family bulletin board or refrigerator door. This is most important.

4. A simplified version of the house rules between the two homes and important aspects relating directly to the children's time with each parent should be written up so the children can read and refer to it. These can be posted above with the calendar.

The parents either independently or together describe the arrangement to the children, including the dates, times, and details regarding clothing, meals, and needed moneys. The parents ask for feedback from the children. If there are serious reservations, the parents may want to confer again and make adjustments. Teenagers are often invited to participate in part of the short-term agreement process. Younger children usually have a chance to be heard—even if they don't vote.

When the trial period ends, adjustments are made in the schedule and another trial period is determined. (Often the original arrangement is extended with few changes.) Again, the agreement is confirmed by both parents, and a new calendar with dates and times is posted for the whole family to refer to.

NEGOTIATING A SHORT-TERM AGREEMENT

PREPARING FOR A SHORT-TERM AGREEMENT NEGOTIATION

Gino and Marlene are the parents of Julia, seven, and Jimmy, ten, both in private school. They have been separated for three months after ten years of marriage. Both are committed to working toward a decent divorce. Both know they have to get some type of schedule for the children. Gino's list looked like this:

GINO'S PREPARATION

Kids in our meetings?   Not for next few months.

Attorney or mediator?   Yes, I want an attorney.

Money for lawyer?   I don't know yet.

Short-term agreement?   For two months to settle things down. Need some ground rules between Marlene and me.

Long-term plan?   Later, I need more time to think about it.

Long-term goals for kids?   Get a college education, stay out of trouble.

What's best for them now?   Try to keep the routine the same, at least for now, go through old house rules again.

I WANT A SHORT-TERM AGREEMENT ON THESE POINTS

1. calendar for two months
2. money to live on for both of us
3. doctors' appointments and medical insurance payments
4. other medical or dental things that need to be settled right now
5. summer vacation dates for both of us
6. try to keep as many things the same as possible for the kids the next few months.
7. some standards of conduct, especially not interfering, and house rules for kids

MARLENE'S PREPARATION

Kids in our meetings?	Maybe the oldest at a special meeting to explain the calendar.
Lawyer or mediator?	Yes, I want a mediator if things don't look good after the first meeting.
Money for lawyer?	Not sure.
Short-term agreement?	Calendar for times, standards of conduct, and safety rules at Gino's.
Long-term plan?	Can't think about this now.
Long-term goals for kids?	Too much to think about now.
What's best for them now?	Keep things stable much as possible.

I WANT A SHORT-TERM AGREEMENT ON THESE POINTS

1. calendar with times with the kids
2. financial support for expenses and the bills that have piled up
3. summer vacation arrangements
4. free time for me and the kids—I need weekend time
5. standards of conduct for us, house rules, and safety rules for the kids

GINO AND MARLENE'S SHORT-TERM AGREEMENT

Before their first meeting, Gino and Marlene each reviewed the checklist "How to Prepare for a 'Parent-Business' Discussion" in chapter 8 and the "Guidelines for Your Negotiations" given later in this chapter.

First Meeting

Marlene and Gino held their first meeting via telephone after the children were asleep. Both were uncomfortable. They had earlier agreed on talking for no more than thirty minutes about things they usually agreed upon anyway: house rules, the calendar for times with the children, and their own ground rules. (See chapter 9.)

Marlene said she would first like to work on the ground rules for the children, and Gino asked her to read off what she had in mind. After hearing her list, Gino added two items. The house rules were very close to what they had when they were living together. Marlene agreed to write them up and fax them to Gino for his review. Gino wanted to post them on the refrigerator door in both homes so the children would see what both parents expected of them. Marlene agreed. Next, Gino wanted to talk about standards of conduct for noninterference and respect for one another's territory, privacy, and parenting. Marlene wanted to get the calendar worked out. They tossed a coin and Gino won.

Gino read off his ideas on standards of conduct. When it came to discussing the level of interference in one another's parenting style, things became tense. This was an old issue. She felt he was too easygoing and didn't supervise the children closely enough. He felt she was never happy with his parenting regardless of how he did it. After a few minutes of "negative intimacy," Marlene realized that they could put this on hold and go on to the other standards of conduct, such as respecting each other's territory and privacy. Gino agreed, and they completed them easily. They had been talking for twenty-five minutes, and it was nearly time to stop. Gino suggested that they do a calendar for the next two weeks quickly and then put that first on the agenda for their next meeting. Marlene agreed. A two-week calendar was no problem. They set another telephone meeting for seven days later. The agenda would be the calendar on the kids' time for at least two months, some issues around the orthodontist, and health insurance. Marlene reminded Gino that they had to make decisions about whether the kids would participate in any of the meetings. They had not yet talked about using attorneys or a mediator. The meeting ended with a greater tone of mutual respect. Even though these were things they had historically agreed upon anyway, Gino still felt more hopeful about future meetings.

Agreements completed: house rules, children; ground rules (for parents) (one remaining item); two-week calendar.

Second Meeting

The agenda was a full one. Marlene suggested that they make some priorities. The calendar was first, the kids' vote second, the orthodontist third, using attorneys or mediators fourth. If possible, they would talk about health insurance. The parents realized their children spent time in many different places. Gino said, "I didn't know how much time the children spend away from home." He wanted the children with him every Thursday night through Monday morning when he brought them to school. Marlene understood that he wanted time with his children, but this didn't leave her with any free time with them. They compromised. They would be with Gino every other Thursday through Monday morning, and on his off weeks he would pick them up at 4:00 P.M. on Thursday, have dinner together, and then bring them back to their mother's home. They agreed Gino would mark up a calendar and send it to Marlene. Once she reviewed it, he would make any changes, then send her a copy. Their thirty minutes were up, but they decided to go five or ten minutes longer. They agreed to tell the children about the calendar and to ask them what they thought about it. Since neither parent had enough cash in the checking account to cover the orthodontist bill, Gino agreed to pay by credit card but said that the responsibility for the bill would be another item to negotiate at a future meeting. Both parents were glad to have their agreements but also relieved that their discussions were over for now.

Agreements completed: calendar—next three months; children's vote on a case-by-case basis; immediate payment of orthodontist bill.

GINO AND MARLENE'S SHORT-TERM PRIVATE AGREEMENT— CHILDREN'S VERSION

Times at Mom's House and Dad's House—February, March, April

Every other Thursday through Monday morning will be with Dad, the rest of the time with Mom. Dad will pick you up after school on Thursdays at 4:00 P.M. and bring you to school Monday A.M.
Times at Dad's House: Feb. 14, 15, 16, 17, 28, 29
Mar. 1, 2, 13, 14, 15, 16, 27, 28, 29, 30.

Homework, bedtimes, and TV rules are the same as before.

Softball: Just like before. Dad will take care of the league activities and will see to practice, transportation, games, and costs.

Ballet: Just like before. Julia will make the arrangements with Mom for transportation and costs. When the lessons are during the time at Dad's house, Dad will provide the transportation.

Extra Times: There may be times when one of us wants to spend extra time together. Let's talk about this when it comes up. If the time is at Dad's house, please remember to talk with him first, and if it is during Mom's time, please talk to her first.

Short-term agreements can be a major relief. They can settle things down. They are a step forward to the legal parenting plan. It may be a big or little step, but it is a step in the right direction. And they may make your negotiations for the permanent plan far easier.

LEGAL AGREEMENTS AND PARENTING PLANS

The long-term parenting agreement or plan and the temporary legal agreement are both legal documents. Unlike the short-term private agreement, these are legal documents and as such bind you to all the conventions and expectations you find in the law. Therefore there is more to think about *and* the consequences are more far-reaching.

THE TEMPORARY LEGAL AGREEMENT

A temporary legal agreement, generally, if you have one, outlines support for the children, the spouse, times with the children, and who gets to stay in the family home, and it makes an assignment of "custody" with "visitation" for the period of time between filing for divorce and final hearing. The expectation is that these are arrangements that will be modified with a permanent marital settlement agreement and attached Parenting Plan.

THE TEMPORARY CUSTODY DECISION THAT IS NOT TEMPORARY

"The lawyer told me it was only a 'temporary' custody order of sole custody—but I was stuck with it permanently." Countless times I have heard fathers who sought a permanent order of joint physical custody report that their desires were undermined by a temporary order that traditionally designated the mother as "sole custodian" and gave her authority over major decisions. If you have a "temporary order" that gives one parent sole custody, you would be wise to check into this. Often what arrangements you have now for the children—if they are working—will continue to stand if they have been in force long enough, regardless of what was promised verbally out of court or explained in conversation. Because judges are usually concerned with preserving continuity and security for a child, a change can be seen as unnecessarily disruptive. If you have a temporary order more than a few months old, beware.

THE LONG-TERM PARENTING PLAN

"I had a great motivation to reach my own private agreement on custody directly with the children's father," said one mother. "I figured if I didn't make these decisions with him, someone else would do it for me. And that someone else just can't know me or my situation as well as I do. The lawyer can hassle the property agreement, but I want to control my private life myself."

This mother was reflecting on a hard fact inherent in our legal system. When people cannot come to their own decisions, outsiders, less knowledgeable about their strengths and needs, will have to make the decisions for them. This fact alone can motivate a parent to plod through the details and negotiations that a good plan requires. Because there is a good deal to think about at once, the usual steps are itemized here.

FIRST, CONSIDER WHAT YOU WANT FOR A PERMANENT PLAN

What you accepted for the short term may not be what you are willing to live with in the long term. This is why it's a good idea to take your time to think it through.

1. Read Chapter 12 on Parenting Plans Again

Give yourself time to go over the different areas that require your decisions. Even if you are feeling impatient, at least read through the list of basic elements of what goes into a parenting plan in chapter 12, including the special provisions. Few people use all the options offered, but you should know what is possible. For some people, getting a handle on it all is quite therapeutic. *Do this first review alone,* without the other parent. This is your time to think things through by yourself.

2. Go Through the Parenting Plan Items in Chapter 12

Ask yourself the following about each item:

- Do I want to *share* this with the other parent? If yes, to what degree?
- Do I want to *divide* this? If so, in what proportion?
- Do I want to let this issue go by, *leave it to chance?*
- How does this *fit into my goals* for my child?
- What would be *best for my child now?* Could I create a better situation?
- *How long* do I want this in effect? Two months, six months, one year, or two years?
- Do I want to put in some "teeth," provisions for *noncompliance?*
- How would I feel if I were the other parent looking at this list?

3. Now Make Two Lists for Yourself, a READY and a NOT READY List

Things I'm ready to talk about—my "ready list."

Things I'm not ready to talk about—my "not ready list."

On the ready list include those decisions and situations where you are clear about what you want, what you would compromise on, what is the least you could accept, and what would be the ideal arrangement. The not ready list is everything else—whatever is explosive, ambiguous, where you need more information. The ready list and not ready list will be of great help to you in discussions with your lawyer and in your negotiations with the other parent.

4. Go Through the Ready List a Second Time

Put a check mark next to those areas you think you and the other parent already *agree upon.* These items should be the first things you talk about with the other parent when you begin to negotiate the plan.

5. Finally, Go over Your Ready List and Ask, *"What Is Best for My Child Here?"*

This second time, think it through from the point of view of your child.

6. Be Clear and Explicit

Your formal agreement must have explicit descriptions of what you mean. Saying your child will be with a parent Thursday evening through Monday morning is barely good enough. It should be from "Thursday at six P.M. to Monday morning when brought to school or to the other parent." Be especially careful with general terms such as "reasonable rights of visitation." This phrase is common in legal agreements. But what does it mean? What is "reasonable"—does that mean three hours a week, a day, a month? Who decides what is reasonable—the father, the mother, a third party? How does "visitation" work—does it mean the other parent has full responsibility during the period the parent and child are together? Can one parent have total authority over the time the child spends with the other parent? Can one parent refuse to exercise his or her visitation rights? When the terms are vague, they are open to many interpretations. People can disagree on exactly how it works, and the avenues are wide open for argument about what is "reasonable" and what is "visitation." Your own formal agreement should be the opposite of this. *While you may agree privately to be more flexible, an explicit formal agreement can provide a starting point for a later give-and-take.*

7. The Clarity of Your Plan Is Your Responsibility

You construct the definitions, make them clear to one another (and to your advisers), and *then put them in writing;* don't transfer this task to a mediator or lawyer. You will all have a better chance to live more happily with what happens in actual practice if you take this extra step of being specific and then writing it out. **If you need to, put in "teeth."**

8. Sleep on Your Decisions

Put the lists aside for a few days. Then review your ready and not ready lists and reconsider your decisions. This second look is important.

9. Keep a Record of Your Lists

Make sure they're dated and placed in your personal legal files. Your future discussions will generate new versions of the ready and not ready lists, copies of which should also go in your records.

If you think you can skip over these steps, consider this: If you don't put in the effort at this stage, you may have to put in three times the amount later. Think of it as having the responsibility for designing a new house for yourself. You have to have decent blueprints and plans for wiring, plumbing, appliances, foundation, drainage, structural integrity. Even when you turn over everything to a contractor, there is still a pile of things to decide on, and they just keep multiplying. Just as in building your own house, you may find that the separation or divorce process can require an extraordinary level of effort and demand for detail. But you are constructing a blueprint of your children's future and your life with them as a parent. It's a worthy effort.

A SAMPLE READY AND NOT READY LIST

Three months after Gino and Marlene negotiated their first short-term agreement, both began their ready and not ready lists. Gino's list is shown here as an example.

Gino's Ready List

Things I'm Ready to Talk to Marlene About

Standards of Conduct	Refine the ones we have now. They seem to be working. Put them in our long-term plan.
Education	Teacher conferences, homework, access to information and records, who checks up on Julia's grades. I want this to be either mine or shared with Marlene.
Medical and Dental	*Insurance*—I'll keep paying it. *Access and information from doctors*—I want full access, and I want to share decisions on major health problems.

Lessons	Julia's lessons—continue as it, I'll pay the bill. Jimmy's karate lessons are okay.
Recreation	Jimmy's softball team—I want to keep doing what I'm doing here and I'll take the expenses.
Communications	No restraints regarding phone calls or seeing kids.
Time Spent with Parent	School week and every other weekend at her house, every other weekend at my house, beginning Thursday nights and ending with my taking them to school Mon. A.M.; I don't know about the exact times.
Transportation	I'll pick them up at the house and bring them back.
Geography	I'm moving two miles away. It's biking distance to school.
Contributions	*Direct contribution*—follow the state's standards for support. *Indirect contribution*— the medical insurance, Julia and Jimmy's lessons, and the softball thing.

Things I'm Not Ready to Talk to Marlene About

Lessons	I think the fencing lessons are a waste of money. Ballet is okay.
Religion	I want them confirmed in my faith, not hers. That means a major argument.
Education	The cost of the private school is just too much. I want them in public school.
College	I'll pay for tuition and living expenses only if they go to state-supported schools. Another major argument.
Life Skills	The kids are too sheltered by their mother.
Holidays	Not ready, too touchy.

Custody	Definitely want joint custody, perhaps even split time.
Contribution	More than $800 a month is too much for me to keep up too long; I won't compromise on this. Marlene should go out and work.

GUIDELINES FOR YOUR NEGOTIATIONS

CHECKLIST: PREPARING TO NEGOTIATE A LONG-TERM PARENTING PLAN

1. Make ready list and not ready list. Check off those things you have already settled or think you agree on. These are what you should start your negotiations with—remember: easiest first, hardest last.
2. Do your homework on money and the cost of raising children. (See appendix 3.)
3. Decide, do you want your children involved in long-term plan decision making?
4. Decide, do you now hire a lawyer or mediator? Who pays the bills?
5. Decide, what are your long-term goals for your child (chapter 9)?
6. Decide, do you want to include any standards of conduct, special provisions (chapter 12)?
7. Decide, do you want anything in a private contract (chapter 12)?
8. Get the information on your state's custody, visitation, and child support laws and decide what you want.
9. Find out the legal route your private parenting plan must take before it can be incorporated into your court order.
10. Obtain a sample paragraph or the advice of a lawyer regarding the change of residence of one parent out of town, to another state, or to another country to put it in your final plan.
11. Take the time to look over the self-test again (chapter 7) on your retreat from intimacy. If your score shows too many hot spots, use a neutral third party for the beginning of your discussions, or delay your discussions until things improve.
12. Try to have at least *one* previous short-term agreement that has given you the experience of how the principles of discussion and negotiation can work for you.

READY? SET? GO.

Review the guidelines "Ten Tips on How to Negotiate" earlier in this chapter. Go through the checklist above. Check your feelings. Cool off if necessary. Give yourself a brief refresher on how to develop a business relationship, as described in chapters 7 and 8. Plan your meeting time, place, and agenda. Take a deep breath. Stay calm and respectful, and start your discussions with the other parent.

FIRST AND SECOND MEETINGS: WHAT TO COVER

1. Bring your versions or your thinking on the following:
   • *All your answers to the "Checklist:* Preparing to Negotiate a Long-Term Parenting Plan" (above)
   • *Standards of Conduct:* privacy, noninterference, your territory
   • *House Rules* for the children
   • *A calendar* for marking times with the children
2. At your first meeting, decide whether or not you will include your children in your discussions or your decisions, whether or not to use attorneys or a mediator.
3. Start with the *easiest decisions where you are most hopeful of agreement.* A good place to start could be any house rules and ground rules where you think you both agree. Then go to your "ready list."
4. Save the difficult decisions for later or the last meetings.
5. When you discuss a subject, *give each other at least two real-life examples of how it would work.* Don't stop at generalities; be specific.
6. Do not expect that the other parent carry out an activity that you and you alone want for your child. (Mom shouldn't be expected to transport their son to the softball game if Dad wants this to be his activity with him.)
7. Select one of you to be the "secretary" for each meeting.

WHEN YOU COME TO AN AGREEMENT

• When you come to an agreement, write it down. A simple sentence will do, but it *must be specific. Get details.*
• If you are uneasy about something you have agreed on, and if it is an issue that lends itself to short-term trials, try it out only for a few weeks before you finalize it in a long-term plan.
• Identify how long you want this agreement to hold. A trial period of two to three weeks is very useful for short-term agreements. But if you are negotiating a longer-term agreement, specify the months or years it should be in force.

- Specify how you will evaluate your agreement or plan down the road and how you will modify it.
- Expect some false starts and some setbacks. No person or discussion is predictable or perfect.
- Each issue you agree on is a building block in the foundation of your new working relationship for your child. Honor this. It is a real accomplishment.

WHEN YOU DISAGREE

- When you disagree, look for the ways each of you could give in a little. A "take it or leave it" attitude is not negotiation—but a reasonable compromise is.
- Try the FASTUR approach explained earlier.
- If you don't come to an easy agreement, don't belabor the point too long. The timing for its resolution may simply not be right for today. Put it on hold, and try again at a later meeting.
- Think about the way you can build trust and good faith with the other parent; try trading assurances, explained in the chapter on mediation.
- If you are attempting your first short-term agreement, this is not the time to settle anything once and for all, especially those things you have not agreed on for a long time. If a settlement and compromise happen spontaneously, consider it a windfall.

AT THE END OF EACH MEETING

- After each meeting, the selected "secretary" should make a copy of your agreement, date it, keep one, and send one to the other parent for confirmation. Keep all your agreements and other paperwork in a special file folder. Careful record keeping is important.
- Set a time for your next meeting. Set a tentative agenda. Try to feel appreciation for the other parent's efforts. Tell this to him or her, and try to be genuine when you do it.

WHEN YOU HAVE REACHED AN AGREEMENT ON ALL YOUR ISSUES

- Make a simplified (and *edited*) copy of your agreement for the kids to read and use. At the least, have a calendar posted at both homes that shows times with each parent.

Congratulations! *Negotiating your own parenting plan is a tremendous accomplishment.*

SOME FINAL CONSIDERATIONS

UPDATING AND MODIFYING PARENTING PLANS AFTER COURT

The legal plan should be as good as you can make it. But parents can relax just a bit when they understand that even the most flawless plans change as the years go by. Parents either do this privately or choose to go through the courts again. As time passes and your working relationship with the other parent becomes a way of life, you may find that it is easier to work out exceptions and changes on your own. When that happens, go ahead and change the plan between yourselves privately. As long as you both agree, this is acceptable. Fall back on the plan if you run into trouble. The court may consider modifying parenting plans when there is a "change in circumstances," or a child's needs have changed. But first try to adjust your plan yourselves or with a mediator.

REVISE YOUR TIME ARRANGEMENTS AT LEAST EVERY TWO YEARS

Children grow, change, go away to school. Babies and stepchildren come into the family, people leave. Make it a point to review and revise your parenting plan at least every two years.

ALL PARENTS DISAGREE SOMETIMES

Parents who develop a working relationship after separation don't agree on how everything will work. Far from it. But neither do other parents who are still together! Disagreements are normal. *What parents do learn is to agree on how to disagree.* Sometimes they reach a compromise, sometimes they simply take turns. "My way this time, your way next time." They may also agree to take no action at all and allow the disagreements to stand as they are. Try to put your disagreements in perspective, and move on to the next chapter, which describes how one couple completed a long-term parenting plan on their own.

Chapter 14

A Long-Term Parenting Plan

Working out an Agreement on Your Own

The Meetings
The Result: A Parenting Plan
Wording Your Agreement
Your New United Front

"Hard work and I are not strangers," said one father in the midst of negotiations with his child's mother. "But this is far more work that I thought it would be. It is not just the information and decision making, it is having to talk to her and controlling myself, being businesslike, trying to do the best for my kids. Every time I think I can cut a corner, it comes back to haunt me, demanding even more of my time. I'll be glad when this is over."

Regardless of whether parents use attorneys to negotiate for them or whether they do it themselves, parents are surprised at how demanding it can be to work out an agreement about the children—not just because of the process itself, but because it brings into play all the things that were so difficult in the relationship: the differences in values, in child-rearing styles, in their hopes and dreams for their child. No wonder many parents decide to use a mediator early in their negotiations. But many other couples do negotiate their plan by themselves or have only one or two unresolved items for their mediator or attorneys.

This chapter gives an example of a couple able to complete a plan on their own. If you are thinking of negotiating on your own, try to have at least one previous private short-term agreement. Prior experience goes a long way toward smoothing the path of negotiations. Our next chapter will help you understand mediation. For now, let's consider the case of the Brown family.

Diane and Tom Brown are the parents of eight-year-old Jason and six-year-old Rachel. To prepare for their initial meeting, they followed the guidelines from part 2 on how to relate to one another and have answered nearly all the questions included in our last chapter's "Checklist: Preparing to Negotiate a Parenting Plan." Here is where they are now.

- Both have updated "ready" and "not ready" lists.
- After seven months of separation, both have a greater appreciation about money and the cost of raising children in two homes.
- Each has an opinion on whether or not to involve Jason and Rachel.
- They have already agreed on when to use a mediator and attorneys and on paying their fees.
- They have had several exchanges on e-mail about their hopes and dreams for their children.
- Each has ideas on whether or not to include any standards of conduct or special provisions in their plan.
- They already have a private contract. Four months ago they put one together on what to do when a child complains to one parent about the other.
- Each parent has obtained information on the custody and visitation laws in their jurisdiction. Tom has already talked to a lawyer about the child support guidelines and has a computer printout on the ranges of payments.
- Diane has found out that their privately negotiated parenting plan, if properly formatted, can be attached to their agreement on property, assets, and debts (the marital settlement agreement).
- They do not have a sample paragraph or the advice of a lawyer regarding the change of residence of one parent out of town, to a different state or another country.
- Diane is somewhat farther along on her "retreat from intimacy" than is Tom. But both are eager to get a long-term plan.
- They have negotiated two previous short-term agreements that have worked out more or less, and they have some ideas about their shortcomings on negotiating.

They have done a good deal of homework, but they still have a lot to do. They know that their previous not ready lists contain some sore subjects that may require the help of a mediator. They are now, seven months after the separation, sometimes acting as parents who can share parenting, sometimes falling back into a "parallel parenting" pattern, where both are active parents but still find it difficult to be at school events at the same time. Diane now has a new love interest in her life, and this is painful for Tom. But Tom feels he is now in control of his feelings enough to start negotiations. They agree on the purposes of their plan.

PURPOSES OF THE PARENTING PLAN FOR TOM AND DIANE

- A long-term legal parenting plan that meets the needs of their children.
- A plan that formalizes a shared parenting relationship.
- A plan that makes both active responsible parents, who maintain two homes where the children belong and are cherished.
- A plan that gives the children a good example of how parents can resolve conflict.

By phone they discuss the information they have received from their local family court services department. They talk about the pros and cons of the private mediators each has seen and talked to and decide to choose one of them if their discussions bog down. They also agree to hold back on negotiating the property settlement until they have completed their parenting plan. (More affluent couples may find this holding back unwise.) Each agrees to contact a separate lawyer for continuing advice but not for negotiating per se. They set up their first meeting with the following agenda: "Compare notes on laws and support guidelines, talk about standards of conduct and special provisions."

THE MEETINGS

FIRST MEETING

At the first thirty-minute session they compare their information on the law, their rights, and support guidelines. Their laws do provide for joint custody, but only if parents agree to it. People they talked to disagreed on what different legal terms meant. Often parents find that the information they have received from different sources may be ambiguous, seem unfair, or even sound contradictory. Recognition of these inconsistencies sometimes helps people to appreciate better the wisdom of private negotiations.

Both parents see that the questions of property, assets, and child support may be the biggest snags in their discussions, and they agree to leave them till the end—possibly for meetings with the mediator or, if necessary, to be left to the attorneys. Even if Diane and Tom decide to leave the money issue to the last, they have done their homework. This will make it easier for attorneys or a mediator to work with them. This couple does not have any past due monies between them, but they do need to think about how later fees for attorneys will be handled. Tom doesn't know it, but Diane may ask him to pay her attorney's fees.

They used up their first thirty minutes just talking about finances, the laws, and the guidelines. They agreed to go another ten minutes to explain their individual views on standards of conduct and special provisions. They would talk on the phone about them later. Diane asked Tom to look at the "Special Provisions" section of chapter 12, especially the part about making appointments and changing schedules. They set a time for their phone meeting. Both Tom and Diane were businesslike in their discussions, even though they were feeling tense. Tom had felt especially anxious.

SECOND MEETING—BY PHONE

In preparing for the phone meeting, Diane felt herself at first resisting all of Tom's proposed standards of conduct. She and Tom had certain standards they followed anyway; she actually agreed with all but one of them. She realized her reaction was not because of the standards themselves, but because Tom wanted them. She wished she had thought of it first. She remembered the FASTUR solution and realized this was where she could be flexible and give Tom something he valued. When they had their phone meeting, she told Tom she agreed with all his standards but one. Tom agreed to keep that one out for now but said he wanted to revisit it later. Diane wanted two special provisions in their plan: "Making Appointments or Decisions That Commit the Other Parent," "Changing Schedules and Trading Times." Tom wanted "Right of First Refusal." Both parents wanted something that expected them to review and update the Plan, perhaps every year. Diane wanted to draft the special provisions. Tom at first resisted, then agreed, knowing he would be looking them over before they agreed on the final version. Tom and Diane had been using the private contract idea for four months. They had put one together on what to do when a child complains to one parent about the other parent. It helped, but both of them felt they needed more. The parents tossed a coin to see who would write up their agreements to date and then fax or mail them to the other one. They set up a date for their next face-to-face meeting. Their agenda: whether the children should be present at any meetings, the legal terminology, and to compare ready and not ready lists if they had time. This meeting was successful but strained. They kept emotional control, were respectful, and looked for ways to be flexible. Both told friends later how tired they felt after the meeting.

THIRD MEETING

Their third meeting, in person, was less tense. They knew that they had already made progress. Both, however, were careful to stay with their agendas and keep their discussions structured. This kept their emotions in check. So far, of course, Diane and Tom had done nothing that they wouldn't have had to do even if they'd had attorneys handling the negotiations— except that they were saving on attorneys' fees.

Diane and Tom talked about the children's participation in their discussions. They believed the children should know about them but were not in agreement about how they might be part of the negotiations. They shelved the question for the present. They also looked at the question of custody and the way their state looked at joint custody. They decided that they wanted to have their plan describe their agreements as clearly as possible. They agreed to push their attorneys for the joint physical custody award if such legal terminology needed to be substituted for their own layman's language of "joint responsibility." Finally, they agreed that if the court needed a temporary custody label, it too would be "joint physical custody." They pledged to one another that they would not undermine their hope for two homes with a sole custody to one and visitation to the other in any initial court order. This gave Tom a big sense of relief. He was fearful that Diane might change her mind and follow her sister's advice and go for sole custody. Their time up, they decided to try some of the next agenda items on the phone. Using the "easiest first, hardest last" rule, they found several items on their ready lists that they had already agreed upon. These would be their agenda items for the next few meetings.

They were wise in not extending their thirty minutes of time together. Privately Tom was feeling some impatience, while Diane was working hard to keep control. A couple needs to stop talking before old feelings begin to grow too strong.

FOURTH MEETING—BY PHONE

Once Diane and Tom began discussing the children, they found their ready lists and the previous negotiations lent themselves to relatively easy early discussions. "Do we divide it, share it, or ignore it?" Education was on both their ready lists. They discussed and reached agreement on which school for the children, costs and supplies, homework, decisions, access to information and records, teacher conferences, report cards, activities, discussions. Tom—the recorder for this session—wrote down: "We agree that the children will continue to attend the ABC Schools in Port Swatterly and continue with the same teachers." Then Diane asked if they needed to think about who would underwrite school costs, supplies, and special expenses. They chose to ignore these items and not mention them at all. If they became a problem, they could try to work out a private agreement. Next they looked at "teacher conferences, report cards, and activities." Although they still sometimes found it hard to be at the same events together, they both decided to attend teacher conferences, receive copies of report cards, and attend or remain active in school affairs. They went on to the next Ready item. The meeting lasted fifty minutes. Both Tom and Diane were feeling a sense of control over the negotiations now.

SUBSEQUENT MEETINGS

With each easy decision and area of agreement, a sense of common interest and respect can grow. Yes, the Browns have their differences and their hurts—but they also have areas of agreement, and these encourage them to continue. Note that as their negotiations go on, the Browns will use the equal status of joint physical custody but will divide the children's time between homes about one-third to two-thirds.

IMPASSE—EXPECT SOME BOTTLENECKS

The real differences between Diane and Tom come out with the not ready lists. It is harder to be businesslike now. The old arguments are back. Tom can't see why the children need so many lessons and special classes; Diane can't see why Tom is opposed to such advantages and wants only to emphasize "real world" skills for the children. Tom thinks the children are overprotected; Diane thinks they are overstimulated.

The "divide it" and "my territory, my philosophy" guidelines can help negotiations. If the couple adopts the principle of noninterference, Diane cannot dictate how Tom spends his time with the children, nor can Tom dictate Diane's parenting style. He has his own time to teach them about insurance, banking, negotiations with salespersons and merchants, and so on. Diane, on her time, and with her money, can arrange for the lessons she feels are important. But she may not arrange such lessons on Tom's time. As you cut the pie together, remind yourself that you can neither have it all nor tell the other parent how to eat his piece of it. But you can show respect and support for one another.

The money issue finally is put on the table. Tom doesn't want his money supporting an activity he disapproves of. Diane doesn't want her parenting style dictated by Tom's withholding of money. They are angry, rigid, and ready to give up. They reach an impasse on child support.

Here is where the out-of-control emotions and the "see why I divorced" justifications can bog down negotiations. Although the Browns had agreed on dollar amounts before separation, each is now having second thoughts. When parents reach no agreement in two meetings, they should cool off, try again, and if then unsuccessful, get in touch with a mediator. The Browns were close to having their entire agreement negotiated by themselves, but they needed some distance from the process and from one another. They agreed to set everything aside for ten days.

When the Browns met again, they were able to agree that they would leave the child support out of their plan and add it to their property and financial discussions with their attorneys. *It's common for a couple to near the end of their agreement process and get held up on even a seemingly minor issue. But it often is a symbol of that "old family feeling," of the reasons why they are divorcing, and sometimes it is also a way to stall the final stage of the move away from their former intimacy.*

The Browns spent several weeks on their parenting plan—drafting it, then reviewing and revising some of the wording. Their document embodies the special feeling that closes one kind of life and begins another. They talk with their children about the calendar and their schools and ask them for their opinions. The children have no serious problems with the agreement, and everyone feels more or less satisfied with the results. The Browns have the agreement typed in its final form and find a witness for their signing ceremony. They are now ready to present copies of the agreement to each of their separate attorneys. If their attorneys recommend changes in wording, they can consider their advice. Since their plan is still a private contract, they can all agree to amend it, if necessary, before marking it legal. They can then begin their property and financial discussions without further involving the child-rearing issues.

THE RESULT: A PARENTING PLAN

The Browns' agreement weaves many of the standardized forms and terminology of the two-home approach into different sections. It is a good example of how a couple can customize their own plan. Provisions missing from this agreement are those of a technical nature—tax exemption, child support, head of household assignment, life and auto insurance (for a child old enough to drive), catastrophic events, and the out-of-state clause. If you want to put these into your plan, consult an attorney and an accountant for appropriate clauses and then see that these provisions are incorporated.

THE BROWNS' PARENTING PLAN

Foreword: We, Diane Brown and Thomas Brown, the parents of Jason Eric Brown* and Rachel Susan Brown,* enter into this agreement in order to better meet our parental responsibilities and to safeguard our children's

---

* Birthdate of child can be added here.

future development. We both recognize that they need to love and respect both of us, regardless of our marital status or our place of residence, and that their welfare can best be served by our mutual cooperation as partners in parenting and by each of us providing a home in which they are loved and to which they belong. We also jointly recognize that court proceedings regarding children and custody and visitation matters can be detrimental to children, and we therefore have decided to resolve these questions ourselves, using this parenting plan. Finally, we have chosen to avoid the traditional terminology surrounding divorce and children by using terms that more accurately describe the reorganization of our family. Accordingly, we wish to instruct our respective attorneys, if necessary, to inform any courts involved in our dissolution that our desires are as follows regarding the custody and upbringing of our children.

1. Terminology

In order to reaffirm our commitment to our two-home status, we choose to use the terms "live with mother" and "live with father" in describing our arrangement, rather than the more traditional terminology of "custody and visitation."

2. Responsibility for Jason and Rachel

Jason and Rachel will be our joint responsibility. Both of us recognize that each of our contributions toward our children's welfare is essential, and we agree to cooperate with one another in establishing mutually acceptable guidelines and standards for development, education, and health. We agree further to discuss and decide all major issues jointly and that day-to-day decisions for the children will be the responsibility of the parent in residence.

3. Our Children's Residences

Jason and Rachel will live with their father every other Friday beginning at 6:00 P.M. through the following Monday at schooltime. The remainder of the time they will live with their mother. During the summer vacation they will live with their father the entire months of July and August with every other weekend with their mother except for an uninterrupted two-week vacation period with each parent. This schedule will continue throughout this year, unless their normal development seems impaired by this arrangement or they express a need for change, in which case we will review and reassess the arrangement. Changes in scheduled times at either home will require substitution of times of equal length and will be subject to our mutual approval. If an acceptable substitute is not found, the parent unable to be home with the children will hire a sitter or make arrangements with friends or relatives to care for the children during the period of his or her responsibility. When a parent needs to engage a child sitter for more than five hours or for overnight, the other parent first has the option to have the child with him or her. The nonresident parent is not obligated to care for the child during the resident parent's absence but does have the first right to do so over that of an appointed child care worker. If the nonresident parent chooses to be with the child, there is no reciprocal trading expected. Neither parent will make an arrangement or commitment that will involve the other parent's time, effort, or expense without first obtaining agreement from the other parent.

4. Standards of Conduct

The parents agree to the following: Both parents agree to always provide an address and phone number where they can be reached to one another and to all child care providers, so that each can be reached in an emergency; each will have access to all medical and school records and direct contact with personnel working with or caring for the children; neither parent shall do anything that would estrange the children from the other parent or impair the child's love and respect for a parent. Both parents are free to attend the children's activities even if the child is not residing with that parent at the time. They agree that each child will have unlimited freedom to communicate with each parent. The parents will regularly discuss the needs and progress of the children. They agree to inform one another of significant events during the time the child is with them and to do so before or at the time the children change residence. We agree to honor one another's parenting style, privacy, and authority. We will not interfere in the parenting style of the other parent, nor will we make plans or arrangements that would impinge upon the other parent's authority or times with the children without the expressed agreement of the other parent. Furthermore, we agree to encourage our children to discuss their grievances with a parent directly with the parent in question. It is our intent to encourage a direct child-parent bond whenever possible.

5. Medical and Dental

It is agreed that the mother will carry and pay all the cost of the children's medical health insurance. The father agrees to pay 75 percent of all medical costs over and beyond that covered by insurance. Dental costs will be paid by the mother. We also agree that transportation to medical appointments will be the responsibility of the parent in residence. We agree that although the parent in residence has final responsibility in making day-to-day medical decisions, the other parent is to be involved in all major discussions and decisions, and consulted and advised about illnesses or accidents.

6. Education and Child Care

Both parents agree that Jason and Rachel will remain in their present schools, and child care arrangements will remain the same for this year. Tuition costs will be the responsibility of the father; child care costs, the responsibility of the mother. We agree to attend teacher conferences on a rotating basis, to be active in school events as our schedules allow, and to both have full access to information and records regarding our children's progress.

7. Holidays

We both agree that the Thanksgiving holiday, beginning with the day before and ending the following Monday morning at schooltime, will be spent this year with the mother and next year with the father. We further agree that for this year Jason and Rachel will live with their father the first week of the December holiday period through to the twenty-seventh of December, when the children will be with their mother. Next year the situation will be reversed, and the children will spend the holiday period first with their mother. Other holidays, three-day weekends, school holidays, and Easter vacation will be shared equally. A master calendar with exact dates and times will be negotiated in March and October of each year.

8. Children's Activities

Summer activities will be the responsibility of the father and will be undertaken at his discretion and expense. School-year activities are anticipated to be ballet and guitar for Rachel and Pony League Softball for Jason. We agree to the continuance of these activities and will share the responsibilities for transportation, costs, and communications in the following manner: Jason's Pony League activities will be supervised by his father, and all costs incurred will be met by him. Rachel's ballet and guitar lessons will be the responsibility of the mother, and all costs will be met by her. Both parents will take responsibility for transporting the children to all activities regardless of where the children are living at the time.

9. Agreement Review, Time Period, and Renegotiations for New Agreement

We agree to review, and if necessary, modify this plan every twenty-four months. We both agree that this parenting plan is to be in effect a minimum of two years and is automatically renewable if no revisions are sought. If revisions are sought after two years, we agree that this agreement will be considered binding until a new agreement is reached. If unusual circumstances arise before the end of the two-year period, all or part of this agreement will be renegotiated, either privately or with the aid of a third party, given thirty days' notice, before either of us seeks modification through the courts. We further agree that, should any serious dispute arise between us relating to our children's education, health, or other aspect of their welfare, before either of us seeks modification through the courts, we will first seek the services of an objective third party, such as a trained mediator.

Date   Signature

Date   Signature

Date   Witness

WORDING YOUR AGREEMENT

Parents have used the sample parenting plan paragraphs in chapter 12 in several ways. Some use the examples just as they are and simply insert their own decisions in their own words. Others redesign paragraphs as the Browns did; still others build a total agreement from scratch. Some parents find the idea of a parenting plan also a good chance to materialize their joint philosophy on raising their children.

I suggest that you consider your own parenting plan in the same way that you might any other public document or ceremony, such as a ritual of confirmation, a graduation exercise, or a wedding ceremony. This agreement is your chance to both deal with the legal requirements and bring some kind of formal validation to your beliefs.

CONSIDER A TRIAL PERIOD

You may want to try out your agreement for two to six weeks or more before you finalize and sign it. Some parents find this test period useful. This should be not a hope tossed to a dissatisfied parent, but a genuine test run. Especially if you have young children, a test run can be a useful way to see how well the time schedule fits your child's needs.

MAKE IT AN AGREEMENT YOUR CHILDREN CAN READ

The words you use will make all the difference in how effective the document can be, both practically and psychologically. The importance of value-laden words and what have been called the "fear words" should not be overlooked. The new vocabulary changes the tone as it clarifies the role. Having "joint and shared responsibility" feels better than having "joint custody."

BEGINNING VOCABULARY FOR TWO-HOME LEGAL AGREEMENTS

Try Saying:	Instead of Saying:
Parenting plan or agreement	Custody agreement
Shared or joint responsibility	Shared or joint custody
Living with, live with, reside with	Visiting or visitation
Primary responsibility	Sole custody
Contribution	Child support
Primary-home parent; parent in residence	Parent with custody
Other parent	Parent without custody

THE EFFECT OF THE PARENTING PLAN ON CHILDREN

Some parents have reported certain calming effects that the actual parenting plan document had on their older children. "It was a pleasure to give it to my teenager to read. It's a positive, accurate document, and it showed her that we could agree on something." Another parent who had typed up a first draft of the parenting plan at home said that her fourteen-year-old son looked over her shoulder as she was finishing the typing and asked what she was doing. She explained that it was a parenting plan about him and his sister. When he asked, "Can I read it?" the mother reported, "It felt so good to say, 'Of course,' and give it to him. He seemed somewhat calmed by reading it." If the son had been handed a traditionally worded legal document, he might not understand the legal terminology or know what the document was for. It might even have frightened him. The simplicity of an agreement written in everyday terms, with the intent and details of decisions clearly spelled out, helps children as well as parents to understand and appreciate what to expect and what will be expected of them.

Since the document is about what will happen to your children, it stands to reason that children should have the right to read it and understand what it means to them.

TEN SIGNS OF A SOLID LEGAL PARENTING PLAN

1. The plan is clear and it details the parents' agreements on
   - time with the children
   - responsibility for their care
   - decision making.
2. The plan reflects the children's needs for continuity and security with both parents, his or her environment, peers, friends, school, child care, important activities, and extended family.
3. The plan contains the parents' intent, goals, or objectives.
4. The plan has examples that illustrate certain arrangements.
5. The plan has provisions for resolving future disagreements.
6. The plan has provisions for evaluating at regular intervals and updating or revising sections to adapt to the children's changing needs and your changed circumstances.
7. The plan has "teeth" when trust in keeping agreements is an issue.
8. There are provisions for trading times and/or unstructured times that the children can have with parents.
9. There are provisions for considering children's opinions and granting their wishes for flexibility regarding times together and activities.
10. The plan reflects the parents' commitment to continued parenting in a businesslike or cooperative manner.

YOUR NEW UNITED FRONT

PRIVATE AGREEMENT AND THE COURT'S APPROVAL

A private agreement, negotiated by parents either alone or with a mediator or by attorneys, can become a legal stipulation. This stipulation is a signed document, the form of which is often open to the creativity of the lawyer or parties themselves. The bottom line in a stipulation is that the parties have come to a mutually acceptable settlement of their rights, responsibilities, and differences. Now they want the court to approve and, if necessary, enforce the agreement.

When the court is presented with a stipulation regarding the care and upbringing of children, it often gives a rubber stamp approval. The general consensus is that parents know what their children need, especially when they can agree and have a plan for how it will work. The courts usually honor this expertise, even though the courts hold the right to review such documents and the power to order a modification if it seems desirable. There are exceptions, however, and some courts have established a review process whereby a trained professional reads every agreement before it is submitted to the judge. Your lawyer should be able to tell you what is customary in the court having jurisdiction in your case.

YOUR WRITTEN AGREEMENTS

A parenting plan often reinforces your family solidarity, increases your children's and your own sense of security, and maintains a sense of family continuity. That agonizing period of indecision or changing positions is finally over, and everyone can relax. Despite your adult incompatibility and disagreements, it shows you can come to a meeting of the minds when it involves the kids.

When parents go through the long and demanding process of thinking through their situation, they go through many steps. They have to take the time, effort, and thought to cover the series of questions about the children and themselves. All by itself this review leads to a sense of accomplishment. When you go further to discuss *and* negotiate your own parenting plan, you earn a well-deserved pat on the back and a sense of true satisfaction. If I could, I would want somehow to reward all the good efforts of parents everywhere who steadfastly, sometimes grimly, persevere in their job of sorting out their personal feelings about one another from the issues of money, children, time, and energy. Their accomplishment is magnificent and worthy of high praise.

"It feels kind of sad," said one father as he looked at his final parenting plan. "I didn't want the talks to end because it was a way for us to be together again, I guess. But if we had to end, then this is the best way I know to do it."

Chapter 15

Family Mediation

Getting Help to Stay out of Court

"I DIDN'T want to go to court, so I knew mediation was my best chance to work out our problems with joint custody," said Elaine, a mother of a fourteen-year-old son. "I was very nervous when I went into the mediation session because my husband can be so dominant. The mediator was good at keeping control of who talked how long, but I was still exhausted at the end of that first session. It took three meetings and all the energy I had, but it was worth it. I have a parenting plan I can support and I feel better about things."

"Mediation was something I thought they did in labor or business disputes," said Richard, a father of twin boys aged seven and a daughter three. "There were so many hard feelings, I didn't think it would work for us, but it did. I think we both calmed down and listened to each other. The agreement we came up with is much better, I think, than what we would have done if we had gone to court."

Most people have heard about mediators who are called in to help resolve disputes between a teachers union and a Board of Education or between employees and employers. Family mediation has the same underlying premises. The mediators usually have a background in law, counseling, psychology, or social work. Their job is to help families in conflict step back, take a look at their circumstances, and, come up with their own solutions. When mediation works, the parents avoid court contests and come away with a written parenting plan they can make legal. The structure of some types of mediation can also help parents build a businesslike relationship with a positive parenting pattern. The mediator can serve as a facilitator and witness to this critical passage.

WHAT IS FAMILY MEDIATION?

Family mediation is a process where an objective and impartial third party works with the family to help them resolve their disputes and come up with a formal written agreement. The parents and mediator meet together from one to three or more hours at a time. Sometimes all it takes is one long session, other times three or more sessions. It all depends on the circumstances of the family and the style of the mediator.

If both the parents have been able to retreat successfully from their former intimacy, they probably don't need a mediator or a third party to resolve their differences. But they might want to use a mediator to help them organize their agreements and a lawyer to formalize them and advise them on legal* or tax considerations. Other couples can agree on all but a few things and use a mediator for those remaining disputes. Mediators are often quite flexible, and many are happy to work with limited issues or specialized aspects of a parenting plan.

Mediation is not for everyone, but when it works it can save you time, energy, stress, and usually money. It is far less stressful and adversarial than going to court, and it helps avoid "being divorced until death do you part." Many, if not most, family courts either require or allow mediation for parents who are deadlocked in disputes over the children. There is good reason for this: Mediation can work to bring about greater understanding and more mutually acceptable agreements. When it works, everyone benefits.

This chapter will describe mediation, answer some frequently asked questions, and then show you how it can work for you.

TYPICAL MEDIATION GROUND RULES THAT FAMILY MEDIATORS UPHOLD

1. Each person has ample opportunity to talk. The mediator should be sure that no one dominates the mediation process.
2. Each person is expected to be courteous and respectful, not just to the mediator, but to one another.
3. Each person is expected to try to put aside stronger feelings and deal with the issues in a systematic, unemotional manner. There should be no threatening attitudes or behavior.
4. Each person is expected to follow the mediator's procedures for the meetings and to complete homework assignments.

---

* For example, the consequences of using terms like "custody" or a clause about a parent moving away with the children.

5. All negotiations are to be based on sound and adequate information. Each person is expected to collect and disclose all of the information pertinent to the issues.
6. Each person is expected to listen to the other person's point of view.
7. Each parent is asked to think first about the children. Their best interests should be the focus.
8. Everything that happens in mediation is considered confidential.

HOW MEDIATION CAN HELP YOUR CHILDREN

A successful, or even partially successful, family mediation can give you two things: first, you will be able to have a full or partial parenting agreement or plan that you can submit to the court for approval and often a written set of private house rules, that you may not have been able to negotiate on your own. Second, you may also emerge with a spirit of compromise and a renewed sense of direction and purpose. The effort alone demonstrates your desire and commitment to do the right thing for your children. The children see their parents cooperate with a clearer sense of which parent does what and when. Things get a new version of "normal." The parents benefit because they have stayed in control of their own decisions, and their family affairs have remained private and confidential.

Tensions are eased. Many people report that they have finally been heard by the other parent, sometimes for the first time. There is a greater appreciation of the other person's point of view and a sense that you can agree to disagree and still be good parents. This all can lead to a gradual calming down of the most intense emotions. Parents can feel that they are more in control of their lives and children can feel a greater sense of security. This change of tone is real progress.

MEDIATION FOR COUPLES WHERE THERE IS VIOLENCE

If there is violence or a serious threat of violence in the relationship, mediation is probably not a good idea unless certain strict conditions are met. More on this below.

FREQUENTLY ASKED QUESTIONS

WHEN YOU SHOULD CONSIDER MEDIATION

Mediation is very helpful when one spouse seems to be successful in retreating from intimacy but the other person is still laboring with negative intimacy, or when both people are still affected by the ups and downs of the emotions of separation or divorce. Some couples, separated for a while, even years, may be trapped in a nasty negative intimacy cycle or even be "hostility junkies." These last situations make communication almost impossible. Sometimes a couple can talk, but nothing important about the children gets resolved, or resolutions dissolve within days or weeks. Believe it or not, mediation helps. Mediators are trained to deal with these dynamics.

"I was skeptical about mediation," said a father of three. "The children's mother overreacts at the drop of a hat, and I lose my patience. We could not seem to have a rational discussion. But the mediator knew how to handle us. I learned some things about how to talk with her, and we got an agreement we both think is best for the kids. I'd do it again."

WHEN TO AVOID MEDIATION

Mediation is not a magic cure, especially when you have the following problems:

- You have experienced incidents of shoving, hitting, slapping, battering, or sexual assault with your former mate.
- You feel seriously threatened, manipulated, or intimidated by your former mate. Most people feel psychologically manipulated at times, but do you fear physical harm? How serious are these threats?
- You have reason to believe that you cannot trust the other parent to be honest in negotiations or to work with you in good faith.
- You believe that if an agreement was made, the other person would ignore it or flout it.

DOMESTIC VIOLENCE AND ABUSE

If you or your family have problems with violence, substance abuse, or child physical or sexual abuse, mediation is not the way to settle your differences about divorce or the children. Assault, battery, and sexual abuse are exceptionally egregious criminal offenses. But also remember that false allegations are also a crime. These are all special problems that require focused investigations and very specific actions from you and from the courts. Working with the resources provided by a battered women's shelter, a rehabilitation program, an attorney, or a counselor is going to be more helpful than using a mediator. Even if the allegations are false, the level of fear or distrust that comes from false allegations will often undermine mediation.

Some courts and private mediators will work with couples who have some of the problems listed here, but only when the physical safety of all is secured. Parents might come to agreement on supervised visitation, a rehabilitation therapy, random drug testing, an anger management group, or parent education. Or the mediator may just be able to calm things down temporarily.

Consider your situation carefully, and don't take unnecessary risks. Ask whether or not the mediator has adequate security backup, and make sure you have ample security traveling to and from the mediator. Does the mediation allow for support people in the mediation itself or for sessions separate from the other parent? Under no circumstances accept a mediation where your safety or rights to due process are compromised or you fear attempts at mediation might make things worse.

I usually give in just to keep the peace. Will mediation work for me?

It depends. If you have a difficult time identifying what you want or what you think is best, you must describe this barrier to your mediator before you begin. A mediator could agree to work with you to help you negotiate or suggest an alternative more suited to your situation. If you do decide to mediate, consider having an attorney in addition to the mediator. If you are still uneasy, see if the mediator and the other parent will allow someone else to negotiate for you. Otherwise, mediation may not be for you.

I don't have much trust in the other parent. Will mediation work for me?

For mediation to be useful, there should be sufficient trust in the other person's willingness to be honest and to play fair. Some relationships have an undertone of threats or intimidation, but no physical violence. People say such things as "If I insist on more time with the kids, she'll run away to her mother's three hundred miles away" or "If I say I want half of the stock options, he'll get very nasty and try to get custody."

On one hand, you could find that mediation is a major step forward because a skilled mediator can cut through the fears and clarify the real issues for you faster and more effectively than the legal system. On the other hand, you might find yourself in a situation where one or both of you are civilized in the mediation session but anything goes as soon as you walk out the mediator's door. If subtle feelings of intimidation or manipulation keep you from articulating effectively, be sure to tell the mediator. When one or both of the parents is unable to speak up for themselves, the mediator must be able to bring some overall balance into the negotiations. If this is not possible, then either that mediator or the mediation process is not for you. Keep an open mind, but be ready to leave mediation if you don't feel it is working for you.

Are there different ways to do family mediation?

Yes. Mediation can differ in both the styles of the mediator and in the circumstances of the family. One mediator may have one or two ways of conducting mediation, while another mediator may work with each family quite differently. While a few graduate schools are including mediation as a discipline, most family mediators are usually attorneys or mental health professionals who have gone on to include mediation as either a subspecialty or as their primary practice. Mediation is usually conducted by a mediator alone and occasionally by two mediators acting as a team—for example, one is a lawyer, the other is a mental health professional, and sometimes a man-woman team. Court-connected mediation may have certain restrictions, such as what can be mediated or the number of sessions. More on court-connected mediation later in this chapter.

What qualifications do mediators have?

A few states or jurisdictions have legal requirements or set standards for training or certification requirements for mediators. Others do not. There are many places where anyone, regardless of background or lack of training, can hang out a shingle and advertise as a mediator. It is wise to beware. Your state or jurisdiction may or may not have standards of practice or require certification or continuing education of mediators. Many courts expect their mediators to meet certain qualifications, such as a master's degree in counseling, social work, or a related field and a minimum number of years of experience. Private mediators may or may not have had formal training followed by a period of supervision. Mediators from any background can obtain training offered by experienced mediators and go through an academic or formal training program.

What is the difference between mediation and arbitration?

In mediation, the mediator is impartial, makes no decisions on the issues. He or she works to help the parties negotiate fairly and come to mutual agreement. Attorneys who represent the parties are rarely present at mediation sessions.

In contrast, arbitration is where the arbitrator, a nonjudicial officer, takes the role of a judge and hears both sides of your case and makes a decision that is either binding or nonbinding. The hearing is usually outside of the court and nearly always about property and support rather than custody. Arbitration is often conducted with attorneys representing each side. You can usually choose beforehand whether arbitration is nonbinding or binding. Nonbinding means you can appeal the arbitrator's decision.

What is the difference between mediation and therapy or counseling?

Therapy and counseling are very private, ongoing processes that explore feelings, emotions, motives, and behavior. Mediation is focused on solving specific problems. It usually takes from one or two to six meetings of one to three hours each. The two parties develop a contract on what they agree to do in the future. It is not about changing feelings or motives, although this may happen as a side effect of reaching agreements or being able to state one's perspective. The goal is to resolve a dispute while managing the emotions surrounding the conflict. Feelings are usually acknowledged, but they do not take center stage.

What is the difference between court mediation and private mediation?

Court mediation is often free. When fees are charged, they are usually based on ability to pay. You are assigned a mediator, you do not choose one. The court may limit the hours or number of sessions available per case and may limit the issues that you can bring to the negotiation table. For example, your mediation may be limited to one to three sessions and will deal only with your disagreements about the children. Each jurisdiction has different policies, so call and ask for information. Most courts have brochures they will send you in the mail. If you decide to use court mediation, ask first what happens if you don't reach an agreement on all your issues. In some courts, the mediator will be required to talk to the judge about your case and make a recommendation to the court. The judge takes the mediator's information under consideration and then, after listening to both parties in court, will make a decision.

In private mediation you select the mediator yourself. You pay the mediator whatever fee he or she sets, and there is usually a good deal of flexibility regarding the number of sessions and where they are held. Some private mediators may limit their practice to child custody mediation, while others may help you negotiate on all matters, including property, support, debts, and assets. With some mediators you may even include other issues in addition to the Parenting Plan—such as developing a private contract for house rules or communications.

What do I look for when selecting a mediator?

Selecting your mediator should be done as carefully as you would select your lawyer or your surgeon. You and the child's other parent should narrow your mediator list to two or three you will interview in person before you choose one. Look for someone who has had more than forty hours of approved training, has been supervised by an experienced mediator, and who has done at least twenty mediations before you. Before you meet, call his or her office and ask for materials that describe mediation in more detail. They may also have materials that outline their confidentiality policy, the mediator's credentials, and suggest readings about mediation, negotiating, divorce, and children. They may also recommend attendance at a divorce education class.

When you and the other parent interview a mediator, ask more detailed questions about mediation and get a sense of whether his or her style will suit you. Tell the mediator what you want. A parenting plan? A property and support agreement? Or both? Obtain information on the mediator's expectations, including preparation for your first meeting and "homework" thereafter. Ask about how the mediator prefers to involve children and how he or she handles the confidentiality of sessions with children. A mediator should agree to maintain specified ground rules for mediation, encourage each of you to have access to attorneys, protect the confidentiality of the mediation, and come to an agreement with you on who will write the final version of the agreement—you, the mediator, or a lawyer. You shouldn't have to spend a lot of time trying just to get basic information. When you ask about the fee and other charges, they should agree to provide services for a fee at a specified rate. They should also describe their billing policies, including how they will bill for services such as telephone calls, secretarial services, and research time. Their billings should be systematic, and charges should be itemized. This should be defined in writing. Experienced mediators will be very clear regarding what you can expect and what they need from each of you.

Are children or other family members involved in the mediation?

It depends on you, the ages of your children, and how the mediator likes to work. Usually children are seen once, perhaps twice. In my practice I liked to give the children aged five and older an opportunity to meet with me alone. They had the opportunity to ask questions about what was happening in mediation and about my role. I would explain that I didn't take sides and that anything they said to me in confidence would not be repeated to their parents—unless it was about something that was dangerous to them or to others. Parents usually reported that the children seemed visibly relieved and calmer in the weeks that followed while the mediation was in process. Children often worry about their parents and can feel relieved when they think that an adult like a mediator is in control of the situation.

Sometimes a relative or close friend attends a mediation session. If one of the parents finds it hard to express himself or herself, that parent can engage a "coach." For example, a mother was concerned that she was not negotiating for herself effectively but did not want to have a lawyer as her coach. Her mediator and her husband agreed to the participation of a mental health professional who attended two sessions as her "coach."

Are mediation meetings confidential?

Your mediator should assure you that everything that happens in the mediation session is confidential and that he or she will not discuss your case with anyone outside of mediation without your written permission. Most mediators will have a written agreement about how information from your mediation sessions will be used and ask you to agree to certain terms before you start. (See appendix 5.) There may also be a law in your state that protects you and the mediator if one of you later changes your mind and tries to subpoena the mediator's records.

YOUR ROLE IN THE MEDIATION PROCESS ITSELF

WHAT TO EXPECT

As parties in a mediation, you will probably be asked to do a number of things. The most common of these expectations are described here:

1. To actively take part in the mediation process. One person should not do all the work. This means making mediation a priority for both of you.
2. To respect and follow mediation ground rules. Typical rules are described at the front of this chapter.
3. To do assigned homework and to come prepared to mediation sessions.
4. To furnish each other with complete financial and personal information, requested by the mediator, in a prompt and accurate manner.
5. To pay all mediation fees promptly and to divide responsibility for those fees either equally or in some proportion.
6. Your mediator may ask for, or you may insist upon, a legal review by an independent lawyer before you sign your final parenting plan. This may be important for determining legal and tax consequences.
7. If you have attorneys, you may be asked to suspend lawyer-to-lawyer negotiations over all matters while you are in mediation.
8. Fill out forms and questionnaires on your circumstances and your concerns.

PREPARING FOR NEGOTIATIONS

1. Review chapters 11, 12, and 13. If you have negotiated even part of a short-term agreement using the guidelines in this book, you will find many of the things that happen in mediation very familiar, and you will have a head start.

2. Reread chapters in part 2 carefully on emotions and your relationship with the other parent. The better negotiators adopt a businesslike manner. Try to keep this attitude and demeanor throughout the time of the negotiations. Yes, it can be difficult. But you have a choice. Strive to do your best. It will be worth the effort one hundred times over for your future.

3. *If* you can discuss your goals for the parenting plan and your children with the other parent before you go into mediation, all the better. If your communications are so strained that discussions are not possible, consider asking the mediator to help you formalize at least one or two of them. When parents can agree on goals, negotiations can be more focused, and difficult issues are more easily resolved.

4. For a step-by-step description of what happens in mediation, see appendix 7, What Happens in Mediation.

EXAMPLE OF A MEDIATION: USING MEDIATION FOR BOTH LEGAL AND PRIVATE AGREEMENTS

BACKGROUND

Emily Sanchez and Eric Sherman have been separated off and on for a year and have been in marriage counseling for eleven months. Three months ago they decided to divorce. They have been married ten years and have two children, Heather, age seven, and Eric junior, age nine. Both parents have full-time jobs, and the children are cared for during the day by Emily's sister, who lives in the neighborhood.

Emily and Eric agree on some things but not on others. They are clear about how to divide the property and on the level of financial contributions for the children, but they have less agreement on what to do about their family residence and the ways to share time and decision making for the children. Emily wants to stay in their home with the children, Eric wants to obtain his share of the equity in order to purchase a condo and wants the children to be with him at least one-third of the time. Emily thinks this is too disruptive for the children. There have been several ugly episodes, with Emily accusing Eric of infidelity during the marriage and Eric calling Emily emotionally unstable. Unfortunately the children witnessed these scenes and were visibly upset.

After three months of trying to reach agreements on their own the couples' counselor suggested using a professional family mediator. Emily then decided she also wanted a lawyer to look over the financial and other property issues with her. Once she got a lawyer, Eric felt he had to have one, too. Both their attorneys encouraged them to settle as much as possible in mediation. The next step was interviewing two mediators, and choosing the mediator best for them.

CHOOSING A MEDIATOR

The mediators each spoke to them by phone, asking about their circumstances and what they hoped to gain from mediation. The mediators explained the way they worked, their ground rules, and their fees. Both mediators seemed competent. Once Eric and Emily met the mediators in person, both of them felt a stronger rapport with the second mediator. They wanted to complete their parenting plan and settle the house issue, but their communications were poor and the children seemed to get caught in the middle. They felt they could benefit from some private contracts. The second mediator had experience working with private contracts as well as parenting plans.

PREPARING FOR THE FIRST MEETING

The mediator sent Emily and Eric materials in the mail. These included a background form they were to fill out and a set of detailed questionnaires on property, assets, incomes, debts, the children, their legal process to date, the names and addresses of their attorneys, and what they wanted to settle in mediation. The questionnaires also asked where they agreed and where they did not. These forms were to be returned before their meeting.

Eric and Emily did their homework. They each reread the chapters in part 2 and part 3. They filled out the mediator's forms. It took time, lots of time. "It had better be worth it," Eric grumbled to a friend.

Each parent independently used the parenting plan lists and examples in chapters 12, 13, and 14 to write down what he or she wanted. Then they looked at how that would work in real life. When Eric did his list he first thought he would like to have the kids with him half the time. Once he tried out his time division on a real calendar, he realized that his travel schedule for work would have to change. On the other side of town, Emily was realizing that she wanted to have all the authority over making decisions. But when she thought about how it would work, she realized that she didn't want to be the only one with responsibility for selecting all the doctors, the schools, the day care. She had done it all when they were married. It could be overwhelming. Because she worked full-time, she realized she wanted Eric to share at least some of the responsibilities.

THE FIRST MEDIATION SESSION

The first meeting had a full agenda. It began with the mediator reviewing the ground rules for mediation and answering their questions. The mediator went on to explain what Emily and Eric could expect and explained how confidentiality in mediation worked. This mediator asked the parents to sign a "Confidentiality Agreement" assuring one another that they would not have their mediation records subpoenaed for any court proceedings, and a "Permission to Release Information" form that allowed the mediator to speak (in generalities) to each of their attorneys about their case. They also decided that they would give any agreement about the house to their attorneys to review before signing the final contracts.

Next the mediator reviewed the forms Emily and Eric had completed and asked each of them in turn for more detail about their issues and concerns. This was very revealing to both of them. They knew the house was their major issue, but Emily was surprised to hear that Eric was also worried that she would find a way to keep the children from him because he had a girlfriend. Eric was taken aback when he heard some of Emily's fears about the negative effect of the divorce on the children and how this would be worsened by leaving the neighborhood and the family home. Emily also admitted it was painful to talk with Eric. The mediator helped them discuss these concerns in more detail so each could get a better picture of what the other was worried about. He stopped Emily from interrupting Eric and kept Eric from discounting Emily's statements.

The mediator suggested that since both felt they were in agreement over many of the issues contained in a parenting plan, they pin this down in writing and "fine-tune" the formal parenting plan later. He explained that negotiations have more clarity if they have a solid foundation of a draft parenting plan from which to tackle the tougher problems of the house and other concerns. Emily could see that their problems with the house involved deeper issues. Eric began to understand that his desire to sell the house would be complicated by issues he hadn't thought about. The mediator said that those issues were possibly the reason they hadn't been able to agree on the house on their own.

Eric and Emily each had done their homework on the purpose of their parenting plan, but because it was hard for Emily to talk with Eric, they had not discussed them together. The mediator drew each of them out, made sure that Emily had as much time to talk as Eric. They spent some time discussing their hopes and dreams for their children. When the mediator suggested that they formalize some of these into statements called "Goals for Mediation," Eric and Emily agreed. The twenty minutes they spent wording their goals in positive terms were rewarding. Some goals would be covered in the plan, others in private arrangements. They actually agreed on something!

GOALS FOR MEDIATION FOR ERIC SHERMAN AND EMILY SANCHEZ

1. To arrive at a mutually acceptable parenting plan that is best for our children and that minimizes the impact of divorce.
2. To assure the children's continuity and security.
3. To identify ways to be active and involved parents.
4. To come to a mutually acceptable arrangement about our family home.
5. To identify ways to work together as parents.

Finally the mediator asked both Eric and Emily to think about one small thing that the other parent could do that would be a symbol of the other parent's good faith toward working toward their goals. Eric chose goal 3 and said that when he called the house to talk to the kids this week, he would like Emily to be supportive of his phone contact. "I get the impression that she lets them talk to me because she has to, not because I have a right to talk to them or them to me. It's demoralizing to me, and it can't be good for the kids." Emily chose goal 5 and said that for this week she would like it if Eric would come to pick up the kids without his girlfriend, Paula. "It's awkward and sometimes humiliating. You know how snoopy the neighbors are," said Emily. The mediator asked Eric about Emily's request, and he agreed to honor it. Then the mediator asked Eric for an example of how he would like Emily to call the children to the phone. Eric answered, "I would like you to sound as if you genuinely support my talking with them." Emily had to agree she had not been enthusiastic. She agreed to try to do better. The mediator congratulated them on two accomplishments: first, reaching consensus on their goals, and second, coming to their first negotiated agreement—a small but important step to reaching their goals.

After a coffee break, Emily, Eric, and the mediator looked at how they would make decisions for the children using the "Parenting Plan List of Parenting Rights and Responsibilities." They agreed that each of them would make the day-to-day decisions when the children were with them alone. To Eric's surprise, Emily agreed that he share major decision making with her. As the parents listed the areas where they agreed, the mediator typed it into a computer, often adding the parent's own words and additional notes for future discussion. At the end of the session the partial draft agreement was printed out and a copy was given to each parent to take home and think about before the next meeting.

The homework for the following week's session was to complete the list of parenting rights and responsibilities and a calendar for the next two years on holidays and summer vacations with at least one alternative or variation. It was now 4:00 P.M., and they had been there three hours. It had been intense, and they were quite tired, but they had something to show for their efforts. They decided that the next session should be shorter.

SECOND SESSION—TEN DAYS LATER

The first part of the session began with the mediator asking how their agreements worked out regarding phone calls and pickup of the children. Emily was agitated. Eric had come alone when he picked up the children, but Paula was with him when he brought them back. Eric was not completely satisfied with the way Emily referred his calls to the children. The parents began to argue, Emily accusing Eric of deliberately baiting her with Paula, and Eric countering with his own accusations about Emily's inflexibility. The mediator intervened and insisted on a calm discussion of the issues reminding them of the mediation ground rules about courtesy and listening to each other's point of view.

At the end of just a few minutes of guided discussion by the mediator, both parents recognized how even small agreements can either support or undermine their working together as parents. For example, Eric was reassured that Emily was making a genuine attempt to be more supportive when he called to speak with the children. But Emily was angrier than ever. She felt Eric was not keeping his part of the deal. The mediator pointed out that they had both made assumptions. Eric had assumed that he could take their agreement about Paula literally. He had overlooked that the purpose of the agreement was to save Emily embarrassment and hurt. Emily had assumed that Eric would accept her needs wholeheartedly and overlooked Eric's needs to move on with his life and be open about his new relationship. They agreed to try the same agreement for another week, and Eric agreed that temporarily Paula would not accompany him either picking up or dropping off the children.

They then set to work on how they would share or divide time with their children. They spent the next forty-five minutes going over the calendars they had prepared, comparing overnights, activity times, recreation, vacations, holidays, and special days. Both had the same ideas on most school nights, special days, activities, and recreation. Emily was surprised that Eric wasn't asking for overnights during the school week but wanted most of his time in the summer and holidays. Eric was surprised that Emily was willing to share the Christmas holiday and that she would agree to his bringing the children to school on Monday mornings some of the time. The mediator used an easel and newsprint to record where they disagreed. The parents then recorded benefits and problems associated with each. This gave them a chance to see everything at once.

The Proposal	Benefits	Problems
Mom, Dad each have five weeks during the summer	Equal time with both parents.	Heather doesn't do well when separated from Mom for long periods.
Most three-day holidays with Dad	Gives Dad longer weekends with the children.	Does not give Mom opportunities to have longer weekends with the children.
All summer with Mom except one week with Dad	Continuity, no big changes, no packing, unpacking, can go to summer school.	There is no consistent, uninterrupted time with Dad except Christmas vacation.
Alternate three-day holidays	Equal time with Mom and Dad.	No Labor Day and Presidents Day family reunion times with Mom.

The parents weighed and discussed each proposal thoroughly. They finally agreed to alternate three-day holidays. When there were family reunions, Emily would trade weekends with Eric. Emily agreed that the children would be with their father for two periods of two weeks each during the summer with a provision for flexibility if this seemed too long for Heather to be away from her mother. These agreements were entered into the computer.

At the end of the two-and-a-half-hour session, the parents came away with a draft parenting plan and plan for the children's time. Eric agreed to put together a new calendar with all the dates to bring to the next session. The homework was to review their draft agreement and to develop at least three different alternatives about the family home.

THE THIRD SESSION

The first two sessions had given Eric and Emily more confidence in their ability to come to solutions together. In this session each presented their three alternatives and used newsprint to write out the pluses and minuses. Eric's alternatives were 1) sell the house, each resettle into new places; 2) Emily buys out Eric's share of the house; 3) Eric moves into the house, Emily lives somewhere else.

Emily's alternatives were 1) Emily and the children stay in the house, Eric's share is deferred until the children graduate from high school; 2) refinance the house, Emily and the children stay, and the equity is used to buy out Eric's share; 3) Emily and the children stay, and Eric's share of the equity is deferred for three years. The pluses for keeping the house for now were that housing values were increasing, the children would have fewer changes (including their relationship with their nearby aunt, who cared for them during the day), and keeping the house was economical. The minuses were that the price for purchasing a new home was rising, thereby making this the wisest time to buy. It was difficult for Eric to rent anything within five miles of the current family home; and Eric did not think he could make a proper home for the children in an apartment. The mediator asked the parents to think about how their alternatives for the house could support their goals for the children, including those for security and continuity.

"Security and continuity," explained Eric to Emily, "is having both your parents in your life after separation, not just one. It's more about having both of us than keeping a house." Emily knew the children loved their father and needed him in their lives. She didn't disagree.

"Of course you are more important than the house," she answered, "but are you saying that if we don't sell the house, they won't have you? Why can't they have their father, the home they are used to, their old neighborhood, and their aunt, too?"

The mediator pointed out that each had proposed an alternative that was similar, namely either to refinance the house or find a way for Emily to buy out Eric's share. The parents agreed this would be the optimum solution. The session ended after two hours with each parent taking responsibility for investigating refinancing and/or finding family or friends to lend Emily money to buy out Eric's share. The mediator also suggested that the next meeting be in two weeks.

THE FOURTH SESSION

The week before the fourth session, Emily and Eric had, on their own, talked on the phone about their findings and about a fair price for the house. They agreed that refinancing would probably be most advantageous in a year when the market price of their house had increased. Refinancing would probably yield about half of Eric's share. Emily thought she had some family who would lend her the other half. Eric wanted to buy immediately and thought he could arrange a lease-to-buy with the down payment due in eighteen months. They arrived at the mediation session with a tentative plan. This was entered into the computer by the mediator at the parents' direction. The mediator pointed out that so far their preliminary parenting plan and arrangements for the house met three of their five goals. Everyone felt a sense of progress.

Next they talked about the problems they had communicating and supporting each other as parents. The mediator asked them "How would an ideal former spouse behave?" The couple knew what was ideal, but they didn't know how to make it work for them. The mediator asked both parents to name at least three things the other parent could do that would show he or she supported the other's relationship to the children.

Eric's list: "Emily's attitude and demeanor tells the children that I am their father and that it is good that they love me; she doesn't complain about me when the children are around; she doesn't grill the kids about my girlfriend; and she accepts the fact that I am dating."

Emily's list: "Eric's backs me up with discipline with the kids. When they complain to him about me, he calls me to find out what happened, he doesn't automatically think the worst; Eric picks up the children on time and has them ready on time when I go to pick them up; he doesn't ask the children how I spend money, he doesn't show up without calling first, and he doesn't have girlfriends overnight when the children are with him."

The mediator led a discussion that ended in agreements on everything except the children and Eric's social life. He suggested that they consider adding regular parent meetings either in person or by phone to talk about the children. He then congratulated them on a job well done and said that he would send them the latest versions of their agreements. They decided to start the calendar immediately and to take the next three weeks to review all their agreements. During this time period, Eric agreed to come alone when picking up or dropping off the kids.

THE FIFTH AND LAST SESSION, THREE WEEKS LATER

The parents had reviewed their draft agreements and had developed an acceptable plan for time, decision making, and the house whereby Emily would buy out Eric's share. The plan for the house was put in a letter of understanding that was sent to each parent's attorney. The only issue that remained was Emily's belief that the children should not have to deal with Eric's social life when they were with him. After discussion, Eric proposed a variation on the provision entitled "Involvement of Children with a New Love." Eric would have no overnight guests while the children were with him until he was in a stable relationship of more than six months. Emily accepted this. The mediator wrote up their private arrangement, and they signed it. The parenting plan was discussed and refined. The final version was printed and turned over to their attorneys.*

The mediation process has ended after eight weeks and five mediation sessions. The parents agree to come back in three months to fine-tune their plan and their private arrangements.

THE FINAL TOUCHES

Eric and Emily successfully negotiated a workable parenting plan. Their attorneys reviewed their plan, suggested some technical wording changes, a legal clause on moving away, and gave it their blessings. The plan was signed in the presence of witnesses. Each parent has a copy in a legal file at home. In some other situations a mediator would have gone on to work with the couple to negotiate all their other divorce matters—property, support, assets, other special provisions, and perhaps more private contracts.

The children appear more settled now and are referring to the calendars in each home frequently. It is as if reading and rereading the calendar is a way to digest all the changes they have experienced in the past few months. The parents have learned something about how to present proposals to one another and how to support one another as parents. Now they settle into carrying out their plan and evaluating how well it is working.

As time goes by, they, like most of us, will have problems with the plan, with one another, and with what the children need. They can then refresh their memories on what works. They will probably need to refer again to chapters 9 and 10 on routines, garden-variety problems, what the children need, danger signals to watch for, family times, and ideas on how to renew their family spirit. When their "negative intimacy" starts to hurt their communications, they should review chapters 6 and 7 and then chapter 8 on how to negotiate.

"It is not as if everything magically becomes better," said Emily, "But it definitely is better with a parenting plan. It makes things predictable. The kids know what they can count on, and so do I. It was a real accomplishment." Eric's view was expressed succinctly: "It worked. I feel I can get on with my life."

Emily and Eric entered mediation with some challenging and complicated decisions to make, some distrust, and a good deal of hurt between them. The

* In some areas mediators may not be permitted to write up formal agreements per se. Instead they write up a "memorandum of understanding" that contains all the same elements of the agreement.

mediation process offered them a bridge to cross over to clearer, more constructive communication and ways to solve problems. In a relatively short time they had eliminated obstacles and created agreements that helped them and their children create a new, meaningful reorganization for their daily lives.

Part 4

YOUR FAMILY,
YOUR FUTURE

Chapter 16

Your Family

Building Family Strength

Your Family
Garden-Variety Complaints
Holidays

YOUR FAMILY

"My family means everything to me," said a thirty-six-year-old father of two sons. "This is what life is all about. When things don't go well with my family, life seems to pull apart." Family is the foundation of our worlds. Family is where love, values, ethics, and meaning spring.

We would like to count on our family to be there when we need them, to prove we are not alone in the world, to protect us, accept us for who we are, to act as a buffer to the stresses of everyday living. And our family members, in turn, would like to depend on us during their times of need. Our families are our treasures. They link us to our past and our present. Our children carry this heritage into the future. Becoming a single parent will change many things, but it does not diminish the importance of your family. This chapter looks first at your immediate family, at garden-variety complaints, how each parent spends time with the children, and the holidays.

BUILDING FAMILY STRENGTH AND A NEW FAMILY FEELING

There are a number of excellent resources for families today who seek support or new ideas. There are parenting classes, parent-child activities that emphasize values that you want for your children; there are specific activities through churches, schools, community groups such as the YMCA and your local recreation centers; and there are some excellent books listed in the "Notes" section for this chapter and in "Further Readings" in part 5. The suggestions that follow are but a few of the things you can consider.

1. Family Meetings—Make Your Family Team Important

Parents who find the time to hold family meetings and build a "family team" are usually very grateful that they did. Regardless of how many children you have, the family team meetings are a good idea. "Our family should set aside a time without interruptions to really talk about things," a parent can say. Then he or she should make the children as important as they would a co-worker at work. Keep it free of TV, phone calls, beepers, outside visitors. Perhaps begin with a meal or with an outing together, with a chance to talk as long as necessary. Demonstrate to your children that what they have to say is important and worth your complete attention. Consider their contributions carefully, just as you would a co-worker's. This can build respect and confidence, and it builds a team spirit. Some good resources for constructing effective family meetings are given in the "Notes" section.

2. When Children Contribute, Everyone Benefits

Earlier chapters have described the dangers of expecting your child to be an adult. There is another pitfall a reader should consider: that is, *not* expecting your child to contribute to the family. Some parents feel so guilty that their child has had to undergo divorce that their child is treated like royalty with the parent as a servant. Children are usually the happiest and feel more in charge of events in their life when they can contribute in a genuine way. Teaching your child how to clean a bathtub or sort papers for recycling is giving your child tools for daily life and showing him or her how to be part of the family team by doing "family work" (a term I like better than "chores"). This is the spirit that helps families develop both a new family feeling and the teamwork that makes a family run well.

3. Routines, House Rules, Safety Rules, and Rituals

Even parents with limited time with their children find that routines, house rules, safety rules, and at least some simple family rituals can strengthen family pride and family identity. Earlier chapters have emphasized how structure and rituals can stabilize things during times of crisis and transition. Expressed with kindness and firmness, rules can also strengthen families in general. Listen to children talk. "In my family, we always turn off the phone during dinner." "In my family, visitors have to leave by nine o'clock." "On Sunday mornings we go to the beach with the dogs. My dad is upset if anyone wants to miss that or just stay home, because except for dinners, that's one thing we all do together every week." "We take turns doing the icky job of cleaning the bathroom." "My mom and I talk every day at four o'clock, even if we are not both home together." These statements usually denote a child's sense of belonging and pride in how *their* family does things.

Routines feel safe to children, even though they may protest at times. Think about routines for when you are together, but also for when you are apart. The nightly or four-times-a-week phone calls from the absent parent are important, as are calls from the resident parent during the day or after school. Many children and parents use the phones, e-mail, or even message machines to coach a school-age child on spelling or to help with homework, a school project, or a sport. It is not the same as being together all the time, but it seems to work nonetheless. Overnights are very important, of course, but without the day-to-day relationship, they are not enough. Make those telephone calls just to touch base. Even when a child says, "I'm playing with a friend," or, "I'm busy now," a parent can answer, "Sounds good, I'll talk to you later [or tomorrow]." No need to insist that a child have a conversation. They know that you called and that you care.

As earlier chapters explained, your involvement in your child's activities can take many roads. You can be part of them, and you can affirm those where they can interact with adult role models and mentors from whom they can learn about values and life. The right activities build skills, teach social values and ethics, shape character, and—whether basketball, ballet, or painting a neighbor's fence—they provide your child with a chance to relate to other adults besides yourself.

4. The Old Family Feeling and the Kids

Some children naturally attempt to re-create the *old* family feeling after the separation, even to their own detriment. Why? Because divorce makes these children feel alone and left out. The old family feeling is familiar to them, it feels like home, and most of all, they know how it works. Children may not yet know how a calmer, more positive atmosphere can work because they don't yet have a *new* family feeling. So in an attempt to keep any kind of continuity, a few children may put the parents in the middle and instigate friction between them. They could carry tales like "Daddy says you spend too much money" or "Mommy says she can't trust you."

One sure way to maintain the old family feeling and to delay rebuilding your own family is to put the children in the middle. Parents can use children as messengers: "Tell your father that his support check is overdue." As tale carriers: "Mom says you spent all our money." As informants: "Is your mother's new boyfriend sleeping over at night?" And as accomplices in secrets: "Don't tell your father that we bought this new TV set." Many parents fall briefly into such behavior at one time or another. But these are bad habits for everyone, especially children.

Nature has equipped children with phenomenal powers of observation and mimicry, abilities that allow them to learn and develop. They know instinctively what gets your goat, what pleases you, and what gives you (and them) a feeling of love, acceptance, and approval. They know the behaviors that will spark your deeper emotions and responses and bring back the "old family feeling."

5. Your Core Values

A family needs "core values" that will guide their thinking, their choices, and their lifestyle and give them a sense of direction, of worth, of purpose. What does your family stand for? Think about your core values—what is uppermost for you? One parent might say, "I want my children to be able to survive ethically in this world," another, "Our family values public service," yet another, "To always support and be loyal to one another. Your values are uniquely your own and reflect what you will pass on to your children. It has been said that what doesn't kill us offers us an opportunity to grow stronger or wiser. Single-parent and remarried families have these opportunities aplenty!

SPEAK OUT: TAKING PRIDE IN YOUR FAMILY

Take pride in your children, emphasize their strengths and contributions. "She can really be a good sister to her baby brother," "He can handle this part of the grocery shopping very well by himself," "He is so thoughtful," "She is so engaging." Motivate your family team. "We can pull together and do this." "We can all do our part. It will work out okay." Attitudes are powerful, especially in adversity. Just as you can adopt positive terms to describe your new status as a single parent, you can also reaffirm your children's abilities and the importance of your family.

GARDEN-VARIETY COMPLAINTS

1. Problems with the Schedule or Calendar

Nearly all families have problems with the schedule at one time or another. Mom starts a second job on Monday evenings and can't be with the children as they do their homework. Dad coaches soccer and wants the kids to stay overnight after practice. If you, your children, or the children's other parent are having problems keeping to your agreement about times together, try this:

1. Take a look at "Changing Schedules and Trading Times," in chapter 12. Do you have an agreement with the other parent on how to handle changes or unexpected lapses in your plan or in a private agreement? If not, have you tried getting these types of ideas down on paper together? Being explicit and finding ways to substitute or trade times can help.
2. Look for ways you can support each other and try to be flexible. If that

doesn't work and if the problem grows more serious, see a mediator and find a solution.

3. As you weigh different options, remember how important continuity of contact is for your children.

2. Not Showing Up or Being Late

Mom gets stuck at work and can't pick up her daughter from Dad's house as planned; Dad has car trouble and is late picking up his son. You are all, after all, only human. But your child needs to trust you now more than ever. Your time with your child is essential to his or her sense of security and self-esteem. You prove that you value your child by being on time, calling if you will be late, and finding substitute times if you have to cancel. Flexibility means that, by mutual agreement, plans can change. It does not mean that capricious cancellations or no-show behavior are acceptable. The same principles hold true for both parents. A parent who forgets to have a child home in time for the other parent's arrival, who cancels out at the last minute, or who sits on the fence about a proposed schedule change also undercuts a child's trust and self-esteem. Your child's ability to trust and to develop relationships later in life depend on you. How you handle your life and commitments teach your children how they can handle theirs.

If you are due to pick up your child at a specific time and you do not show up at all, you risk hurting your child deeply. Too many times I've heard parents tell of watching their child sitting outside on the doorstep or by a window, waiting for a parent who never came. The pain children bear and the rejection they suffer when this happens are devastating. One caveat, however. Sometimes parents want to make the child feel better by making up excuses for the parent who has not shown as promised. It may be better for the parent to be honest and say he or she doesn't know why the other parent isn't there. Then assure the child of his or her love and that the parent will be able to explain what happened later. Be sure your child does not feel that the parent's lateness or absence is their fault. Children, especially during the first year of separation, need parents who follow through with plans. Your child's sense of trust, of security, and of being worthy of being loved is at stake.

If you say you are going to be there, or if it is on the schedule, follow through. Be on time, be back on time, and if you are late or need to cancel, make substitute plans immediately, giving your child reasons for the change. The standard is: *Be on time, call if you will be late, explain the problem.*

3. It's Your Fault!

Blame games flourish when one parent believes the other parent is encouraging the children's resistance to being at one home or the other. It can also lead to estrangements between the other-home parent and the child—when perhaps each one accuses the other of being uncaring and insensitive or each withdraws in silent hurt or resentment. This is exceptionally hurtful to children. In some situations, a child can become oppositional. He or she won't go to the other home, see the other parent, and won't accept other arrangements. When parents are overwhelmed with feelings of guilt, blame, and fear of losing their children's love, they may be afraid to provide needed limits to discipline their children, or to be the cause of any disappointment. In such circumstances, children learn how to be manipulative. Blaming and guilt are rarely constructive.

4. I Don't Want to Go

Children, especially teenagers, may say they are too busy or too involved to go to their other home. "I don't want to go," "There's nothing to do," "It's no fun there," or even, "I don't want to be there." Reluctance to go to their other home or unhappy returns from one home to the other are common the first year or so. Children go through their own emotional wounding and healing process, and having to say hello to one parent and good-bye to another during all this is not easy for them. It reminds them that what they don't have is what they want most—both parents living together. In most cases this resistance dissipates. But it is nearly always cause for a thoughtful reconsideration of your child's circumstances. A six-year-old who refuses to stay overnight with his father soon after the separation is not rejecting him. He or she needs time to get adjusted to the separation and what it means. You know your child. Respect his or her need. Give your child a say here, hear him or her even if later you gently but firmly insist that your child go with the parent as planned.

Some children resist going to the other home because they feel they must protect or reassure the parent they are leaving. Perhaps they worry that the parent will be lonely without them, and they feel responsible. Or parents may need reassurance from their child that they are still important or even that the child favors them over their former mate. Some parents can be sitting ducks for an all-or-nothing reaction to the "I don't want to go" wail. When these parents tell about how their children refused to come and live with them during regularly scheduled time, they show feelings of anger, hurt, and rejection. Some are ready to retaliate with, "I don't want you, either." Sometimes when parents tell of the child's reluctance or refusal to go to their other home, there is a tone of triumph in their voice when they say, "They just don't want to be with him or her. They want to stay with me." Sometimes they are bewildered. "Can I make them go if they don't want to?" Sometimes they are angry: "I planned a weekend with a new friend without children and now they won't go." Some children seem to say, "Either make coming to your house worth my while, or I'll not come at all. If you force me to come, I'll be miserable and hard to handle and you will be sorry you didn't give me my way." Or, "You got a divorce, not me—I hate this moving around. You do it."

When children are difficult and angry, sometimes the parent who is expecting the child can admit to honest relief that the kid is not going to be there for three or four days. However, put it all in perspective. The "I don't want to go" wail is typical behavior in *any* home.

5. Difficult Parents

Sometimes children resist going to the other parent's home because the parent is acting like an adolescent or is in the off-the-wall stage. And he or she is hard to be with. A parent once good for giving advice may now seem more like a parent in need of some advice. "I don't like the way my father looks now." "Mom acts like she's a teenager instead of a mother." Parents do change after divorce, and children may resist adjusting to their parents' new routine, style of dressing, activities, or social circle. A new lover often upsets teenagers. "I'm not coming to your house as long as you have a woman there," a fourteen-year-old son might say to a father. Is the son upset with his father's new behavior? Are there sexual overtones that are too hard for the son to deal with? Or is he being loyal to his mother? Is the son caught in that classic father-son tug-of-war often seen in the teen years? These are common questions posed during the first years of separation. It also happens that children are sometimes reluctant to go to a parent's home because they will have to share him or her with a friend, a lover, or a job. It hurts to miss a parent when apart only to find that when together, someone or something else is the focus of attention.

6. Your Children Have Their Own Lives

Children do have their own lives, and the older they get, the more separate and independent they become. How many never divorced parents have heard their teenagers say, "I don't want to go to Uncle or Aunt So-and-so's place for dinner—I have plans." When parents live separately, the script is the same, but the object of complaint is now the parent who makes them go (or stay) and miss out on something they want.

The mother with the teenage son who says, "Mom, I can't go to Dad's house this weekend, I have a game," can hear him out for a minute and say, "Well, that's up to your dad, not to me." If the son persists with, "Dad won't listen to me, Mom," Mom can persist as well. "That's something you and your dad have to work out, son. I can't speak for either you or your dad— only you two can do that for one another." Son at this juncture may stomp out of the room, saying, "Oh, forget it," and make that phone call himself to

Dad or try a little guilt induction with, "You don't understand how awful it is for me." If that mom runs interference for her son, she may be putting herself in the middle. No matter how much Mom may sympathize with her son's cry of "He doesn't understand me," she needs to remember that her objective is for the son to talk to the father directly. This is Dad's time and his decision. The son knows that, may not think Dad will cooperate with him, or just doesn't want to bother. Furthermore, if Mom interferes, it might make Mom somehow responsible for his behavior, his feelings, and his schedule. No matter how strongly the mother may inwardly agree with her son about the father's lack of tact, understanding, or ability to communicate (she did divorce him, after all), she should try and step back. Mother will not make the father perfect for the son, nor will the son make his eventual peace with his father's foibles or personality unless he puts out some effort. Help your teenager develop a responsible approach to his or her growing independence.

7. Be in Charge

A parent must play a firm role when the child says, "I don't want to come to your house." Remember, the days that the child lives with you are your days of responsibility and authority. If your teenager wants to go off with friends surfing or on a camping trip on your time together, it should be you who gives or withholds permission, not the other parent. If you say yes, you sign the emergency medical slips and you pick up at the bus stop, you let people know how you can be reached in an emergency. It is your time for supervision.

Perhaps a parent hasn't seen his or her child in more than a month and says "Not this time" to the request to stay at the other home or be somewhere else. The child may be angry, disappointed, or even rebellious. But many a firm parent has found that a yelling, hurt teenager dissolved in tears and relief when that parent cared enough to stand his or her ground. Teenagers need parents to be parents.

Parents need to clear up for themselves and for their children what part of the time together is negotiable and what is not. "Matthew is sixteen, he has his own life," said his father. "He can negotiate with me for Saturday nights out, using the car, and staying overnight with friends. He doesn't have any choice about whether or not this weekend is with me or not, though. He knows it is our time, even if sometimes I hardly see him." Matthew knows what to expect. He has the safety and comfort of his father's attention and authority, even if it seems that there isn't much together time apart from sleeping in the same home for a few nights.

Parents who are not living with their children the majority of the time can fear losing their children's love. They also miss them and are far more willing to respond to their requests than they might have been when they all lived together as a family every day. Flexibility and support for a child's plans can be an especially rewarding way for parent and child to begin to get reacquainted and renegotiate their new relationship. But such accommodations should not be entered into out of fear of losing a child's love.

If you are a second-home parent and your teenager lives a full and busy life that competes with your time together on weekends, don't always settle for the "convenient" thing and arrange for him or her to stay at the other parent's house. You will miss the breakfast chatter and the surprise secret revealed while you exchange car keys. "He's never here, anyway," is not the point, Dad or Mom. *He or she doesn't need to be home, but you do.* Those weekends when you hardly see your kid are still precious because that child is yours, and if you are not sleeping under the same roof, you'll miss some opportunity, that brief exchange, glance, or hug that reaffirms that "parents are forever."

When a child is able to call all the shots about where his or her time is spent, many things can deteriorate over a period of time. The children, even teenagers, must learn how to check their plans with the appropriate parent as automatically as they put on a pair of shoes. This strengthens their relationship and teaches them the benefits of going directly to the source and, if necessary, how to compromise.

8. The Parent Who Fades Away

Some parents who move out of the family home may stop seeing the children for a while. These parents often feel confused or depressed, but their unexplained absence can create serious problems for their children. Children have to struggle with whether or not they are lovable, whether the parent left because of their lack of importance or worth. Their self-value, self-esteem, suffers. Each parent is an essential source of love, security, and continuity for a child. Even though parents may feel powerless or inadequate, their children need to know that they are not gone forever and that they have not taken their love away from their children.

If you are separated by many miles, make your contact frequent and tangible—chapter 18 will show you how.

From time to time, it's helpful to give yourself a checkup on some of the most common sources of problems with the schedule.

Checklist: Children's Time with Each Parent

	Yes	No	Sometimes
Is your schedule written down on a calendar with copies posted at each home where the children can easily read it?	___	___	___
Does each parent have some activity time with the children?	___	___	___
Does each parent have "together" time with the children?	___	___	___
Do the older children stay overnight with each parent?	___	___	___
Do the children eat at least one meal a day with a parent?	___	___	___
Are the children usually picked up or returned at the agreed-upon time?	___	___	___
When a parent cancels plans, are substitute times set up within a short period of time?	___	___	___
When a parent doesn't show up or cancels a planned time with the children, does he or she call ahead with plenty of notice?	___	___	___
When a parent doesn't show up or cancels a planned time with the children, is there an important reason?	___	___	___
When scheduled plans are changed on one parent's time, is that parent asked permission to do so?	___	___	___
Can you usually count on the other parent to follow through with scheduled plans?	___	___	___
Can your children count on getting some extra time (or dropping some time) with the other parent on occasion?	___	___	___

"Yes" answers are excellent. "Sometimes" answers mean a little more attention could be paid to this area. "No" answers are calls for renewed attention. No family can do all of these things all of the time. But things seem to go better if they can do most of these things most of the time.

HOLIDAYS

A holiday or a holiday season can be a time of spiritual renewal, a reinforcement of what is most important in life, an opportunity to deepen bonds with friends and family. The hope is that a shared holiday can renew the spirit, heal old wounds, bring us closer together with those we love. The chance to sit next to a brother or sister you haven't talked to for several months, share a meal, and swap kid stories has meaning and renewal beyond the words themselves. Holidays are a time when some people seem to be more willing to be open, more tolerant. They can also be a time of dismay and deprivation—not enough time, money, energy, too many unrealistic expectations, and irritation at the materialism and hype. There can be a keen sense of loss of what once was or might have been.

"Holidays are the times when you are supposed to be with those who belong to your inner circle of loved ones," offered the father of a teenage daughter. "Divorce dissolves that circle, and you can be left devastated and alone." The effects of separation become exaggerated during the holiday period. Though separated parents may have been progressing nicely through their transition, they seem to be especially vulnerable during this period. The holiday season offers opportunities to fan the flames of anger and old resentments and to reignite unfinished emotional business. But think back to your preseparation days. Be honest now: How relaxed, fulfilled, and rewarding were your holidays? Do you remember ever feeling rushed, pressured, discouraged, disappointed, irritated? Did you ever vow that next year it would be different?

TOO MUCH

The Thanksgiving to Christmas and Hanukkah period usually mean more people, activity, sweets, and special outings. Routines, schedules, and familiar food are replaced with later nights, more parties, the excitement of unopened gifts, Santa Claus. More seems better, but is it? As exciting as this can be for many children, especially the younger ones, it can lead a child to more outbursts of anger, frustration, disturbed or interrupted sleep, and susceptibility to colds or illnesses or accidental poisonings. Plan ahead, keep the schedule reasonable, taking care to be home with your children to break up the holiday stress. Too much of a good thing will make the holidays hard for everyone.

The holiday season can also bring with it unreasonable expectations for loyalty and attention, competitiveness over gift giving, an onerous anxiety or compulsion to do things "right" and to overdo. Debilitating stress becomes the rule. People feel grumpy, jealous, angry, unappreciated. Some people are renewed, rested, comforted. For others, however, a last-minute cancellation by a sister at a family gathering is devastating, a fight between preteen cousins leads to an argument among their parents. For some people, the get-togethers over the holidays are painful and old wounds are deepened. No one can hurt you like a family member.

The old married feeling and the old family feeling often surface again, bringing a sense of loss along with fond memories. Such feelings and rituals are familiar and perhaps quite dear to your heart, but they are not the only good feelings around. Your new family feeling can also be satisfying and can begin to take over those old feelings. If you haven't yet updated your sense and meaning of family to fit your new life, you might have to face the holiday blues.

PRACTICAL PLANNING SUGGESTIONS

Go to your parenting plan and update your calendar. What do you have in writing about how to share or divide these holidays or special days?

If your parenting plan is not explicit enough, or if it doesn't spell things out at all, it's time to try to work things out. But before you talk things over with the other parent, get some idea of what *you* want yourself, then think about other alternatives you might accept. Then prepare to be reasonable and flexible.

If you and the other parent are on poor terms, it is critical that you both agree to some plan for the holidays. Everyone has a right to make plans, and that includes the other parent as well as you.

SUGGESTIONS

1. Try to plan your holiday times well ahead. Three to six months' notice is not too much time, especially if extensive travel is involved.
2. Consider your hopes for the holiday or the season—the times with and without the children and transportation. Have several versions, all acceptable to you.
3. Present these alternatives to the other parent. (If you don't communicate well, use the mails.) Give the other parent time to think about your proposals and to respond.
4. If you talk in person or by phone, follow up your understanding of the conversation with a brief and informal note of confirmation.
5. Be very specific when making plans. Which parent will have the children, which day? For how long? What about transportation?
6. Be flexible. Unscheduled or spontaneous times together can be mutually rewarding. Mom says she would like to take her daughter to a concert at a

time when she is to be with her dad. Son misses his dad and would like to see him more this week. Discuss the proposed change first.

A special note about the increase in accidents involving children: Keep a sharp eye out for guests or hosts unaccustomed to small children. There may be breakables or medications within reach of explorers' inquiring hands.

THINNER SLICES OF THE SAME PIE

After divorce, the slice of children's time and affection is cut thinner than before. "My mother always did dislike the idea that holidays had to be shared with my husband's family as well," said one mother. "Now that we are divorced, she sees even less reason for sharing." Even if you have grandparents, uncles, and aunts with more realistic expectations, the slice of time is still smaller. This is one of the prices of parenting apart.

FEELINGS IN THE PIT OF YOUR STOMACH

When you attend gatherings of friends and family, with or without your children, be prepared for a surprising resurgence of old memories and some wistfulness of feelings. "I was having a mellow time," said Peter, "until I saw my brother lean over and whisper something in his wife's ear, and I thought I was going to break down and cry right then and there." A gesture of tenderness between a couple, a child's tugging at a parent's sleeve, just about anything can bring back an old memory at a holiday time. Being with other couples, families, and friends brings many warm and good feelings. There are exchanges of camaraderie and that sense of continuity so welcome and nurturing at holiday time. But many parents find that it's just too difficult to be around married families, especially when it's their turn to be without the children. Weigh the alternatives and consider having an alternate plan for the day or the evening.

YOUR NEW HOLIDAYS AND "FAMILY FEELING"

The exact "old holiday feeling" will not be possible when divorce has separated the parents. The "new family feeling" means a gradual but deliberate (in many cases) sense of a new family pride by thoughtfully developing new traditions, new customs, and a reinforcing of some of the old ones. Children love ritual. A dad who always read *A Christmas Carol* can't do it if the kids are with Mom this Christmas Eve, but he can read it when he and the kids do get together. As a result, much of the old tradition has been transplanted into new ground, where it can take new root.

Holidays and special days have great potential for joy and for sadness. As one father said, "If we do it right, it is the way we show our kids the importance of celebrating one another and of giving to others."

Chapter 17

Your Family Network

Opening Your Family to Others

Common Barriers to Extending Families
How to Begin an Extended Family and Acquaintance Network
When There Is No Other Parent

"I HAD to fill out one of those emergency cards for David at nursery school today," one father told me with unconcealed pleasure. "When I came to those three lines where you list people to call in case you can't be reached, it really hit me how my life has changed since the days I was married. Then I would have had to really search around, wondering whom I could 'impose on' for my son. Maybe there'd be each of the grandparents and the lady up the street. But now, after four years as a single parent, I can list at least twelve families I know who would be there for David if he needed them. Now, that's a real community."

David's father had a closed-family system when he was married. Now that he is divorced, he has chosen to develop a more open family system. Friends, neighbors, associates, and other families are involved with David's family, and his family is involved in their lives as well. Over the course of history, people have always banded together to give each other mutual support or protection. This process can be especially crucial when a big life change such as ending a marriage disrupts or fragments close relationships or a way of life. When you have the responsibilities for a child, that mutual support and social life becomes even more important. While old bonds can be strengthened, it is also likely that if one is open to new relationships, new ones can form. New standards need definition. The extended family of choice and "open family" provides the validation for these new and necessary standards.

AN ACQUAINTANCE NETWORK

This is a group of people who know one another, give and get things from one another, spend time together, and in general act toward each other as the social beings they are. This can be limited to a circle of people such as neighbors who are not necessarily close friends in the usual sense of the word but who support one another in material, emergency, and child-rearing tasks. An extended family can grow from this network, and it can be folded into one's relationships with relatives and kin.

The significance of these networks should not be underestimated. Many single parents who seek counseling two or three years after their divorce are frequently parents who have "closed" families. But, when a person can call out in time of personal need and be assured of assistance in the form of funds, emotional or practical aid, help or advice with the kids, or perhaps the daily demands of living, a sense of security and well-being can't help but be enhanced. Sometimes it is just two families, often five, six, or more who interweave their lives, tasks, and activities around one another, redefining and maintaining standards, providing interpretations to everyday events, and in general acting as a buffer to the outside world. Our links to others can be made up of co-workers, old and new friends, relatives, and neighbors. The network can be formal, informal, of long or short duration.

The more supportive a network is to a parent, the easier it is for the parent to survive a crisis—and the more confident that person will feel as a parent. To the extent that a person's sense of competence as a parent affects how he or she behaves toward the children, it also follows that the kind of people Mom or Dad has as friends affects the children's personal adjustment. Studies and common sense both show that when parents feel good about themselves and their lives, they usually have children who feel competent and self-assured as well.

COMMON BARRIERS TO EXTENDING FAMILIES

The idea of an extended or open-family style often delights and enchants people. But when they ask, "How is it done?" or, "What do people do?" some find that certain attitudes and past beliefs stand in their way. Here are some of the most common barriers:

MAKING IT ALONE

This is a traditional do-it-yourself approach. The original ideal of family includes only mother, father, the children, and maybe—but only maybe—a grandparent or one uncle or aunt. For this making-it-alone view of the family, the fewer people a tight nuclear family unit depends on, the better. Ideally, those rugged individuals are so strong and independent that they never have to say to anyone but a mate or child, "Help," or, "I need a friend." In this version they need only one another. For those who want to remain ruggedly independent, uneasy feelings are associated with being a joiner or part of a group. "I don't want a person to tell me his troubles," people say, "I've got enough of my own."

The difficulty with this closed system is that families have many personal needs, many responsibilities, and too little time for fun and for enjoying one another. For some families, it becomes a merciless cycle where there are too many needs and too few people to meet them. If such isolation continues over a very long time, family members may become afraid to deal with the outside world and their demands on each other become excessive. Sometimes quarrels are extreme and physical violence erupts. During the first part of a crisis, a family's closed ranks may be a healthy response to the challenge to new and sometimes threatening situations. But later, as the family settles down, it can relax and open itself to the advantages of new relationships in the outside world. Family members may be unaware of the ways and means available for establishing an open-family style. "I've been in a closed-ranks position so long," said one father, "I've forgotten how to be any other way." A closed system may have its disadvantages, but it is familiar, and he knows exactly what to expect. An open-family style, on the other hand, may be one that he will have to teach himself to develop.

FEAR OF IMPOSING UPON OTHERS

Old habits of reserve can be very powerful deterrents to building an open family. I've heard many horror stories about parents—faced with accidents, serious illness, or sudden calamity—who had no one to turn to. These parents were unwilling to impose on neighbors or acquaintances, so they struggled through endless hours of aloneness, fear, and even danger. But their isolation and lack of help were usually avoidable. Louise, for example, talked in a workshop of the time her young son had required hospitalization in the middle of the night because of a serious asthma attack. She left her two other children, aged two and four, alone asleep and rushed her son to the hospital emergency room. Ada, an acquaintance who lived two blocks away from Louise and was also a member of the group, said, "You should have called me. I would have stayed with the babies." Louise replied that she didn't want to impose on Ada in the middle of the night. When I asked Louise if she would call Ada tonight if the same thing happened again, Louise answered honestly that she would still be reluctant to disturb Ada's sleep in order to ask her for help with her children, even in an emergency.

MR. RIGHT AND MS. WONDERFUL

To many newly divorced parents, the search for new social relations is limited to a search for a new mate. Every new person they meet is evaluated as to whether or not he or she is a potential lover or can help in the search for a new lover. But building a network or friendship circle is not an adolescent dating situation. If you are constantly asking yourself whether every new person is a potential mate, you will not be able to see the other qualities the person has. Standards for a mate are usually high, often too complicated for friendship. "Too young," "too old," "he's a doctor and I'm a programmer," "she's too plain," "he's too macho," are quick judgments made by some singles when identifying the mate potential in another. But are these same standards realistic when considering a new acquaintance or friend? Just because a person is not attractive as a mate does not mean he or she is not kind, honest, companionable, sensitive, helpful, or fun-loving. To build an open family, you need to shift your emphasis from finding a lover to connecting with new acquaintances. Don't let the search for Mr. Right or Ms. Wonderful keep you from building your own circle of good friends.

DISCOURAGEMENT, THE FIRST YEAR

Building an acquaintance network or open family takes time, a commodity always in short supply; it is especially scarce during the first year after separation. Some single parents reported that while they often made three good friends that first year, others came more slowly. The time and effort you spend will often seem one-sided. "I seem to be making all the efforts," some people complain. Laments about time, work, fatigue, and the absence of baby-sitters are common. These words often mask inner reservations. What many parents really mean is: "What guarantee do I have if I make the effort? The risk is high; what if I'm rejected? I don't want to be disappointed. I don't want to cope with other people's problems, and besides, I feel guilty about leaving my children. Yet I want friends."

If this could be you, just try to remember that the time and effort you do spend during that first year will most probably pay off in years two, three, or four.

YOUR OWN NEEDS AND PERSONAL STYLE

An extended family with friends and relatives is not just for the kids' benefit, it's for the grown-ups, too. Sometimes the people who become close to your children are your close friends, too, but they can also be acquaintances whom you know and trust with your children but with whom you are not close.

Take a look at the following questions. First answer them for yourself, then go back and answer them for each of your children.

A SELF-TEST: YOUR EXTENDED FAMILY

A. Whom Do You Count On?

1. If some calamity such as a severe auto accident were to befall you, whom would your family immediately call on to help out while you were out of commission?
2. How many other families could your children stay with if you suddenly had to go out of town tomorrow for three days? Would there be more places for the children to stay if you could give two weeks' notice?
3. Who besides yourself could talk to your children like an aunt or an uncle if you needed some adult support with a problem at school or in the neighborhood?

B. What Is Your Personal Style?

1. When you are lonely and feeling blue, do you have a friend or set of friends to talk with? Do you want to be by yourself or participate in some activity to give your mind a rest from your troubles?
2. If you want to relax and have fun, with whom do you share this time? With your children, your friends, other family, neighbors, or usually alone or with one other person?
3. Who shares your holidays, such as the Fourth of July or birthdays?

Look at your answers to A. Ideally you could have some immediate family and some other family friends or acquaintances who could step in in an emergency or who could (and would) feel comfortable with your children over a weekend period. Furthermore, to have other adults your child can trust and confide in is also a healthy expansion of a child's world. If you have such options, you probably already have (or have the makings of) an open family. If you do not have such alternatives, you may have a more closed-family system.

In B, when it comes to your own feelings and private life, do you depend on yourself, perhaps on one other person and your children, for support or fellowship? If so, yours may be a closed-family system, but you may also be a person who prefers to live quietly and privately. What was your human income score back in chapter 5? Was it well over 100, or was it hovering around 90 or 80 or even lower? If you had a high score, was it high because you had people you could count on? Your answers can give you another indication of your open or closed style.

If you feel you have an open family now that you can reinforce and enrich, the next few pages will seem old hat to you. But if you are interested in exploring it further, here are some simple ways to begin.

HOW TO BEGIN AN EXTENDED FAMILY AND ACQUAINTANCE NETWORK

An acquaintance network is essentially low voltage, requiring no emotional disclosure. Children are a natural way of opening up a network. The children are out playing with other children in the neighborhood—you meet the children, you can meet the parents. Children's teams, classes, church groups, school projects—all are natural ways to make connections.

Asking for information is another dimension for building a network. This is very different from asking for time or effort, and most people are glad to share. Requesting the name of a good family doctor is not an emotional overture, yet it makes a liaison that establishes you in the fellowship of neighbors, particularly if you call later and report a successful contact. Take a look at the following lists and picture yourself asking nearly everyone you meet or know for their recommendations of at least one on the following list. For example, "Whom would you recommend as a good car mechanic?" "Could you recommend a gym where I could work out?"

Ask for recommendations for:

1. a doctor, a dentist, an attorney, a tutor
2. a dance or music studio, sports leagues, discussion groups, classes (any activities that interest you)
3. schools, teachers, supplies, day care, baby-sitters, public transportation (children's needs)
4. a good mechanic, a good place to shop for groceries, children's clothes
5. contacts for the "neighborhood watch," emergency procedures
6. referrals for child care: jobs, household repairs, and the like

After trying this approach for several months, some people say, "I didn't realize that I didn't have to tell anyone my private business in order to develop a network and a sense of belonging." When the exchange of information and request for recommendations lead to casual conversations, acquaintanceship can sometimes blossom to friendship. Giving an acquaintance a lift home from the car repair shop, sharing names of doctors, dentists, and places to shop, all build trust and caring. An acquaintanceship expands to friendship, spontaneous potluck suppers or birthday parties appear, often drawing in more new acquaintances. Your children meet. Perhaps they play together for longer and longer periods of time. Then they ask to sleep over. All these steps happen naturally enough.

WAYS EXTENDED FAMILIES AND ACQUAINTANCE NETWORKS BEGIN

Once parents begin thinking about their connections with other people and other families, they find connections all around. It's like finding a four-leaf clover. When you find one, you're in the middle of a patch.

"I started thinking about this open-family business," said Frank, father of two teenage sons. "After I took stock of whom I could count on, I realized that we have a ready-made one now because of our soccer league parents. We met one another naturally at games, and the boys really got on well. You know how kids are. Pretty soon one or the other of their soccer buddies is coming along on a weekend we go out of town, or they are invited to go somewhere with another family. When I started counting, I found three other families the boys could spend three days with on ten minutes' notice."

Frank had not become good friends with the other parents over the last two years of the soccer league, but he did trust them with his sons. One of the fathers had some business in common with Frank, and they sometimes had lunch, but the open family was one the boys had built themselves. I asked Frank if any of the parents provided a confidential ear for his sons. He answered, "I honestly don't know. If they do, I'm for it because they are really fine folks. But I never even thought to think about it." When I asked Frank about his own circle of friends, he answered, "I kept most of my friends from the marriage. I have a lot of people I have known for many years, but they aren't especially interested in children."

Some people say their open families began because their neighborhood was so friendly. Others talk about some neighborhood crisis that brought them together. In a neighborhood, the least people can do for one another is look out for one another's safety and interest. For some areas, "neighborhood watch" refers to property, but when you have children, it should refer first to caring about the kids.

In one community, a small group of single mothers canvassed their five-block area to count the other single parents. They found thirty! They asked if the single parents were interested in forming a twenty-four-hour emergency service so that those who needed help would know the names of neighbors close by. Most of the parents agreed willingly. Many had found that living alone and without friends or other family nearby had made it almost impossible to deal effectively with emergency situations.

CARING ABOUT OTHER PEOPLE'S CHILDREN:
HOW TO GIVE WHAT YOU GET

"Carla came bouncing in from the Datterleys' house, saying Mrs. D. was going to teach her how to sew if it was all right with me," reported Carla's mother, a mother of five. "It was fine with me. The more people loving and caring for my kids, the better I like it. Furthermore, the Datterleys are a blended family, and Carla can see firsthand what happens in some families after remarriage. I bless the day those people moved in down the street, because they are showing my kids graphically that there are other stages beyond the divorce stage that we're in now." Children such as Carla are getting new role models, new points of reference, and an added sense of security from adults who are interested in them. Families such as the Datterleys are generous people. They share their lives with other people and other people's children. They don't see time with other people's children as a duty, a favor, or baby-sitting. Mrs. D. genuinely related to Carla, who glowed from her warmth. Children are fortunate when they find such an adult friend.

HAVE YOU WELCOMED A KID TODAY?

You can duplicate Mrs. D.'s kindness and be a friend or mentor for a child. This relationship is not baby-sitting. It has its own intrinsic value. Welcoming your friend's child while you play, relax, or work is a traditional way adults have transmitted skills to children while enjoying the human interchange. Both generations have their worlds expanded, and sometimes, as trust grows, children will disclose parts of themselves to you—their adult friend—away from the day-to-day interaction of their homes. You need not meddle or give advice. Instead be a good ear or judiciously share your own experiences. Many parents have recounted how a small friend has given them insight into their own situation. Here's an example of how it works for some parents.

"My little friend John came over to help me polish my car," said a father about an eight-year-old neighbor child. "As he worked alongside me, I found myself far more patient with him than I was with my own children. He began to show up more often after that, for about an hour or so at a time. Eventually he asked me why daddies sometimes go away and don't phone or call children. I knew his dad had not dropped out, and I didn't at first know what to say. I did tell him that I had a time a while back when I didn't call my children because I was so sad and lonely. I wondered why he hadn't asked his own father, but I didn't want to meddle. Then I began to wonder why my children had never asked me that question. I initiated conversations with my own kids after that about how they had felt. I found that there were still some unfinished feelings."

Parents are often suspicious of adults who befriend their children. This is a normal protective reaction. Get to know the parent first. Do not rush things along. Being an adult friend for a child is not surrogate parenting, nor should it be a challenge to the natural parent's role or authority.

Many children who have adult friends do not share private feelings or thoughts with them. Instead, times together may be to show off a new skill or ask for a drink of water, or just a quiet time of occasional companionship while the adult washes a window, walks the dog, or waters the lawn. Later, if the relationship between you and the family develops further, you might become part of one another's acquaintance network or even your own open-family network. You might become closer to your young friend, gradually becoming a mentor, or an adopted uncle or aunt. Each relationship with a child can have its own special qualities and be a powerful lift for a child. Studies show how even limited contact with a caring adult can reduce teen pregnancy, substance and alcohol abuse. Many parents speak of brief contacts over a week's time with other people's children who come in for a visit, a play date, or youngsters who want contact with a safe and warm adult. The need, hope, and thirst for human affection runs deep. Children have much to teach us adults about directness, spontaneity, and a sense of wonder. When we limit our involvements to children who call us Mom or Dad, we limit ourselves.

WHEN THERE IS NO OTHER PARENT

Doris, Alice, and Harry are the names I'm using to describe three parents whose former mates are out of the picture. These are parents who are going it alone. For example, Doris had hoped that since the children's father did at least make contact with them on their birthdays and was faithful in sending the support checks that she would eventually be able to develop a working relationship with him. She had taken many of the steps necessary to develop a working relationship. Doris's efforts had brought her a release from her former anger and resentment. But despite her good efforts and some eased tensions, the children's father did not choose to become reinvolved with the children. As another mother said in the same situation, "Dead or alive, he's gone."

TURN YOUR ENERGIES TO INCLUDING OTHERS

Doris began to turn more of her energies toward reinforcing her already functioning extended-family system. Her parents lived two states away, but her sister and her family lived in the next city, twenty miles away. She also had friends from her church and some close friends. She began to pay more attention to their families and how she and her children could become closer. For example, her sister's children were younger than her children, but she offered to come over with her kids and give her sister some time off on a Saturday while she cared for the combined brood for three hours. During the separation, her sister had been there for her. Now she could reciprocate. Her children loved their cousins and their auntie Carole and uncle Mel. This was what family was about.

Alice and Susan are solo parents. They have known each other for seven years and have been close friends. They have shared child care, holidays, even a vacation together with their children. What is different now is that Alice (now Aunt Alice) proposed to Susan that they have a clear under-standing regarding what they would and would not do with one another's children. Alice felt constrained in how she related to Susan's children. Each mother wanted more. They wanted to be more like aunts than like adult friends. They wanted to be more supportive to each other as parents. This was an important step. "Now, I can say, 'I don't like it when you talk back to your mother like that,' when Susan's daughter starts with her mouth," said Alice. "Before I felt constrained. I wasn't supposed to interfere." "We know this will be messy sometimes," said Susan. "We probably will have some disagreements. But working these things out is what will make us closer. And we need each other to be honest." The two women settled on some basic rules for how they would relate to each other's children and jotted them down. They were on their way to another form of cooperative parenting.

The situation Harry typifies was somewhat similar to Doris's in that his son's mother had dropped out four years ago, and he had never received any communications from her. Harry had no hopes that his former mate would ever again reenter his son's life. In contrast to Doris's more gregarious personal style and her relish for an open-family system, Harry was a loner and probably would continue to be so. His approach toward an open family was to give his son the opportunity to develop a network as Frank's sons had. Harry made the opportunity available for his son while maintaining his own personal quiet style.

"I was surprised to see how I had insulated myself from others," said Harry. "I wanted to be by myself when I felt punk, I totally relied on Jay's grandmother for anything unusual that happened. I shared my birthdays with her, my son, Jay, and Betsy, the woman I'm going with. I either went places alone or with Betsy." Harry's world suited him, but it wasn't especially helpful to his son or to him as a parent. Betsy was pleasant enough but not particularly interested in Jay. Harry was her focus. Grandma kept good contact with her grandson but lived on the other side of town. Jay needed more places where he could stay over if an occasion arose, more people to give him a hug now and then, perhaps an uncle he could look up to and feel safe with.

Harry, for example, can give Jay the opportunity to meet other families by joining a father-son activity like Little League or some club like those found at Boys' Clubs or the YMCA. These are easy and fun ways for someone with Harry's more private lifestyle to meet other parents and children on safe, nondemanding terms. The schedules are structured, the activity supervised by other adults, and parents and children alike can make as much or as little of this focus as they wish. Jay can meet the kids and their parents with his father's blessing and scrutiny. Harry's initial presence is his stamp of approval that encourages his son. Once Jay gets started in such activities and becomes friends with some of the others, Harry's presence will be less necessary. If Harry helps Jay make contacts with his new friends outside of the activity after a few meetings, he will be launching Jay on his own open circle of friends.

Solo parenting—where you are parenting alone—is a common occurrence. Nevertheless the children need education, affection, emotional and physical security, standards, and limits. The parents' needs are similar. Basic human needs are the same, whether there is one involved parent or two. All parents—married, single, remarried—can give their children second and third homes by developing a working relationship with a relative or close friend. The tie doesn't matter; the love and caring do.

Chapter 18

Long-Distance Parenting

How to Feel Close When You Are

Far Apart

To Move or Not to Move Away
How to Feel Close When You Are Far Apart
Partings and Reunions

"SHE'S taking the kids to Michigan," cried Phil, a forty-four-year-old engineer, in a fury. "She's taking them away from me! She knows damned well I can't hop a plane every other weekend or fly them out here to California. She's crazy to do this to the kids and me."

Phil knew about two homes. His children had two homes for three years while he and the boys' mother had been living in the same city. He was shocked at the prospect of being separated from his sons by more than 2,500 miles, and he didn't know how he could continue his relationship over such a long distance. Although he was an involved parent, the children's mother held the title of "sole custodian." And his original legal agreement had neglected to make his permission necessary for the other parent's out-of-area moves with the children, nor did it spell out mutually acceptable standards for such a change. He feared he had no formal or legal authority in his parenting plan to block his former mate's decision to move with the boys to another state. He was angry, hurt, and frightened.

TO MOVE OR NOT TO MOVE AWAY

Any major geographic move by one parent is going to affect the children, as well as the other parent. It is one of the most difficult, most heartrending decisions a parent may have to make—or be powerless to stop. Yet it is inevitable that for many families there will be new jobs, new relationships with ties in other parts of the country, a longing to be closer to one's roots and extended family, or just the need to start afresh. "The kids need the stability of aunts, uncles, cousins, grandparents," say parents. Or, "I have a

Linda's Worksheet on the Pros and Cons of Moving Away

What	Problems	Solutions—Stay	Solutions—Move
Neighborhood and living quarters	Unsafe, not enough room, no money to move.	Move to safer location and larger place, but more expensive.	Safer location, can afford larger quarters.
Children's school	Too crowded, not enough money for private school.	New school in new location, or private school.	Public schools are better, maybe can afford private school for one child.
Day care	Expensive, kids in too many hours.	John has children more in afternoons; I change jobs.	Grandmother will provide after school and sick care.
Kids have their father in the same city. He is available in emergencies.	Kids don't see John very much now.	John sees kids more often, calls them more.	John has kids summer and holidays. Calls them more. Family helps with emergencies.
Overnights with John now that he has remarried.	Down to 4 nights a month from 8.	Increase overnights.	Lump time with kids during summers and holidays.
Together time and activity time with John now that he has remarried.	Down from 5–6 hours a week to 5–6 hours a month.	Increase together and activity time.	Phones, e-mail, and time during summers and holidays.
Support extended family	Aside from friends and John, no support, no help with kids.	New neighborhood and school. John has to be more involved.	Extended family will provide support.

(continues)

(*continued from previous page*)

John and Lisa's Worksheet on the Pros and Cons of Linda's Move

What	*Problems*	*Solutions—Stay*	*Solutions—Move*
Neighborhood and school	Not the best, could be better.	The children could come and live with Lisa and me. Maybe subsidize better housing.	Less expensive there. Neighborhoods are safer. Don't know about schools.
Continuity of place and having both parents		Children have both parents, and a stepmother here.	Father and stepmother are missing. Mother's parents and sister's family are there.
Linda's working hours	Hours are too long, kids in day care too long.	Kids could be in more supervised activities or more with us.	No guarantee Linda's work hours will be less. Not so sure about Grandma as sitter.
Dad's time with the kids	New responsibilities have meant less contact lately.	Step up a new schedule where the kids are with me more.	Can't afford more than two or three trips a year.
Dad's help in an emergency.	My out-of-town travel schedule means I'm gone a lot.	Use my beeper. Lisa is backup.	Grandparents and sister's family can help.

They reviewed the charts together. Everyone was surprised at what the other was thinking! By the end of the second session, John and Lisa heard Linda say 1) she desperately needed to leave the current neighborhood and to put the children in a better school, 2) she did not feel she had a working relationship with John and Lisa about the children, and 3) John was not seeing the children enough. She was overstressed and exhausted parenting alone. Linda heard John say that he 1) recognized the neighborhood was going downhill and that they definitely needed to make some changes, 2) he thought that Linda's desire to move had to do with his remarriage and her feelings about Lisa, and 3) he felt torn between wanting to spend time with his new wife and his new life, and time with his children.

All three parents agreed that the children needed to get into a better school and a better neighborhood, but Linda couldn't do this on her current salary. Nor was there any chance of advancement in her current job. The three parents with the help of the mediator began to generate as many options as they could. These are listed below.

OPTIONS IF LINDA AND THE CHILDREN STAY

John pay for private school tuition; Linda and/or John and Lisa take out loans so Linda and the kids can move to a better neighborhood with better schools; the kids move in with John and Lisa, and Linda goes to advanced professional training at night school for a year; or John and Lisa become more involved with the children's activities and have them after school two or three days a week.

OPTIONS—MOVE AWAY

John and Lisa move to the same city as Linda; the children fly back to Dad's four times a year, Dad comes to their city two times a year, Dad pays less support in order to afford the plane tickets or Linda pays for two-thirds of the transportation; the kids spend at least four weeks in the summer with Dad and half of the major holidays, more time in the summer as they reach age ten and older. This is more time than he has now.

At the end of the mediation process John, Lisa, and Linda agreed to an arrangement whereby Linda would move to her former hometown, and the boys would be with their father and stepmother for a total of five weeks in the summer, half of the major holidays and three-day weekends (which would be stretched to four days each). They arranged a calendar with additional times so that the boys would never go more than six weeks without seeing their father. Costs for these trips would be shared three-fourths by John, one fourth by Linda. They would reevaluate how this plan was working for the boys in six months. John wanted the boys to live with him for the school year when they began high school. Linda was open to this but a final decision was not reached.

If the move is going to happen, parents need to answer the following questions, following the rule of answering easy questions first, hardest last:

1. Where will the children live? How will we make decisions for them now? Go back to chapters 10, 11, 12. Look at your own parenting plan clauses—many of them need to be revised now. For example, look at time: during the school year, during the summer, for long holidays.
2. Who will pay for travel: the parent who moves? both parents? In what proportions? What about rising costs? What priority will travel money have in family budgets? What happens if somebody fails to come through? Will older children contribute? Will certain money-conserving measures be written into the renegotiated agreement to ensure the lowest fares?
3. How long is too long for parent and child to be separated? Will time be increased?
4. How will communications be handled: between each parent and each child? between parents? Access to school and health records?
5. Who will arbitrate disagreements over money or time, and how?

There are poignant emotional consequences to big geographic separations. *Distance feels final* and gives tangible proof that the family has changed and the parents are separated. If one member of the family has harbored, however unconsciously, a hope for reconciliation, long distance will bring that false hope painfully to the surface. *The physical separation hurts.* Many miles means no way to hug, to brush back a forelock of hair, to drop in on football practice, or to witness the writing of a first book report. The parent separated from the child feels this pain, and so does the child. Some children, veterans of this experience, can describe how it feels.

"It was not too bad when my dad lived in Seattle," said Robert, aged thirteen, who lived the school year with his mother. "That was only five hundred miles away. Now he's moved to Houston, and I feel lonely." He touched his solar plexus. "Do you know about those lonely feelings?"

I nodded, touching my own place of knowing emptiness. "Two of my children are 2,500 miles away, too."

"Then you know how it is. Right about two months since you've seen them last you get to miss them like crazy, but you can't do anything," adding, "My dad and I are close, even though we don't see each other in the usual ways."

CHILDREN MUST KNOW WHEN THEY WILL SEE THE ABSENT PARENT NEXT

When children separated by many miles from a parent show signs of strain, I ask them, "When will you see your mother [or father] next?" If they answer, "I don't know," I ask, "What about letters?" Often they answer,

"Sometimes I get a letter. I don't write much, and phone calls cost too much. Mom [or Dad] doesn't have much money." Children can be adrift on their lonely feelings, not knowing when they will have that all-important contact with Mom or Dad. Some parents do an excellent job of explaining why they are moving away. But these same parents may not say when or how they will next see or talk to each other again. The absence of even a tentative timetable can hurt.

Both parents and children need factual clarity. A flexible but well-understood parenting plan and a set of parental priorities to make this plan work are basic to successful long-distance parenting. Even so, the separation hurts, the wail of children on the telephone sobbing, "You are so far away and I can't hug you." "You are more like an aunt than a mom." The strain of such times can be balanced somewhat by a parent's ability to keep in touch during long stretches of separation. And parents can learn to express more openly their deep appreciation of shared times.

LONG-DISTANCE PARENTING IS DIFFERENT FROM IN-HOUSE PARENTING

The parent on the other end of the telephone line many miles away has a unique but important role in the rearing of his or her child. It takes commitment, follow-through, but it is an amazing role. It is a different type of parenting. For older children, a parent can become a very special confidant. With younger children, however, it is harder to hold a strong bond.

When the link holds, parents talk about breakthrough periods when, as one father put it, "You know inside that it's working out okay for everyone."

CHECKLIST: FOR THE PARENT SEPARATED BY MANY MILES

1. Review chapters 6 and 20 on the emotions of divorce. The move may cause a flashback bringing back the negative expectations and emotions of past difficulties.
2. Review chapter 10 on children's fears and on needs during big changes. They need your reassurance as well as your permission to go with the other parent.
3. Explain the "why," "how," and "when" of the move. If the child is old enough, include him or her in discussions on how time together will be shared.
4. Reassure your child with detailed information on when you will be together next, when you will call and how you will be in touch. Give him or her a calendar with dates.
5. Give your child immediate, tangible proof of your connection with him or her—the phone call on arrival at the new place. Have a private phone line installed in the child's room (with an answering machine, if possible).
6. Make contact with the child's school; it is a way for you to know a little and care a lot about his or her world.
7. Brace yourself for the inevitable reactions from your children, and take the time to reassure and listen well. Remember that children past the age of eleven may have a harder time adjusting to new areas than those still in elementary school.
8. Plan from the beginning on the dollar costs and allocate enough money to make travel plans work.
9. Be conscious of how long is too long for you and your child to be separated.
10. Make travel between homes a top priority in both parents' budgets, not to be minimized short of major surgery or major emergency.

THE SCHOOL-YEAR PARENT

"In many ways, the move to Michigan was difficult," said Nancy six months after her arrival. Her sons were back with their father, completing their school year, and Nancy had started a new job without family or friends to lend a hand. "I felt anxious, unbearably lonely at first. I missed the boys far more than I expected. But I also felt a tremendous surge of excitement, and it wasn't all the new job, either. I was relieved to start over again somewhere without the reminders of the past staring at me in that little town. I loved the time alone and savored it, but was happy when the boys settled in for the school year with me."

Nancy's story reflects the common patterns parents experience after they replant themselves far away from the other parent and old surroundings. It feels like a fresh start. "No one knows about your past; they only know your present. It feels great," said one father.

"What I wasn't prepared for was how much the children would miss their old neighborhood, their father, and their old school," said Nancy when the boys had rejoined her to start the new school year. "It was exasperating. Some of their obstreperous behavior during the early weeks of the separation seemed to come back. The youngest became withdrawn, and the oldest picked fights at school. I tried to remember that they were really feeling a huge change in their lives and that this would pass, but it was hard. And there was no Dad on the scene to help me out when the going got rough. It was day-in, day-out parenting without a break. I began to wonder what I had let myself in for. Then I became furious with their father. He must have put them up to this resistance so they would agitate to go back to the old hometown. I was back in the off-the-wall, distrustful place of three years before."

Such experiences are common to many parents who make the move away with the children—the excitement, the newness, the delight, the release, and relief; and the stark reality of the children's seesaw behavior, happy one day, miserable the next, all without a day off. But while some parents do lobby and pressure children to reject the new arrangements and so return to them, most of the hurt and confusion is because drastic change is hard on children, and because they genuinely need and miss the other parent.

THE SUMMERTIME PARENT: COMMUNICATIONS—THE KEY

No matter who moves away, the parent separated by five hundred or five thousand miles during the school year cannot watch the children grow and develop day by day or be there to share those spontaneous moments proximity allows. This absence is felt by both parent and child, so that frequent communications with phone calls, e-mail, voice mail, answering machines, letters, snapshots, and video- or audiotapes become especially important. If you are parenting long-distance, try not to dwell on the time you're apart. Obviously the only solution is to find new ways to relate, to use time and communication avenues wisely and well, so that your children can know that you really are still their parent and that you are still a family.

HOW TO FEEL CLOSE WHEN YOU ARE FAR APART

People can communicate over long distances in as many ways as they can imagine and put into action. Some parents and older teenagers, influenced by the instant travel on television and movie screens, sometimes assume that distance won't bother them or their missing family members. "I can't do anything about it anyhow," marks the attempt to be brave or stay cool. Make no mistake. It matters. And it matters what you do. Although these long-distance ways of connecting can't beat a hug or a pat, they take on their own vitality.

We live in an age where technology provides many forms of access. Parents have many possibilities to choose from, and so do the children. The success of the contact, however, lies in its consistency even in the face of a child's seeming disinterest or nonresponse. If you are the parent who moved away, you may have to earn your way back to reciprocal communications by keeping up your end in the face of initial disinterest.

THE MAILS

E-mail and regular mail. Both are excellent ways for the resident parent to let the other parent know what is happening at school or with the latest doctor visit. It can even help with homework. With older children, e-mail is an easy way to have frequent, even daily contact. Let your child know about your day, where you have been, what you saw. If you watch the same TV shows or sporting events, you can share reviews.

Short letters with lots of pictures sent by surface mail (along with some self-addressed, stamped return envelopes) are another unbeatable bargain for continuity and contact with children, especially young children who are enthralled with having their very own mail coming to the door. Many parents write letters laced with travelogues and weather reports, riddles, and jokes along with impressions and feelings. The subjects need not relate directly to the parent-child relationship. It is enough to share some of your daily life with them. Content of the letters depends on the ages of your children. Small children love photographs, stickers, and postcards. They can't read, but they know when something comes that is for them, from you, whether it is a dead bug, a picture cut from a magazine, or a drawing signed with your symbol or name, and the XXXs and OOOs of kisses and hugs.

Children don't often answer letters. Most of the time it is too exacting to sit down and write. And it may hurt to have to think about the parent who is so far away. Nonetheless, enclose a stamped, addressed envelope with all your correspondence or, better yet, send them in batches. Small children love the independence that comes with putting a scrap of paper with their mark on it in your envelope and mailing it back to you themselves! A child can answer your letter easily and independently without the cooperation of the other parent. Your relationship with your child is not the responsibility of the other parent. But it helps immensely when you have his or her support.

MAILS AND THE SCHOOLS

The same technique you use to establish communication with your children also succeeds with their school. Some parents initially wonder what good all this information can do when they are hundreds, even thousands, of miles away. First, when you have pertinent information like a school calendar, you know what's happening and can ask intelligent questions of your child concerning events, school, and the like. You can be a support to the other parents as well. Second, your child knows that you know and that you care enough to know. This is most important for his or her sense of your caring and of your continuing relationship. But what if one of your children begins to fail in school and bad reports arrive in the mail? Your involvement is already part of the solution. Even though long-distance parenting does bring a sense of helplessness about your child's day-to-day events, your knowledge and attention, even from a distance, can nevertheless be most reassuring to both your child and to the other parent.

THE PHONES: VOICE MAIL, BEEPERS, ANSWERING MACHINES

The phone rings in the girls' room. They know it is either one of their friends or their father. How do they know? Because Dad saw to it that the phone was installed in their new room after they moved away, along with an answering machine. And he pays the bill. He can call and leave a message or talk to them anytime. They can reach him anytime—or at least leave a message. Dad has voice mail at work and an answering machine at home. This is a very useful practice whether or not the homes are separated by many miles or not. It can give both children and parents a sense of security and continuity.

A beeper vibrates on your belt, you check the number. It is from your son, age thirteen, living two hundred miles away. "Dad, I made the team!" Your son can pass this triumph along to you just as quickly as if you were living in the same town. True, you can't pop by the house to give him a hug, but he knows you know and that he will talk to you about it soon. You can ask him about the tryout, his teammates, how he feels—all on the phone. But you can't watch the first game, unless you travel two hundred miles to do so. A beeper does not substitute for a parent's physical presence, but it can be a meaningful presence nonetheless.

Voice mail and answering machines are indispensable. Unfortunately, they do malfunction. Messages are lost or not deposited on time, power fails. And, voice mail hell—where a caller cannot reach a living soul—is no place for a child who needs to reach you *now*. So be sure that your child has an alternate number or two to call that will certainly reach you.

THE THINKING-OF-YOU BOX

The thinking box is a collection of little things that you give to your child when you reunite. Extra or particularly special postcards or pictures; a pressed flower from a particularly colorful place; a small piece of driftwood; a book; an idea you had, dated with time and place . . . anything can be put in a special box or container, awaiting your child's presence. "I still have the seashells you sent me five years ago," a child reveals. A teen confesses, "I have all these things my dad has given me in a special place." When we tell our children who are far away that we are thinking of them, and that even though we are far away they have a home with us, we can back up our assurances with a special memento in a special container. The voice-to-voice communication is a daily treasure. But physical, tangible, collectible things appeal to the other senses of touch, smell, sight, and sound. These things stand as concrete, retouchable, re-readable evidence of caring.

Some parents keep a journal, putting in written entries for the child now and then: "I saw a sixteen-year-old girl who looked like you. I wondered if in four years you would have your hair as long as she did. Did you know our aunt Jane wore her hair like that—long and silken—until about a year ago?" A journal is a concrete way of imparting belonging, of talking with your child, of keeping your child part of your daily life.

Parents who have been denied total access to their children can collect these treasures for the day when they will be united with their children. When the reunion comes, and it most often does, even if it is years later, these dated mementos stand as testimony of the parent's steadfastness and love and provide both parents and child with a vehicle for making up part of their lost time together.

VIDEOTAPES, CASSETTES

These are very helpful and eagerly awaited by children. The VCR and tape deck are common household items. Many families own videocameras. Making audio and videotapes and receiving them can be a lot of fun, and the children's friends can play, too. Yes, videotapes are more costly than e-mail or letters, but they can be quite wonderful for children. If you are separated from your child, a video of you, your home, neighborhood, friends, family, will become a favorite. They can show their friends what their absent parent looks like, what he or she is doing, and show that he or she thinks enough of them to make this tape. The parent separated from his or her children can see how much the children have grown, see the new neighborhood, the room, the school. "Dad now knows what my school looks like. When we talk on the phone, I know that he knows." "Mom sent a videotape of her new apartment and of our room there and her new office." Some of these videotapes will definitely take a cooperative resident parent, but if you must be separated by many miles, please try to cooperate for the sake of the children, especially those first difficult months of the move. Older children can do the taping themselves. Younger ones can be the directors for a willing adult camera operator and can do the narration. Videotapes can help everyone adjust.

One child's lonely feelings were eased considerably when he decided to use his friend's audiotape recorder to make an hour-long audiotape for his father. He even recorded interviews with his friends. His father was delighted with the tape, and a better communications system began to grow between them. The children's production of such tapes can be surprising, so much so that parents are amazed their children's antics could be so sophisticated. "These kids should have their own TV show," said one parent. Some parents read bedtime stories or the classics to their children through audio- or videotapes. One mother found that the sound of the absent father's voice on an audiotape he had made for their two-year-old was especially soothing for the child.

SHARING PROJECTS AND EVENTS LONG-DISTANCE

When child and parent separated by miles make a date to watch the same TV programs, read the same article or newspaper, or cheer for the same baseball team, these sentimental and spontaneous links give double pleasure. You can discuss them in letters, compare notes on the phone, and use them as bridges when you first get together again. Many projects generate even more concrete evidence of family solidarity. I, for instance, had my daughter Amy's fish in my care, following her telephone instructions about new snails, food, and what to do with baby guppies.

CHECKLIST: LONG-DISTANCE COMMUNICATIONS

1. Continually reassure the child of your love, but do it in simple terms and gestures. The key here is to show *and* tell.
2. Call and talk to the child at least twice weekly, and if possible much more often. Consider a private phone and answering machine in the child's room just for your calls.
3. Set up a telephone or beeper signal so the child can let you know if he or she needs to talk to you.
4. Provide the child with stamped, self-addressed envelopes.
5. Use video- and audiocassette tapes for correspondence, reading bedtime stories, and so forth. Mail pictures of your life and environment.
6. Use e-mail, beepers, voice mail, and answering machines for frequent written communications.
7. Start a "thinking-of-you box"—dated items, mementos, and unmailed letters to give the child when reunited, if you're out of touch with him or her at present.
8. Make connections long-distance with the child's school and if possible with doctors and coaches.

PARTINGS AND REUNIONS

HOME FOR THE SUMMER

"I stood waiting for them to get off that plane from New York," said the father of two teenagers, "thinking, 'My God, I'm shaking with pure excitement. It's been three months since we've been together, and finally, at long last, here we are.'" A teenage girl admits, "I was standing waiting to get off the plane and my heart was pounding so hard in my chest. I was going to see my mother!" The feelings of reunion are sweet. Those of parting again at the end of the summer, with another long expected absence, are wrenching. But as one mother put it, "What's the alternative? I won't go without seeing them. They are my family. It hurts, but we take the hurt of separation as part of what we have to put up with. It doesn't keep us from coming together again."

THE PHYSICAL STRAIN OF TRAVEL AND REUNION

Traveling is tiring. Sheer nervous energy and the fatigue that follow the trip add to the physical strain. "The kids need a lot of rest those first few days," say parents. Then, gradually, the reality of being with the other parent sinks in, and within a week or two they settle into the old routine. A word to the parent putting the child on the plane, train, or bus to the other home: Try to see that the child has had plenty of sleep and rest before the trip. The child's energy and excitement often mount before the trip, making the reentry period more fatiguing. Transition anxiety need not be a negative thing and does respond to rest and calming schedules rather than late hours and excessive activities. Reread the parts about safety rules and house rules, and when your child arrives, take the time to walk the neighborhood again with your children (chapter 9). All these things make everyone feel at home and relaxed again.

Parting at summer's end can be hard. As one child said somberly, "The day you think will never happen is here." The hard reality of saying good-bye again for another two, three, or six months can be softened with phone calls on arrival and more frequent talks during the transition period of the next few weeks. Still, the transition is difficult, especially for sensitive children. "It is so confusing," said one preteenage girl. "You get up in the morning and you are with one parent, you get on a plane and by lunch you are in a different city, different climate, and with your other parent. It is so fast. I don't like it. I feel weird."

HOME FOR THE SCHOOL YEAR

The school-year parent has the routine and home base of school. For the children, it's time to find out what other kids have been doing over the summer. The traditional routine makes reentry much easier for everyone. But even so, children will show signs of missing the other parent, signs of withdrawal or of sadness.

"It takes about two weeks," Cindy said confidently, describing her own experience, "for me to get past some of those missing feelings and some of the weird feelings of being in two places at once. Then it's okay." Many children feel that the first year of separation is the hardest, since they must cope with the unknown, the differences between the two places, plus missing the other parent and other family members. But school's demands and the excitement make up for a good deal of the emptiness and sense of strangeness.

Younger children do not reenter as easily as school-age children. They, after all, have concrete expectations of life. And if one parent's routine is rigid while the other's is exceptionally loose, relocation is much harder. They can be bewildered, even disoriented.

BE PATIENT, BE UNDERSTANDING

For all parents: Have patience with your children's behavior when they reenter. Remember they no longer have access to both homes and both parents within one week as they may have had when you all lived in the same city. Long distances between their homes, sometimes with drastically different climates and time zone changes, can be disorienting.

Children must face again and again the fact that their parents live very far apart. When they say good-bye to one and hello to the other, they know they may be separated from the other parent for a long time. This is hard for children, but they do handle it more or less. "The only option is not seeing my dad at all," said sixteen-year-old Craig of his situation, in which one parent lived in England and the other in Ohio, "and that is no option at all. I have a mom and a dad and that's that." The inconveniences and the discomforts of travel and readjustments are far better than having one parent unavailable altogether or only on a very limited basis.

If you have been communicating regularly with your children while they are at the other house, reentry troubles will be smaller for everybody. The more the two homes have been connected by good communications, the less difficult the transition will be.

As both children and parents adjust and expand to the different circumstances of their lives and the experiences of two homes in two different locales, many reactions emerge. Children have said such things as "It hardly bothers me now. I've gotten so used to it, I don't even think about it anymore," "It's neat having two homes so far apart," and "I missed my dad at first when I was at school at Mom's house, but he has been seeing me more this year and it's easier."

"I do it because they are my parents and I haven't much choice if I want to be with them," said one twelve-year-old girl. "But I'd like it better if they lived only twenty miles apart instead of two thousand." When I asked her to describe an ideal two-home situation, she and her friend, also with widely separated parents, described homes within easy driving distance where they could be with each parent no less often than once a week. "After a month, I get to feeling bad and sad inside and I either have to call my mom or write her a letter before I feel better."

Other children describe a merciful amnesia that temporarily blocks out their need for physical contact with the other parent. "I got to missing Dad so much that I was crying a lot, and then all of a sudden it was over and I never thought about him anymore—I couldn't even remember what he looked like. Then when I got off the plane and saw him, I cried a lot." For some children the distance continues to be painful, something they have to live with. Absence cannot continually make the heart grow fonder and more tender. Children have few choices when parents move away and they must cope as best they can with the consequences that accompany their parents' decisions.

Both parents and children will meet new experiences, new friends, new ties that can all enrich the child's sense of family and home. Children have an opportunity to become more flexible, to be totally immersed in one lifestyle when with one parent, without having to give up forever the other parent. Older children often report a growing sense of independence. "You have to be more independent," said one teenager. "There's no hopping on a bus so you can drop by Dad's office and talk a problem over with him at a moment's notice." You make the effort to communicate in other ways.

Parents report varying degrees of satisfaction with the two-home arrangement. "I don't like it. I'm the one separated from the kids the most. I put up with it and make the best of it, but I don't like it," said thirty-two-year-old Les. "No matter what anyone says, the parent who has the kid for the school year is the parent who exerts the biggest influence on the child's life. I know that sounds competitive and it probably is, but that's how I feel."

"I like it very much," said thirty-seven-year-old Carole. "I don't have to look at my ex-husband's presence three or four times a month when he comes to pick up the children. In fact, I never have to see him at all. The kids are the ones who have made all the adjustments. I knew they would have to make the biggest sacrifices, and they have. But I think it's the best way for us."

"I like it." "I don't like it." "It's not what I expected of parenthood, but it is parenthood nevertheless." There are no easy answers. As with so many of the choices that follow the reorganization of a family, you must consider all the alternatives and choose the best for all of you.

Chapter 19

When an Absent Parent Returns

Things to Consider

How Children Feel When They Lose a Parent
The Price of Reentry—For Both Parents
When Reinvolvement Does Not Work: Two Homes with
Friends and Relatives

"My 'ex' has faded away. He pays child support, but he never sees the kids. The children miss him, ask about him. I never made it difficult for him to see the children. I encouraged visitation; he just wouldn't respond." The only reason for the absence appears to be that the parent doesn't care. A deep resentment can grow in a mother who survives the rapids of parenting alone, holding afloat children suffering the loss of a parent. Some finally get their life together only to have the absent father call, announce his new marriage, and expect instant reinvolvement with the children as if nothing had happened. I've heard such mothers say: "Fat chance he has of seeing these kids."

Some parents are not absent by choice. Some have been pushed out or left behind by a parent who abducts their child. Pushed-out parents are those parents who want to be with their children, but the resident parent or the expense of travel prevents it. There are also a number of situations where a resident parent has made the access to the child nearly impossible. Over time, the "outside" parent is effectively removed from the child's life. "My wife was so unreasonable and possessive that I just gave up trying to see the kids. I figured it was easier on everyone." A number of parents have a deep concern and love for their children but feel they hurt themselves and their offspring by being in the family picture. Some actively seek ways to someday again become active parents. For others, a partial amnesia appears to block out their children, with many making no effort to see their offspring for years at a time.

When a parent has dropped out, a child nearly always struggles with pain, bewilderment, and a loss of self-worth. For the remaining parent, parenting solo may mean trying to be everything to the child—mother and father—psychologically as well as financially. Unless resident parents want the other parent out of the picture, they also suffer a loss. There will be no one to share the joys and problems of parenting, no other parent to call to help with emergencies, and often no child support.

REENTRY IS COMPLICATED!

The reinvolvement process is often a complicated one deserving at least several volumes by itself. It usually calls for some professional consultation or advice. Commonly there are unsettled issues between mother and father—often debts around property or child support, bad feelings, negative intimacy, and old frozen ways of looking at each other. Even parents who say "What is the use?" at attempting to reinvolve the other parent often admit that the resignation they profess on the surface overlays anger, hurt, and feelings of resentment, even revenge.

HOW CHILDREN FEEL WHEN THEY LOSE A PARENT

ABUSE, NEGLECT, VIOLENCE

When a parent is absent because there has been violence, neglect, or abuse, the separation from that parent can be a blessed relief. Nonetheless, many children who have suffered may still harbor a longing for that absent parent. Some even blame the residential parent. Dealing with abuse, neglect, and violence is very complex. If your child is separated from you or the other parent because of these circumstances—regardless of whether these are unfounded allegations or the real thing—seek counseling with an expert in these matters. And seek it again before you attempt to reenter the child's life or seek to reinvolve the parent. Your situation is special, and this book cannot cover the information you should have to make measured judgments.

CHILDREN CAN FEEL ABANDONED, RESPONSIBLE, RESENTFUL, DEEPLY HURT

In nonabusive situations, many children, regardless of their ages, can also carry with them a sense of deep hurt and fear. Younger children cannot express their feelings of loss in words. Their behavior is altered, they regress to earlier developmental stages. Something very important is missing. As a child grows into preschool and school age, there may be even deeper feelings of abandonment, loss, and confusion. Many children secretly fear they are the reason their parent has disappeared. A few mix these feelings with sharp resentment at being so unimportant. It's one thing to feel you are responsible for your parents' separation, but it is even worse to feel that you made the other parent disappear. "What did I do to make them hate me so much, they don't want to see me?" a younger child may wonder.

Older children usually know the parent is absent because of choice or a personal weakness. Perhaps this is due to a remarriage or lifestyle that has supplanted them in importance. These children long for a parent to say, "You are really important. I do want to be in your life." When it doesn't happen, they make judgments. Sometimes they are realistic, sometimes they are not. "He left me and my mom and never even remembered my birthday or my graduation," said one eleven-year-old girl. "Now he wants to be my father? No way." Yet underneath all this, there is the void. She does want and need a father who cares and whom she can relate to.

RETURNING USUALLY MEANS HAVING TO SAY "I'M SORRY"

Some reentry situations are relatively clear-cut even if drawn out. "I went off to graduate school," said one twenty-six-year-old father of a five-year-old daughter. "And although I would call now and then, I hardly saw her. And I stopped paying support, arguing that I wasn't working full-time. After I graduated, I faced up to what I had done to her, and to her mother. Those two years had been hard ones for both of us. Without my financial contribution to help out, they were forced to ask my former in-laws for help. My daughter must have thought I had abandoned her." This father had the good sense to contact the mother first (not the daughter) and to tell her he came to the realization of what he had done. He was man enough to say, "I realize now that this must have hurt Melanie and been hard for you. I am sorry. I do want to be an active father. I want to make it up to Melanie and you. How can I do that?"

The mother needed time to recover from the shock of the phone call and the apology. She talked it over with her parents and with a close friend. "If he had called and pulled one of those 'I'm her father and I'm coming to get her, I have my rights' type of thing," said Melanie's mother, "I would have called a lawyer fast. But he said he was 'sorry.' I can understand his situation with school and all, but to drop out like that was irresponsible and hurtful. I've been really angry." The mother suggested that they meet face-to-face later in the week and talk it through.

They met. It was emotional. They both survived and agreed to meet again. After three meetings they had a plan. Dad agreed to reinstate his support payments and to pick up additional costs for day care as a way to repay his past child support. He also agreed that he would eventually thank and apologize to Mom's parents for standing in for him. Mom agreed that Dad would reenter Melanie's life gradually. First she would tell him that he had finished school and that he was going to be calling her on the phone to see when she wanted him to come and visit. Mom felt that Melanie should feel some control over Dad's reentry since she had no control over his dropping out. Once Melanie consented to see her father, he would visit Melanie at home with Mom present. At first this would be just for thirty minutes, then, within a week or two, an hour. At the end of two months, overnights could be tried, depending on how Melanie was responding.

This reentry father is fortunate: the child's mother is supporting his reentry. The mother is fortunate: the father is owning up to his responsibilities. Each needs to be careful over the months to come that past guilt or resentment doesn't take over in tough times. Their child is fortunate because with any luck she will have both parents again. And both are looking to her for cues to regulate the speed of the reconnection with Dad. The father knows that even if it is slow going, the mother will support an eventual two-home situation.

The primary parent also has to say "I'm sorry" if they have kept the other parent from his or her children. Perhaps it is "I'm sorry it has been so difficult for you, and for our child" or "I'm sorry, I misjudged you" or "I was doing what I thought was the best for our child. But I'm sorry it was so hard on you." You don't have to say "It was my fault" unless it was. If you are seeking to reinvolve the other parent, or are thinking about his or her wishes to come back into your child's life, think hard about how you can acknowledge their pain. They, too, have borne a loss.

IF YOU WANT TO REINVOLVE AN ABSENT PARENT . . .

1. Do not let up on your efforts to develop important adult-child relationships for your children with relatives or friends. Look for ways they can have second, third, and fourth homes. This should go on regardless of what happens with the other parent.
2. Move away from negative intimacy, in your mind, in your heart, and in your actions. Take your children out of the middle.
3. If and when you have dealings with the other parent, make them businesslike and courteous.
4. If he or she doesn't respond within a reasonable amount of time, shift your attention to other good people in your life who will be open and caring about you and the children. You can, with effort, build two homes for your children with a relative or friend.
5. If the other parent later comes back into the picture, keep an open mind, but keep your open family. Your children might end up with it all—the other parent, extra homes with relatives and friends, and an open family!

BECOMING AN ACTIVE PARENT AGAIN

Parents who want to come back into their children's lives need to first contact the parent the children are living with and make an initial attempt at a civil and businesslike conversation. Even if the initial attempt is unsuccessful, a follow-up letter, stating your intent and desire to become an active parent, can be sent. Persistence and a show of good faith on your part are important. There may be tension and distrust. "Is this just a false display of interest? Will my custody be challenged?" a mother might ask herself. "Will the children be persuaded not to see me?" a father might think.

Once you have passed the first hurdle by contacting the other parent, you can begin to work out a plan together to begin contact. If you haven't seen your child in years, this should be a gradual process. If your separation has been a matter of months, then your timing will be different. In either case, a simple "I was thinking of you" when contacting a child is not enough. You need to explain why you've been away and apologize. Tell them how much you have missed them and how important they are to you.

After the children and the other parent have had a chance to get used to more frequent contacts, time alone together can resume. Sometimes parents religiously stick to the original court order's specifications of designed time. This is a known quantity, a beginning framework. Even if the old agreement was a troublemaker before, it's something that might temporarily work while another short-term schedule is discussed.

Concurrently, the person regaining active parenthood can begin to establish the child's new, other home. The groundwork, house safety rules, and house rules discussed in chapter 9 should be worked out or negotiated with the other parent.

The first four or five months of a trial period are a time when trust is being reestablished, and little by little, pieces of the old puzzle of those past events may fall into place. "Why did you really stop calling me?" a child might finally ask of a parent. Parents need to answer these questions.

Most children want both parents involved in their lives. The lost parent who reenters the picture after several years of silence can often become an active parent again despite the other parent's disbelief and possible resentment. If the former parent is willing to start from the ground up and rebuild trust and respect with the children, he or she can, in time, establish another home for them. If the resentment of the other parent is a continual barrier, perhaps professional counseling can point the ways to a trial parenting agreement. The unfinished business of the past should be put to rest for all concerned. The change, when it works, is worth the time and the effort.

IF YOU WANT TO RETURN
CHECKLIST FOR THE RETURNING PARENT

First, think things over and consider the consequences:

1. Think about seeing a mediator to explain your situation and ask for guidance on how to bring the other parent into a mediation process with you. If the other parent agrees, mediation could help everyone.

2. Think about how you will say "I'm sorry":
   - If you felt "pushed out," you can say to your child, "I'm sorry things happened the way they did." Don't blame the other parent. If pressed by an older child, you can say that the other parent was doing what they thought was best.
   - If you faded away and are back now, say you are sorry that you have been gone. Don't weasel out of it by acting as if it should not be a big deal. Ask how you can make it up. If you get an "It's okay," don't believe it. Your child may not want to estrange you by exposing hurt or anger.

3. Rebuild trust by being trustworthy. Actions speak louder than words. Start with one thing you know you will be sure to do, then do it.

4. Be prepared to weather some emotional storms with both your child and the other parent.

5. Reenter your child's life in gradual stages. Let the child and the other parent set the pace, at least for the first year.

A SMALL STEP—INVESTIGATE SHARING INFORMATION

The granting of information privileges by the custodial parent to the other parent does not give the other parent the right to make decisions for the children, but it does give him or her the right to have information about the children. The custodial parent has lost nothing, but the other parent can gain a good deal of respect and status as a result. When this works, both the renewed parent and the child can receive a boost of positive reinforcement of their relationship from this action. Remember that under most state laws, unless you have an agreement that states otherwise, the parent with sole custody, primary custody, primary care, and sometimes primary residency usually has the most (or unquestioned) authority. Sharing information can be a small but helpful step forward.

SHARING CERTAIN DECISIONS

The next step for the parent with custody is to ask yourself how willing you are to give your former mate the title of a joint legal custodial parent instead of a visitor. What would this change really mean to you? Titles are status. A visitor is a person who doesn't belong, who must obey the rules. Being a joint custodian—even if that word "legal" modifies its clout in the real world—is better than and different from being a "visitor." Would you share decisions?

You might consider sharing decisions from many angles. You could offer to go all the way to a modification of your previous court order; you could offer it as a sincere gesture of seeking a more balanced scale of power as parents. You could offer and give information, access, and status but still retain all the legal authority. The more you can give (hoping to work out your shared authority), the greater the risk and the greater the potential benefits. (Chapters 10, 11, 12, and 13 can be useful here.)

Often, the inside parent who seeks the other parent's reinvolvement is more than willing to share authority. But the outside parent may not be willing, at least at first. "I'm giving you joint legal custody and I'll put it in writing, too," said one mother. "What do I have to do?" growled the father. "Nothing," she replied, "it's just there if you ever choose to be more involved than you are now." A year later this father returned from his fading status and became a two-home parent. This change was not without the usual ups and downs of a working relationship, but it might never have happened if Mom had not opened the door. Please note that this mom didn't open the door just to reinvolve the dad. She confessed she wanted to feel that she had done all she could. "If he decides not to take the option, no one can blame me."

CUSTODY LABELS

If the nonresident parent feels the major impediment to involvement is the initial award of sole custody, however reasonable the custodial parent may be, the other parent's relationship with the children can feel tenuous. In the end, a noncustody parent may feel stripped, defeated. They might think they can parent only at the pleasure (or whim) of the other parent. The other parent, often unaware of the psychological power of their position, may find the sole custody award a silly reason for his withholding behavior. "I'll give him/her more authority." Or even the classic "All she/he has to do is ask."

While some see no reason for anyone to be so bullied by legal terms, the truth is that the loss of legal status is often at the root of the absent parent's feelings of invalidation, defensiveness, or sense of powerlessness. In my experiences, parents with specific joint custody arrangements don't seem to fade away in the same numbers as do sole custody/visitation parents. A vague legal agreement that calls for "reasonable visitation" to the noncustodial parent is not much help. Try to at least negotiate a calendar for times together.

REACTIONS

When reinvolvement does become a reality, the wonder of watching the past right itself and old wounds heal feels like a miracle. The healing, however, also shows how deep the hurt. There are often unexpected reactions from one or more members of the family. Knowing about what these reactions may be and where they may appear is useful.

The skepticism of friends and family may show itself. "I'd just wait and see if he really means it this time." "Where does she get off acting as if nothing happened all those years when she denied him seeing his children?" "I'd never forgive a woman like that." "I'd make him pay dearly for what he's done." Or, "I'm surprised at him even wanting to have her back in the children's lives after all she's done."

Others do not understand the complexities of the inside story of a family. Not even the people directly affected by such a situation understand it completely. A father can feel real guilt when he sees how his children have suffered because of his absence. A mother can feel deep remorse when she sees that her behavior denied her children their father. These honest feelings need not take over the show, however; they are there, they can be felt, and you can then get on with a better plan. If you find you have a series of amends to make, perhaps you could begin by saying simply, "I'm sorry it all happened the way it did. What can I do to help make it up?"

THE PRICE OF REENTRY—FOR BOTH PARENTS

Part of reinvolvement means paying a reentry price. As already mentioned, this may mean that at some juncture you have to admit that you were wrong and genuinely apologize. You may see that some of your old decisions or behavior were not wise or generous or benign. You may have hurt people badly, especially your children. You may have yelled, "I never want to see you again," and meant it five years ago. But you don't mean it now. One day at a time. One meeting at a time. Reinvolvement usually happens gradually over months, even years. As one mother said when her children's father became reinvolved in their lives after a two-year absence, "It became clear to me that the natural relationship between the children and their father was just not canceled by the emotions that I had been through with him. The kids needed him, he needed them. I began to see how he needed to feel in order to be a real father. I hadn't given him a chance. I had taken the kids out of state. Why should he support them so far away from him?" When the mother described the end of their first two weeks together in three years, she said, "When I saw John and Lisa with their father, it was so clear to me how important they were to one another. It was easier to forget all those times when I needed him to be their father and he wasn't there. I thought, There is another person who is just as responsible as I am for these children. I didn't feel so alone." A year later she said, "Seeing my son with his father is so revealing. They look and act so much alike. Now I'm not threatened by the thought that he may want to live with his father someday."

A year later, when the son went to live with his father, the father was delighted. The mother did not see it as an insult to her.

WHEN REINVOLVEMENT DOES NOT WORK: TWO HOMES WITH FRIENDS AND RELATIVES

Not all parents who seek reinvolvement will get it, and not all parents who investigate it will want it. Some mothers with sole custody awards have initially sought consultations for the express purpose of reinvolving the father and then changed their minds when they began to explore what this would actually mean. A few said, "I don't want him to have any authority at all. He should just see them like the agreement says." A few admitted that getting a break from parenting was their prime concern. A few more tasted the implications of reinvolvement and decided to think about it more before they made any changes.

On the other side of the coin, fathers who sought reinvolvement were also of various minds. Some had romantic fantasies of freshly scrubbed cherubs who would complete their lives with their love and childlike wonder. These fathers didn't want the children when they were ill, poorly behaved, or cranky. They wanted a form of joint custody that gave them fully one-half of the child's time but would not agree to hire a baby-sitter or make arrangements for after school. Some still called the other parent their "wife" and still expected that their "wife" would act like their executive secretary. This doesn't mean that a little history behind them or a change of heart wouldn't put them in a more favorable frame of mind, but as of now, the timing is not right and perhaps may never be so.

"THE FEELINGS CAN EAT YOU ALIVE"

Each parent can have a load of hard feelings that seems unending. "The anger and resentment will eat you alive if you don't watch out," said one mother of four teenagers whose father had dropped out. "I have good reason to be angry—no child support, no father for the kids, and no help from the authorities on any count. But you can't let these feelings become a part of you. They will destroy you."

This mother, like countless others who are "solo" parents, has gone through the toughest knothole. She knows that she must change her situation for herself and her children regardless of what the law or the other parent does. If this effort results eventually in the reinvolvement of that other parent, fine, but if it doesn't, she has still liberated herself from the insidious poison of pervasive bitterness. She can go on to build an extended family for herself and her children, one that can include a second, third, or fourth home for the kids with relatives or friends.

Chapter 20

Moving On

Bottlenecks and Breakthroughs

The Second Wave: Flashbacks
Remarriage: Your Own or the Other Parent's
Another Ending
A Change in School-Year Residence
Your Place in the Community
Graduations, Weddings, Family Fiestas
And Thanks for the Memory

"MY divorce had been over and done with for more than two years; what a shock it was to find myself feeling depressed again! On top of it, I now feel hopeless, too. I had made so many changes and had done so well with my life, I don't understand this." The speaker was Sondra, a woman in her thirties, talking openly to a group of women who had come to a "Seasoned Single Parent Seminar" I was holding at a family agency. Other women nodded their heads; more than half of the women present had experienced the same type of feeling. Just when they should be feeling good about the fact that they have made it, they didn't feel good at all.

THE SECOND WAVE: FLASHBACKS

Over the years of working with families, I have continued to observe a phenomenon of flashback periods sometimes triggered by certain circumstances and events. These flashbacks were so predictable that I christened them the "second wave." Each flashback contained many of the same feelings and behaviors that had been problematic during the separation. If parents had yelling sprees during this initial period, they might be tempted to do a repeat performance during a flashback period. If a child was a bed wetter those months after the separation, during a flashback period he may regress to the same behavior. Some flashback episodes were tied to self-evaluation, others to specific events.

"HOW FAR HAVE I COME?"

The second wave of feelings, thoughts, and circumstances has been described by people as a more sophisticated confrontation with the changes that the divorce has brought about. One woman described it this way: "I know I'm surviving and coping now. That's been established. I'm calmer, I'm thinking more clearly, and the intensity of my emotions has finally wound down. Now—without all that extra energy—I can take a longer look at what's happened and where it's going to take me."

The pace of this more measured reevaluation differs with each individual. Some say this second wave experience hits them just about the time they get over the crisis months and survival is assured. Others have no clue that this is connected with their separation and attach their feelings to a current situation with their child or with the job. If the counselor asks about the divorce, they dismiss it with, "It was two years ago," or, "I'm over all of that." Children, too, seem to have these second wave experiences—sometimes more like delayed reactions to changes in their lives and the uncertain future. "I'll never again be able to wrap my arms around both my parents at the same time," said twelve-year-old Beth. The true dimensions of the change divorce has brought about are beginning to sink in.

For everyone in the family, the second wave means finally having to face the fact that the parents probably aren't going to reunite. Some hearty optimists hold on to this hope for many years. One teenager, her parents divorced for six years, burst into tears when her father announced his coming marriage to his longtime steady. When her father asked her about her feelings, she replied that she liked her intended stepmother, but she had kept hoping secretly that she would have him and her mother again under one roof.

For others, the flash of the singles scene and the promise of new horizons has not worked out as hoped. The hours at the job are longer than they realized, advancement slower, and acceptable companions hard to find. The single life has ended up looking just as complicated as the married life they left. "I've gone through all that hell of the divorce just to get to this," said one angry and hurt woman. "It wasn't worth it."

WHAT ARE THE TRIGGERS?

Sondra came into my office clearly depressed. As she talked, Sondra revealed several flashback triggering events happening simultaneously: she had been evaluating herself and the consequences of the divorce, her former husband was now making twice as much money as when they were married, and he was now seriously involved with another woman. The result was not just one flashback trigger, but three. No wonder she felt so depressed!

HERE WE GO AGAIN: FLASHBACKS AND WHAT TRIGGERS THEM

1. A more measured evaluation of the past two or three years, a "What have I done?" "What has really happened?"
2. A new partner or marriage for the other parent.
3. Another child born from the other parent's new union.
4. A change in residence—by either parent—that makes easy access to the children difficult or inconvenient.
5. A change (or threatened change) in where the children will live the majority of the year.
6. Any other major life change—serious illness, job loss, income loss, income increase, and so on.
7. Another divorce or the ending of a major relationship.
8. The reinvolvement of a dropout or pushed-out parent.

ONE AT A TIME OR ALL AT ONCE

The biggest flashbacks often come in sequence. The first major flashback may come two or three years after the separation, followed in a year or two by a remarriage and, even later, a change in residence. But sometimes these changes come together, as they did for Sondra. A common combination of flashbacks is that of a thoughtful reevaluation produced by the news that the other parent is going to get married again and now wants to have the children for the school year. "Josh's mother said to me, 'I'm getting married and I want Josh to come and live with us for the school year,' " reported Josh's father, Sam. "I couldn't believe how bad I felt. I was scared, angry, hurt, and now I'm depressed. What's wrong with me? I don't want to remarry her and I'm not against Josh living there for the school year." Sam has a heavier task of reevaluation than Sondra—the remarriage of the former mate is one of the most demanding of the flashback situations.

HOW LONG DOES IT LAST?

Some people take a long weekend and do their reevaluation in a few days' time. Others never look back and never think about it. The remarriage of a mate means a month-long funk for one person and a good excuse to binge for another. The longer you were married, the more children you had together, the longer lasting the different flashbacks seem to be and the more intense the old feeling. When a person is living a satisfying family and intimate life, a serious relapse into depression or difficulty is less likely. The flashback can often be short-lived, even informative and enriching. But if the working relationship with the other parent is shaky or nonexistent, if your personal life doesn't meet your hopes, the second wave can rekindle and intensify many of the same problems that proved difficult earlier. Any crisis may bring back old habits, feelings, and fears.

TREATMENTS FOR FLASHBACKS

The treatments for the flashback periods are the same ones you used during the first months of separation. Don't be misled by a four- or five-year period of a reasonably peaceful and cordial working relationship. *A recurrence of negative intimacy must be treated by a return to an acquaintance/business relationship.* "He is such a sneak," a woman might say. "He's been so civil and cordial for five years, and now that he's married he's being sarcastic and snotty. He never changed at all." The dialogue and the intensity of feelings put the two parents back into a form of their former negative intimacy. Those five years were good years as parenting partners. They can have more good years, too. After a cooling-off period, parents can usually regain a more cordial working relationship. But during flashback periods, they should strive for business as usual, nothing more.

CHECKLIST FOR THE FLASHBACK PERIODS

1. *Your feelings:* You may be going through the same stages of the wounding and healing process as you did at first. The treatments are the same.
2. *Your working relationship with the other parent:* A renewed sense of dislike, hurt, or resentment can flare. Return to the business guidelines.
3. *Communications:* When tales and dubious information from children and friends increase, go back to a scrupulously direct and neutral style.
4. *Your own human needs:* During a flashback, just as during the initial crisis, you need to increase your human income.
5. *That old skeleton notebook:* If you have one from the initial period, take it out and reread your notes to remind you of troublesome, repeating behaviors and feelings.
6. *Your family and extended family:* During flashback periods, friends and close loved ones can restore your equilibrium.

(continues)

(continued from previous page)

7. *Your old family feeling:* The old family feeling may be back. Children may put themselves in the middle; parents may want them there. A sense of the old family comes back. Reach out for your new family feeling for strength.

8. *Taking stock of your life so far:* Use the spurt of energy a flashback can bring to take stock and make some changes or renew efforts.

9. *Flashbacks should be short:* With the exception of responses to the other parent's remarriage or some drastic residential shift, flashback periods are short. If a flashback period lasts more than one or two weeks, or is particularly intense, then seek professional help. It may be telling you more than you yet know.

10. *Flashbacks recur:* Be alert to how you go through these periods. Knowing your reactions and what helped may shorten the next one.

REMARRIAGE: YOUR OWN OR THE OTHER PARENT'S

Remarriage, your own or that of the other parent, nearly always unbalances your old working relationships and sets off a flashback period where you eventually reach a new perspective, a new equilibrium.

YOUR REMARRIAGE

Your remarriage brings on flashbacks for everyone: you, your children, your stepchildren, and the other parent. Everyone may feel a renewed burst of old fears, myths, and feelings. These flashbacks can be a conduit to a reopened, off-the-wall stage. Your two-home arrangement can be endangered, and so can your new marriage.

Remarriage adds new complexities: yet another family history, family feeling, and probably a string of expectations for a happy ending, dreams of instant love between stepparents and stepchildren, and a longing to "get back to normal." There are many local seminars and good books on remarriage and stepparenting (part 5, "Further Readings"). I urge you to seek these out. In the meantime it is helpful to remember that your remarriage is not a step back to your old family history, but a step forward to a newer version with its own unique values, customs, and family feeling. Your new family can thrive with a good working relationship between the two homes or be crippled by spiteful former mates and children caught in the middle.

Your remarried family life is different from the single or never divorced family in certain important ways. The biological parent and children have had their own long history together, their ways of doing things. When a new mate comes into this picture, standards for personal territory, discipline, chores, and personal attention change. How will they be now? Whose closet space will be reduced, who decides on discipline, who sets the final house rules, who does the dishes, the lawn? Logistically, if both adults have children, there will be times with his, hers, and even their children, and additions to the open family, with new cousins, aunts and uncles, friends, and grandparents. Finances are often tight.

The kids may wonder, Will the new mate pull his or her weight, throw it around, compete with them for the parent's affection? Will the new mate become part of the old group or will a whole new grouping emerge? Most of all, the children fear the threat a new mate poses to their other parent in their second home. Is this new spouse a replacement parent, one who will shut out their other parent? Or an additional parent, a special adult friend or relative? Loyalty to a biological parent is paramount for children, and new mates who attempt to usurp this bond are often in for a well-deserved rough time.

The biological parents have their share of grief from the kids, too. They must watch while the children may yell at the stepparent, "I don't have to, you're not the boss of me, you're not my real mother [or father]." The children may constantly point out the shortcomings of the new mate and be jealous or defiant.

If this sounds depressing, take heart. Your remating can also mean a new family, one that reorganizes itself for your present life, not for your past. Your new family can nurture constructive and creative ways of communicating with one another, of cooperating, and of solving family problems. Even though you may not begin with a long history of shared experiences, you will develop them eventually. "How we always did things" can change to "How will we do them now?" Review chapter 9. Remember the suggestions for groundwork for house and safety rules, for chores? Remember chapter 10 on easing children's fears, on communications? These can work for you again here in your new family.

THE OTHER PARENT'S REMARRIAGE

The remarriage of the former mate may be one of the most painful and longest-lasting flashbacks of the second wave. You may not want to remarry the former mate, you may not even like him or her very much, but remarriage closes a door on the past in a way that says you have been replaced and any illusory option to return is gone. Even when one spouse has been married happily for some time, the news about the other spouse's impending marriage brings about surprising inward reactions. "I'd been happily married for four years," said a father of two teenagers. "I wanted to be rid of the alimony payments and I wanted the children's mother to be happy. I felt a little guilty that she was alone and I was not. But I didn't expect my reaction when I heard the news of her coming marriage. I didn't like it, and I hated the idea of the children calling anyone but me Dad."

Some people have no conscious reaction to the new marriage, but they catch the flu or are short-tempered for a few days. Other people feel sad; still others are surprised that they have any feelings at all left over for the former mate. Still others find themselves in a full-blown, off-the-wall state, angry, suspicious, hurt, and ready to do battle. This is a bad time to make decisions, but the temptation often seems too great to resist.

The idea that remarriage mends the broken home, that the family is now back to normal, the view of one home with all the authority often reemerges. "The first one married can get dibs on the kids" is not too far from the truth when a parent sees this as an advantage in the arguments about who should now have the primary residence.

As before, there are fears about the wicked stepmother/stepfather or of losing custody or easy access to the children. Worries about changes in agreement and in financial dealings are common. Suspicions arise as the validating blanket of tradition settles on the other parent's married household. The worry about losing the children's love, affection, and loyalty sometimes surfaces. Someone has indeed taken your old place. How complete will this substitution be? When the parent is unmarried, doubts can arise, bringing questions. "Is there something wrong with me because I'm still single?" Will the children want to be primarily in a "traditional" home again instead of your home?

The list can be long if the flashback is severe, and an off-the-wall former mate can sometimes successfully sabotage the new union. Conversely, an about-to-be-married mate or parent can push old buttons, saying again, "The only thing wrong with the kids is you."

Remarriage can also bring about a shift in the time the newly married couple wants to spend with children. For some, this is a first marriage, and they do not want to spend their weekend time with children who are not their own flesh and blood. While the ethics of such behavior are debatable, when the new spouse says "me or the kids" at a strategic point in time, the two-home arrangement can go into temporary (or permanent) limbo.

Fears around remarriage can be subtle and hidden, but everyone, even the new bride and groom, has them. The danger is that these anxieties will be pinned on the two-home arrangement as a scapegoat instead of tied to the reality of remarriage.

CUSTODY AND MONEY

The months surrounding one parent's remarriage are sometimes punctuated by one or both parents consulting attorneys about protection of rights, changes in custody, child support, and alimony.

Child support payments can become a bone of contention. If the payment is late or not made, the interruption may be blamed on the other parent's increased expenses or the new mate's unhealthy influence. Or if it's the parent where the children has greater residency who has remarried, the other parent can be late or absent with payments because he or she doesn't want to contribute to the support of a stranger. "They bought a new camper with my money," spouted one irate father. "That money isn't going to the kids, it's going into that family pot. I resent it and I'm not sending another dime! Furthermore, I'm not taking the kids to be their baby-sitter anymore, either! See how their sweet little love nest thrives on that!" This father calmed down when he and the children's mother adopted the accounting procedure suggested in appendix 3.

Sometimes parents find that their parenting agreement has to be renegotiated. In other cases, entirely new financial arrangements must be worked out. If the question of accountability for child contribution funds becomes a problem, perhaps it needs addressing in a more specific and formal way. When issues of custody and money arise, remember that this is a common flashback reaction to remarriage. Reread the "Checklist for the Flashback Periods" a few pages back, then review chapters 6, 7, and 8 and if need be get some outside help. Try not to let the flashback emotions get the upper hand. Stick to your business relationship instead.

"WHAT DO I CALL YOU?"

"Mom" and "Dad" are magical words, a symbol of honor, connectedness, ownership. These words have a very special meaning. Some biological parents do not want to share their titles of "Mom" or "Dad" with stepparents, and some stepparents don't want to be called by these titles, either. In other families, however, the situation is reversed. Children, sensitive to their parents' and stepparents' needs, call stepparents by either their first names, special nicknames, or Mom or Dad. No one rule will suit everybody.

If you can let your children choose their names for their stepparents (including the title of "Mom" or "Dad"), it will be a relief for them. Children seem to find their own names for stepparents more easily if they don't think they have to protect your feelings as a parent or stepparent. Beware of using the title "Mom" or "Dad" as a weapon against the other parent. "I want you to meet the children's new father," said one insensitive mother to her former husband. The natural father told this tale with fresh pain and fear months later. This woman not only hurt her former husband unnecessarily, she put him on the defensive to the point where he considered legal action so his sons would live primarily with him lest the stepfather usurp his parental relationship.

Another remarried woman admitted that her renewed flashback anger after the subsequent remarriage of the other parent led her to a drastic move. She insisted that her children call their stepfather "Dad" and their biological father by his given name. "I reasoned that 'Dad' should be reserved for the person who lived with the kids." Fortunately her resolve was as short-lived as her flashback, and she averted any disastrous, long-term consequence with everyone—especially her children.

Finally, children's usage of "Mom" or "Dad" has a good deal to do with their age. Teenagers who see their mother's new mate as a special adult or as a stepfather may call him both Dad and Larry, while little ones will probably stick to Dad or Daddy because, as one stepfather said, "That's what men my size are called."

RE-CREATING THE HOLIDAYS AFTER REMARRIAGE

Remarriage isn't a return to the original family, it is a brand-new family, one that has to blend and choose from each individual family tradition that which it will retain. The Jones father married the Smith mother, and the Christmas or Passover they celebrate needs to be a blending of Jones *and* Smith, not all Jones or just Smith traditions. If one family always had Thanksgiving dinner with Grandma and the other always had it with just the children and parents, what will they do this Thanksgiving now that they are Jones-Smith? Perhaps they will alternate ways, perhaps they will bring in many other relatives besides one grandma, perhaps they will do both somehow. Families can make priorities—which traditions seem the most important, then the next important, and so forth. Then they can more easily make decisions about what to keep, what to compromise, what to blend with the other family. New traditions—those that combine the most important traditions of both families—emerge with their own unique "new family feeling."

THE CARDINAL GUIDELINES—A REVIEW

You may have one home, but your child has two. Remarriage or remating can replace a spouse, but it does not replace the child's other original parent. Regardless of how pleased and secure the child may be with the in-house stepparent, the child still knows he or she has a natural parent living somewhere else.

A strong, two-home arrangement reduces doubts and fears during flash-back times. The new stepparent is seen as an additional parent, not as a replacement or a competitor.

CHECKLIST FOR REMARRIAGE

1. *Remarriage usually triggers a flashback.* This time can be a full-blown crisis period, or it can just be a brief squall. Take good care of yourself in either case and go over

   a. the earlier checklists on flashbacks in this chapter. Then, as a protective measure,
   b. the self-tests in chapters 7 and 8. You may have to take another step away from reborn negative intimacy. If you do, look at it as a way to further personal growth, not as failure.

2. *Give and expect respect and privacy* from the new mate, the other parent, and yourself. Discourage gossip and "soap operas."

3. *Expect issues of custody, support, and authority to be either discussed or reopened.* New discussions and perhaps agreements may be needed. Chapters 6–12 may help.

4. *Reach out and give the other biological parent some reassurances:* that you want the working relationship to continue; that he or she will not be replaced or shut out; that any change can be taken care of in a businesslike manner. Don't take him or her for granted.

5. *The new mate can help by being sensitive and open with the former spouse.* Listening, comprehending, and staying off the defensive and on an acquaintance level help.

6. *The new mate can adopt a neutral position* with the parents' ongoing relationship as parents and let them make their own arrangements.

7. *Let the stepparents and the biological parents develop their own relationship at their own pace* without interference from either other adults or the children. Let stepparents and children do likewise. It's not uncommon for the mother and stepmother to develop a strong working relationship by themselves. When this works, it is a true bonus for everyone.

8. *Similarly, let stepparents and stepchildren develop their own relationship at their own pace* without interference from either the natural parents or other children. This is most important.

(continues)

(continued from previous page)

9. *Watch for hyper-fairness in the children.* They can become preoccupied with fears that one or the other parent is not getting a fair break.

10. *Newlyweds, take time to be alone as a couple.* Try to get at least one weekend alone each month. Sounds impossible? Well, that's where the children's time at their second home comes in. If that doesn't work now, then make it a priority to make other arrangements. You need time alone, not just sometimes, but regularly.

11. If you are now going through the other parent's remarriage, *find a way to have your own good times.*

ANOTHER ENDING

What if major relationship number two hasn't worked out? Or even number three? When that lover leaves, or another marriage ends, the combined effects of the original parting and the new separation can be hard to handle. The second blow may fall on a wound that never healed properly the first time around. The survivor now may have two unfinished endings to deal with—an incredible double whammy of strong feelings, old skeletons, memories, and self-doubts.

"This relationship was going to be the one that was going to last forever," said one woman about her second marriage. "When it began to come apart, I asked, 'How could this be happening to me again?' I hadn't done my review work the first time around. I had tiptoed around my feelings and plunged headlong into this quick replacement marriage. I dismissed the end of my first marriage as incompatibility but secretly blamed it all on him. Now a two-time loser, I feel like a total failure. Maybe I was to blame for the first marriage's failure."

This woman's original resistance to dealing with her unfinished emotional business from her first marriage before remarrying undermined her next relationship and has caused a good deal of her present emotional turmoil. Now she has the job of cleaning up two relationships. The process of setting the past in order demands its due when important relationships end. If the job is ignored or minimized, it continues to poke and prod until attention is properly paid and the wound finally cleansed of its major debris.

Some people have few symptoms of the wounding and healing process of divorce the first time around but find themselves incapacitated by the end of their first meaningful love affair. "Breaking up with Ron was far more difficult than separating from my husband," said one mother of three teenagers. "I couldn't believe my feelings; they were strong and I was so hurt and angry." The feelings she had stored up from her original separation finally came out disguised as sorrow over the end of the second relationship.

Despite the comfort and companionship of a quick replacement marriage, such a union has a lot of strikes against it, as the unfinished business from the past can spill over to the new relationship. "I couldn't sleep on one side of the bed because his former wife had slept there," said one quick replacement wife. "He really didn't see or know me, he only knew what his former wife had been, and he didn't want me to be the same. It was confining, discouraging; even the way I held a coffee cup bugged him."

Many people are attracted to others who have the same characteristics as former partners, whether in appearance, manners, or bearing. But often the likeness is more hidden. When the layers of social amenities peel off and the inevitable disagreements arise, it's surprising how the new lover displays the same old disagreeable traits!

By the time a person has experienced a divorce and the ending of an important love affair, the reaction may be to pull back and be alone for a while. The desire for companionship may be countered by the still-fresh memory and pain of those past relationships. Consequently when a likely acquaintance shows promising signs for a relationship, the reaction may be one of aversion instead of attraction. "If my marriage had all that promise and commitment and ended in so much pain, what is to keep this new relationship from ending up the same way?" If you feel this way, you might want to look to your open family and your friends for companionship, forget about romance for a while, and let nature take its healing course.

A CHANGE IN SCHOOL-YEAR RESIDENCE

Changes in jobs, health, and personal circumstances often bring about a necessary change in where a child will go to school. When a child changes a primary residence in order to be in one school during a year, a flashback often occurs. This flashback can be short-lived, as seen in chapter 16, or it can be a full-blown crisis. For example, when a mother's last child at home goes to live the school year with his father, she faces both the life stage adjustment of the empty nest and the flashback legacy of her divorce. This combination can be heavy going.

When a two-home arrangement has been in operation for some time, a parent can switch to the "other home" role more easily. The shift feels natural. It is the other parent's turn. "It's Dad's turn" or "Mom's turn" describes the happiest shifts. The change need not become a tragedy or crisis. Even if financial difficulties or a child's behavior initiate a parent's decision to have one or all of the children live with the other parent, don't overemphasize these reasons. Most important, the children have two homes;

taking turns is part of the process. When Mom is in debt and temporarily unable to raise a family alone and Dad takes over, calling it "Dad's turn" is still a good idea. Too much focus on the parenting burden makes a child feel like an albatross, whereas a turn is easily understood. Fair is fair.

"I CAN'T HANDLE HIM, YOU TAKE HIM"

One reason frequently cited when children take a turn at the other parent's house is: "I can't handle him, you take him." Or: "Send her to me, I'll straighten her out."

If this is happening to you, and a change in homes for the school year seems the best answer, take a look at your language and the attitude it connotes. "I give up, you take him/her," or, "You obviously are not effective, let me take over," are all win-lose phrases. "Sending" a child to the other parent's home implies exile, banishment, and failure for both the resident parent doing the sending and the child being sent. Avoid the temptation to wipe your hands of the whole situation. A mother of a combative six-foot-two-inch son now living with his father still has her responsibilities to her son. Her relationship will go on, and anger, resentment, and fear left over from their stormy past together will not make it less of a relationship. The problems won't dissolve automatically with just the passage of time. A poor attitude can spell failure for both parent and child. The child needs help, and so do the parents who are dealing with the situation.

TEENS AND THEIR DADS

Most parents, married or single, disclose feelings of frustration and inadequacy when discussing teenage behavior. A number of teenagers seem to need a close relationship with their father during these years. There are, again, no standard rules on this. "I want to live with Daddy," said a fourteen-year-old girl. "I was five years old when he and Mom were divorced, and I want to see what it's like to wake up a lot of mornings in a row and know that he will be there."

Young teenage boys seem to especially need their fathers, the girls their mothers. Those who feel the separation acutely might even agitate at school or get in trouble, trying unconsciously to make a separated parent pay attention to them.

A father responding to a child's need has a special role here. There may have been some extenuating circumstances, such as unruly behavior, that have resulted in the change of residence. But if there are any leftover emotions of divorce, here is where they can surface. A father might say, "I had to admit I was feeling some secret delight that their mother couldn't handle our daughter [or son] anymore. I knew it would happen sooner or later. You see, she/he doesn't dare act that way with me. The kids' mother has always been a pushover." There it is. The new, primary-residence parent has the old blame game all set up to play again. The other parent failed; he, of course, thinks he will succeed.

Children know how to play blame games with each parent. Often teenagers will set up perfectly capable mothers (or fathers) to be failures by getting into trouble in order to involve the other parent. Parents have been labeled as failures who were nothing of the sort. More accurately, these parents were sacrificed by a child who desperately needed somehow to get the commitment of their *other parent.* If you do a change of school-year residence with your child, resist the temptation to compete over who is the better parent.

Focus on your child's best interests. Under such forthright conditions, blame games are hard to play and nobody can easily evade responsibilities as a parent or as a child.

As the months go on, you can give yourself a quick checkup every once in a while by answering the following eight questions as honestly as you can. Answer "Good," "Fair," or "Not Yet."

A FINAL CHECKUP

1. Your home and day care is safe, comfortable, healthy, nurturing.
2. You have a daily routine, provide the children with house and safety rules. You have family fun times together. You are involved with your children's activities or their school.
3. You and your children have established or retained selected traditions and rituals, perhaps established new ones.
4. You have a positive pattern for parenting with the other parent. The children can have both of you without fear of hurting, losing, or making one of you angry. You make it easy for the other parent to be a parent.
5. You are responsive to your children's needs, watch for danger signals, and take corrective action.
6. You have, or are building, an extended family or a friendship circle. You have people who support you and your children. You, in turn, support them.
7. You have a renewed sense of pride in your family, your children, yourself. You know that you, your family, and your children are important, not just to yourselves but to your neighborhood and community.
8. You have found opportunities to help your children build character and skills and have provided them with other healthy adult role models.

YOUR PLACE IN THE COMMUNITY

Perhaps you are a person who is quite active in the community and have continued to be so despite everything. But, if you have dropped out or have not been involved at all, now is the time to reconsider.

What you have learned in order to get that decent divorce can be a powerful asset to your community as well as a personal achievement in making tough times work for you. You and your children *can* begin to bring strength to other families besides your own and, in so doing, help yourselves. In the process, you can update your image from struggling new single parent to fully functioning family that can now reach out and contribute to their neighborhood and community. Just as you or your child are touched or inspired by the adults and children around you, you can also have that positive effect on others.

Parents and their children find time to volunteer at school, to become active in a neighborhood watch or a sports league, to look after an aging neighbor, to help another single parent. Parents have started support groups for children whose parents are going through separation or divorce, or volunteer to support established groups. The months or years that you have spent in this reorganization process have probably resulted in more effective and sensitive parenting, more personal skills in dealing with tough situations, a greater ability to muster resources, a stronger appreciation of the power of negotiation, and a stronger sense of self and family. No matter how tired or discouraged you might be at times, these heightened skills and sensibilities are sorely needed everywhere in today's world. You have a lot to offer.

The pace of our world is accelerating. Major changes appear every week. As time passes, more and more demands will be placed on all parents and children to adapt. What you have learned about relating to others and reorganizing your lives during a very difficult time is a skill that you will be able to call upon again and again. Every time you deal with conflict or a new situation effectively, you are also showing your child how to survive and thrive in this new age. Every time you provide an example on how to assess a situation and arrive at a sound judgment, you also help your child grow. Every time you help someone else build an extended family network or work with other adults to solve problems, you provide your child with an example on collaboration for their future. You show that a good family can triumph over hard times and grow stronger—and have a solid place in the community.

GRADUATIONS, WEDDINGS, FAMILY FIESTAS

Family gatherings are times when an intense, often short-lived flashback may occur. Be prepared for a poignant tug at your heart. A son's wedding or a daughter's graduation are traditional rites of passage. We are all reminded of how quickly life passes, how soon we grow older, how vulnerable our children still seem. Flashbacks from the divorce are quite common at such times and may add to your deep feelings. Experience the feelings that properly belong to the traditional event. Ignore the past. The child's rite of passage is what should captivate your heart.

"We were all there—the other family, my family, the kids, everyone. . . ." The rewards of a solid working relationship, or even one that is shaky but resolute, appear concretely at family gatherings such as a child's wedding or graduation. A history of a good working relationship between parents can mean a relaxed and rewarding family celebration together. At the least, a civil containment of tensions enables the child to have the day without the parents' soap opera intruding. Regardless of how the child's time has been divided over the years of school and summers, the child usually wants both parents there at the grand event, behaving themselves. Such events should never be a showcase for parents' unfinished personal business.

Some events can include both sets of grandparents, new grandparents from second and third marriages, aunts and uncles, cousins, neighbors, and members of the open families from both Mom's house and Dad's house. The tone of the day is set by the parents' respect for one another and their separate relationships with the children and the respect of the stepparents for the old and new families. This mutual respect will give guests and friends a sense of security and guide their own behavior.

When a working relationship has a few years behind it, this respect, no matter if periodically shaken, does grow. The positive changes in the children's behavior and attitudes are usually proof enough for parents that their independent relationships with the children and hands-off policy with the other parent's parenting style and personal life have worked as a sensible solution to parenting after divorce. This allows parents, when they must, to coexist at a family fiesta. It even allows the two families to share the planning, the work, and the cost. Some parents spend a few private minutes together sharing the feelings that come with their child's growing up and going out into the world. Some cry together for a few minutes, others speak only in generalities. Whatever works in their ongoing parenting relationship can also be a guide for the party. Some flashback feelings will arise and may be painful. Don't let them spoil either your day or your child's event.

OTHERS TAKE THEIR CUES FROM YOU

Despite the ups and downs of a working relationship, children, confident enough of their parents' relationship and proud enough of their two-home life, often insist on both parents' active involvement in important occasions. "About four years after Paul and I had developed a working relationship, our son announced he was getting married," said a mother of three. "Paul and I talked about wedding plans the same way we talked about other things in the children's lives. As is our habit, we talk infrequently, come to decisions quickly, and then go our separate ways. We did the wedding the same way. What I didn't expect at all was how delighted all our relatives and old friends were to have a reason to be together again in one place with no sides to take. His parents and my uncle were talking away like old times; old friends were chatting.

"People came up to me and said things like 'This is wonderful,' first with one of us, then with the other. At first I didn't understand what they meant. I came to understand that while Paul and I took our working relationship for granted, there were others who had not. They took their cue from our behavior and relaxed. Our children loved it all, moving between their two families easily. I never expected that the wedding would bring such an unexpected bonus. We all saw how we had healed."

When a set of families survives a shared family event without serious repercussions, an additional dimension of confidence and respect is added to the parents' working relationship and to the children's sense of security. But when a family thrives in it, as this set of families has done, it is an indication of a job well done and a special blessing.

AND THANKS FOR THE MEMORY

"I was cleaning out the closet the other day," said Betty, happily remarried for two years, "when out tumbled an old baseball cap of my first husband's. I just found it falling in my hand. I don't know why it was there after six years. I started to cry, cry hard, and think, Why couldn't it have worked out? I don't want to remarry him. I'm very happy in my present marriage. It was just those years together, the kids. I finally said, 'Oh, damn,' and then it was over."

Countless times I have heard people tell of such brief but deeply touching flashbacks, bringing a sense of love, of sadness, and of loss. Sometimes it's an outpouring of feelings never before expressed or of difficulties never admitted. Most people regain their balance within a few minutes and their normal perspective on life in an hour. But the impression lingers, reminding you that you did have a history together. They are poignant and purgative moments when history demands its due.

Such families, and each person in them, know that life's changes can season and strengthen them. Like many people who survive the end of a marriage, they have found that pain is bearable after all.

As one mother said, "I now know from my experience that I can choose to learn from life. I discovered that it was what I learned since the end of my relationship that determined what I did—not other people's opinions, not my memories. I'm not a statistic, I'm a mother, we are a family. If I'm anything, I'm a new age pioneer."

With parents like these and their families beside them, the family is not in danger of extinction. These families have not in any way been broken. They have been reorganized, reassessed, and revitalized.

The parents' intimate relationship ended.

But the families, and the parents and children in them, continue.

Part 5

REFERENCES AND RESOURCES

For Professionals

The first edition of *Mom's House, Dad's House,* published in 1980, set forth my experiences in the 1970s working with students, clients, and training professionals in the field of divorce, custody, single parenting, and mediation. Now, in 1997, after twenty-seven printings of *Mom's House, Dad's House,* I find myself finishing a new edition.

Over these seventeen years this book has been used as a self-help guide, reference, and text. Some of the concepts and frameworks originally offered in the first edition took flight on the wings of others and are now represented in the daily workings of law, mental health, counseling, and mediation. This edition revisits the original concepts and then incorporates what I have learned since the 1980 edition—not only from students and clients but from later studies and research, including my work at Stanford University, and, more recently, the perspective of an administrator overseeing a statewide office on family court research and education. The following is an overview of the additions and revisions from the first edition:

Two homes for children after separation or divorce, regardless of how the children's time is divided between them, was proposed in the first edition. Two homes is now an accepted alternative to the one-home, one-authority view. This edition expands this approach to more fully include unmarried parents, separated and remarried parents, as well as solo parents who are encouraged to make two homes for their children with relatives or friends.

Replacing negative terms such as "broken home," "custody," "visitation," with positive everyday terms was proposed in the first edition. This view generated interest quickly and has found its way into common usage as well as some family laws. This edition continues its commitment to the new positive vocabulary.

The "businesslike working relationship" between parents originated in the first edition as a way for parents to structure their new relationship and is now taught widely: in parent and divorce education classes, in family court orientation classes, in psychotherapy, legal, and mediation sessions. Journalists and mental health professionals have also made it a feature in their own work. There are expanded sections in several chapters on this approach and its relationship to a successful healing process, structuring interactions, mediation, supporting successful negotiations, and the children's adjustment.

The concept of a "parenting agreement" was originally presented in the first edition and served several purposes: *first, as a legal contract* negotiated out of court between separated or divorcing parents that specified how parents would share or divide their responsibilities; *second, as an agreement that used common everyday terms in place of legal terms and that parents could write themselves;* and *third, as a name for a process (now called "mediation" or private negotiations) through which parents themselves developed arrangements for raising their children.* The term "parenting agreement" was adopted by many jurisdictions in the 1980s and early 1990s. It receives an additional name in this edition: the "parenting plan," a term now also in common usage. There is also a new chapter on the structure of effective parenting plans, including actual clauses for special provisions and private contracts for parents to consider. *Family mediation,* still new in 1980, was proposed in the first edition as one way parents could develop a "parenting agreement" outside of court. This edition reaffirms its enthusiastic support of mediation for parents and adds a chapter that takes the reader step by step through the mediation process, including how to decide if mediation is their best alternative.

The goal of a "good divorce" was proposed in the first edition and is amplified here as the "decent divorce." A decent divorce is considered synonymous with a good working relationship between parents and a healthy outcome for the children. This view of divorce says that families can reorganize successfully after separation or divorce and raise their children with honor and dignity. This new edition upholds this belief with renewed energy.

New pioneers. The notion that separated/divorced families are pioneering a new form of family life was put forth in the first edition. This edition reemphasizes this perspective and goes on to promote the central role our new families can play in bringing stability and strength not just to themselves but to their communities.

The chapter notes that follow are for those readers who seek to know more about the first edition, pertinent research, references, specifics on adaptations and the new material added to this edition.

—ISOLINA RICCI
San Francisco, California

Chapter Notes

PREFACE

First edition: Isolina Ricci, *Mom's House, Dad's House: Making Shared Custody Work* (New York: Macmillan Publishing Company, 1980). The revisions and expansions of the original concepts in the first edition for this edition are those of the author. New material is noted.

PART 1

CHAPTER 1—BUILDING A NEW FAMILY LIFE

How it began—the first edition: The conceptual and educational/clinical models in the first edition (*Mom's House, Dad's House,* 1980) were tested and refined with approximately 1,500 parents in seminars, workshops, and counseling sessions, including the UCLA Extension Series on Divorce and Single Parenting (1974–1980) and in New Family Center Parent Education Seminars, Palo Alto, California (1977–1980). Seminars and classes training professionals in these approaches began in 1975 (UCLA Extension, graduate level). Subsequent study is described in "For Professionals."

Two-home approach: See Isolina Ricci, "Dispelling the Stereotype of the 'Broken Home,'" 1976; this article includes material from Ricci's course for professionals (UCLA Extension, graduate level), 1974–1975. Some others (in the late 1970s) who supported the involvement of both parents in a child's life after divorce include Constance Ahrons, "Binuclear Families: Two Households, One Family," *Alternative Lifestyles,* 2 (1979): 449–515; Miriam Galper, *Co-Parenting: A Source Book for the Separated or Divorced Family* (Philadelphia: Running Press, 1978); Henry H. Foster and Doris Freed, "Joint Custody: A Viable Alternative," *New York Law Journal,* November 9 and 24, December 22, 1978; and Douglas F. Grote and Jeffrey P. Weinstein, "Joint Custody: A Viable and Ideal Alternative," *Journal of Divorce,* fall 1977.

Contact with both parents: A number of U.S. state laws include terms stating that, whenever possible, a child should have close and continuing contact with *both* parents.

Divorce rate: U.S. statistics on first marriages ending in divorce range from 40 to 50 percent, depending on the region. Divorces in other countries have been on the rise since 1954.

"Divorce is forever": Personal communication to Ricci from the Honorable Douglas McNish, Family Court of Maui, Hawaii, 1996.

A decent separation/divorce: See also the work of Constance Ahrons, *The Good Divorce: Keeping Your Family Together When Your Marriage Comes Apart* (New York: HarperPerennial/HarperCollins, 1995); Lois Gold, *Between Love and Hate: A Guide to Civilized Divorce* (New York: Plume/Penguin Books, 1992); and Craig Everett and Sandra Volgy Everett, *Healthy Divorce* (San Francisco: Jossey-Bass, 1994).

Family bill of rights: Updated from the first edition.

CHAPTER 2—BELIEVE IN YOUR FAMILY

Myths: These are expansions of the stereotypes put forth in the first edition (*Mom's House, Dad's House,* 1980, chapter 2).

CHAPTER 3—FROM ONE HOME TO TWO HOMES

From one home to two homes: The diagram and the stages are updated from the first edition (*Mom's House, Dad's House,* 1980, chapter 4). The diagram originated with the author, was published in Isolina Ricci, "Dispelling the Stereotype of the 'Broken Home,'" *Conciliation Courts Review* 12:7–15, 1976, and was rendered by artist Theresa Abramian for the first edition.

Unmarried parents: New to this edition.

CHAPTER 4—WATCH YOUR LANGUAGE

Need for new positive terms: This chapter first appeared in the *Single Parent News* (later called the *Journal of the One Parent Family Community*) as a series of articles, beginning in December 1975, entitled "Where's Noah Webster Now That We Really Need Him?"; "Some Adults Should Have Their Mouths Washed Out with Soap"; and "Stinkweeds and Roses." The articles were later reprinted under the title "A New Language" and then appeared in the first edition as chapter 5.

Legal language: One of the strongest statements calling for a revision of language can be found in "Parenting Our Children: In the Best Interest of the Nation, A Report to the President and Congress," *U.S. Commission on Child and Family Welfare* (Washington, D.C., 1996). Also see the updated legal language used in U.S. Washington State family code. Lowell Halverson and John Kydd, *Divorce in Washington: A Human Approach* (Mercer Island, Wash.: Eagle House Press, 1990).

English language: John Kydd in "Language and Family: The Poverty of English," *Family and Conciliation Courts Review,* 1996, 34(3):351–372, explored the "poverty of English," expressing concern over the increasing propensity of the English language to migrate away from terms of family relation and love toward commerce, reason, technology, and a narrow form of law. Other languages have many more terms for family relations than does English. For example, English has 36 terms of family relation (aunt, uncle, sister, brother, and so forth); in Chinese there are 137 such terms, including 5 types of uncles and 5 types of cousins.

CHAPTER 5—YOUR HUMAN INCOME

Your human income: Based on *Mom's House, Dad's House,* 1980, chapter 6.

Laughter and healing: See, for example, Norman Cousins, *Anatomy of an Illness* (New York: Bantam Books, 1979).

PART 2

CHAPTER 6—THE EMOTIONS OF ENDING A RELATIONSHIP

The emotions of ending a relationship: Based on *Mom's House, Dad's House,* 1980, chapter 7.

Decision to divorce: See Isolina Ricci, *An Exploration of Parents' Post Divorce Relationship and Child Behavior* (Dissertation Abstracts International, 1984).

Boot camp: This construct is new to this edition.

Dynamics of wounding and healing: This model appeared in the first edition (*Mom's House, Dad's House,* 1980, chapter 7) and has continued to be helpful to readers and clients. It was developed in collaboration with Lorraine Sanchez, RN, MPH, from 1969 to 1973 and was based on the loss and crisis intervention literature. The "adult adolescence" concept was first presented by Ricci at a lecture series entitled "Human Development" at Pacific Oaks College, fall 1973. Other durable models include Emily M. Brown, "A Model of the Divorce Process," *Conciliation Courts Review,* 1976, 14(2); Reva S. Wiseman, "Crisis Theory and the Process of Divorce," *Social Casework,* April 1975, vol. 56(4):205–212.

Betrayal: See also John Amodeo, *Love and Betrayal: Broken Trust in Intimate Relationships* (New York: Ballantine Books, 1994).

CHAPTER 7—THE RETREAT FROM INTIMACY

The retreat from intimacy: This chapter describes a relationship model developed by Ricci in 1975 and published in the first edition of *Mom's House, Dad's House,* 1980, chapter 8. The "businesslike relationship" is now used widely in parenting classes, family court orientation, or education classes—for example, some family court education programs in California; the Key Bridge Center, Arlington, Va.; Peacemakers, Ft. Smith, Ark.; Families First, Atlanta, Ga.; and Johnson County Mental Health Department, Kans.; and promoted by other authors—for example, Melinda Blau, *Families Apart: Ten Keys to Successful Co-Parenting* (New York: G. P. Putnam's Sons, 1993), and Stephanie Marston, *The Divorced Parent: Success Strategies for Raising Your Children after Separation* (New York: Pocket Books, 1994).

Predictors of divorce: John Gottman's work with couples over twenty years captures the ascending spiral of criticism, defensiveness, distressing thoughts, emotional flooding, contempt or disgust, and stonewalling. See John Gottman, *Why Marriages Succeed or Fail* (New York: Fireside, 1994).

"Hostile takeover": Quoted from *The Barletter,* April 1996, Johnson County Bar Association.

CHAPTER 8—THE NEW BUSINESSLIKE RELATIONSHIP

How to relate to the other parent: Additional material has been added to this chapter to further illustrate and expand upon the business relationship principles presented in the first edition (*Mom's House, Dad's House,* 1980, chapter 9).

Emotional control: An effective business relationship is driven not by emotion but by structured interaction. Recent research supports the use of structure to help keep

---

volatile emotions in check. For example, Kathleen A. Camara and Gary Resnick in "Styles of Conflict Resolution and Cooperation between Divorced Parents: Effects on Child Behavior and Adjustment" (*American Orthopsychiatric Journal,* 1989, 59:560–575) found that parents' "successful renegotiation of relationships was forged around a high degree of structure and ritual which served to prevent outbursts of animosity and recrimination" (p. 573). Further, "the strategies that parents employed to resolve conflicts [with each other] were significantly associated with parent-child relationships" (p. 570). Fathers who used verbal attacks or physically expressed their anger toward their spouses/former spouses not only escalated the conflict with the other parent, but damaged their relationship with their children. Mothers who verbally attacked the other parent ended up having poorer relationships with their children and these children also had poorer relationships with their fathers. Verbal attacks and/or physical expressions of anger toward the other parent by either parent adversely affected their children's social functioning.

Lack of repair abilities: See John Gottman, *Why Marriages Succeed or Fail* (1994).

Chronic anger toward children: See Matthew McKay, Kim Paleg, Patrick Fanning, Dana Landis, *When Anger Hurts Your Kids: A Parent's Guide* (Oakland, Calif.: New Harbinger Publications, 1996).

CHAPTER 9—MOM'S HOUSE, DAD'S HOUSE

Making two homes for your child: Based on *Mom's House, Dad's House,* 1980.

Goals for parents: This section is new to this edition.

Safety rules: A helpful resource is Rae Tyson, *Kidsafe: Everything You Need to Know to Make Your Child's Environment Safe* (New York: Times Books, 1995).

Family work: I prefer the term "family work" to "chores," as recommended in Jane Nelson, Cheryl Erwin, and Carol Delzer, *Positive Discipline for Single Parents: A Practical Guide to Raising Children Who Are Responsible and Respectful* (1993). Lynn Lott and Riki Intner, *The Family That Works Together: Turning Family Chores from Drudgery to Fun* (Rocklin, Calif.: Prima, 1994), is also an excellent book on developing family cooperation.

Parenting patterns: This new section is adapted from the author's work with clients. First presented by Ricci at the Association of Family and Conciliation Courts International Conference (Boston, May 1986). Quoted in a California Appellate Court decision (see Lyne Ellinwood, "In Re Marriage of Salmen & Birnbaum: Order Modifying Children's Residential Timetable Is Not a Custody Change," *California Family Law Monthly,* 1989, 6:45–56, and later published in Isolina Ricci, "Mediation, Joint Custody and Legal Agreements: A Time to Review, Revise and Refine," *Family and Conciliation Courts Review,* 1989, 27:47–55).

School communication: James Austin, in his study of seventy-nine randomly selected public school districts, unfortunately found that in almost half of the schools studied, noncustodial parents were excluded from their children's educational process (see James F. Austin, "The Impact of School Policies on Noncustodial Parents," *Journal of Divorce & Remarriage,* 1993, 20:153–168). See also Isolina Ricci, "Divorce, Remarriage, and the Schools," *KAPPAN,* March 1979:509–511. Appendix 1 has a special form for parents to use with schools.

CHAPTER 10—YOUR CHILDREN

Your children: giving them security and continuity: This chapter was originally published in *Mom's House, Dad's House,* 1980 (chapter 13). New sections include "Choices and Changes for Your Child," "Give Your Child a Say," "Children Need Parents to be the Grown-Ups," "Together Time," "Know Your Family History," "Danger Signals," "What Affects Children," "Children's 'Ready' and 'Not Ready' Lists," and "Remember to . . ." checklist.

Successful parenting: Parenting classes are popular and helpful resources. Call your local adult education program, your community college, high school, family court, or family services for referrals. Also see the "Further Reading" list after these notes.

Choices and changes for your child: This section has been expanded from the first edition (*Mom's House, Dad's House,* 1980, p. 176) to include a new section on the child's TLC.

Temperament: McKay, Paleg, Fanning, and Landis have a helpful description of the traits that make up "temperament" in their book *When Anger Hurts Your Kids: A Parent's Guide.* (See "Further Readings.")

Keep children out of the middle: This section is expanded from the first edition (*Mom's House, Dad's House,* 1980, p. 182). See also Kevin P. Kurkowski, Donald A. Gordan, and Jack Arbuthnot, "Children Caught in the Middle: A Brief Educational Intervention for Divorced Parents," *Journal of Divorce & Remarriage,* 1993, 20:139–150.

Pain games: Kansas's Johnson County Mental Health Center, a pioneer in parent education, developed and identified seven "pain games" in 1975; the center continues to use them successfully with parents referred for mandatory parent education. See Carol Roeder-Esser, "G.R.A.S.P.: General Responsibilities as Separating Parents," Johnson County Mental Health Center, Mission, Kans., 1986, and Carol Roeder-Esser, "Families in Transition: A Divorce Workshop," *Family and Conciliation Courts Review,* 1994, 32(1):40–49.

Living arrangements for children after separation and divorce: For in-depth discussion, see Mitchell A. Baris and Carla B. Garrity, *Children of Divorce: A Developmental Approach to Residence and Visitation* (De Kalb, Ill.: Psytec, 1988); James H. Bray, "Psychosocial Factors Affecting Custodial and Visitation Arrangements," *Behavioral Sciences and the Law,* 1991, 9:419–437; and William F. Hodges, *Interventions for Children of Divorce: Custody, Access, and Psychotherapy* (New York: John Wiley and Sons, Inc., 1991).

Children's adjustment to separation and divorce: For further discussion see Kathleen A. Camara and Gary Resnick, "Styles of Conflict Resolution and Cooperation between Divorced Parents: Effects on Child Behavior and Adjustment," *American Orthopsychiatric Journal,* 1989, 59:560–575; Andrew J. Cherlin, et al., "Longitudinal Studies of Effects of Divorce on Children in Great Britain and the United States," *Science,* 1991, 252(5011):1386–1389; Paul Amato, "Life-span Adjustment of Children to Their Parents' Divorce," in *The Future of Children: Children and Divorce* (Los Altos: David and Lucille Packard Foundation, 1994); E. Mark Cummings and Patrick Davies, *Children and Marital Conflict: The Impact of Family Dispute and*

Resolution (New York: Guilford Press, 1994); Ketty P. Gonzalez, Tiffany M. Field, David Lasko, Jeffrey Harding, Regina Yando, and Debra Bendell, "Adolescents from Divorced and Intact Families," *Journal of Divorce & Remarriage,* 1995, 23:165–173; Janet R. Johnston, "Children's Adjustment in Sole Custody Compared to Joint Custody Families and Principles for Custody Decision Making," *Family and Conciliation Courts Review,* 1995, 33:415–425; Janet R. Johnston and Linda E. G. Campbell, *Impasses of Divorce: The Dynamics and Resolution of Family Conflict* (New York: Free Press, 1988); Joan B. Kelly, "Current Research on Children's Postdivorce Adjustment: No Simple Answers," *Family and Conciliation Courts Review,* 1993, 31:29–49; Stacy R. Markland and Eileen S. Nelson, "The Relationship between Familial Conflict and the Identity of Young Adults," *Journal of Divorce & Remarriage,* 1993, 20:193–206. Also see *Journal of Family Psychology,* June 1993, vol. 7, no. 1, which has a special section of seven articles titled "Families in Transition," by James H. Bray, E. Mavis Hetherington; Sanford L. Braver, Sharlene A. Wolchick, Irwin N. Sandler, Virgil L. Sheets, Bruce Fogas, R. Curtis Bay; Eleanor E. Maccoby, Christy M. Buchanan, Robert H. Mnookin and Sanford M. Dornbusch; John M. Gottman; E. Mavis Hetherington; James H. Bray and Sandra H. Berger; and Nicholas Zill, Donna Ruane Morrison, and Mary Jo Coiro.

PART 3

CHAPTER 11—THE LEGAL BUSINESS

The legal business is your business: The concepts presented in the first edition (*Mom's House, Dad's House,* 1980, chapter 12) have now been expanded here to two chapters to include "Ways to Think about Time," and a chapter on negotiating your own agreements (chapter 13).

Child-support levels: Child-support levels may not be negotiable below a certain guideline amount. In Hawaii, for example, child support is considered the child's right, one that parents cannot negotiate away.

The best agreement can be the parents' agreement: Exceptions exist when parents agree on a plan that is not in their child's best interests. For example, parents may devise a plan where an infant moves between homes with different sleeping schedules or where no effort is made for children to have contact with one parent for an extended period.

Attorney involvement: The "unbundling" of legal services is becoming increasingly popular; this pertains to the use of an attorney as a consultant for a single issue or service rather than as an "attorney of record" for all legal matters. Contact your local bar association and request information on whether or not this is available in your area.

Washington State laws: For an excellent reference on law, parenting plans, and self-help, see Lowell K. Halverson and John W. Kydd. While the book was written for Washington State, it has a number of useful sections for the general reader.

Differences in custody laws: 28-U.S.C.-1738A and international treaty implemented in the United States under 42-U.S.C. (11601–11610) provide that the custody order issued in one jurisdiction be honored in another jurisdiction.

Ways to think about time: Adapted from material presented by Ricci at the Association of Family and Conciliation Courts Conference (Boston, May 1986) and later published (see Isolina Ricci, "Mediation, Joint Custody, and Parenting Plans: A Time to Review, Revise, and Refine," *Family and Conciliation Courts Review,* 1989, 27:47–55).

Role models: See Reginald M. Clark, "Effective Families Help Children Succeed in School" (1987); Reginald M. Clark, "Why Disadvantaged Students Succeed: What Happens Outside School Is Critical" (1990); and Sanford Weinstein, *Family Beyond Family: The Surrogate Parent in Schools and Other Community Agencies* (New York: Haworth Press, 1995).

CHAPTER 12—PARENTING PLANS AND AGREEMENTS

Parenting plans: Based on the parenting agreement concept developed by Ricci (1974–75) and described in *Mom's House, Dad's House,* 1980, chapter 12.

The basic elements: The special provisions and private contracts are from Ricci's private mediation and mediation training materials. See also Robert Thompkins, "Parenting Plans: A Concept Whose Time Has Come," *Family and Conciliation Courts Review,* 1995, 33:286–297.

Parenting agreements/plans and the legal system: A number of states in the United States either require or accept parenting agreements and/or parenting plans. See Susan Notar, "Unpublished Internal Review of State Family Law and Custody Statutes," *U.S. Department of Health and Human Services, Administration for Children and Families,* May 1995. The *U.S. Commission on Child and Family Welfare* recommended that all "parents attempt to develop parenting plans that clarify and formalize their parenting responsibilities (parental decisionmaking, parenting time, and residential arrangements)." "Parenting Our Children: In the Best Interest of the Nation, A Report to the President and Congress" (1996). (Also see Isolina Ricci, "Parenting Plans: Making the Family Court System Work for People," *Testimony before the U.S. Commission on Child and Family Welfare,* San Francisco, Calif.: U.S. Commission on Child and Family Welfare, 1995.)

Disclosure of phone numbers, addresses: If there are concerns about violence or child abduction, this information should *not* be given out.

Life insurance: Parents often name their children as beneficiaries to their life insurance. When determining the amount of life insurance, consider an amount that would cover that parent's share of college as well as remaining child support payments.

CHAPTER 13—HOW TO NEGOTIATE YOUR OWN AGREEMENTS

Negotiations: This chapter is new to this edition. Excellent references on negotiations and conflict resolution are Joel Edelman and Mary Beth Crain, *The Tao of Negotiation: How You Can Prevent, Resolve and Transcend Conflict in Work and Everyday Life* (New York: HarperCollins, 1993); Roger Fisher and William Ury, *Getting to Yes: Negotiating Agreement Without Giving In* (New York: Houghton-Mifflin, 1981).

CHAPTER 14—A LONG-TERM PARENTING PLAN

The legal parenting plan: This chapter continues to expand upon the concept of parenting agreements presented in the first edition (*Mom's House, Dad's House,* 1980, p. 164). The sample plan is taken from composites from the author's private mediation practice and mediation training materials. For an excellent workbook on parenting agreements and plans, see Mimi Lyster, *Child Custody: Building Agreements that Work* (Berkeley, Calif.: Nolo Press, 1995). Also see Isolina Ricci, "Parenting Plans: Making the Court System Work for People" (1995).

Custody terminology: The word "custody" is omitted entirely in the parenting agreement presented in the text. If your attorney feels the need to include this term, it is very important that you understand the ramifications of the custody term that will be used.

Child support terminology: Your attorney may advise you to use the legal term "child support" along with another term such as "contribution."

Cost-of-living clause: Some people add a cost-of-living clause under contributions when determining what to include in their parenting plan.

Parenting plans—having a witness to the signing: When signing a parenting plan with the other parent, some people choose to have a witness present who also signs the plan. While this is probably not necessary, it does add a more formal tone to the procedure.

CHAPTER 15—FAMILY MEDIATION

Mediation: This chapter, new to this edition, is adapted from material used in Ricci's private mediation practice and professional mediation training programs at the New Family Center in Palo Alto, California. See also "Isolina Ricci on Family Mediation: 1984 Masters Series," *American Association of Marriage and Family Therapists* (videotape), and Isolina Ricci, "From the Client's Point of View: Some Interpersonal Elements of Client Satisfaction with Mediation," presented at the California Family Court Services Statewide Educational Institute, Monterey, Calif., 1993.

Mandated/permitted mediation: In the United States, currently five states mandate mediation in *all* contested cases (California, Florida, Maine, North Carolina, and Wisconsin), and another twenty-two states permit courts to offer mediation or to order it from the bench. The U.S. Commission on Child and Family Welfare recommended to the president and Congress that mediation be made mandatory in all disputed child custody cases where domestic violence was not an issue.

Client satisfaction with mediation: Parents usually report high satisfaction with mediation. For further discussion, see Statewide Office of Family Court Services, *Report 6—Future Directions for Mandatory Child Custody Mediation Services: Considerations from Two Statewide Representative Studies of Court Users* (Administrative Office of the Courts Judicial Council of California, February 1996), and Jessica Pearson, "Family Mediation," *National Symposium on Court Connected Dispute Resolution Research* (Baltimore, Md., 1991).

Mediation—special circumstances: An increasing number of juvenile courts are instituting a specialized form of mediation when neglect, abuse, or violence is present in a family. This type of mediation may include parents, attorneys, social workers, and court investigators. These mediations are usually held at the courthouse under secure conditions.

Mediation—developing your skills as a negotiator: Self-defeating patterns should alert a mediator to the absence of knowledge or skill in negotiations. See Isolina Ricci, "Mediator's Notebook: Reflections on Promoting Equal Empowerment and Entitlements for Women," *Journal of Divorce,* 1985, 8(3/4):49–61.

Standards for mediators: California, Florida, and Virginia are examples of states with legal standards for court-connected mediators.

Mediators—training programs: For example, the Academy of Family Mediators approves trainers for divorce and separation mediation who meet specific guidelines. Training typically involves a forty-hour program and subsequent supervision.

Mediation—exceptions to confidentiality: Confidentiality should be legally supported within the mediation process (therefore no information can be shared with those outside of the mediation without written consent); however, since both parents participate in the mediation process, this same standard for confidentiality may not exist between the parties and the mediator (unless the mediator has a rule that keeps each person's communication with the mediator confidential). For instance, if Dad tells the mediator privately that he is getting remarried, the mediator may be required to tell Mom.

Preparing for mediation: In addition to the guidelines suggested here, see *Getting to Yes* (1980) and *The Tao of Negotiation* (1993).

Trading assurances as an indicator of good faith: Ricci first described this approach to dissolving resistances in her 1980 presentation entitled "Parenting Agreements" to the first mediation conference of the Association of Family and Conciliation Courts in Ft. Lauderdale, Fla. Also see Isolina Ricci, "Mediator's Notebook: Reflections on Promoting Equal Empowerment and Entitlement for Women" (1985).

PART 4

CHAPTER 16—YOUR FAMILY

Your family: Adapted from *Mom's House, Dad's House,* 1980, chapter 14, "The Open Family." The "Family" section has been added.

Believing in your family: A helpful book suitable for both parents and professionals is C. Margaret Hall, *New Families: Reviving and Creating Meaningful Bonds* (New York: Harrington Park Press, 1994).

Family cooperation, family meetings, and family work: See Betty Lou Bettner and Amy Lew, *Raising Kids Who Can: Using Family Meetings to Nurture Responsible, Cooperative, Caring, and Happy Children* (New York, HarperPerennial, 1989); Jane Nelsen, Cheryl Erwin, and Carol Delzer, *Positive Discipline for Single Parents: A Practical Guide to Raising Children Who Are Responsible, Respectful, and Resourceful* (1994); and Lynn Lott and Riki Intner, *The Family That Works Together: Turning Family Chores from Drudgery to Fun* (1994).

Protecting your family: For further reading, see Mary Pipher, *The Shelter of Each Other:*

Rebuilding Our Families (New York: Grosset/Putnam, 1996), and Richard Louv, *Childhood's Future* (San Diego: Anchor Books, 1992).

Holidays: The "Holidays" section is adapted from the first edition (*Mom's House, Dad's House,* 1980, appendix II) and a two-part series: Isolina Ricci, "How to Avoid the Holiday Blues" and "The Emotional Strings Attached to Christmas Gifts," *New York Times Syndicate,* 1981.

CHAPTER 17—YOUR FAMILY NETWORK

Your extended family and acquaintance network: This section, updated from the first edition (*Mom's House, Dad's House,* 1980, chapter 14), originated with Isolina Ricci, "Primary Communities among Middle-Class Americans: Toward an Analysis of an Emerging Phenomenon," *Marriage and Family Counselors Quarterly,* no. 9 (1974). Also see "Social networks" below.

Extended family: Grandparents are an especially important part of the extended family for children and for parents. For example, see Carolyn Cogswell and Carolyn S. Henry, "Grandchildren's Perceptions of Grandparental Support in Divorced and Intact Families," *Journal of Divorce & Remarriage,* 1995, 23:127–149, and Raeann R. Hamon, "Parents as Resources When Adult Children Divorce," *Journal of Divorce & Remarriage,* 1995, 23:171–183. A caring adult can have a powerful effect on children. Studies have shown a reduction in the initiation of drug use by 46 percent and alcohol use by 27 percent. "Making a Difference: An Impact Study of Big Brothers/Big Sisters," Public Private Ventures, 1995.

Social networks: Updated for this edition. Originally based on Ricci, 1974. Ricci's UCLA Extension series, "The One Parent Family Community" (1976) and *The Single Parent News,* published from 1974 to 1978 (Arthur Herman, ed.). For a more recent discussion, see also Geoffrey Nelson, "Women's Social Networks and Social Support Following Marital Separation: A Controlled Prospective Study," *Journal of Divorce & Remarriage,* 1995, 23:149–167.

CHAPTER 18—LONG-DISTANCE PARENTING

The decision to move away and long-distance parenting: This chapter, published originally in *Mom's House, Dad's House,* 1980, has been updated for this edition. For further discussion, see Joyce Munsch, John Woodward, and Nancy Darling, "Children's Perceptions of Their Relationships with Co-residing and Non-coresiding Fathers," *Journal of Divorce & Remarriage,* 1995, 23:39–53.

Relocation and custody issues: The legal right of a parent with sole or primary custody to relocate with the children is currently a subject of increasing litigation and shifting legal presumptions. Attorney Leslie Ellen Shear points out that the high courts of the three largest North American jurisdictions (New York, California, and Canada) "relied heavily on the labels 'custody,' 'visitation,' and 'access.' These labels obscured rather than illuminated the realities of the children's lives. . . . Too often labels, formulae, and doctrines are substituted for careful attention to the particulars of families' lives." From "Life Stories, Doctrines, and Decision Making: Three High Courts Confront the Move-Away Dilemma," by Leslie Ellen Shear, *Family and Conciliation Courts Review,* vol. 34, no. 4, October 1996, 439–458.

CHAPTER 19—WHEN AN ABSENT PARENT RETURNS

Reinvolving a parent or becoming reinvolved: This chapter, published originally in *Mom's House, Dad's House*, 1980, as appendix I, has been updated and expanded.

When reinvolvement doesn't work: For further discussion, see Geoffrey L. Greif, "When Divorced Fathers Want No Contact with Their Children: A Preliminary Analysis," *Journal of Divorce & Remarriage*, 1995, 23:75–85.

CHAPTER 20—MOVING ON

Your place in the community: Based on Isolina Ricci, "Relationships after Divorce or Separation: Crossroads for the Community and the Family," Family Mediation Conferences, Melbourne and Sydney, Australia, 1990.

Emotional flashbacks: The "flashback" phenomenon of the second wave of emotions was part of an educational and clinical model used by Ricci beginning in 1975 and recorded in *Mom's House, Dad's House*, 1980, chapters 7 and 16. The subsequent refinement of the "second wave" theory has been a useful framework for educating professionals and parents on the emotional responses that can threaten previously working agreements or relationships.

Remarriage/stepparenting: See "Further Reading" for a list of helpful books.

PART 5

APPENDIXES 1, 2, 3

All are updated from the first edition, 1980.

APPENDIX 4

Private Contracts. Based on the author's private mediation practice and training materials. New to this edition.

APPENDIX 5

Mediation Confidentiality Agreement. Based on the author's private mediation practice and training materials. New to this edition.

APPENDIX 6

Finding a Mediator. Updated from the first edition.

APPENDIX 7

What Happens in Mediation. Based on the author's private mediation practice and training materials. New to this edition.

APPENDIX 8

Choosing Child Care
Updated from the first edition.

Further Reading

Ahrons, Constance. *The Good Divorce: Keeping Your Family Together When Your Marriage Comes Apart.* New York: HarperPerennial/HarperCollins, 1995.

Amodeo, John. *Love and Betrayal: Broken Trust in Intimate Relationships.* New York: Ballantine Books, 1994.

Baris, Mitchell A., and Carla B. Garrity. *Children of Divorce: A Developmental Approach to Residence and Visitation.* De Kalb, Ill.: Psytec, 1988.

Berman, Claire. *Making It as a Stepparent: New Roles/New Rules.* New York: Harper & Row, 1986.

Bienenfeld, Florence. *Helping Your Child Succeed after Divorce.* Claremont, Calif.: Hunter House, 1987.

Blau, Melinda. *Families Apart: Ten Keys to Successful Co-Parenting.* New York: G. P. Putnam's Sons, 1993.

Brazelton, T. Berry. *Infants & Mothers.* rev. ed. New York: Bantam Doubleday, Dell Publishing Group, Inc., 1983.

Brinkman, Rick, and Rick Kirschner. *Dealing with People You Can't Stand: How to Bring Out the Best in People at Their Worst.* New York: McGraw-Hill, 1994.

Burns, Cherie. *Stepmotherhood: How to Survive without Feeling Frustrated, Left Out, or Wicked.* New York: Times Books/Random House, 1985.

Clark, Reginald M. *Family Life and School Achievement: Why Poor Black Children Succeed or Fail.* Chicago: University Press, 1983.

Edelman, Joel, and Mary Beth Crain. *The Tao of Negotiation: How You Can Prevent, Resolve and Transcend Conflict in Work and Everyday Life.* New York: HarperCollins, 1993.

Everett, Craig, and Sandra Volgy Everett. *Healthy Divorce.* San Francisco: Jossey-Bass, 1994.

Eyre, Linda, and Richard Eyre. *Teaching Your Children Responsibility.* New York: Fireside, 1994.

Garrity, Carla B., and Mitchell A. Baris. *Caught in the Middle: Protecting the Children of High-Conflict Divorce,* New York: Lexington Books, 1994.

Glenn, H. Stephen, and Jane Nelsen. *Raising Self-Reliant Children in a Self-Indulgent World: Seven Building Blocks for Developing Capable Young People.* Rocklin, Calif.: Prima Publishing and Communications, 1989.

Gold, Lois. *Between Love and Hate: A Guide to a Civilized Divorce.* New York: Plume/Penguin Books, 1992.

Goleman, Daniel. *Emotional Intelligence: Why It Can Matter More Than I.Q.* New York: Bantam Books, 1995.

Gottman, John. *The Heart of Parenting: Raising an Emotionally Intelligent Child.* New York: Simon & Schuster, 1997.

————. *What Predicts Divorce: The Relationship between Marital Processes and Marital Outcomes*. Hillsdale, N.J.: Lawrence Erlbaum Associates, Inc., 1993.

Hall, C. Margaret. *New Families: Reviving and Creating Meaningful Bonds*. New York: Harrington Park Press, 1994.

Halverson, Lowell K., and John W. Kydd. *Divorce in Washington: A Humane Approach*. Mercer Island, Wash.: Eagle House Press, 1990.

Hickey, Elizabeth, and Elizabeth Dalton. *Healing Hearts: Helping Children and Adults Recover from Divorce*. Carson City, Nev.: Gold Leaf Press, 1994.

Johnston, Janet, Baris, Mitchell, Garrity, Carla, and Karen Breunig. *Through the Children's Eyes: Healing Stories for Children of Divorce*. New York: Free Press, 1997.

Johnson, Janet, and Linda E. G. Campbell. *Impasses of Divorce: The Dynamics and Resolution of Family Conflict*. New York: The Free Press, 1988.

Kottler, Jeffrey A. *Beyond Blame: A New Way of Resolving Conflicts in Relationships*. San Francisco: Jossey-Bass, 1994.

Lansky, Vicki. *Vicki Lansky's Divorce Book for Parents*. New York: Signet, 1991.

Lofas, Jeanette, and Dawn B. Sova. *Stepparenting: A Complete Guide to the Joys, Frustrations, and Fears of Stepparenting*. New York: Zebra Books, 1985.

Lott, Lynn, and Riki Intner. *The Family That Works Together: Turning Family Chores from Drudgery to Fun*. Rocklin, Calif.: Prima, 1994.

Louv, Richard. *Childhood's Future*. San Diego: Anchor Books, 1992.

————. *101 Things You Can Do for Our Children's Future*. New York: Doubleday, 1994.

Lyster, Mimi. *Child Custody: Building Agreements That Work*. Berkeley, Calif.: Nolo Press, 1995.

Marston, Stephanie. *The Divorced Parent: Success Strategies for Raising Your Children after Separation*. New York: Pocket Books, 1994.

McKay, Matthew, Paleg, Kim, Fanning, Patrick, and Dana Landis. *When Anger Hurts Your Kids: A Parent's Guide*. Oakland, Calif.: New Harbinger Publications, 1996.

Nelson, Jane, Cheryl Erwin, and Carol Delzer. *Positive Discipline for Single Parents: A Practical Guide to Raising Children Who Are Responsible and Respectful*. Rocklin, Calif.: Prima, 1993.

Paul, Margaret and Jordan. *Do I Have to Give Up Me to Be Loved by My Kids?* New York: Berkeley Publishing Group, 1995.

Pipher, Mary. *The Shelter of Each Other: Rebuilding Our Families*. New York: Grosset/Putnam, 1996.

Rogers, Fred, and Clare O'Brien. *Mister Rogers Talks with Families about Divorce*. New York: Berkeley Books, 1987.

Seligman, Martin E., Reivich, Karen, Jaycox, Lisa, and Jane Gillham. *The Optimistic Child: A Revolutionary Program That Safeguards Children against Depression and Builds Lifelong Resilience*. New York: Houghton-Mifflin, 1995.

Silverstein, Olga, and Beth Rashbaum. *The Courage to Raise Good Men: You Don't Have to Sever the Bond with Your Son to Help Him Become a Man*. New York: Penguin Group, 1994.

Taffel, Ron. *Why Parents Disagree and What You Can Do About It: How to Raise Great Kids While You Strengthen Your Marriage*. New York: Avon Books, 1994.

Threck, Stanley, and Leslie Tonnel. *The Difficult Child.* New York, Bantam Books, 1985.

Tyson, Rae. *Kidsafe: Everything You Need to Know to Make Your Child's Environment Safe.* New York: Times Books, 1995.

Unell, Barbara C., and Jerry Wyckoff. *20 Teachable Virtues: Practical Ways to Pass on Lessons of Virtue and Character to Your Children.* New York: Perigee, 1995.

Visher, Emily B. and John S. *How to Win as a Stepfamily.* Chicago: Contemporary Books, 1982.

Weinstein, Sanford. *Family Beyond Family: The Surrogate Parent in Schools and Other Community Agencies.* New York: Haworth Press, 1995.

Whiteside, Mary F. *Custody for Children Five Years of Age and Younger.* (Pamphlet). San Francisco: Statewide Office of Family Court Services, Administrative Office of the Courts, Judicial Council of California, 1996.

Wallerstein, Judith S. *Second Chances: Men, Women, and Children a Decade After Divorce.* New York: Ticknor & Fields, 1989.

Appendix 1

INFORMATION FOR SCHOOLS
(TO BE UPDATED ANNUALLY BY PARENTS)

This is a form that *all* parents—married, divorced, or remarried—can use with their children's schools. It can eliminate guesswork on "whom to call" or "who makes decisions" and can encourage more home and school cooperation.

1. Please write in the names and phone numbers of the adults who will have dealings with this school this year.

Natural mother	Name_____	Phone_____
Natural father	Name_____	Phone_____
Stepfather	Name_____	Phone_____
Stepmother	Name_____	Phone_____
Adult friend	Name_____	Phone_____
Relative	Name_____	Phone_____
Guardian	Name_____	Phone_____
Other	Name_____	Phone_____

2. Please indicate how these adults may be involved with the school by writing their names next to the activity listed below. The adults below have the following rights and responsibilities with the child:

Teacher-parent conferences:
    1. Name_____
    2. Name_____

Classroom visitations or observations:
    1. Name_____
    2. Name_____

Emergency release to this adult from   1. Name_____
the schoolgrounds
                                              2. Name_____

Adult to contact regarding discipline   1. Name_____

                                             2. Name_____
Adult to contact regarding placement
and education matters   1. Name_____

                                             2. Name_____

3. What is your own legal status or relationship to the child you are registering?

   Please mark all that apply:
   _____ I have sole legal custody
   _____ I have joint legal custody
   _____ I have joint physical custody
   _____ I have educational rights specified in my divorce agreement
   _____ I have a private agreement with the other parent
   _____ I am a stepparent
   _____ I am a legal guardian
   _____ I am the _____
   _____ I am the adult the child is now living with
   _____ I am a natural parent

4. Which adult that you have listed can the school release the child to in case of an emergency?

   Name _____   Phone _____

   Name _____   Phone _____

   Name _____   Phone _____

   Which adult listed here should be called first if you cannot be reached?

   Name _____

   Your name _____   Child's name _____

   Your address _____   Grade _____

   Your phone _____

Appendix 2

ATTORNEYS

Attorneys are usually in private practice and rarely are formally employed by the courts. Attorneys may act as litigators, consultants, advisers, and less frequently as mediators and arbitrators. Choose your attorney with great care. The closer his or her philosophy is to yours, the happier you will be with the results.

HOW TO FIND A KNOWLEDGEABLE ATTORNEY

First: Ask as many friends as you can whom they would recommend as an attorney for a separation, divorce, custody, or paternity matter. Be curious. When a name is suggested, go further by asking, "Have you used this person yourself?" "How did you hear about this person?" "What did you or your friend like most and least about him/her?"

Second: If you like the answers you receive, you can make phone contact with the law office and ask questions. Don't be surprised or put off if the secretary asks you to make an appointment so you can pose your questions in person. Think of how much free phone time you can afford during your own working hours. Your goal is to find a knowledgeable attorney, not necessarily one with low rates. When you do talk to the attorney, prepare in advance by reviewing the following questions.

QUESTIONS TO ASK ON THE TELEPHONE

1. Are you a family law specialist? Do you practice other types of law? If yes, what kind? What percentage of your cases is in family law? How long have you been practicing law? How long have you been practicing in this county or parish? (It is not necessary that an attorney spend 100 percent of his or her time on family law cases, but it should be a substantial percentage.)
2. What experience have you had in working with couples who attempt to work out a parenting plan on their own or with a mediator? Would you format a privately negotiated agreement in the necessary legal form? What number of cases during the past two years or percentage of your practice was devoted to this type of case?

3. What has been your experience negotiating shared custody arrangements?
4. How do you handle your fees? Do you require a retainer? What types of billing procedures do you use—monthly? Do you provide a detailed billing of your services each month? (It should be monthly and detailed.)
5. Could a potential client drop by for fifteen minutes or so to get acquainted? (This would be not for legal advice, but for the lawyer and potential client to get to know one another.)
6. Would you be working on my case, or would you refer it to an associate?
7. If you were my attorney, and I called to speak with you, what is the maximum time that will elapse before you will return my call?
8. If you were my attorney and I needed to see you, what is the maximum time that will elapse before I can obtain an appointment to see you?

Listen carefully to the responses and decide if you want to meet with this attorney for an initial interview. The choice of mediator or attorney will be one of the biggest decisions you will make during these months. *You want this person to have values and beliefs similar to yours.*

QUESTIONS TO ASK AT THE FIRST FORMAL MEETING

1. First ask the questions outlined above that are still outstanding.
2. Does our jurisdiction use child support guidelines to determine ranges of child support?
3. Does our jurisdiction use spousal support guidelines to determine ranges of spousal support?
4. Ask all questions in chapter 11, in the section entitled "Know Your Laws."

Appendix 3

MONEY—THE COST OF RAISING CHILDREN

FANTASIES ABOUT MONEY AND THE OTHER PARENT

When parents are caught in that unreasonable off-the-wall period and at the same time are feeling the financial pinch, some of them develop self-serving fantasies about how well the other parent is getting along. I have listened to some fathers say that the child's mother and the child can live comfortably on $500 a month "because she knows how to do this" or that money sent for the children is being used for new furniture. I have listened to mothers sure that the father has spirited away cash in secret accounts, angry that he has a new suit of clothes.

The truth is often overlooked in such tales. Parents are often deep in debt, confused, fearful. Yes, some are dishonest, looking for revenge, but most are not—at least not initially. It's easier for people to keep their fantasies that everything is comfortable at the other house than to face the guilt that might surface when confronting the hardships that divorce has brought the children and the other parent.

The fantasies serve one purpose—they avoid reality. They allow the parents to sidestep their responsibilities to be specific about who contributes what for the children and their needs. In reality, probably neither parent will be particularly solvent, and even if one has some money stashed away, it is unlikely the secret cache is the grand windfall the other imagines. Distrusting or not, both parents will usually have to rebuild their economic lives with reduced resources. Unfortunately this economic rebuilding is often far more difficult for a woman than for a man. In spite of some changes, women still earn considerably less than men earn for the same jobs. Their eight hours of labor still purchases less food than can be bought by a male doing the same work. This inequity takes a heavy toll when the mother has the primary financial responsibilities.

A REALISTIC FINANCIAL PICTURE: A GOOD START

A realistic financial picture is one way parents can help themselves through the maze of competition and fears about money. A startling number of divorcing parents are unaware of how much money they spend on clothing, food, and other necessary expenses and what proportion actually goes for the children. This lack of knowledge seems to cause half the problems and misunderstandings. What parents find very helpful is to estimate the cost of living with and without children. This list of expenses should be a good "guesstimate" of the more hidden costs of child rearing in both the primary and secondary residence. This same list can be a good help in determining the hot spots that might flare up around the triple issues of money, time, and energy. Finally, the list can be used as a personal checkup on your own financial condition and as a precursor for legal requirements to itemize expenses.

It has been helpful for some parents to fill in this form from two perspectives: first their present situation, and then what it would be like to be in the other parent's shoes. If the other parent will be making a new home, check into the cost of housing with children, scan the ads, make a few calls, see what it feels like to hear the answer "No children, no pets." Take a look at the area—would you really want to live there with your children? Make inquiries about the availability and costs of really good child care and baby-sitters. Take the time to visit one of these places and look around.

The double assessment is time-consuming but well worth it. Once you have completed that, evaluate your priorities. Where do you rank your children and their need to be with each parent? How high on the list is the two-home system? What about funds for adequate communications? for being together? child care? These items should be your highest priority, counted along with the survival needs of food, shelter, and clothing.

ACCOUNTING FOR DIRECT FINANCIAL CONTRIBUTIONS: WHERE IS THIS MONEY GOING?

The contributing parent usually pays the other parent by check based on a guideline or a negotiated amount. But the paying parent can be suspicious. As one father said, "That money is going to support her and her new boyfriend." True enough, even where you can trace the dollars spent on the children's clothes and the like, the joint consumption by parent and child of food and shelter is a part of living together.

Since no parent has the right to a complete financial accounting of the other's income outside of court, many contributing parents feel they have good right to be angry. There is a possible solution to this problem. Consider a simple accounting of where the money is going.

This accounting is given to the contributing parent by the other parent and describes how—in theory, at least—that contribution check is used. This can be done on one sheet and given to the other parent once every three to four months. Or, the contributing parent pays for costs directly. Instead of giving the other parent a certain flat amount that goes for bills, that parent pays those bills directly, often absorbing rising costs.

The accounting is done simply. For example, one mother received $350 from her child's father and gave him a simple one-page statement every four months that read like this:

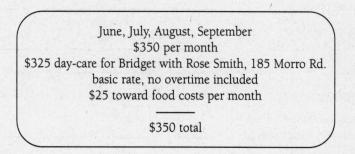

June, July, August, September
$350 per month
$325 day-care for Bridget with Rose Smith, 185 Morro Rd.
basic rate, no overtime included
$25 toward food costs per month
———
$350 total

The father's response was one of embarrassment. Somehow he had not heard her when she had verbally told him the amount of the child care costs. He was assuming the money was all going for food and clothing, and he knew that his child could not eat on less than a dollar a day. The formal accounting made a difference in his attitude and in his later willingness to assume increased child care costs.

Cost of Raising Children

Expenses	Parent Living Alone	Parent Living with One Child	Parent Living with Two Children	Parent Living with Three Children
Housing (including insurance, taxes, upkeep)	_____	_____	_____	_____
Household help, janitorial services	_____	_____	_____	_____
Food, household supplies	_____	_____	_____	_____
Clothing	_____	_____	_____	_____
Child care	_____	_____	_____	_____

Medical, dental,
co-payments, and
prescriptions _____ _____ _____ _____

Medical insurance _____ _____ _____ _____

Education, K–12, tuition,
related costs _____ _____ _____ _____

Higher education, college
tuition, related costs _____ _____ _____ _____

Utilities _____ _____ _____ _____

Telephones, beepers _____ _____ _____ _____

Transportation (include
insurance, fuel, upkeep) _____ _____ _____ _____

Insurance: life, disaster,
fire/theft _____ _____ _____ _____

Recreation, entertainment,
equipment _____ _____ _____ _____

Cultural and educational
enrichment (lessons,
classes, outings) _____ _____ _____ _____

Sports (fees, equipment,
transportation) _____ _____ _____ _____

Taxes (personal, state,
federal) _____ _____ _____ _____

Alowances—children _____ _____ _____ _____

Miscellaneous, incidentals _____ _____ _____ _____

Religious training (classes,
events, donations, aid,
special clothing) _____ _____ _____ _____

Spousal support (past
marriage) _____ _____ _____ _____

Child support (past
marriage) _____ _____ _____ _____

Books, toys, games, gifts
to child and from child   _____   _____   _____   _____

Pets and related costs of
food and vet   _____   _____   _____   _____

Appendix 4

PRIVATE CONTRACTS

More ideas for customized private clauses are itemized below. The variety should encourage you to develop your own clauses or to modify what you see here to suit your circumstances.

1. Parent Cooperation Plan and Ground Rules for Interaction

When there is a good deal of negative intimacy or a long history of misunderstandings, some parents can articulate what they expect from one another. For example, Theresa and Taylor decided to write down an agreement that they would both try to stop the "neighborhood soap opera" their divorce had become. It was degrading to them and very hurtful to their children. They identified three major actions they would take: talk about the divorce only to close friends and family; support each other to the children; not speak badly about the other parent in public. They found it easier to do these things when they wrote them down and agreed upon them formally.

2. Sharing Responsibilities

"Rosie has the decision-making responsibilities for choosing the doctors and taking care of regular checkups," said a father of two toddlers, "but I don't want her to announce to me that I have to bring them in for booster shots next week when they are with me. She wanted the medical responsibilities, so she should do that on her own time. Or at least ask me about it! She just dumps it on me and says, 'Do it.' " This father was willing to take the kids to the doctors, but he wanted to schedule the time himself.

A few couples are so locked into their negative intimacy (or old married habits) that who will be responsible for what is clouded by their competitiveness. This can happen even when the decision-making responsibilities have been identified. There are disagreements over the details: who will take time off from work to drive the children to appointments, who will fill out applications, pay for certain bills connected to activities, buy special clothing, pay those pesky, out-of-pocket costs that spring up without warning. These couples have found it helpful to list their trouble spots where schedules and making decisions collide. They try to decide who will do what ahead of time. Some couples decide to rotate some of these responsibilities from year to year. They often use a chart like the following one:

Assignment of Lead Responsibility Chart

	This Year			Next Year		
	Mom	Dad	Both	Mom	Dad	Both
Special school projects	——	——	——	——	——	——
Medical appointments	——	——	——	——	——	——
Dental appointments	——	——	——	——	——	——
Orthodontist appointments	——	——	——	——	——	——
Children's income taxes	——	——	——	——	——	——
School admissions applications	——	——	——	——	——	——
Activity applications	——	——	——	——	——	——
Activity fees	——	——	——	——	——	——
School bills	——	——	——	——	——	——
School/activity fees	——	——	——	——	——	——
Equipment, instruments	——	——	——	——	——	——
Special clothing	——	——	——	——	——	——
Other	——	——	——	——	——	——

3. Coordination of Children's Activities

"We have four kids ten to sixteen, and it was a coordination marathon when we were all living together," said the father. "What are we going to do now?" This parent could make his own chart like the one just shown. Then he could think about how he and the children's mother coordinated their activities in the past, then ask "Who will coordinate things now?" For example, Dad coordinated the search for summer jobs and summer camps and was responsible for getting the brochures and filing the applications. He was also heavily into the team sports for the sixteen- and fourteen-year-olds. Mom coordinated school activities, oversaw the completion of long school papers that were due, arranged the standard parent-teacher conferences. This couple could formalize their agreement in writing and put it in a private contract.

COORDINATING CHILDREN'S ACTIVITIES

1. *Transportation to an activity.* The parent the child is with at the time is responsible for transportation to the child's activity, school, or appointment (even if that parent is not the parent who is the overall coordinator of that activity or has the final say). The parent who is either responsible or coordinates an activity or appointment is to tell the "transportation parent" for that event at least several days before the event.

2. *Attendance at a child's activity.* Both parents can and should attend a child's activity where parents usually attend, such as a game, open house, concert, play, or tournament. Neither parent should be excluded from these activities at any time (unless safety is a concern).

4. Involvement of a Child with a Parent's New Love Interest

"I had no idea the kids would be so obnoxious about my engagement and impending remarriage. And their father is worse than they are about this," said a mother separated six months. "He doesn't even want them sleeping over if Gary is going to be at the house. He thinks it has all been too sudden for the children. His attitude has slowed down our negotiations considerably."

There is nothing quite like having to deal with the reaction of a parent or a child to the other parent's dating or new love. If the couple is newly separated, it can be shocking to the former mate and the children. It is a major second wave event if the couple has been separated for a year or two. Many a parenting agreement process has been held up while parents battled over the propriety of having children around a parent and "friend" too soon after the separation. Others have serious reservations about consenting adults romping around the children, enjoying their "adult adolescence," but unaware that they are embarrassing and confusing the children. "It's not right," said one father. "It is a bad example for the children. And she's not behaving like a parent, either."

A number of parents have solved their pitched battles over how new people are introduced into children's lives by coming to some clear conditions they both agree to follow. Often, once parents have come to terms with one another on this delicate situation, other things—like overnights or making decisions—are far easier to resolve. The aggrieved parent feels heard and respected, the parent in the new relationship feels there will be some end to the conditions. Both want to do what is best for the children.

Following are some guidelines to consider and reword to fit your situation.

THE CHILDREN AND A PARENT'S NEW LOVE

Level One: The child meets the new person in the parent's life. The new person is introduced as a "friend" or "friend from work" (or church or club), not as a new "girlfriend" or "boyfriend." The meeting is brief. The parent and friend are not openly affectionate with one another. Affection is saved for private times away from the children. (This period can last for a number of months.)

Level Two: The second or subsequent meeting: The child spends a hour or so together with the parent and the "friend." The adults continue to be reserved. (This is important.)

Level Three: Third or subsequent meeting. The child, parent, and friend go to an event or on an outing, such as a picnic. (This seems to work best for three or four hours, not for a full day.) The adults are less reserved regarding their affection for one another but are nonetheless discreet and not effusive.

Level Four: There is increasing involvement and proximity, depending on the child's age and temperament and your circumstances. Begin with a full day spent together, then graduate to more than one day. But no overnights while the child is present.

Level Five: Once the parent and friend are in a stable monogamous relationship, the friend is staying overnight while the children are there.

5. When a Child Complains About a Parent

A child's complaints or criticisms about a parent can be unsettling. Some parents, when confident that there is no abuse present, use these guides.

WHEN A CHILD COMPLAINS ABOUT A PARENT

1. If our child complains to a parent about the other parent, is eight years or older and capable of expressing himself or herself, the resident parent will ordinarily refer the child back to the other parent for resolution.
2. We will not send verbal messages through our children to the other parent, or automatically side with a child against a parent.
3. If a child's complaint persists, the resident parent can help the child be direct and facilitate the needed discussion with the other parent. We will telephone the other parent to encourage the child and parent discussion.
4. If a child's complaint is of a serious nature, we will call the other parent and ask what they think is going on. We will give each other the benefit of the doubt.
5. Whenever possible, we intend to foster in the child an appreciation of the other parent.
6. We will have _____ (weekly, monthly, bimonthly) contact with one another to discuss the children's needs with regards to direct parent-child contact. This will begin with the month of _____. Dad/Mom will initiate contact this month.

6. Life Skills: Preparation for Adulthood

Life skills can mean learning about finances, opening a checking account and balancing a checkbook, working in Dad's shoe store as a clerk, or taking on an apprenticeship. Although most parents take one another's educational responsibilities for granted and do not feel the need for such a clause, others find that it helps to think these things out. Parenting goals are often helpful in determining these provisions. For example, in the parenting goal example in chapter 9, Randy wanted his daughters to be prepared for the world. He and their mother could agree that he would be responsible for lessons in self-defense, opening their first savings account, or working closely with them in competitive sports.

Appendix 5

MEDIATION CONFIDENTIALITY AGREEMENT

1. All communications between (your name) _____, (spouse's name),
   _____ and (mediator name) _____ are confidential. In the event of
   litigation, regarding any matters you have discussed with your mediator,
   neither of you shall call or cause anyone else to call the mediator as a
   witness or to subpoena his or her records.

2. In the event either of the parties named above calls the mediator named
   above as a witness, despite this agreement, the party who calls the
   mediator as a witness will be responsible for paying all of the mediator's
   reasonable costs, including attorneys fees and a fee for the reasonable
   value of the mediator's time.

Appendix 6

FINDING A MEDIATOR

You may write to the following organizations and ask them for members who list mediation or divorce counseling as their specialty or who hold groups or workshops for divorcing people in your area.

- Your own family court, Family Court Services Department, county Department of Family and Child Services, or Conciliation Court may list mediators or mediation centers that they recommend in your area.
- Check your telephone directory under "Mediation" or "Divorce" and "Attorneys," each of which may list a specialty in mediation.
- You can also call your local bar association, family law section.

You may also want to contact a national organization for mediators in your area.

Academy of Family Mediators
4 Militia Dr., Suite 6
Lexington, MA 02173
(617) 674-2663

American Arbitration Association
140 West 51st St.
New York, NY 10020-1203
(212) 484-4100; fax (212) 307-4387

Association of Family and Conciliation Courts
329 West Wilson
Madison, WI 53703-3612
(608) 251-0604; fax (608) 251-2231

Conflict Resolution Center, Inc.
2205 E. Carson St.
Pittsburgh, PA 15203
(412) 481-5559; fax (412) 481-5601
e-mail: crcii@igc.apc.org

Mediate.Com Information and Resource Center
e-mail: admin@mediate.com

Society of Professionals in Dispute Resolution
815 15th St. NW, Suite 530
Washington, D.C. 20005
(202) 783-7277; fax (202) 783-7281

Appendix 7

WHAT HAPPENS IN MEDIATION

THE FIRST MEETING: CONFIRMING WHY YOU ARE THERE

- The mediator confirms the information you have given and your areas of dispute, answers your questions, and lays out the mediation ground rules in detail.
- You will be asked what it is that you want to come out of this mediation.
- Option: You may also want to use mediation to develop goals as described in chapter 15.

ALL MEETINGS: EXPLORING YOUR AGREEMENTS AND DISAGREEMENTS IN DETAIL

- You will detail what you already agree upon and what you do not.
- You both lay out the information you have collected regarding your circumstances, point of view, or issues. Follow the instructions on the parenting plan checklist in chapter 13.
- Your areas of disagreement are discussed from both points of view: yours and the other parent's.
- The mediator works with your concerns and proposals, helps you hear one another, narrows the field of alternatives, proposes new options.
- You may leave your first meeting with "homework."
- There may be discussion on how the options relate to your goals.

REACHING AND WRITING AND REVIEWING YOUR AGREEMENTS

- The mediator facilitates your negotiations, adding options for your consideration.
- One of the three of you writes down what you have agreed upon.
- You should take ample time to review your agreement. You may ask an attorney for a review or to draft the final agreement in a legal format.

WRITING THE PARENTING AGREEMENT AND MAKING IT "LEGAL"

- The plan is formalized either as a private contract or as a memorandum of understanding. Later it can be made part of a legally binding formal decree by referral or inclusion or become a part of your marital settlement agreement. Either may be drafted by an attorney.

- Copies of your legal forms and your signed parenting agreement/plan should be given to your attorney. A copy goes to each parent.

FOLLOWING THROUGH

- Regular private meetings in person or by phone between the parents to evaluate how children are doing with the arrangements.
- An annual meeting to review and revise your agreement/plan to keep up with your child's needs and development.
- Option: Meet with the mediator for "fine-tuning" your arrangements at two, three, or six months after your last meeting.

Appendix 8

A GUIDE FOR CHOOSING CHILD CARE

First, find out if there is a Child Care Council in your area. Many of them have free booklets on how to choose child care providers. The information may also be obtained through Web pages on the World Wide Web. Many states have regulatory systems that set standards for the health and safety of children in licensed centers and child care homes. These are usually limits on the number and ages of children in a center, requiring that caregivers be checked for child abuse convictions, criminal records, and infectious diseases. Usually there are requirements for training in CPR and the homes or centers are checked for health and safety. The National Association for the Education of Young Children lists criteria for parents to review.

1. *Don't delegate the job of choosing a provider.* Visit the day care center, the home of the day care family, or the home of the sitter who may be coming to your house. Ask yourself one question only: How comfortable do I feel in this setting, with this person? Deep down, do I feel welcome, safe, and at home? Children can learn a lot in good day care. But bad day care can be disastrous for a child.
2. *Most important:* Is this center or caregiver licensed? How well trained is the staff? What is the ratio of adults to children? What is the level of cleanliness, especially for infants and toddlers? Is there a low turnover of teachers so that a teacher has enough time to make a relationship with a child? Try the "floor test." How many teachers are actually on the floor, interacting with a child? (The more the better.) Once you make your choice, drop in unannounced on a regular basis to observe. Volunteer. Go to parent meetings, field trips. Good child care providers can sometimes become part of your family's extended family.
3. *Spend at least two to three hours, three times* at the center or home that has made your top two possibilities. Just stay there with your child. In a day care setting, observe
   a. *the physical setting:* Is it clean, pleasant, with adequate bathrooms, fire exits, safety fixtures? Does it provide good places to play and nap, even in bad weather?

b. *the program:* Would your child enjoy the activities, learn from them? Notice the basic approach—educational and social. Which takes precedence?

c. *meals and snacks:* Are they appealing and healthy? What happens if a child wants something different? More? How much variety is planned?

d. *interaction of adults and children:* Do the children seem happy? How does the staff handle discipline? How are children (and parents) greeted?

e. *fees and parent participation:* How much? Are there any discounts, any hidden costs? Do you have to pay for absences due to illness or family vacation?

f. *what kind of extended time arrangements have been made for parents* who (regularly or occasionally) will be working past regular closing time. How expensive is this service, and what is expected of your child and you?

g. *emergency procedures:* What provisions are made for the emergency needs of children?

4. *Ask yourself these questions:*
   a. Would my child fit in this group?
   b. Would my child's emotional, social, and learning needs be recognized and developed here?
   c. Do I feel comfortable with the style, methods, and philosophy?
   d. Will my child be physically safe and comfortable here?
   e. What do my instincts tell me about this place?

5. *Ask for references,* license information, a copy of the child care standards they follow.

FOR SITTERS WHO WILL COME TO YOUR HOME

1. Ask for references and check them out before you spend time talking to any prospective sitter.
2. Ask for information regarding the sitter's emergency procedure if you cannot be reached. (This is especially important if the sitter is a teenager.)
3. Have the sitter you are considering take charge in your home with the children while you observe. Do this several times.

ONCE YOU HAVE MADE YOUR CHOICE

1. Drop in unexpectedly a few times. Do you like what you see and feel?
2. Watch your children. Watch their reactions: their reluctance to go in the

morning or a joyful anticipation of the day to come is an important indicator of what is happening during the day while you are away.

3. If problems do develop, don't hesitate to change arrangements. Your kids are worth the time and trouble.

Index

HIRT test, 201
holidays, 170, 177–78, 228, 265–68
    remarriage and, 316
homes, *see* stages of transition from one
        home to two; two-home
        arrangements
homicidal thoughts, 70
house rules, 12, 21–22, 121, 132, 153,
        194–95, 256–57
housework, 122, 132, 151
human income, *see* stress
humor, 54, 154

illness, stress and, 47–48, 53
independence, businesslike relationship
        and, 95–96
infants, 176–77
information form for schools, 347–48
information sources, in
        communications, 99–101
inner self, caring for, 52
insurance, in parenting plan, 188
intimacy, 77, 82–83, 124
    negative, 76–77, 82, 83, 90, 144,
        196, 199, 235–36, 311
intimacy, retreat from, 36, 76–93,
        235
    and acting like a guest, 90–91
    and appreciation from other parent,
        91
    communications in, 91–92, 98
    continuing effort needed in, 92
    courtesy and respect in, 90
    family feeling and, 77–78
    feeling strange about, 92
    first steps in, 84–85
    guidelines for, 89–93
    initiation of, 86
    language and, 89
    negative intimacy and, 76–77, 90,
        235–36, 311
    privacy and, 89–90
    self-test for, 87–88
    and time with children, 90
    when to begin, 87

see also business relationship
    between parents
isolation, 51, 124

joint custody, 160, 165, 166
    equal time in, 167
    and return of absent parent, 304,
        306
    see also two-home arrangements

language, 38–45, 54
    "broken home" label, 39–40, 41
    changing old habits in, 43–44
    and divorce as contest, 41
    and divorce as crime, 40–41
    effects of, on children, 40–41
    legal, 160–61, 165, 187
    new vocabulary for post-divorce
        family life, 41–43, 44–45
    power of, 45
    in retreat from intimacy, 89
    "stinkweed" and "rose" words in,
        38–40, 44, 45, 54
laws:
    ambiguities in, 158
    differences in, 160–61, 165
    knowledge of, 160–61
    state guidelines, 161
lawyers (attorneys), 162–64, 165, 198,
        349
    finding of, 349
    questions to ask, 349–50
legal business, 157–82
    ambiguities in, 158
    attorneys and, 162–64, 165, 198,
        349–50
    avoiding court hearings, 159–60,
        163–64
    emotions and, 158–59
    information collection and, 51–52
    and knowledge of laws, 160–61
    language in, 160–61, 165–68,
        187
    limitations of, 7–8
    major decisions in, 162

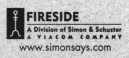